Also in the Variorum Collected Studies Series:

ANGUS MACKAY
Society, Economy and Religion in Late Medieval Castile

PETER LINEHAN
Spanish Church and Society, 1150–1300

JACQUES FONTAINE
Culture et spiritualité en Espagne du IVe au VIIe siècle

ELIYAHU ASHTOR
East-West Trade in the Medieval Mediterranean

ELIYAHU ASHTOR
Technology, Industry and Trade

KATHERINE FISCHER DREW
Law and Society in Early Medieval Europe

ANTHONY LUTTRELL
The Hospitallers of Rhodes and their Mediterranean World

JEAN GAUTIER DALCHÉ
Économie et société dans les pays de la Couronne de Castille

DAVID ABULAFIA
Italy, Sicily and the Mediterranean, 1100–1400

HENRI BRESC
Politique et société en Sicile, XIIe–XVe siècles

I.A.A. THOMPSON
War and Society in Habsburg Spain

BÉATRICE LEROY
Le royaume de Navarre à la fin du Moyen Age

ELENA LOURIE
Crusade and Colonisation

MANUEL C. DÍAZ Y DÍAZ
Vie chrétienne et culture dans l'Espagne du VIIe au Xe siècles

GILES CONSTABLE
Monks, Hermits and Crusaders in Medieval Europe

ROGER COLLINS
Law, Culture and Regionalism in Early Medieval Spain

JOHN J. CONTRENI
Carolingian Learning, Masters and Manuscripts

Also in the Variorum Collected Studies Series:

ANGUS MACKAY
Society, Economy and Religion in Late Medieval Castile

PETER LINEHAN
Spanish Church and Society, 1150–1300

JACQUES FONTAINE
Culture et Spiritualité en Espagne du IVe au VIIe siècle

ELIYAHU ASHTOR
East-West Trade in the Medieval Mediterranean

ELIYAHU ASHTOR
Technology Industry and Trade

KATHERINE FISCHER DREW
Law and Society in Early Medieval Europe

ANTHONY LUTTRELL
The Hospitallers of Rhodes and their Mediterranean World

JEAN GAUTIER DALCHÉ
Économie et société dans les pays de la Couronne de Castille

DAVID ABULAFIA
Italy, Sicily and the Mediterranean 1100–1400

HENRI BRESC
Politique et société en Sicile, XIIe–XVe siècles

I.A.A. THOMPSON
War and Society in Habsburg Spain

BEATRICE LEROY
Le royaume de Navarre à la fin du Moyen Age

ELENA LOURIE
Crusade and Colonisation

MANUEL C. DIAZ Y DIAZ
Vie chrétienne et culture dans l'Espagne du Ve au Xe siècles

GILES CONSTABLE
Monks, Hermits and Crusaders in Medieval Europe

ROGER COLLINS
Law, Culture and Regionalism in Early Medieval Spain

JOHN J. CONTRENI
Corolingian Learning, Masters and Manuscripts

The City and the Realm: Burgos and Castile 1080–1492

Professor Teofilo F. Ruiz

Teofilo F. Ruiz

The City and the Realm: Burgos and Castile 1080–1492

Routledge
Taylor & Francis Group
LONDON AND NEW YORK

First published 1992 by Variorum, Ashgate Publishing

Published 2017 by Routledge
2 Park Square, Milton Park, Abingdon, Oxon, OX14 4RN
52 Vanderbilt Avenue, New York, NY 10017

Routledge is an imprint of the Taylor & Francis Group, an informa business

A CIP catalogue record for this book is available from the British Library and the US Library of Congress.

ISBN 13: 978-0-86078-329-9 (hbk)

COLLECTED STUDIES SERIES CS375

CONTENTS

This book consists of xii + 315 pages

To my parents

Amelia M. Alum y Valenzuela (1921–)
Fabian I. Ruiz y Estrada (1909–1965)

PREFACE

This volume includes most of my published articles on the history of Burgos and northern Castile which have appeared in learned journals throughout the last two decades. As is the case with most historians, I can think of numerous ways in which they can be improved or changed for the better. Although, in some cases, I no longer embrace some of my earlier interpretations, or, at least not as sweepingly as I once did, I have refrained from altering these essays, with the exception of two articles translated from the original Spanish into English. They can thus serve as guideposts to my intellectual development and, I hope, to my growth as a scholar. My research interests, as this collection shows, have shifted over the years from the study of Burgos to that of the region of northern Castile, from economic and social history to the examination of symbols, colours and popular culture. These changes synchronized with similar transformations in the discipline of history, and reflected my concerns with new methodological and interdisciplinary approaches to historical issues.

In the last twenty years, there has been an almost revolutionary change in the manner in which scholars study and write about medieval Castilian history. With some noticeable exceptions, the normative works in early Castilian historiography focused on the areas of institutional and legal history. In the late 1960s, García de Valdeavellano, García de Cortazar, Valdeón Baruque and others, influenced by the works of Vicens Vives and of the French *Annales*, published methodological and historical landmarks which addressed the role of social and economic structures in the development of late medieval Castilian society. My early articles on the city of Burgos, on its ruling elites and on the crisis of late medieval Castile owe a great debt, first and foremost, to my teacher Joseph R. Strayer at Princeton, but also to the works of these scholars. Since then there has been a veritable flood of local studies, carefully researched monographs on rural, urban social and economic life, as well as the first serious attempts at providing a synthesis of the history of Old Castile. Among the best examples of this new vision of Castilian history, one may mention Hilario Casado's book on the Burgalese countryside and María Asenjo and Adeline Rucquoi's books on Segovia and Valladolid.

To an extent, some of my early articles may seem dated in the light of these new findings. I am thinking specifically about the essays on the economic structure of the region of Burgos and on rural life in the region of Campóo. Others, such as "The Transformation of the Castilian Municipalities," have stood, I believe, the test of time. I have also come to realize, as I reread through many of these essays, the abiding perversity of my scholarly interests. Although I sought, in most cases, to examine important issues in Castilian history from a novel perspective, there was also an underlying desire, almost a mischievous wish, to provoke, to ignite scholarly debate and to overthrow or at least to shake up long held orthodoxies. This certainly was and still is the case with three of the articles included in this collection.

"The Transformation of the Castilian Municipalities," (chapter VII), challenges the long held belief on the democratic character of Castilian municipal life before the reign of the Catholic Kings. "Expansion et changement," (chapter VIII), argues that the conquest of Seville and the problems of Christian expansion and settlement of al-Andalus shaped the subsequent course of Castilian history. "Unsacred Monarchy," (chapter XIII), shows that the kings of Castile did not legitimize their power through anointment and/or crowning but through ceremonies of marked popular flavour.

These last two articles have provoked a great deal of controversy and, in some cases, vehement reaction. Commenting on "Expansion et changement," Manuel González Jiménez pointed out, correctly I should add, that the crown's policies of resettlement of Andalucía sought to encourage the formation of a small and free farmers society. It was the failure of repopulation and not the conquest of Seville which led to the emergence of the latifundia. Based on information from Avila and some localities in Burgos, García de Cortazar has disputed my suggestion that there was a demographic crisis in the period before 1350. My answer to that is twofold.

First, the main thrust of my argument was that the conquest of Seville and the expansion into the South led to a rearrangement of political relations between the crown, the nobility and the non-noble knights. On the emergence of this new political arrangement in Castile, I have not been challenged and my main argument was and is, I think, correct. González Jiménez's assertions of the nature of the early repopulation policies are quite valid, but they do not necessarily alter my conclusions. Whether in the mid-thirteenth century or later, the latifundia became the normative form of agricultural production in southern Spain, and this pattern of economic development was exported to the New World with tragic consequences.

Second, regarding the demographic crisis, I have just concluded a rather long and detailed book, the labour of the last ten years, in which

I examine the question of whether there was a demographic crisis or not in northern Castile. My conclusions are that, as far as the documentation for northern Castile shows, the kingdom, notwithstanding some local exceptions, suffered a series of demographic upheavals which were to a large extent responsible for the late medieval crisis. Contrary to the usual Malthusian argument which has been advanced, erroneously I should add, as the main reason for the late medieval European crisis, my article shows that Castile faced serious economic and social problems in the late thirteenth and fourteenth centuries, because it did not have the demographic resources to support its unprecedented territorial expansion.

"Unsacred Monarchy" brought a sharp response from the young and talented José Manuel Nieto Soria. He argued that the Castilian monarchy was sacred, even though it lacked the outward symbols and rituals of anointment and coronation prevalent elsewhere in the West. The fact remains that the kings of Castile were, with few exceptions, neither crowned nor anointed; moreover, the arguments for sacral kingship even without the usual rituals are found mostly in fifteenth-century sources and not in the crucial period running from the late twelfth century to the rise of a new dynasty in the 1360s. In any case, I have already addressed his objections in an article published in the *Proceedings of the International Workshop on Frederick II* at Erice. Far more eloquently, Peter Linehan's new book on history and historians in medieval Spain deals with Nieto Soria's arguments far better than I can ever hope to do. Linehan nevertheless also shows that the mechanical statue of St. James, which medieval chronicles and myself had busily knighting kings from the early thirteenth century on, was not even present in Castile until the 1330s.

The seventies and eighties were heady times for historians. Inspired by the borrowing of new methodological tools from allied disciplines, historians sought to rewrite the past anew. We are less confident now, as the very validity of our texts, the heart of the medievalists' craft, is under question. Yet, if I am delighted and honoured to put these articles forward for the consideration of readers, it is because I have an abiding belief in the importance of texts and in the possibility of reconstructing the lives of medieval men and women and of understanding the social, economic and cultural structures of the world in which they lived. A belief which I learned long ago from Joseph Strayer and from my colleague Elizabeth A.R. Brown.

Individual articles already acknowledge the suggestions, advice and support of scholars and friends who, through the years, have helped me to be, I hope, a better historian. Here I wish to express my thanks to the different journals and publishers that have kindly permitted the reprinting of these articles by *Variorum*. Chapter I, "Burgos and the Council of 1080," which appeared in *Santiago, Saint-Denis, and Saint Peter: The Reception of the Roman Liturgy in León-Castile in 1080* (edited by Bernard F. Reilly and published by Fordham University Press in 1985) is reprinted by permission of Fordham University Press. Chapters II and VI are the English translations of "La estructura económica del área de Burgos," *Boletín de la institución Fernán González*, 186 (1976), 819–30, and of "Prosopografía burgalesa, 1248–1350," which appeared in the *Boletín de la institución Fernán González*, 184 (1975), 476–99. They are translated and reprinted with the kind permission of la Institución Fernán González. Academia Burgense de Historia y Bellas Artes in Burgos, Spain, Chapters III and V, "Burgos y el comercio castellano en la Baja Edad Media," which appeared in *La ciudad de Burgos. Actas del Ier congreso de historia de Burgos* (León, 1985), pp. 37–55, and "Notas para el estudio de la mujer en el área del Burgos medieval," in *El pasado histórico de Castilla y León*, 3 vols. (Burgos, 1983), I, 419–28 are reprinted by permission of the Consejería de Cultura y Bienestar Social of the Junta de Castilla y León. Chapter IV, "Una nota sobre la estructura y relaciones fiscales del Burgos bajomedieval," appeared in *En la España medieval, III. Estudios en memoria del profesor D. Salvador de Moxó* (Madrid, 1982), II, 387–97 and is reprinted here with the kind permission of the Universidad Complutense and of the editor, Profesor Miguel Angel Ladero Quesada. Chapter VII, "The Transformation of the Castilian Municipalities. The Case of Burgos, 1248–1350," World Copyright: The Past and Present Society, 175 Banbury Road, Oxford, England. This article is reprinted with the permission of the Society from *Past & Present: A Journal of Historical Studies*, no. 77 (November 1977), pp. 3–32. Chapters VIII and XV, "Expansion et changement: la conquête de Séville et la société castillane 1248–1350," *Annales E.S.C.*, (1979), 548–65, and "Festivités, couleurs et symboles du pouvoir en Castille au XVe siècle. Les célébrations de mai 1428," *Annales E.S.C.*, (1991), 521–46 are reprinted with the permission of *Annales E.S.C.* Chapter IX, "Castilian Merchants in England, 1248–1350," which appeared in *Order and Innovation in the Middle Ages. Essays in Honor of Joseph R. Strayer*, eds. William C. Jordan *et al.* (Princeton, N.J., 1976) is reprinted with the permission of the Princeton University Press. Chapter X, "Une note sur la vie rurale dans la région d'Aguilar de Campóo," which appeared in *Les Espagnes médiévales. Aspects économiques et sociaux. Melanges offerts à Jean Gautier-Dalché* (Nice, 1983), pp. 13–20 is reprinted with the permission of Professor Denis Menjot, director of the Centre d'Etudes Médiévales de l'Université de Nice and of the Association des Publications de la Faculté des Lettres de Nice. Chapter XI, "La formazione del mercato della terra nella Castiglia del basso medioevo," *Quaderni Storici*, 65 (1987), 423–52 is reprinted with the kind permission of Professor Edoardo Grendi, editor of the *Quaderni*. Chapter XII, "Oligarchy and Royal Power: The Castilian Cortes and the Castilian Crisis 1248–1350," *Parliaments, Estates and Representation*, 2 (1982), 95–101 is reprinted with the permission of Pageant Publishing. Chapter XIII, "Unsacred Monarchy: The Kings of Castile in the Late Middle Ages," which appeared in *Rites of Power. Symbolism, Ritual and Politics since the Middle Ages*, ed. Sean Wilentz (Philadelphia: University of Pennsylvania Press, 1985) is reprinted with the permission of University of Pennsylvania Press. Chapter XIV, "Images of Power in the Seals of the Castilian Monarchy: 1135–1469," which appeared in vol. IV of *Homenaje a Don Claudio Sánchez Albornoz* is reprinted with the permission of the Instituto de Historia de España of the Facultad de Filosofía y Letras of the Universidad de Buenos Aires. Chapter XVI, "The Holy Office in Medieval France and in Late Medieval Castile: Origins and Contrasts," which appeared in *The Spanish Inquisition and the Inquisitorial Mind* (Highland Lakes, N.J.: Atlantic Research and Publications, 1987) is reprinted with the kind permission of the editor, Professor Angel Alcalá. I must also thank Scarlett F. Berkowitz, friend, *compañera* and kindred soul, who helped me with the preparation of this manuscript.

TEOFILO F. RUIZ

Brooklyn, New York
December, 1991

PUBLISHER'S NOTE

The articles in this volume, as in all others in the Collected Studies Series, have not been given a new, continuous pagination. In order to avoid confusion, and to facilitate their use where these same studies have been referred to elsewhere, the original pagination has been maintained wherever possible.

Each article has been given a Roman number in order of appearance, as listed in the Contents. This number is repeated on each page and quoted in the index entries.

I

Burgos and the Council of 1080

THE COUNCIL that met in the city of Burgos in 1080[1] brought to an end the long and arduous process by which Castile turned from its allegiance to the Mozarabic rite to the observance of the Roman ritual.[2] As such, the council of 1080 was not a unique benchmark in the ecclesiastical history of the realm but rather a final step. Already under Fernando I, the Roman liturgy had made permanent inroads in the Cluniac monasteries in Castile,[3] and a series of councils and synods of the Castilian and other Iberian churches (Nájera, 1067; La Llantada, 1067; Burgos, 1073) made a commitment to the acceptance of the Roman rite in the kingdom.[4] This early success had already been noted by the *Crónica Najerense*, which reports that in 1075 the prayers of the Lenten festivities were chanted according to the Roman rite.[5] Furthermore, the example offered by the kings of Aragón and Navarre in abandoning the Mozarabic rite, the growing influence of Cluny and the threatening demands for compliance with the Roman ritual hurled against Alfonso VI by Alexander II, and, above all, Gregory VII had a decisive impact in the final outcome of the liturgical controversy.[6]

Almost two years before 1080, the *Chronicon Burgense* announced in a laconic entry that "intravit lex romana in Hispania."[7] Therefore, 1080 did not signal a revolutionary change in the ecclesiastical history of Castile; yet in Burgos Alfonso VI, who for political and personal reasons had resisted the adoption of the Roman forms, bent his will before Gregory VII's threats. Soon afterward the rich Mozarabic ritual faded away from the altars of Spain, although fortunately for antiquarians and historians Cardinal Ximénez de Cisneros rescued the liturgical books of the Mozarabic rite from oblivion in the fifteenth century, allowing the daily celebration of a Mozarabic Mass in a side chapel of the cathedral of Toledo.

The politics and religious implications of the introduction of the Roman rite in Castile have long attracted the attention of scholars. My task in the following pages is, however, more mundane and pedestrian.

First, I wish to describe, in as much detail as the extant documentation allows, the Burgos where the papal legate, the bishops of Castile–León, the abbots of nearby monasteries, and the king and his court met to transact the business of the council. Second, I will also suggest some reasons which may help explain why they met in Burgos, i.e., what made Burgos an attractive and convenient place for their deliberations.

Unfortunately we know little about Castilian cities in the early Middle Ages, and Burgos is no exception.[8] The documentation is scarce and so are secondary works on the subject. In the municipal archive of Burgos there are no documents from before the twelfth century and the *fuero* of Burgos has long been lost. One must depend, therefore, on documents from nearby monasteries and on those ecclesiastical documents which offer, from time to time, a glimpse into the social and economic life of the region. Interestingly enough, the years around 1080 marked the beginning of Burgos' rise to a position of primacy among the urban centers of northern Castile. This was due to many factors, among which one must not ignore the enhanced position of its bishop in the hierarchy of the kingdom resulting from the success of the council of 1080.[9]

Burgos had grown slowly from its foundation in the late 880s, when it comprised a few scattered homesites around the castle, to the end of the eleventh century. Most of the dynamic changes in the structure of the city took place, however, in the period around 1080. Burgos already had well-defined neighborhoods or parishes, numerous churches, and a low wall.[10] The city was ruled by a *concejo*, or city council, but we lack direct information about its composition or jurisdiction in the late eleventh century. There is evidence of the existence of *concejos* in the small villages around Burgos.[11] Documents show *concejos* serving as witness to transaction of property and, in other instances, the entire male population of the village serving.[12] The practice testifies to the size of the hamlets around the city, small and limited to a few families. In the contemporary documentation of the monastery of Cardeña, ten kilometers from the center of Burgos and possessor of by far the richest collection in the region, the *juez* and the *merino* of Burgos are mentioned, conclusive proof of the existence of a well-organized *concejo*. Their jurisdiction, or at least that of the *merino*, extended far beyond the city walls into the Orbaneja valley 50 kilometers north of the city. This may indicate that even then the city had an extensive *alfoz* or area under its control, a fact not uncommon in Reconquest Castile.[13] The city—for it must be emphasized that it was a city in spite of its small size, and was described as such in the documents[14]—was always part of the royal domain. Royal control was assured by the towering castle which, high upon its hill, dominated Burgos.[15]

Burgos had begun its life as a frontier outpost and never knew the blessings of security until early in the eleventh century. After Almanzor's death († 1002) and that of his son, Abd al-Malik († 1008), the firm establishment of the lines of the Arlanza and Duero rivers placed Burgos well beyond any Muslim attack.[16] The counts of Castile and, later on, its kings found the geographical location of the city ideal, as evidenced by their frequent visits and residence there.[17] In 1080 the city probably served as military headquarters. From Burgos to Toledo, which, if we are to believe Menéndez Pidal, Alfonso VI already planned to attack, is just over 300 kilometers in a straight line. The Guadarrama range with the pass of Somosierra was the only obstacle. Burgos was also conveniently located to keep a watchful eye over Castile's recent acquisitions in the Rioja (1076). It was equally well placed for communication with the Bay of Biscay region, and, at the same time, overlooked the troublesome borders with Navarre and Aragón.[18]

Even before 1080 Burgos had played an important role in the political life of Castile. Both King García of Galicia in 1071 and Alfonso VI in 1072, when he was just king of León, had been imprisoned in the city's castle by order of their brother, King Sancho.[19] After the latter was assassinated at the siege of Zamora, Alfonso VI, now king of Castile, León, and Galicia, came to Burgos to swear at the church of Santa Gadea his innocence in his brother's death.[20] After all, the survival and promise of his rule depended on Castile and not on León. This need to gain Castilian support became more necessary since in the early years of his reign he faced the hostility of some of the chroniclers of the monasteries around Burgos. Furthermore, Sancho had been a well-loved and quite successful king in the short time he ruled.[21] That Alfonso VI overcame this early resistance is clearly demonstrated in his exile of the trouble-maker Ruy Díaz de Vivar, and under his orders the city of Burgos closed its gates and refused aid to the Cid as he rode away from Castile.[22]

In 1080 Burgos had not yet reached the position of unofficial capital of Castile which it enjoyed later on. It had neither the size and prestige of imperial León, the commercial importance of Sahagún, nor the spiritual position of Compostela, but it was clearly advancing toward some such status.

Economically and socially the city was about to undergo a radical transformation. Early in its history there is evidence of trade. Burgos served

I

even then as a key intermediate point on the east–west and north–south trade routes which followed the old Roman roads.[23] The Andalusian chronicles mention the bazaars and commercial activity of the city. We also have documentary evidence of permanent stores (*tiendas*) and blacksmith shops within the city walls.[24] Burgos served as a regional market for the agricultural goods of the surrounding countryside, drawing a wide clientèle from areas as far away as Oña, Silos, and Aguilar de Campóo.

More important still, the labors of San Domingo de la Calzada and his followers, the growing security of the roads, and Cluniac promotion and propaganda were at the point of making the pilgrimage to the tomb of St. James in Compostela into a most popular excursion and the road to Santiago into a busy thoroughfare. In 1080 Burgos had just become a stage along the road and was beginning to benefit from the influence and expenditures of foreign pilgrims. Undoubtedly foreign merchants—the *francos*—settled in Burgos, even though, unlike Estella, Logroño, Sahagún, and other Navarrese and Castilian urban centers, these *francos* did not, so far as we know, gain a *fuero* of their own in Burgos.[25] One cannot underestimate the importance of the "Way of St. James" in ultimately turning the city into the most important trading center of northern Castile.[26] At the same time, the undeniable impact of the pilgrimage had hardly converted Burgos into a large, bustling urban center by 1080. In fact, its size and commercial importance in the late eleventh century must still have been relatively diminutive.

When the see of Burgos was relocated from its original site in Oca, it found a home not in the city but in Gamonal, a suburb of Burgos today. Although Gamonal was also on the road to Compostela, it was in the Middle Ages no more than a hamlet and well outside the city.[27] Coinciding more or less with the council, and thanks to Alfonso VI's generous gift of his own palace in Burgos, the bishops of Burgos–Oca found a lasting home in the city. Had Burgos been a thriving commercial center in the late eleventh century, there would have been no difficulty in attracting the wandering bishops of Oca–Valpuesta–Burgos. Thereafter, however, the city had no problem in retaining its bishops. Moreover, Alfonso VI and his foreign wife with their predilection for eccentric French holy men brought St. Lesmes to the city. This obscure figure became the city's resident saint and later its patron. Alfonso VI granted him and his monastery, San Juan, splendid donations, contributing greatly to the well-being of the city.[28]

Despite French settlers and incipient commerce, Burgos retained, as will be the case later on in the thirteenth and fourteenth centuries when it had indeed become a rich trading center, a predominantly rural character. The extent to which the countryside around the city remained unchanged in its economic and social organization, from its early settlement in the late ninth century to the years of crisis and change in the fourteenth century, is remarkable.[29]

The plain extending around the city was crisscrossed by *carreras* (small roads) and royal roads which allowed for the easy movement of goods.[30] The arable was given mainly to the production of cereals such as wheat, barley, and rye, and of wine, the typical pattern of agricultural production in northern Castile. In addition, flax, fruit trees (especially apple trees), and small gardens were common. Some livestock was run on the grazing lands and the fallow. The woods were exploited as always. Some of the most important salt wells of Castile are also found in the region of Burgos: Anaña, Poza de Sal, and others.[31] This basic, sturdy pattern of rural economic activity remained essentially unchanged for the next three centuries.

The scarce documentation still extant reveals a pattern of land-holding in which property was widely scattered over the countryside. The concentration and consolidation of property through the purchase of contiguous lands, so characteristic of the late thirteenth century and afterward, had not yet begun in 1080. As far as one can ascertain, the basic unit was rather small—as was the average price paid for it. Unfortunately in Burgos and in all of Castile the documents do not show the size of the land bought or sold. In the late eleventh centuryy, the terms *agro* and *divisa* were widely used in the documents. In 1062, a *divisa*, a cow, mills (probably backward horizontal mills), vineyards, and gardens were sold for 70 silver *solidi* (*ss.*).[32] In 1064, an *agro* and pasture land went for just 4 *ss.*; a *divisa* brought 60 *ss.* On the other hand, a year later a *divisa* was exchanged for a mule.[33] *Agros* were generally sold for amounts ranging between 20 and 30 *ss.*, but lower or higher figures are not uncommon.[34] Clearly, no general conclusions can be drawn from this fragmentary evidence. The price of horses, as always, seemed to command a rather high price, and therefore furnishes at least another basis of comparison. In 1069 a mare was sold for 15 *ss.*; and in San Millán de la Cogolla a horse and a mule were appraised at 1,000 *ss.*, though, since it was a donation, the value was probably exaggerated.[35]

As I have shown elsewhere, one found numerous mills in the area of Burgos. Most of them were the inexpensive and traditional horizontal mills, but there is evidence of more technically advanced vertical mills.[36] Rights to the use of mills were quite fragmented. These milling rights, sometimes as small as a few hours of grinding, were often sold or exchanged as outright property. The same can be said of salt wells.[37] The undeniable existence of a large number of small, free farmers and the widespread fragmentation of grinding rights alike point to the limits placed upon the feudal rights of the nobility. The nobles, a large majority of them illiterate as shown by the crosses with which they sign their donations but already with a taste for such expensive items as ermine coats and silver spurs, enjoyed special privileges. Their conduct and rights were regulated by a special *fuero de infanzones*, but in 1080, or afterward, they did not hold the extensive bans and economic prerogatives which were common to the nobility north of the Pyrenees.[38]

Socially, Burgos was also at a crossroads. Its early inhabitants, of Basque and Cantabrian origin, were well on their way to adopting Castilian names and identities.[39] As these changes were taking place, French and other northern merchants began to settle in the city, and their impact on the social and economic life of Burgos was still felt two hundred years later.[40] The city also had an important Jewish population, which found mention in Arab chronicles, in the *Poem of the Cid*, and in contemporary documents. We know little about its economic and social role but certainly enough to dismiss the stereotyped portrayal of Raquel and Vidas in the *Poem of the Cid.* Some Jews were both money-lenders and farmers.[41] It is probable that they served, as Thomas Glick has shown, as intermediaries between the Christian and Muslim world.[42] Furthermore, one finds a few references to *conversos*, perhaps an indication of growing religious pressure on the Jewish population coinciding with the introduction of the Roman liturgy.[43]

This rather broad and impressionistic sketch of Burgos in the late eleventh century suggests some reasons why Burgos was chosen as a site for this important council. The city did not rank with other urban centers such as León, Compostela, or even Sahagún; nevertheless, its strategic location made it a favorite of the Castilian kings. Alfonso VI displayed a marked interest in the city and appreciated its importance for the success of his rule. Bishop Jimeno of Burgos became, despite his lack of learning, the champion of the Roman rite in Castile and gained the favor of the Pope by his loyalty to Rome. Thus, he was given the task of spearheading the final adoption of the Roman liturgy.[44] The Roman Church had a great deal to gain by holding the council there and by having it labor under the watchful supervision of a well-known friend rather than somewhere else where the local bishop or abbot might not be as well disposed as Don Jimeno was. The ecclesiastical authorities in Rome could not have forgotten the pretensions of the archbishops of Compostela a few decades earlier and the unexpected attitude of the monk Robert after becoming abbot of Sahagún.[45] At another level the choice was ironic because, as Menéndez Pidal describes, Burgos was one of the hotbeds of resistance to the introduction of the Roman liturgy. How appropriate, then, to have the council ban the Mozarabic rite in Burgos itself.[46]

These are the familiar explanations. I would add here yet another which, although quite obvious, has not been pointed out by previous historians of Burgos. Within the diocese of Burgos, or close to its borders, one finds most of the important monasteries of northern Castile: San Pedro de Cardeña, San Salvador de Oña, Santo Domingo de Silos, San Salvador del Moral, San Pedro de Arlanza, and, a bit farther off, San Millán de la Cogolla and Santa María de Najera.[47] If one looks at a map of the province, one sees that, geographically, Burgos was the natural meeting-place for the powerful abbots of these monasteries. The road from Silos to Oña, from Nájera to Cardeña, passes through Burgos. The monasteries form a wide circle around the city.

The documents of the period also show the close connection between the bishops of Oca–Valpuesta–Burgos and the abbots of Cardeña, Arlanza, Silos, and the other monasteries in the region. The bishop of Burgos often appears as witness to important transactions of Cardeña, and there are numerous accounts of the abbots of these monasteries coming to Burgos to meet the king.[48] The heads of these monastic houses had great influence in the realm: partly because of their reputed saintliness (for example, St. Sisebuto and St. Domingo, abbots of Cardeña and Silos, respectively), partly because they had been the vanguard of Cluniac reform in central Castile, and finally because of their wealth. It is reasonable to think that they favored Burgos as the place for the meeting of the council. Burgos, just a short trip away from their monasteries, was to witness their final victory over the traditions of the past and to vindicate their own early embrace of the Roman ritual.

All Castile was responding and reacting to the influences of the Holy See and French culture.[49] Just so did Burgos to the dynamic impact of northern traders and pilgrims. The council of 1080 brought to an end the liturgical controversies over the validity of the Mozarabic rite. But the city of the council had already been noted for its advantages. The latter would carry it to future primacy among the cities of northern Castile.

NOTES

1. There are doubts as to the exact dating of the council or synod of Burgos. See Ramón Menéndez Pidal, *España del Cid*, 7th ed. (Madrid, 1969), I:246; Luciano Serrano, *El obispado de Burgos y Castilla primitiva desde el siglo V al XIII* (Madrid, 1935), I:305. Vicente de la Fuente in his now badly outdated *Historia eclesiástica de España*, 2nd ed. (Madrid, 1873), III:367–73 places the council in 1078 and the final acceptance of the Roman rite later than 1080. For a general background to the period and to Alfonso VI's reign see Joseph F. O'Callaghan, *A History of Medieval Spain* (Ithaca, 1975), pp. 193–214.

2. On the Mozarabic rite itself see William C. Bishop, *The Mozarabic and Ambrosian Rites* (London, 1924); Germán Prado, *Historia del rito mozárabe* (Madrid, 1924), and also his *Manual de liturgia hispano-visigótica o mozárabe* (Madrid, 1927).

3. Serrano, I:256.

4. Ibid., I:278, 289.

5. ES, XXXVIII:319.

6. Augustin Fliche and Victor Martin, *Histoire de l'église* (Paris, 1940), VIII:45–47, 53, 106, 129. See also Gregory VII's fierce attack against the Castilians, accusing them of heresy. *The Correspondence of Pope Gregory VII*, trans. Ephraim Emerton (New York, 1932), pp. 29, 123–25, 144. Luis García de Valdeavellano, *Historia de España*, 1st ed. (Madrid, 1952), pp. 807–20.

7. ES, XXIII:372.

8. On Castilian cities in general the recent published book by Jean Gautier-Dalché is useful though it does not have enough information on Burgos during the late eleventh century. Gautier-Dalché, *Historia urbana de León y Castilla en la Edad Media (siglos IX–XIII)* (Madrid, 1979), pp. 78–79. Also Claudio Sánchez-Albornoz, *Una ciudad hispano-cristiana hace un milenio. Estampas de la vida de León*, 5th ed. (Madrid, 1966). See also Bernard F. Reilly, *The Kingdom of León–Castilla under Queen Urraca, 1109–1126* (Princeton, 1982), pp. 314–51.

9. Gregory VII and Alfonso VI's satisfaction with the outcome of the council is reflected in the nomination of Don Jimeno, bishop of Burgos, for the dignity of metropolitan, an idea later rejected because of Don Jimeno's lack of learning. The king also gave to the bishop his palace in the city. Serrano, I:309–10; *Correspondence of Gregory VII*, p. 177.

10. Luciano Serrano, ed., *Becerro gótico de Cardeña* (Madrid, 1910), p. 241 (neighborhood of San Esteban), 346 (neighborhood of San Martín); Gautier-Dalché, p. 78 and the often quoted mention of Burgos' wall in the *Poem of the Cid.*

11. For *concejos* in general see María del Carmen Carlé, *Del concejo medieval castellano-leones* (Buenos Aires, 1968).

12. Serrano, *Becerro de Cardeña,* pp. 95–96 (1079), 53–54 (1080), and 47.

13. Serrano, ibid., pp. 175–76, and 18–20. The documents of Cardeña appear as volume III of the Fuentes de la historia de Castilla series. There are few or no documents for the period under discussion in volumes I and II of the Fuentes. These two volumes contain the documents of San Salvador del Moral and the Infantado de Covarrubias. On the *alfoz* of Burgos see Teofilo López Mata, "El alfoz de Burgos," *Boletín de la Institución Fernán González,* 154 (1961), 416–30; 155 (1961), 512–29; and 156 (1961), 618–34.

14. Burgos was already described as a city in the documents of the late eleventh century. Segovia, on the other hand, remained a *villa* well into the late thirteenth century.

15. On the castle of Burgos see Teofilo López Mata, *La ciudad y castillo de Burgos* (Burgos, 1949).

16. For a general overview of Castilian history in this period see O'Callaghan, pp. 193ff.

17. Burgos had clearly played an important role in the Castile of Fernán González. See the numerous mentions of his visits and stays in Burgos in Justo Pérez de Urbel, *El condado de Castilla* (Madrid, 1970), I:306; and Menéndez Pidal, I:169, 195, 209, 219, and 246.

18. Menéndez Pidal, I:224; García de Valdeavellano, p. 814.

19. López Mata, *La ciudad y castillo,* pp. 14–15.

20. Menéndez Pidal, I:195.

21. Ibid., I:197.

22. *Poema del Cid,* Biblioteca de Autores Espanoles, 57 (Madrid, 1966), p. 1.

23. Nazario González, *Burgos: La ciudad marginal* (Burgos, 1958), p. 87.

24. Ibid. See also Teofilo F. Ruiz, "La estructura económica del area de Burgos," *Boletín de la Institución Fernán González,* 186 (1976), 819–30 and my collection of essays on Burgos, *Sociedad y poder real en Castilla* (Barcelona, 1981). There are mentions of *herrerias* (blacksmith shops) in Serrano, *Becerro de Cardeña,* p. 274; and Antonio Ubieto Arteta, ed., *Cartulario de San Millán de la Cogolla (759–1076)* (Valencia, 1976), pp. 376–77.

25. On the pilgrimage to Compostela see Luis Vázquez de Parga et al., *Las peregrinaciones a Santiago de Compostela,* 3 vols. (Madrid, 1948–49). For Burgos specifically, II:181–99. On the *fueros* to the *francos* see Gautier-Dalché, ch. 8.

26. Luis García de Valdeavellano, *Origenes de la burguesia en la España medieval* (Madrid, 1969), pp. 87–102.

27. Serrano, *El obispado,* I:290–92.

28. For Alfonso VI's grants to St. Lesmes and to the Hospital of San Juan see *El "becerro" del monasterio de San Juan, Burgos* (Burgos, 1950), pp. 19–25.

29. Ruiz, "La estructura economica," 824–25; also my "Expansion et changement: La conquête de Seville et la société castillane (1248–1350)," *Annales E.S.C.* 3 (1979), 385–401.

30. Serrano, *Becerro de Cardeña*, p. 277.

31. Ibid., pp. 206–208, 199–203, 287, 62, 197, et passim; Ruiz, "La estructura economica," 825. See also Salustiano Moreta Velayos, *El monasterio de San Pedro de Cardeña. Historia de un dominio monastico castellano (902–1338)* (Salamanca, 1971); J. A. García de Cortazar, *El dominio del monasterio de San Millán de la Cogolla (siglos X a XIII): Introducción a la historia rural de Castilla altomedieval* (Salamanca, 1969).

32. Serrano, *Becerro de Cardeña*, p. 203.

33. Ibid., pp. 91, 197, and 290.

34. Ibid., pp. 163, 170, et passim. One also finds *agros* sold for 6 *ss.*, 31 *ss.*, and other diverse figures.

35. Ibid., p. 234; *Cartulario de San Millán*, pp. 316–17.

36. Ruiz, *Sociedad y poder real*, ch. 4. A document from Cardena mentions iron machinery in one of the mills of the monastery. It probably refers to an *acena.* Serrano, *Becerro de Cardeña*, p. 370. See also Thomas F. Glick, *Islamic and Christian Spain in the Early Middle Ages* (Princeton, 1979), pp. 92–99.

37. Ruiz, *Sociedad y poder real*, ch. 4; Serrano, *Becerro de Cardeña*, pp. 206, 260, 295–96, 370, et passim; *Cartulario de San Millán*, pp. 326, 359–60.

38. The *fuero de infanzones* is mentioned in a document of 1071. Serrano, *Becerro de Cardeña*, p. 330. For their illiteracy and blatant consumption pp. 262, 346, 349–50.

39. See the numerous Basque and Cantabrian names in the documents of the period in the area of Burgos. Also J. A. García de Cortazar, *Historia de España Alfaguara: La época medieval*, II (Madrid, 1974), 135.

40. T. F. Ruiz, "The Transformation of the Castilian Municipalities. The Case of Burgos 1248–1350," *Past & Present*, 77 (1977), 10.

41. *Poema del Cid*, p. 3. See below n. 42.

42. Y. Fritz Baer, *A History of the Jews in Christian Spain* (Philadelphia, 1961), I:43, 51; F. Cantera Burgos, "La juderia de Burgos," *Sefarad*, 12 (1952), 61–62; Serrano, *El obispado*, III:68–70; Glick, pp. 176, 258, 286, et passim.

43. Serrano, *Becerro de Cardeña*, p. 370.

44. Serrano, *El obispado*, I:298.

45. García de Valdeavellano, *Historia de España*, ch. 15.

46. Menéndez Pidal, p. 239.

47. Serrano, *El obispado*, II:227ff.

48. Ibid., I:296, 300, 306; Serrano, *Becerro de Cardeña*, pp. 161, 241, 284, 360, 260, and 340; Menéndez Pidal, I:169; *Cartulario de San Millán*, pp. 343, 376–77.

49. García de Valdeavellano, *Historia de España*, pp. 807–808.

II

THE ECONOMIC STRUCTURE OF THE AREA OF BURGOS, 1200-1350

One of the fundamental problems in the study of late medieval Castilian history is the process of reconstructing the social and economic structures of a particular region. As the works of the *annalistes* and of English historians have shown us, medieval history is, above all, the study and understanding of local conditions. We can see only the general patterns of development of a kingdom--in this particular instance Castile in the late Middle Ages--when, through many individual efforts, we can integrate different regional studies into a broad vision of the kingdom as a whole.[1]

My aim here is, simply, to present a preliminary inventory of the economic history of the area of Burgos in the late Middle Ages. It is important, however, to emphasize the economic peculiarities of the region of Burgos, as well as its relations with the Castilian economy at large. This inventory of the Burgalese economic resources must also be placed within the geographical and climatic history of the area. Both, geography and climate, limited and, to a point, shaped the economic destiny of Burgos and of its hinterland in the late Middle Ages, as they do at present. Fortunately, there is no need to examine these topics in detail. Teófilo López Mata's *La provincia de Burgos en la geografía y en la historia* and Nazario González's *Burgos. La ciudad marginal* provide excellent guides to the climate and geography of Burgos.[2] A few comments, however, would help illustrate the impact of climate and geography on the economy of the region of Burgos. The frequency and lateness of frost (an average of three in April) was a factor in the orientation of Burgos towards trade and the relative (by Castilian standards) secondary role played by agriculture in the region. In terms of its geographical location, Burgalese trade with Flanders and Andalusia flowed through the ports of Laredo, Santander, Castro Urdiales and other coastal towns on the shores of the Bay of Biscay. These locations, a mere 150 kilometers north of the city, were under the jurisdiction of the bishop of Burgos to whom they paid the tithe.[3]

---

1 Since the publication of this essay a large number of articles and monographs have been published on urban and rural local history. For a bibliography see my *Continuity and Change: Northern Castile in the Late Middle Ages* (forthcoming).

2 See Nazario González, *Burgos. La ciudad marginal*. (Burgos, 1958), pp. 47-61; Teófilo López Mata, *La provincia de Burgos en la geografía y en la historia* (Burgos, 1963), pp. 42-49.

3 See Archivo de la Catedral de Burgos (ACB), vol. 4, p. 1, f. 1 (10-VII-1192), published by Luciano Serrano, *El obispado de Burgos y Castilla primitiva desde el siglo V al XIII*, 3 vols. (Madrid, 1935-36), III, doc. #206. Confirmation by Alfonso X in ACB, vol. 71, f. 16, (25-II-

Moreover, a considerable number of the royal officials collecting custom duties in these ports, as well as of the merchants trading there were citizens of Burgos.[4]

What is obvious from the preceeding discussion of the geography and climate of Burgos is that the city had--more than any city in northern Castile--a commercial orientation. In fact, most historians agree that Burgos' mercantile orientation was unique in the context of the northern Castile's economy in the late Middle Ages.[5] This, as shall be seen below, is an assessment which needs to be modified.

The commercial life of Burgos was closely linked to its maritime outlets in the Bay of Biscay and to its location on the Road to Compostella. Manuel Basas Fernández and Luis García de Valdeavellano have already noted the importance of the pilgrimage to Santiago as the catalyst for the rise of the bourgeoise in northern Castile and for the emergence of Burgos as a commercial center. The Milky Way, as the Road was also called, traversed Burgos, following the streets of San Juan, Sanct Llorente and Tenebregosa. As I discuss elsewhere in this volume, the ruling oligarchy of the city resided along these streets during the thirteenth and fourteenth centuries. These were also the streets where most of the commercial activity took place. Burgos was a city where, as a letter of Fernando IV indicated with certain exaggeration, most of its inhabitants lived from the profits of trade.[6]

1255), and by Alfonso XI: ACB, vol. 4, p. 1, f. 13 (25-X-1333).

[4] See Mercedes Gaibrois de Ballesteros, *Historia del reinado de Sancho IV de Castilla*, 3 vols. (Madrid, 1922-28), I. This volume includes the accounts of some northern ports in 1293-1294. Also see chs. III, VI and VII.

[5] Manuel Basas Fernández, *El consulado de Burgos en el siglo XVI* (Madrid, 1963), pp. 29-31; María del Carmen Carlé, "Mercaderes en Castilla, 1252-1512," *Hispania*, XXI-XXII (1954), 175.

[6] Basas Fernández, pp. 29-31; Carlé, "Mercaderes en Castilla," 175; Luis García de Valdeavellano, *Orígenes de la burguesía en la España medieval* (Madrid, 1969), p. 88. See also Ismael García Rámila, "Estudio topográfico-histórico del Burgos de los siglos pasados," *Boletín de la comisión de monumentos de la provincia de Burgos* (hereafter *BCMPB*), XVIII-XIX (1939-40), 261-69, 305-16, 356-66, 396-404; Antonio Ballesteros y Beretta, "Datos para la topografía del Burgos medieval, *BCMPB*, XX-XXII (1941-43), 609-18, 1-9, 33-44, 73-82, 113-18, 145-52. See also ch. VII below. Eloy García de Quevedo, *Ordenanzas del Consulado de Burgos de 1538* (Burgos, 1905), p. 23, note 1.

FOREIGN TRADE

The city functioned as the center for the distribution of foreign trade along a north-south axis. Burgalese merchants linked the ultramarine textile centers of England and Flanders with the ports of the Bay of Biscay and, either overland or by sea, with Andalusian markets in the south. These activities can be easily illustrated. Burgalese merchants appeared prominently among the Castilians trading in Flanders.[7] Elsewhere in this volume, I also examine in detail the role of Burgalese merchants in England and their activities in the triangular trade which connected England, Flanders and Castile.[8] One must notice, above all, the commercial activities of Andrés Pérez de Castrogeriz, "merchant of Burgos," whose name appears in an extant document of 1313 as having loaned 1,000 *mrs.* to the city for the rebuilding of the walls. Andrés appears in the English documents as a "merchant of the king" of England, and he served Edward II in important political and mercantile missions abroad. His example is just one of the many which show Burgalese merchants trading and even settling in England and/or Flanders.[9]

Numerous references point to the privileged position of the city in the commercial life of the realm. In 1240 Fernando III granted to Burgos the right to a market "in la glera in illo loco qui est inter Relanzone (Arlanzón) et rivum de Vena."[10] We know little about the later life of this

---

[7] Jules Finot, *Etude historique sur les relations commerciales entre la Flandre et l'Espagne au Môyen Age* (Paris, 1899), pp. 6-7, 19, 47; *Calendar of the Patent Rolls, 1317-1321* (London, 1903), p. 605; Américo Castro, "Unos aranceles de aduana," *Revista de filología española*, VIII-X (1921-23), 5; Claudio Sánchez Albornoz, *España. Un enigma histórico*, 2 vols, (Buenos Aires, 1956), I, 123; Charles Verlinden, "Contribution a l'étude de l'expansion commerciale de la draperie flammande dans la peninsule iberique au XIII-siécle," *Revue du Nord*, 85 (Feb. 1936), 6; and also his *El comercio de paños flamencos y brabanzones en España durante los siglos XIII y XIV* (Madrid, 1952), pp. 8-9.

[8] See Chapter IX below for Castilian merchants in England.

[9] *Ibid.*, chapter IX.

[10] Julián García Saínz de Baranda, *La ciudad de Burgos y su concejo en la Edad Media*, 2 vols. (Burgos, 1967), I, 420-21.

particular market. Located outside the city walls, the market on the Arlanzón river must have served, primarily, as a place for the exchange of agricultural goods, but its charter of foundation may also serve as an indication of Fernando III's acceptance of the city as a distribution center for international trade.

This assumption is somewhat verified by subsequent evidence. In 1281, Rodrigo Ibáñez de Zamora, as representative of Castilian and Leonese merchants, and Pedro de la Riba Gordon, as a spokesman for the foreign merchants trading in Castile, protested to the king because of the abuses perpetrated by the royal officials in charge of collecting the tithe and the custom duties. Alfonso X prohibited the imprisonment of merchants because of debts which these merchants or their fellow citizens may have owed to municipal councils throughout the realm. The king also limited the collection of the tithe to the port of entry. Alfonso X sought, though with little success, to remove barriers to the free movement of goods within the kingdom. According to Carlé, Rodrigo Ibáñez de Zamora had commercial interests in Burgos. Pedro de la Riba Gordon resided in Burgos and served in the city council after 1281.[11]

On 15 February 1281, Alfonso X exempted foreign and local merchants from paying "*portadgo*" on their own goods. That same day the representatives of mercantile groups in Burgos, Santander, Casto Urdiales, Laredo, Medina de Pomar, Vitoria and foreign realms agreed to pay to the crown a fine of 101,000 *mrs*. This they paid in return for a royal pardon of the charges of exporting goods which had been fobidden to be taken out of the country by the cortes. The king accepted the fine and lifted the sanctions against the merchants.[12] Burgos and its representatives, Guillén Trapaz and Asensio García, headed the list of cities and delegates, attesting to the primacy of Burgos in the commercial network linking northern ports with the interior. These ties were already in place more than a decade before the establishment of the well-known brotherhood or Hermandad de la Marisma of 1926, which joined the commercial centers on the Bay of Biscay into a defensive league.[13]

On 21 May 1285, Sancho IV confirmed two privileges which had

---

11 Carlé, "Mercaderes en Castilla," pp. 224, 297, *Memorial histórico español*, 49 vols. (Madrid, 1851-1948), II, 29-31; Archivo Municipal de Burgos (AMB), clasif. 134 (13-II-1281). See also chapter VI below.

12 AMB, clasif. 2689 (15-II-1281); clasif. 2690 (15-II-1281).

13 See chapter VI, 487.

been previously granted by his grandfather, Ferdinand III. Besides ratifying the concession of a market, the king exempted from taxes those Burgalese merchants carrying their wares to Palencia by the royal road. Fernando IV, Sancho's son, also added other privileges to the long list of previous concessions. They attest to the importance of long distance commerce in the economic life of the city. The king allowed the merchants of Burgos free movement throughout the realm with "their carts and mule trains." At the same time, royal officials were restrained from detaining merchants unless it was for a personal debt. As the document states, the merchants of Burgos traveled freely within the kingdom with "all their merchandise, food (*viandas*) and cloth (*pannos*).[14] As shall be seen below, Burgos did not produce enough food or manufactured enough good quality cloth to support an export economy. The goods the merchants carried across the plains of Castile came from elsewhere. This role as distributors of foreign and regional trade is confirmed by two further privileges, granted by Ferdinand IV on 7 April 1304 and 28 February 1309, the latter granted exclusively to Burgos. By these grants, the king renewed the merchants' freedom of movement within the kingdom and exempted their goods from inspection except in the borders of the realm.[15]

Thirty years later, in 1339, Alfonso XI granted to the merchants of Burgos the right to sell abroad without penalty one horse (*rocín*) a year (up to a value of 400 *mrs.*). This particular document raises a series of questions. The merchants benefitting from this privilege carried their trade to Flanders and Montpellier.[16] Although trade with Flanders can be documented from a variety of other sources, this is the only reference to Burgalese trade with a Mediterranean French city. Common sense would indicate that trade there was, most probably, in the hands of Italian, Occitanian and Catalan merchants. Because the references to Burgalese trade in southwest France are so meager, there is little one can say about its nature or extent, except that it existed.[17] As corroborating evidence, there is a mention in the Burgalese archives of a citizen of Montpellier, a certain Johan, who settled in Burgos as a doctor and married a Burgalese

---

[14] AMB, clasif. 120 (21-V-1285); clasif. 104 (28-I303).

[15] AMB, clasif. 103 (7-IV-1304); clasif. 100 (28-II-1309).

[16] AMB, clasif. 96 (28-XI-339).

[17] For trade in Montpellier see A. Germain, *Histoire du commerce de Montpellier*, 2 vols. (Montpellier, 1861).

woman. In 1282, Johan sold some properties in Val de Casa to provide a dowry for one of his four sisters-in-law.[18]

To bring an end to this rather long list of examples, we should note that Alfonso XI granted to the city the right to hold an annual fair. It was to begin on St. John's Day and to last for fifteen days afterwards. The royal peace protected merchants bringing their goods to the fair, and, as an added incentive, the payment of tolls was also commuted.[19] The fair of Burgos never became successful, and there is not enough of a documentary record to study its history. Few years after its foundation, the Burgalese fair was eclipsed by the extraordinary success of the fairs at Medina del Campo.[20]

As I noted above, Burgos' commercial orientation in the late Middle Ages allowed for patterns of development which were almost exceptional in the context of the economic and institutional life of northern Castile. Its mercantile structure decisively influenced the emergence of an urban oligachy and the eventual transformation of its municipal institutions.[21] And, yet, for all my emphasis on the importance of long distance trade in thirteenth and fourteenth centuries Burgos, one should not accept too eagerly this one sided vision. The commercial proclivity of Burgos' economic structure was balanced by the existence of other forms of economic activities and by the unavoidable links of Castilian towns to agriculture and to the land.

LOCAL TRADE AND OTHER ACTIVITIES

If foreign trade was the most significant element in the economy of Burgos, providing the merchants with the financial foundations for their political hegemony, local commerce also played an important role in the life of the city. In addition, employment in the nascent royal and municipal bureaucracies brought prestige and economic rewards to Burgos and to its leading citizens. In this respect, one must remember that a large number of the royal tax collectors and tax farmers in the extensive

---

[18] ACB, vol. 49, f. 81 (23-IX-1282).

[19] AMB, clasif. 98 (24-XI-1339).

[20] On the fairs of Medina del Campo see C, Espejo and J. Paz, *Las antiguas ferias de Medina del Campo* (Valladolid, 1912).

[21] See below chapter VII.

jurisdiction of the diocese of Burgos were residents of the city. They belonged to the few families who monopolized the social, economic and political life of the city.[22]

As other towns in late medieval Europe, Burgos had a substantial number of its inhabitants engaged in local commerce and artisan pursuits. There are numerous references to butchers, shopkeepers, fishmongers and other similar economic activities, but for this period there is little one can say as to the volume of their business. One must simply assume that it was enough to satisfy the demands of the city itself. Because of the frequent royal visits to the city and Burgos' role as the unofficial capital of the realm, Burgalese shopkeepers and artisans must have also experienced marked fluctuations in demand and in the volume of their businesses. Moreover, the annual cycle of pilgrimages--mostly in Spring and Summer--must have also dictated important seasonal changes.

The city was, in any case, not a manufacturing center. Claudio Sánchez Albornoz has indicated that Burgos had a textile industry, but I have found no evidence that the city exported or produced textile in any meaningful quantity.[23] Although not an industrial town, in the medieval sense of the word, Carlé, in her article "Mercaderes en Castilla," also cites documents which reflect the economic diversity of the city in the twelfth and thirteenth centuries. Other documents from this period allow for the listing of additional forms of economic activities: millers, surgeons, doctors, tilemakers, moneychangers, harnessmakers, lawyers, charcoalmakers, dyers, sheathmakers, wood and salt merchants and others.[24]

Clearly, the city enjoyed a complex mercantile, artisanal and service economy more than adequate to satisfy the material needs of its population, and the municipal council had the resources and the will to engage in such ambitious projects as the rebuilding of the city walls. In 1313, don Domingo de Ramos--who had been *alcalde* of the city in 1296--bought the right to collect municipal taxes for the sum of 46,677 *mrs*. The city council ordered Domingo to pay two thirds of that amount to a large

[22] See chs. III, VI, and VII in this collection.

[23] Sánchez Albornoz, *España. Un enigma histórico*, II, 120.

[24] Carlé, "Mercaderes en Castilla, p. 171; González, *Burgos La ciudad marginal*, p. 113. Also ch. VI and ACB, vol. 45, f. 145 (15-XI-1300): *cirujano*; vol. 49, f. 81 (23-IX-1282): *médico*; vol. 50, p. 2, f. 145 (?-XI-1283): *tejero*; vol. 42, f. 35 (20-I-1299): *monedero*; AMB, clasif. 2941 (15-XII-1300): *brisoneros*; ACB, vol. 40, f. 251 (6-XI-1320): *abogado*; vol. 42, f. 8 (13-II-1323): *carbonero*; vol. 44, f. 5 (8-I-1324).

number of Burgalese citizens (113 altogether) who had advanced money for the work on the city walls. Most of the individuals listed were merchants, non-noble knights, as well as municipal and/or royal officials.[25]

References to "*tiendas*" (stores or shops) are numerous in the Burgalese documents; they provide a glimpse into the city's local commercial life. These, the shops, were places where daily economic changes took place, and the frequent mentions of these establishments reflect the bustling atmosphere of the medieval city. The first references to the existance of shops date from 982, and, characteristically, they were located on those streets which were part of the Road to Compostela. Similar evidence can be found in the following centuries.[26] Although a great deal of this information has already been studied by Ismael García Rámila and Antonio Ballesteros in their respective studies of the topography of medieval Burgos or can be found in the published documentation of the monastery of Las Huelgas and of the Hospital del Rey, it has not yet been examined for its economic significance nor placed in an adequate chronological framework.[27]

The first mention of a shop after 982 is found in an undated document, probably of the late twelfth century. In it, Pedro González donated two shops to the cathedral chapter of Burgos. The stores were located in the "*cal mayor*," towards the street of San or Sanct Llorente.[28] For 1212, 1213 and 1222 we have a good number of references to butchershops in the neighborhood of San Esteban, and a document, already cited by Carlé, shows other shops in the streets adjacent to the cathedral.[29] In 1222 a butchershop in the neighborhood of San Gil was exchanged for a piece of land plus 15 *mrs.*[30] This last transaction points to the relative

---

[25] AMB, clasif. 652 (19-XII-1313). Also ch. VI below.

[26] González, *Burgos. La ciudad marginal*, p. 8; Carlé, "Mercaderes en Castilla," p. 119.

[27] See footnote 6 above.

[28] ACB, vol. 70, f. 97 (c. XIIIth century.)

[29] Amancio Rodríguez López, *El real monasterio de las Huelgas y el Hospital del Rey*, 2 vols. (Burgos, 1907), I, 411; ACB, vol. 70, f. 75 (?-IV-1212); vol. 70, f. 68 (?-I-1213); vol. 70, f. 74 (?-IV-1213); vol. 70, f. 22 (?-I-1223).

[30] ACB, vol. 70, f. 92 (?-IV-1222).

value and economic importance of shops within the general economy of the region. Fifteen *mrs.* was the price of a modest piece of land, and to that, one must add the other portion of land. Further evidence of the importance and size of the stores is provided by a royal letter of 1257. That year Alfonso X ordered that the butchershops and fish stores located in the vicinity of the cathedral be moved to the area near the bridge of Santa María. Seemingly, the volume of business, the noise and the problems of sanitation disrupted the celebration of the liturgy.[31]

One additional indication of the financial importance of stores in general and butchershop in particular can be found in a royal charter of 1261. Alfonso X donated the usufruct of four stalls in the main butchershop of Burgos, located in the street of Tenebregosa, to the cathedral chapter. The following year the king granted jurisdiction over all the butchershops to the city council, with the exception of the aforementioned four stalls.[32]

Elsewhere I have already identified by name a good number of shopkeepers and artisans, living in Burgos between 1200 and 1350.[33] To this list we could add two cloth sellers, Don Vidal and García Ordóñez, as well as a leather shop in full operation during the first half of the fourteenth century.[34] García Saínz de Baranda has also identified two other centers of Burgalese commercial life: the Red, located in the neighborhood of San Esteban, where fish and other seafood was sold, and the Rastro, a special market located near the bridge of San Pablo, where every Saturday, between the feast of St. Michael (28 September) and Christmas, goat and lamb meat was sold.[35]

THE HINTERLAND OF BURGOS.-THE RURAL ECONOMY

To this summary of commercial activity in the region, one must add an inventory of the complementary rural economy. In the late Middle

---

31 ACB, vol. 2, p. 1, f. 8 (11-XI-1257).

32 ACB, vol. 2, p. 1, f. 5 (10-IV-1261); AMB, clasif. 116 (12-IV-1262).

33 See ch. VI below.

34 *Ibid.*; ACB, vol. 49, f. 4 (18-IX-1326); vol. 44, f. 550 (9-XII-1326); vol. 42, f. 39 (1-III-1330).

35 García Saínz de Baranda, *La ciudad de Burgos*, I, 288.

Ages the *alfoz*, the region around Burgos under the jurisdiction of the city, produced the usual diversified cereal crop common to the medieval rural economy: wheat, rye and barley. These cereals were sold at la Llana of Burgos, the local grain market of the city, located near the cathedral. In the thirteenth and early fourteenth centuries, the level of rural production, above all grain, seems to have been sufficient to supply the city, but with little margin to export to other regions or to provide relief in times of penury. In 1334 and 1346, to give just one example, bad weather and endemic nobiliary violence brought famine to the area of Burgos.[36]

Besides grain, Burgos and its alfoz produced a commodity of great commercial value: salt. Two of the most important saltwells in Castile were within a relatively short distance of the city. Although they were under the jurisdiction of the monastery of Las Huelgas and of the king respectively, the trade in salt added an important dimension to the economy of Burgos.[37] Salt was an indispensable item in human diet and an useful commodity for exchange in southern markets.

Burgalese documents for the period between 1150 and 1350 also include numerous references to vineyard and viticulture. Altogether there are more than sixty different vineyards mentioned in the extant record.[38]

---

[36] See footnote 6 above.

[37] *Cortes de los antiguos reinos de León y Castilla*, 5 vols. (Madrid, 1861-1903), I, 287; Antonio Benavides, *Memorias de Fernando IV de Castilla*, 2 vols. (Madrid, 1860), II, 608-09; Rodríguez López, *El real monasterio de las Huelgas y el hospital del rey*, I, 515, 542-43.

[38] Luciano Serrano, *Fuentes par la historia de Castilla*, 3 vols. (Valladolid, 1906-10), II, 7, (6-I-974); 9, (974), Serrano, *El obispado de Burgos*, II, 117 (1139); ACB, 70, f. 180 (1146); vol. 70, f. 21 (?-IX-1172); vol. 70, f. 21 b (?-IX-1172); vol. 70, f. 183 (?-V-1174); vol. 70, f. 202 (?-I-1175); vol. 70, f. 200 (?-III-1175); vol. 70, f. 181 (?-IV-1184); vol. 49, f. 35 (?-XII-1186); vol. 70, f. 184 (?-V-1195); vol. 50, p. 2, f. 134 (?-X-1200); Rodríguez López, *El real monasterio de las Huelgas*, I, pp. 341-42; ACB, 70, f. 38 (?-XII-1205); ACB, 70, f. 179 (?-julio-1206); Rodríguez López, *el real monasterio de las Huelgas*, I, 407-08; ACB, vol. 70, f. 192 (?-VIII-1208); vol. 70, f. 194 (?-III-1209); vol. 70, f. 176 (?-VI-1209); vol. 70, f. 39 (?-VIII-1209); vol. 70, f. 193 (?-VIII-1212); vol. 70, f. 185 (?-III-1213); Rodríguez López, *El real monasterio de las Huelgas*, I, 382; ACB, vol. 70, f. 191 (?-XII-1214); vol. 70, f. 195.(?-I-1215); vol. 70, f. 199, (?-V-1216); vol. 70, f. 204 (?-V-1216); vol. 70, f. 198 (?-VI-1216); vol. 70, f. 197, (?-XII, 1216); vol. 70, f. 196, (?-III-1221); vol. 70, f. 102, (?-XII-1222); vol. 70, f. 177 (?-XI-1227); vol. 70, f. 187, (?-I-1228); Rodríguez López, *El real monasterio de las Huelgas*, I, 455, 448-49; ACB, vol. 50, p. 2, f. 141 (25-VII-1253); Rodríguez López, *El real monasterio de las Huelgas*, I, 462, 471; ACB, vol. 48, f. 277 (4-XII-1270); vol. 49, f. 96 (28-XII-1292); vol. 49, f. 98 (4-II-1293); vol. 70, f. 175 (no date); vol. 48, f. 298 (25-II-1300); vol. 49, f. 27 (29-VII-1311); vol. 41, p. 1, f. 450 (27-III-1319); vol. 43, p. 2, f 17 (27-III-1319); vol. 30, f. 594 (21-IX-1324); vol. 30 f. 821 (25-IX-1324); vol. 30, f. 584 (23-X-1324); vol. 30, 596 (23-X-1324) vol. 30,

Some of them, such as the vineyard bought by Sancho García, the goldsmith, from the chapter of Burgos, were located right outside the walls of the city.[39] These references are even more remarkable if we consider that the area of Burgos, because of its soil and climate, was not really suited for viticulture in the Middle Ages or even today.

In the economy of rural Burgos, watermills also played an important role. At the end of the tenth century, the first references to watermills appear in the Burgalese documentation, and they grow rapidly in number in succeeding centuries.[40] Undoubtedly, in the Burgalese hinterland and within the city itself, mills were a familiar sight to the inhabitants of the city in the late Middle Ages, and, as I have already examined elsewhere, the fragmentation of milling rights in the area of Burgos shows the broad participation of diverse social groups in the use and rights over mills and in the economy of the region.[41]

Far less important than watermills, which required considerable financial investment and maintenance, was the large number of gardens which were cultivated within the city itself, just outside its walls or in the area of the *alfoz*. They balance, somewhat, the one sided vision of Burgos as a mercantile city. The gardens supplied produce for the needs of the city, but they also tell us about the importance of agriculture even within the urban setting. Moreover, their location, in what should have been a valuable urban space, provides important clues as to Burgos' demographic density.[42]

---

f. 583 (19-V-1325); vol. 30, f. 592 (31-V-1325); vol. 25, f. 23 (13-IV-1328); vol. 48, f. 275 (29-VI-1329); vol. 30, f. 588 (22-IV-1333); vol. 36, f. 650 (23-XI-1334) et passim.

39 See ch. VII, fn 40 below.

40 See my "Tecnología y división de la propiedad. Los molinos de Burgos en la Baja Edad Media," in *Sociedad y poder real en Castilla* (Barcelona, 1981), pp. 73-93.

41 Ibid., pp. 82-85. WIthin the city itself or just adjacent to the walls one finds the following mills: that of Atga near the gate of San Juan; that of Santa Agueda; a mill in the Vega of Burgos; the mill in the Huerta; one mill in the bridge of Santa María; a mill in the neighborhood of San Gil; the mills of Guillermo Arlanzón in the neighborhood of San Román, etc.

42 ACB, 70, f. 163 (?-XII-1213); vol. 70, f. 164 (?-I-1214); Rodríguez López, *El real monasterio de Las Huelgas*, I, 471-72; vol. 70, f. 154 (?-X-1206); vol. 70, f. 159 (?-VI-1212); vol. 70, f. 170 (?-VII-1212); vol. 70, f. 161 (?-XII-1212); vol. 70, f. 152 (?-II-1213); vol. 70, f. 165 (?-I-1214); vol. 70, f. 157 (?-V-12140; vol. 43, p. 1, f. 31 (14-IX-1259); vol. 50, p. 1, f. 57 (4-IV-1261); vol. 49,

CONCLUSION

From the information above, one can conclude that in the thirteenth and fourteenth centuries, Burgos was a city with a strong mercantile orientation, perhaps, far more than any other northern Castilian city, but, at the same time, this evidence must be balanced by the heterogeneous character of the Burgalese economy. The merchants of Burgos, as merchants did elsewhere, invested their profits in the land. The city, for all of its commerce, retained, without a doubt, its rural character.[43] One must point out, once again, the numerous areas within the city dedicated to the growth of produce or of the vine. Many of the inhabitants of the city worked in the fields adjacent to the walls. Above all, in spite of the numerous royal privileges and of the obvious prosperity of the ruling commercial oligarchy, there is no indication of an active building program, except for the rebuilding of the walls, or of any expansion of the city's boundaries beyond its walls. The documents show that gardens under cultivation within the city walls in the early thirteenth century remained unaltered in the mid-fourteenth century.

Although Burgos had enough resources to supply its own market, it lacked the volume of agricultural production for export of rural goods. Together with geography and climate, the limitations of Burgos rural resources determined, to a certain degree, the economic structure of Burgos and its *alfoz* in the Middle Ages. The economic orientation of the city was directed towards foreign trade, in addition, it also served as distribution center for northern Castile. In truth, regardless of the ties to the land and the marked rural character of the city, a reduced number of merchants dominated the commercial life of the city. These merchants controlled the patterns of economic development in the region; they also controlled the political and social life of Burgos.

---

f. 63 (15-VI-1277); vol. 19, f. 515 (18-XI-1284); vol. 50, p. 1, f. 61 (5-X-1286); vol. 43, p. 1, f. 4 (19-I-1295); vol. 43, p. 1, f. 29 (?-II-1314); vol. 43, p. 2, f. 102 (25-II-1317); vol. 40, , f. 212 (17-XI-1335); vol. 42, f. 221 (10-III-1346); vol. 43, p. 2, f. 7 (27-VI-1347); vol. 40, f. 223 (16-VIII-1348). See also ch. VII, below.

[43] See an engraving of early sixteenth century Burgos, still a time of demographic growth, when the city showed only a limited number of buildings outside the walls in Teófilo López Mata, *La ciudad y castillo de Burgos* (Burgos, 1949).

III

BURGOS Y EL COMERCIO CASTELLANO EN LA BAJA EDAD MEDIA: ECONOMIA Y MENTALIDAD

En su estudio pionero sobre los orígenes de la vida urbana en el norte de la Europa medieval, Henri Pirenne, el gran historiador belga, afirmaba que «las economías urbanas, propiamente dichas, se caracterizaban por su función como intermediarias de contactos comerciales a larga distancia» [1]. Estos lazos que unían a diferentes focos comerciales e industriales en el medioevo no se limitaban, sin embargo, sólo a relaciones comerciales sino que incluían tipos de intercambios culturales decisivamente influentes en la formación de nuevas actitudes mentales. Los centros urbanos del medioevo europeo pueden a la vez ser definidos, empleando ese lenguaje en boga hoy en día en las ciencias sociales, como «centros heterogenéticos donde encontramos ideas originales con autoridad más allá y en conflicto con formas culturales del pasado» [2]. Ajustándonos a esta definición, Burgos y algunas otras villas y ciudades del norte de Castilla pueden ser categorizadas, sin duda alguna, como centros urbanos cuyos mercaderes distribuían los frutos del comercio exterior y regional a todo lo largo y ancho de Castilla. Este carácter de intermediarios entre diferentes ejes económicos significó al mismo tiempo la transformación de actitudes tradicionales así como la adopción de nuevas formas de pensar, de nuevos tipos de dieta, y nuevos modelos de conducta.

Hoy en día, quizás no estemos tan dispuestos a admitir como algo real la pronunciada dicotomía entre el mundo urbano y el mundo rural que numerosos historiadores han enfatizado en el pasado. En su lugar, ciertamente en la Castilla del nor-

---

[1] Citado en John Langton y Göran Hoppe, *Town and Country in the Development of Early Modern Western Europe* (Historical Geography Research Series), 11 (nov. 1983), p. 6.

[2] *Ibid.*, p. 7.

te y probablemente en otras partes de Europa medieval, la demarcación entre lo que hoy consideramos el campo y lo que al presente definimos como ciudad no fue siempre algo fácil de indentificar. Cuando examinamos las ciudades y villas de Castilla septentrional y particularmente Burgos, debemos de pensar en términos regionales, pues la ciudad a orillas del Arlanzón mantuvo una compleja relación con otras villas, así como con su campo circundante durante toda la Baja Edad Media y aun más en tiempos de los Austrias [3]. Estos lazos se extendían mucho más allá de la inevitable interdependencia económica, marcando una multitud de aspectos políticos, culturales y sociales.

No es éste, sin embargo, el momento para explorar en detalle todas las facetas de estas relaciones o la hegemonía comercial de Burgos en el norte de Castilla a finales del siglo XIII y principios del XIV. En estas páginas, mi proyecto es más limitado. Desearía explorar, aunque someramente, detalles específicos de la vida comercial de Burgos y del norte de Castilla. Apartándome de mis investigaciones anteriores sobre este tema, me propongo ahora reexaminar este comercio tomando en cuenta un ámbito regional e internacional. Al mismo tiempo, aunque sólo sea a la ligera, deseo explorar hasta qué punto la vocación comercial afectó la mentalidad no sólo de las élites mercantiles, sino de otros sectores o grupos sociales en Burgos y otras villas en la región.

I. Entre las tipologías que frecuentemente se emplean para diferenciar entre formas de organización urbana una de las más favorecidas es la que distingue entre villas mercaderas y villas rurales —o en el lenguaje de los procuradores de los concejos de Logroño, Navarrete, Nájera, Treviño, Haro, Briones y otras villas de la Rioja definiéndose a sí mismas «que en las dichas e en otras villas que son en sus comarcas... que no son villas mercaderas» [4]. Hay que añadir que mientras estos concejos reclamaban la protección del rey, con la excusa de no ser villas de comercio, no cejaban en sus esfuerzos de vender su vino en otras regiones.

De todas formas esta tipología que distingue entre lo rural y lo comercial resulta de poca utilidad si señalamos una vez más que aún ciudades con una inclinación mercantil tan marcada como Burgos, conservaron a todo lo largo del medioevo y hasta el presente un importante componente agrícola. Con esta atenuación, podemos entonces afirmar que existía en el norte de Castilla una red de centros urbanos en la que podemos identificar una marcada orientación comercial. Se pueden ver con claridad el vigor de estos contactos inter-regionales en dos instancias particulares. Primeramente tenemos a la famosa Hermandad de las Marismas —hermandad de los puertos de la costa de Cantabria y del País Vasco, Santander, Laredo, Castro Urdiales, Bermeo, Guetaria, San Sebastián, Fuenterrabía y Vitoria en el interior. La segunda instancia se trata de la reunión de los mercaderes de diversas villas castellanas

---

[3] Vid. Carlos Estepa et al, *Burgos en la Edad Media* (Valladolid, 1984), pp. 261-73 y el libro de Paul Hiltpold sobre la ciudad de Burgos en el siglo XVI de próxima publicación.

[4] Diego Ochagavia Fernández,«Notas para la historia de los vinos riojanos», *Berceo*, 10 (1949), p. 14.

y extranjeras, quienes bajo el liderazgo de Burgos y con representación de Castro Urdiales, Laredo, Santander, Aguilar de Campoo, Vitoria y Medina de Pomar presentaron en Burgos una serie de peticiones al rey en 1281[5].

En el primero de estos casos, las villas mencionadas, con la excepción de Vitoria, constituían los puertos más importantes del mar de Castilla, y junto con Lequeitio, Portugalete, Plencia y Bilbao después de 1300, sirvieron como puntos de acceso y partida para el comercio ultramarino de Castilla. En cada uno de estos lugares, a pesar de que la escasa documentación de la época no nos permite reconstruir las élites comerciales, encontramos mercaderes y marinos activos en el comercio internacional. A ello debemos añadir, aunque sea de paso, que muchos de ellos eran vecinos de Burgos. Los mercaderes y hombres de mar —que en muchos casos significaba lo mismo— de los puertos del Cantábrico, así como de las ciudades del interior, mantenían un vigoroso comercio por tierra y mar con Andalucía, Inglaterra, Francia, Italia y, sobre todo, con los centros fabriles de Flandes y Brabante. Las obras de Jules Finot y Charles Verlinden sobre el comercio castellano-flamenco, el reciente libro de Wendy Childs y uno de mis artículos sobre el comercio anglo-castellano ilustran claramente este punto[6]. En el caso de la relación comercial entre Castilla e Inglaterra el gran número de mercaderes y naves del norte de Castilla que podemos identificar a través de los *English Calendars* y de otros documentos es francamente impresionante. Y todavía nos queda un gran número de mercaderes, identificados sólo como originarios de Hispania —o sea de Castilla pues en la documentación medieval ambos términos eran sinónimos— que es lógico suponer eran vecinos de esos pueblos de la costa o de villas en las redes comerciales centradas en Burgos o en Vitoria. Un poco más difícil es identificar a los mercaderes que comerciaban en Andalucía o Flandes aunque también podemos identificar a un buen número de ellos y trazar sus actividades a diversas ciudades del norte de Castilla, aunque en su mayoría a Burgos. Hay que suponer, y esto es algo que se puede demostrar en algunos casos, que la mayoría de los mercaderes castellanos con intereses en el comercio inglés traficaban al mismo tiempo con Flandes[7].

En el pasado he enfatizado el papel de estos puertos como punto de entrada de un comercio en manos de mercaderes burgaleses. Aunque en muchos sentidos esta conclusión es correcta, debemos re-examinar este comercio en un ámbito regional. Hasta cierto punto, algunas de las villas al norte de Burgos, tales como Medina de Pomar, o al este o al oeste, como Aguilar de Campoo, Orduña, y sobre todo Vitoria, para sólo mencionar algunas, poseían intereses comerciales propios que los llevaban en ciertos casos a circunvenir a Burgos. Es obvio que Santander, Castro Ur-

[5] Antonio Benavides, *Memorias de Don Fernando IV de Castilla*, 2 vols. (Madrid, 1860), II, 81-85; Archivo Municipal de Burgos (A.M.B.), clasif. 2.690 (15-II-1281).

[6] Vid. Jules Finot, *Etude historique sur le relations commerciales entre la Flandre et l'Espagne au moyen âge* (París, 1899); Charles Verlinden, «Draps des Pays-Bas et du Nord de la France en Espagne au XIVe siècle», *Le Moyen Age* 3.e série, 8 (1937), 21-36; «Paños belgas en fuentes literarias españolas medievales. Poesía e historia económica», *Cuadernos de historia de España*, 29-30 (1939), 218-30; Wendy Childs, *Anglo-Castilian Trade in the later Middle Ages* (Manchester, 1978); Teófilo F. Ruiz, *Sociedad y poder real en Castilla* (Barcelona, 1981), cap. VII.

[7] Ruiz, pp. 205-06.

diales, Laredo, San Sebastián, Bilbao, Vitoria y otras localidades en la costa o cerca de ella, también tenían élites comerciales en contacto con la de Burgos, pero también independientes de ella.

Entre los signos de esta independencia relativa a las villas del norte en sus relaciones con Burgos podemos señalar entre otras el comercio marítimo como Sevilla, el comercio de Logroño —una villa en teoría no mercadera— con el sur por vías de Arnedo, Yuste, Soria y Guadalajara, o las relaciones comerciales de San Vicente de la Barquera con la meseta central a través de Reinosa y Aguilar de Campoo[8]. En todo este período, a pesar de lo largo y peligroso de la travesía, comino, pimienta, canela, miel, cueros y frutos viajaban de los puertos andaluces al mar de Castilla. En los puertos del Cantábrico se vendía o cambiaba parte de estas mercancías, se recogían otras, por lo general hierro, cueros, un poco de lana, y de ahí rumbo al norte, a puertos franceses, ingleses y flamencos. Este modelo lo podemos ilustrar con numerosos ejemplos. En 1337, para sólo mencionar dos casos, Domingo Pérez y Sancho Fernández de Frías, mercaderes burgaleses, transportaron en diferentes bajeles miel, cueros de Sevilla, canela, sebo y cereales a Inglaterra y Flandes[9].

En los documentos ingleses encontramos más de 70 mercaderes de Bermeo, Fuenterrabía, Guetaria, Lequeitio, Plencia, Portugalete y San Sebastián y más de 40 mercaderes de tales villas del interior como Vitoria, Tolosa, Miranda de Ebro, Orduña, Medina de Pomar y Valmaseda.

CUADRO I

MERCADERES DE LA COSTA Y DE VILLAS DEL INTERIOR

A. **Villas de la costa**	**Número de mercaderes en la documentación inglesa**
Bermeo	12 *
Bilbao	6 *
Fuenterrabía	7
Guetaria	10
Lequeitio	2
Plencia	4 *
Portugalete	2
San Sebastián	11 *

B. **Villas del interior**	**Número de mercaderes**
Medina de Pomar	3
Miranda de Ebro	1
Orduña	6 *
Tolosa	2
Valmaseda	3
Vitoria	20 *

* Indica que la documentación menciona otros mercaderes de estas villas sin especificar los nombres o el número.

C. **Barcos (Lugar de origen)**	**Número**
Bermeo	10
Bilbao	3
Fuenterrabía	2
Guetaria	5
Lequeitio	1
Plencia	3
Portugalete	1
San Sebastián	8

Podemos así mismo identificar más de 40 barcos, y esto es en adición a los numerosos mercaderes de los Cuatro Puertos y de Burgos que ya he identificado en mi artículo «Mercaderes castellanos en Inglaterra»[10].

Hay que reconocer, al mismo tiempo, que el nombre del barco nos revela a veces la procedencia del capital. La Santa María de Burgos, propiedad de Juan Sánchez, un mercader de Castro Urdiales, era probablemente un barco financiado por intereses comerciales burgaleses. En todo caso, la Hermandad de las Marismas y otras evidencias documentales indican que a pesar de la diversidad que hemos apuntado con antelación existía una comunidad de intereses políticos y mercantiles en el norte de Castilla. Poseemos una lista de la tripulación y pasajeros de una nave de Guetaria que es bastante indicativo de la unidad indiscutible de las villas marítimas del interior. En 1296 el dicho bajel transportaba mercancías con destino a Inglaterra y entre la tripulación encontramos a cuatro mercaderes, Juan Ortiz de Bermeo, y otros tres de Valmaseda, Martín Juánez, Lope y Rodrigo. El maestre de la nave, Bertram Pérez, era probablemente de Bermeo y de sus hombres, una tripulación de 15, 6 eran de Guetaria, 4 de Fuenterrabía, 2 de Bermeo, 2 de San Sebastián y el último era Edward le Engleys, o sea un nativo de Inglaterra[11]. Hay que suponer que este amasijo de marinos de diferentes lugares de la costa, del interior, y aun del extranjero era representativo de otras tripulaciones y compañías mercantiles del norte de Castilla.

Temo que aunque mi intención en esta ponencia es examinar aspectos específicos del comercio burgalés y castellano, me he desviado un poco de mi propósito en esta discusión del comercio del mar de Castilla. Sin embargo, para ilustrar el tipo de comercio que promovió a las villas y ciudades del norte de Castilla a ser algo más que meros centros de distribución para sus respectivos alfoces, tenemos por necesidad

---

8 Vid. Ruiz, pp. 221-23.
Sobre Vitoria véase también E. Fernández de Pinedo, «Aspectos económicos y sociales de Vitoria y su entorno en la Baja Edad Media», en *Vitoria en la Edad Media* (Vitoria, 1982), pp. 65-73, y la comunicación de César González Mínguez publicada en las actas del Congreso de Historia de Burgos.

9 Ruiz, pp. 208-09.

10 Cuadro. La documentación proviene de los Calendar of the Patent, Fine and Close Rolls para el período entre los años 1250 y 1360. Véase asimismo, T. F. Ruiz, «Mercaderes castellanos en Inglaterra, 1248-1350», *Anuario Juan de la Cosa*, vol. I (1977), pp. 11-38.

11 *Calendar of the Patent Rolls, 1292-1301* (Londres, 1895), p. 207 (16-IX-1296).

que comenzar en los puertos del Cantábrico. La estructura de este comercio nos explica en gran parte la naturaleza peculiar de los grupos mercantiles en la región y el tenor de la vida en algunas de las ciudades de Castilla septentrional. Afortunadamente poseemos documentos que reflejan, aunque sólo sea parcialmente, este comercio. Me refiero en particular a las «Cuentas y gastos del Rey Don Sancho IV (1293-94)» publicadas por Mercedes Gaibrois de Ballesteros. Dicho documento representa una fuente valiosísima para la historia de Castilla todavía por ser utilizada en su totalidad. Como anexo a las *Cuentas* debemos notar también los aranceles de aduana que datan de la misma época editados por Américo Castro [12]. A pesar de las limitaciones de ambos documentos —la información que ellos contienen se limita a sólo unos cuantos puertos— ambos son representativos del comercio castellano en el período anterior a 1350 y del inicio de la exportación masiva de lana a puertos flamencos.

Siguiendo la información de las *Cuentas*, los productos importados pueden ser clasificados en dos categorías: telas y otros productos no textiles. En un interesante artículo, Gual Camarena ya ha examinado el origen, volumen y precio de las telas importadas, en su mayoría de Flandes, pero también de Inglaterra, Francia e Italia. Las cantidades de paños importados en un año y la inversión monetaria que esto representó, aun cuando nuestra información se limita a sólo una pequeña fracción del total, no deja de ser francamente asombrosa. De estas telas la mayor parte correspondía a las llamadas Valencinas, o telas de Valenciennes, pero que a finales del siglo XIII ya eran producidas en otros centros textiles del norte de Europa y que según Gual Camarena eran empleadas para la vestimenta de sirvientes y escuderos [13].

No por esto debemos de ignorar la importancia de las telas de lujo en el comercio castellano. Los testamentos e inventarios, así como las leyes suntuarias de la época, dan vívido testimonio de la función social y estimación que los estamentos nobiliarios y burgueses conferían a las telas de lujo, tales como la escarlata, la seda y los paños tintos. Aunque trabajo sobre este tema al presente, sin embargo, lo debemos dejar a un lado para concentrarnos en el papel del tráfico de telas de la actividad comercial del norte de Castilla [14]. En las *Cuentas* podemos seguir casi día a día las actividades de la aduana de San Sebastián desde el 20 de enero de 1293 al 1 de octubre del mismo año, lo que nos permite compararlas con las de otros puertos mencionados en las Cuentas.

CUADRO II

REGISTROS EN EL PUERTO DE SAN SEBASTIAN 20-I-1293 AL 1-X-1294

Enero	3	Mayo	14	Septiembre	11
Febrero	34	Junio	8	Octubre	2
Marzo	10	Julio	16		
Abril	6	Agosto	13	Total	117 [15]

El mes de febrero con 34 declaraciones del diezmo es el mes de más actividad comercial. No poseemos información alguna sobre el período del 1 de octubre al 20 de enero, pero basados en los datos de Fuenterrabía y la Nao, debemos suponer que febrero es el mes de más tráfico en toda la costa. No se produce, sin embargo, una distribución equitativa a través del mes, sino que las declaraciones de mercancías se concentran en unos pocos días; el período entre el 12 y 21 de febrero incluye todos los registros, con 19 el día 17 y 8 el día 19. Las cifras sugieren una travesía en grupo —pequeñas flotas en realidad— desde los puertos ingleses y flamencos a los del Cantábrico; unas pocas naves adelantándose y otras rezagándose durante el viaje. No por eso debemos pensar que cada declaración de diezmo representaba a un barco. La mayoría de las mercancías, telas, agujas, pieles, arenques, etc., no eran de gran volumen y ya hemos visto con anterioridad como grupos de mercaderes compartían un barco. Ni tampoco podemos suponer que todos los mercaderes cuyos nombres aparecen en las listas abonando el diezmo viajaban de Flandes a Castilla. Por ejemplo, un Juan de Beunza aparece en los registros el 25 de junio, el 8 de julio, el 21 de agosto y el 10 de septiembre lo cual no le hubiera dado tiempo suficiente para la travesía marítima. Juan de Beunza fue quizás un agente permanente o semipermanente en San Sebastián, quien recibía mercancías del extranjero para después llevarlas o enviarlas a otros puntos en el interior para su distribución y venta [16].

Creo que el registro del día 17 de febrero merece un estudio detallado, porque aunque un día excepcional en términos de volumen, dicho registro modela el comercio castellano en la Baja Edad Media. 19 mercaderes se nombran en las declaraciones del diezmo de ese día con sus respectivas mercancías. El importe total, 307.249 mrs., representa casi el 43 por 100 del costo de todas las mercancías introducidas en el reino por el puerto de San Sebastián del 20 de enero al 10 de octubre. De las 19 declaraciones, 11 consistían en mercancías tasadas en más de 10.000 mrs., lo cual resulta extraordinario, pues en lo que resta de año en sólo otras cuatro ocasiones se rebasa dicha cifra. Poseemos ejemplos similares para el Figuer de Fuenterrabía que nos lleva a pensar que aunque importadas durante todo el año, la mayor parte de las telas y otras mercancías entraban al reino en cuestión de unos pocos días, algo que nos recuerda las grandes flotas que de Sevilla y Cádiz a América y de América a Sevilla y Cádiz mantenían el pulso del imperio en los siglos XVI y XVII [17].

Si examinamos los nombres de los mercaderes mencionados en los registros del 17 de febrero específicamente y para el resto del año en general, no siempre podemos descubrir su lugar de origen o reconstruir su posición social o política a través de la documentación local. De los 19 mercaderes que aparecen en el registro del día 17, hay que destacar a Giralt de Prestines quien declaró mercancías por valor de 17.500

---

[12] En Mercedes Gaibrois de Ballesteros, *Historia del reinado de Sancho IV de Castilla*, 3 vols. (Madrid, 1922-28), vol. I; Américo Castro, «Unos aranceles de aduanas del siglo XIII», *Revista de Filología Española*, VIII (1921), pp. 1-29, pp. 325-56; IX (1922), pp. 266-76; X (1923), pp. 113-36.

[13] Miguel Gual Camarena, «El comercio de telas en el siglo XIII hispano», *Anuario de Historia Económica y Social*, I (1968), pp. 85-106.

[14] Trabajo al presente en una monografía sobre el norte de Castilla titulada tentativamente, «Patterns of development in late medieval Castile».

[15] *Cuentas*, pp. iii xiii.

[16] Idem.

[17] *Ibid.*, pp. iii-vi.

mrs. Giralt pertenecía a una de las familias más destacadas de Burgos, los Prestines, emparentados con la familia de los Bonifaz, el grupo familiar dominante en la ciudad a principios del siglo XIV y nombre estrechamente vinculado con la historia de Burgos. Giralt debió ser bastante joven en 1293, pues más tarde lo encontramos nuevamente entre un buen número de ciudadanos burgaleses quienes en 1313 arrendaron los impuestos de la ciudad o prestaron cantidades importantes de dinero al concejo para la reconstrucción de la cerca. En 1338, ya al final de su vida, Giralt era alcalde de la ciudad y miembro, junto con sus hijos y otros parientes de la prestigiosa y exclusiva cofradía del Santísimo y Santiago, una hermandad reservada para los «buenos de la ciudad», los caballeros —o sea, aquéllos poseedores de la fortuna necesaria para mantener un caballo de guerra y armas. Como la mayoría de los mercaderes y caballeros de Burgos, Giralt residía en la Cal de Sanct Llorente, cerca de la catedral [18]. Juan Pérez de Carrión, otro mercader burgalés mencionado el 17 de febrero, importó mercancías ese día por valor de 8.790 mrs. Como Giralt de Prestines, Juan pertenecía a uno de los clanes familiares que dominaban la vida de Burgos en esa época, el clan de los Cambranas-Pérez de Carrión. En 1273 Juan fue miembro del concejo de la ciudad y junto con su hermano, García Pérez de Carrión, aparece también en la lista de 1313 anteriormente citada. La cantidad con que ambos contribuyeron a la reconstrucción de la cerca, 5.000 mrs., fue la más alta de las registradas. Con anterioridad en 1293-94, lo encontramos al servicio del rey, y diez años más tarde, en 1303, como alcalde de la ciudad. Otros miembros de la familia Cambranas-Pérez de Carrión aparecen prominentemente como oficiales del concejo de Burgos, mercaderes y miembros de las cofradías de caballeros de la ciudad [19].

Los mercaderes de Burgos no monopolizaban el tráfico de San Sebastián. El registro del 17 de febrero nos muestra a un Ferrán Iváñez de Vitoria, junto a no menos de cuatro mercaderes a quienes podemos identificar como vecinos de Vitoria. Esto unido a la presencia de otros mercaderes burgaleses, entre los que debemos destacar a Juan García de Frías, nos indica en líneas generales, la dirección del comercio castellano de importación [20]. Debemos suponer que una vez que las mercancías eran desembarcadas en San Sebastián, proseguían hacia el interior, vía Orduña y Vitoria, y de Vitoria en dirección a Burgos o a la Rioja. La presencia en los registros de San Sebastián de por lo menos 10 mercaderes de Burgos a quienes podemos identificar con certeza con posibilidades de que su número fuese aún mayor; o sea casi 10 por 100 del total de mercaderes mencionados en las *Cuentas* de San Sebastián —nos indica la importancia de Burgos en el comercio del norte de Castilla. De mayor importancia aún es que sabemos que la mayor parte del comercio burgalés con ultramar llegaba a tierras de Castilla a través de los Cuatro Puertos, y eran transportados ha-

[18] *Ibid.*, p. v; Ruiz, *Sociedad y poder real*, cap. V; A.M.B., clasif. 652 (19-XII-1313); *Texto cronológico de las tres reglas, por la que sucesivamente rigió su vida corporativa la Real Cofradía del «Santísimo y Santiago» de la ciudad de Burgos*, ed. Ismael García Rámila (Burgos, 1970), p. 17. De ahora en adelante referido como *Texto*.

[19] *Texto*, p. 17; *Cuentas*, p. v; A.M.B., clasif. 652 (19-XII-1313); A.M.B., clasif. 806 (4-VIII-1273); Ruiz, *Sociedad y poder real*, cap. V; A.H.N. Clero, carpeta 185 // 11 (17-III-1303).

[20] Entre los mercaderes de Vitoria debemos destacar a Johan de Vitoria, John Yñeguez de Vitoria, M. García de Vitoria, y Lope de Vitoria. Para Juan García de Frías. *Cuentas*, p. vi.

cia el sur casi siempre por el camino que unía a Laredo con Burgos. Quizás los burgaleses que operaban en San Sebastián importaban telas y otros productos con destino a mercados en la Rioja y Navarra, y compartían clientes o pugnaban por ellos con los intereses comerciales de Vitoria, Orduña y Valmaseda. Por otro lado, la navegación en el Golfo de Vizcaya no ha sido nunca una empresa fácil, y San Sebastián representaba, junto con Fuenterrabía, los primeros puntos de llegada para la navegación costera que, de Flandes o Inglaterra, hacía puerto en Bordeaux o Bayonne. Debemos recordar que siglos más tarde en 1512, la flota de Carlos I con destino a Santander, ancló cerca de Villaviciosa por equivocación [21]. Cualquiera que fuese la razón, lo que nos importa, es que San Sebastián, como los otros puertos del norte, atraía mercaderes de toda la región: hombres de Guetaria, el más importante de ellos, Juan de Ochoa, mercaderes y marinos de Castro Urdiales, de Francia, de Gascuña, de Navarra, Vitoria, de otros lugares y, sobre todo de Burgos. De estos contactos más allá de las fronteras políticas, el mejor ejemplo es el de Lop de Roncesvalles. Por sí solo, o con otros mercaderes de Navarra, Lop recibió o trajo mercancías a San Sebastián el 28 de enero, el 21 de abril, el 6 de junio y el 10 de septiembre. Las mercancías importadas eran por lo general más bien modestas: 12.000 arenques por un valor total de sólo 480 mrs. y 70 piezas de Valencinas a 170 mrs. la pieza, tan sólo por un total de 12.380 mrs. por los cuatro viajes. Podemos imaginar a Lop transportando sus mercancías hasta Vitoria, dirección suroeste, donde sabemos que pagó el diezmo en uno de sus viajes, y después probablemente por el camino de Santiago hacia Navarra [22].

Asimismo debemos considerar quiénes eran los compradores de telas importadas. Como Gual Camarena ha indicado, la Valencina, una tela cuyo costo es relativamente bajo, representaba una gran parte del volumen de las importaciones. Sin embargo no debemos pensar que era tela de pobres. Los pobres, como nos muestran numerosos testamentos, se vestían de estopazo o sayal [23]. Además, los paños producidos en Castilla, en su mayoría en Segovia, Avila o Soria, se vendían a precios muy inferiores a los de las telas importadas. Por ejemplo en 1268 cuando la vara de Valencina costaba 6 1/2 mrs., la mejor tela segoviana se vendía a sólo 4 sueldos la vara [24]. Las telas que podemos considerar como más caras entre las mencionadas en las *Cuentas* —y ellas no incluyen tela escarlata la más cara y codiciada de todas— paños tintos, blaos y otros, representaban una porción considerable del precio total de todas las telas. En este sentido los paños asignados a los funcionarios de la casa real, único ejemplo que poseemos de los años 1293-94, nos indican el consumo excesivo y ostentoso que constituía un desgaste continuo de las finanzas reales y que añadido a los cuantiosos gastos de los ricos hombres debió representar una importante porción del déficit del comercio exterior castellano. Casi 140.000 mrs. fueron desti-

21 *Viajes de extranjeros por España y Portugal*, ed. J. García Mercadal, 3 vols. (Madrid, 1952-62), I, p. 673.

22 *Cuentas*, pp. iii, vii, ix, xii.

23 Entre los muchos testamentos que he examinado baste ahora mencionar uno de 1315. A.H.N. Clero, carpeta 241 // 1 (29-IV-1315).

24 María del Carmen Carlé, «El precio de la vida en Castilla del rey Sabio al Emplazado», *Cuadernos de historia de España*, XV (1951), pp. 143-44.

nados a vestir y calzar a los hombres del rey en 1293, y esto sin tomar en cuenta otras cantidades similares devengadas en el séquito de la reina, amén de otras asignaciones para ropa de oficiales y sirvientes que encontramos dispersas en las cuentas de 1293-94[25].

La diferencia considerable entre los precios de telas extranjeras y las producidas en Castilla explica en parte el porqué, las ganancias derivadas del comercio de textiles flamencos debieron ser muy superiores a las derivadas de las ventas de telas castellanas a pesar de los gastos de transportación, diezmos y derecho de peaje. Y esto es lo que llevó a estos mercaderes a enfatizar un comercio de distribución y su papel de intermediarios en el comercio castellano más que la inversión en el desarrollo de actividades fabriles. Recordemos también que en Burgos y otras villas mercaderas del norte de Castilla, dichas ganancias sirvieron de base económica para la hegemonía política y social de los mercaderes[26].

Aunque no tan importante como el comercio de telas, toda una serie de otros productos entraban también por los puertos del Cantábrico con destino a los mercados del interior. La preponderancia del comercio de telas, claro está, aseguraba la regularidad de los contactos comerciales entre el norte de Castilla, Flandes, Inglaterra y Francia; pero la presencia de otros productos nos muestra una compleja red de vías comerciales. Por el puerto de San Sebastián, como por los otros, entraban otros productos que una vez más podemos clasificar en dos categorías: productos alimenticios y fabriles. Entre los primeros debemos destacar a los arenques, probablemente del mar del Norte, 121.000 en total a un precio promedio de 35 mrs. el millar. El pescado se vendía bien en la región, sobre todo en el interior donde sabemos por disposiciones testamentarias que se donaba dinero para la alimentación de los pobres y por las cuentas de monasterios, que se consumía en abundancia. Mucho más caro que los arenques era la pimienta, alrededor de 5 mrs. la libra, el azúcar de 3 a 5 mrs. la libra, y pequeñas cantidades de azafrán que entonces, como hoy, demandaba un alto precio (12 mrs./lb); también de alto precio eran otros productos de franca procedencia meridional, como el jengibre y el añil. Aunque no encontramos mención de cereales en las cuentas de San Sebastián de 1293, otras fuentes nos muestran que eran importados cuando la producción castellana no era suficiente. Tal fue el caso en 1346 cuando mercaderes castellanos importaron 160 toneladas en una instancia, y 1.000 cuartos de trigo inglés en otra oportunidad[27].

Lo que hay que destacar, sin embargo, es que con la excepción de los arenques, los otros productos alimenticios procedían del sur, probablemente por vía de Sevilla. La pimienta, por ejemplo, era fácil de adquirir en toda Castilla, como lo demuestran entre otras evidencias, las cuentas de mecaderes navarros que en 1352 viajaban a través del norte de Castilla, de Estella a Sevilla, y que nos muestra, aparte de los numerosos privilegios de que disfrutaban los mercaderes del norte de Castilla

[25] *Cuentas*, pp. lxxiii-lxxv et appsim.

[26] El ejemplo de Burgos es sólo el más evidente. Véase Estepa et al, *Burgos en la Edad Media*, pp. 140-45, o el ejemplo de Pedro Pérez, tendero y alcalde en Miranda de Ebro. A.H.N. Clero, carpeta 242 // 16 (6-VII-1342).

[27] *Cuentas*, pp. iii-xiii; *Calendar of the Patent Rolls*, 1345-48 (Londres, 1903), pp. 58, 201 (18-III-1346) y (8-XI-1346).

que viajaban por tierra a Sevilla, la constante comunicación, ora por vía terrestre, ora por mar, con los mercados andaluces [28].

La estructuración del comercio inter-regional norte-sur era mucho más compleja que un simple intercambio de especies y productos subtropicales, cueros y pequeñas cantidades de lana de Andalucía por el hierro y cáñamo de Castilla septentrional. Así lo demuestra la labor de Pero de la Riba y Pedro Pérez, dos mercaderes burgaleses y funcionarios de Sancho IV, quienes por orden del rey enviaron hierro y cáñamo por mar de Laredo a Sevilla en 1293. Pero más allá de esta gestión básica del comercio castellano-andaluz podemos observar una elaborada estructura de transferencias comerciales que incluía telas de alto precio y artículos de lujo de Italia, tintes de Montpellier, seda y toda una gama de productos que a través del estrecho de Gibraltar iban de Sevilla a los puertos del Cantábrico y de ahí al extranjero. Tal lo indican los mercaderes castellanos y maestres que transportaban granadas para el deleite nostálgico de la reina castellana de Eduardo I de Inglaterra, o los que cargaban sus navíos con lana inglesa destinada a Italia [29].

Parte de este comercio con centro en Sevilla se encontraba pocos años después de la conquista de la ciudad, en manos de mercaderes y banqueros italianos quienes jugaban un papel vital en el comercio andaluz. Debemos enfatizar, sin embargo, que éste no fue el caso en el norte de Castilla, pero aunque un buen número de los comerciantes castellanos descendían de mercaderes extranjeros establecidos a lo largo del camino a Santiago durante el siglo XII, en la época que estudiamos, sus intereses y perspectivas eran netamente castellanas. Hay que añadir que la ruta marítima hacia Andalucía y el Mediterráneo no sustituyó del todo las antiguas vías comerciales que cruzaban la península de norte a sur; eso sí, ofrecía alternativas en una época tan turbulenta como las minorías de edad de Fernando IV y Alfonso XI, compensando de esa forma los peligros del mar.

Tenemos que considerar la segunda categoría de productos importados a través del puerto de San Sebastián en 1293. Estos incluían grandes cantidades de agujas, peines, mondadientes, cuchillos, y otros utensilios de mesa, espadas, cáñamo, botones de París, sombreros de Toulouse, sortijas, dedales y mercería. Por lo general eran objetos de poco valor y de fácil distribución. Algunos de estos productos, como por ejemplo, los sombreros importados de Toulouse, quizás fuesen transportados por tierra hasta Bordeaux, y de allí por mar a San Sebastián. Las espadas y los cuchillos, quizás eran de manufactura andaluza, con su antigua tradición en la producción de armas blancas [29].

El comercio no puede, sin embargo, consistir solamente en importaciones. Si nos guiamos por las Cuentas de 1293-94, Castilla sufría entonces de lo que hoy en día describiríamos como un balance deficitario en su comercio exterior. Estos conceptos están muy lejos de la mentalidad medieval, por lo que nuestra visión moderna resulta un impedimento y no una ayuda. En esa época se favorecía la importación y se obstaculizaba la exportación. Si examinamos los registros de Orio, Oyarzun y Segu-

---

[28] *Desde Estella a Sevilla. Cuentas de un viaje (1352)*, ed. María Desamparados Sánchez Villar (Valencia, 1974).
[29] Véase Ruiz, «Mercaderes castellanos», pp. 11-38; *Cuentas*, pp. iii-xiii.

ra podemos observar que el volumen de exportación sólo representa una fracción del total de las exportaciones castellanas. En las cuentas de dichas tres estaciones de recaudación del diezmo encontramos casi exclusivamente evidencia de la exportación de un solo producto, el hierro. En ellos alrededor de 800.000 lbs. de hierro fueron declarados en sólo unos pocos meses, lo que nos da una idea de la gran cantidad de hierro que se exportaba al exterior desde otros puertos en el Cantábrico. Parte de este metal se transportaba al sur, otras cantidades eran asignadas a la construcción de navíos en los puertos del Cantábrico —como por ejemplo los 29 quintales de hierro enviados a San Sebastián por Pedro Juánez de Aperreguín el 3 de agosto de 1293 para los marcos de las ventas de un «halop» bajo construcción en ese puerto. La mayor parte del hierro, sin embargo, se enviaba al norte de Europa en pago parcial del gran volumen de telas importadas. En los registros de Segura encontramos también pequeñas cantidades de cuero, cáñamo y herramienta, a lo que podemos añadir, gracias a la evidencia que nos proporcionan otras fuentes, caballos — cuando no lo prohibían los edictos reales de las Cortes. Además se exportaba sebo, arroz, mercurio, alumbre, miel, almendras, higos, dátiles, frutas en general, anís, platos, madera, comino y otras especies, armaduras, vino, en especial vinos dulces de Andalucía, un poco de lana, y en contadas ocasiones, trigo [30].

Entre los mercaderes que dominaban el comercio del hierro encontramos un buen número de ellos, Juan Ochoa de Guetaria, Miguel de Beunça, Pero Ortiz de Osunsulo, Juan Bono, Martín Orduña, Domingo de Berrio, Juan Iñiguez de Vitoria, quienes eran así mismo importadores de telas. Como en el caso del comercio de paños, unos cuantos de estos mercaderes, Pero Martínez en Segura, Martín Orduña, Pero Ochoa y otros en los demás puertos, casi monopolizaban el mercado de hierro. Junto a ellos encontramos mercaderes de Guetaria, San Sebastián, Vitoria, Orduña, Burgos y otras villas del norte de Castilla compartiendo las ganacias y mostrando una vez más la existencia de una élite comercial regional dispuesta a cooperar hasta cierto punto en empresas comerciales.

Hasta el presente he concentrado mi atención en los puertos del Cantábrico y en el comercio marítimo, aunque como ya hemos visto, mercaderes de las villas del interior participaban de forma activa en este comercio. Ahora debemos dirigir nuestra atención a otros tipos de alianzas, que nos revelan en parte la dinámica comercial del norte de Castilla y la preponderancia de Burgos en ella. No existe un tipo de alianza similar a la Hermandad de las Marismas de 1296 para las ciudades del interior. Las grandes Hermandades de 1295 y 1315, aunque reflejaban ciertos intereses comerciales eran esencialmente ligas políticas que incluían entre sus miembros localidades con poco o ningún comercio de larga distancia. Una serie de privilegios reales a principios de la década de 1280 nos muestra por otro lado la interdependencia del comercio del norte de Castilla.

A principios del año 1281, Alfonso X otorgó un privilegio a los mercaderes castellanos y extranjeros que es indicativo del espíritu de cooperación que existía entre

[30] Ruiz, «Mercaderes castellanos», pp. 25-29; Finot, p. 303.

ellos, así como las dificultades a las que tenían que enfrentarse en la gestión de sus negocios. Rodrigo Ibáñez de Zamora y Pedro de la Riba de Gordón por sí mismos, y como procuradores de los otros mercaderes, presentaron una larga lista de quejas al rey. El tenor de éstas, que podemos deducir de la respuesta del rey, expresaba las usuales y justificadas protestas contra los abusos de los recaudadores del portazgo y de los diezmos en los puertos de mar y tierra. Al mismo tiempo los mercaderes se lamentaban de la violencia endémica —recordemos que la fecha coincide con el inicio del conflicto entre el rey y el Infante don Sancho— que amenazaba a las actividades comerciales. Estos abusos, como los mercaderes enfatizaban y el rey estaba presto a admitir, obstruían el intercambio comercial y ponían en peligro el bienestar económico del reino. Alfonso X prometió protegerlos contra los abusos de los recaudadores reales y municipales, al tiempo que les autorizaba a exportar mecancías por valor similar a las que importaban. Las barreras a la exportación evidentes en este decreto son dignas de notar, pues depósitos de gran cuantía eran requisito para garantizar los productos a exportar. Por otra parte, los pagos del diezmo debían ser abonados en plata, una condición bastante onerosa para los mercaderes en una época en que la moneda castellana sufría una seria devaluación[31].

El 15 de febrero del mismo año Alfonso se reunió una vez más con los representantes de grupos mercantiles del mar de Castilla y de las villas mercaderas del interior. Los mercaderes de estas localidades eran en este caso acusados de exportar productos vedados por las Cortes, y de no haber depositado las cantidades en plata requeridas. El rey ordenó a dos de sus oficiales, Domingo Pérez de Burgos y Arnalt de Castro, que efectuasen las apropiadas pesquisas. Entre los procuradores en reunión con el rey encontramos una vez más a Pero de la Riba Gordón por los mercaderes extranjeros, Asensio Guillén y Guillén Trapaz por los de Burgos, Martín Salcedo y don Ochava por Castro Urdiales, Bernalt Pelegrino por Laredo, Domingo Pérez de Precianes de Santander, Don Quirze de Aguilar de Campoo, Juan Martínez de Çamarra y Lope Juánez de Vitoria, Don Bartolomé y Domingo Pérez, ambos de Medina de Pomar. Ellos acordaron pagar 101.000 mrs. al rey como compensación y a cambio del cese inmediato de las investigaciones[32].

Podemos deducir lo siguiente de estas negociaciones: lo primero es enfatizar, una vez más, el carácter regional del comercio castellano. Al mismo tiempo, hay que destacar también que las ganancias derivadas del comercio internacional debieron ser suficientemente elevadas como para que los mercaderes estuviesen dispuestos a pagar una multa en plata equivalente a 101.000 mrs. para poner fin a las pesquisas, en especial a la investigación de la exportación de productos prohibidos. Finalmente, podemos afirmar que a los mercaderes les apremiaba exportar. En un período cuando la moneda castellana carecía casi de valor, la compra de paños en Flandes requería o metálico aceptable en el exterior, el equivalente moderno de divisas, o productos de fácil comercialización. Es por esto que a pesar de las amonestaciones

---

[31] A.M.B., clasif. 134 (13-II-1281), publicado en *Memorial Histórico Español*, II, p. 293.
[32] A.M.B., clasif. 2.690 (15-II-1281).

de las Cortes y los decretos reales —su misma frecuencia nos indica la naturaleza del problema— los mercaderes castellanos continuaron sus esfuerzos para exportar caballos, seda, halcones y otros productos cuya venta al exterior estaba terminantemente prohibida. Aunque nos es imposible estimar el balance negativo del comercio exterior de esta época, no cabe dudas que no beneficiaba al reino y, como sucedería en una época posterior, Castilla se convirtió en un exportador de metales preciosos —el oro y la plata de las minas de Africa que por tierras de Castilla iba a enriquecer a los protocapitalistas de Flandes e Italia.

Hay otros aspectos del comercio inter-regional castellano que merecen señalarse, pero que debido a las limitaciones de tiempo y espacio debemos posponer para otra ocasión. En lo que resta desearía examinar, aunque sólo sea superficialmente, la estructura social y la mentalidad de los mercaderes del norte de Castilla, privilegiando sobre todo a Burgos. Para comenzar debemos seguir la ruta marcada en páginas anteriores, o sea, reconocer a dichos mercaderes e integrarlos en la vida diaria de sus respectivas ciudades. Si examinamos la lista de los representantes de mercaderes reunidos con el rey en 1281, encontramos en ellos, una vez más, a Pero de la Riba y a Rodrigo Ibáñez de Zamora. El primero, probablemente un comerciante extranjero, o por lo menos con importantes contactos con el exterior, se estableció en Burgos y era vecino de la ciudad con todo lo que esto implicaba: propiedad dentro de la cerca y derechos políticos. En 1293 y 1294, junto con Pedro Pérez, alcalde de Burgos, encontramos a Pedro de la Riba como recaudador del diezmo en los Cuatro Puertos, así como supervisor de las cuentas de los recaudadores locales. El 14 de julio de 1294 presentó sus cuentas, que incluían gestiones en nombre del rey, tales como el envío de hierro y cáñamo a Sevilla y la supervisión del decorado de la capilla de Santa Bárbara en Burgos. Casi 40 años más tarde, otro Pero de la Riba, probablemente un hijo, aparece como miembro de la cofradía de la Real Hermandad —la exclusiva cofradía de caballeros de la ciudad— y como residente de la cal de Sanct Llorente, la residencia habitual de la oligarquía de la ciudad. Su compañero en las gestiones de 1281, Rodrigo Ibáñez de Zamora, mercader y oficial del rey, fue también a pesar de su nombre, residente de Burgos [33]. Asensio García recaudó impuestos, o lo que es más probable, los arrendó en 1279, 1281 y casi seguro en 1293 cuando recibió 2.000 mrs. en pago parcial por los 13.000 mrs. que Asensio y otros hombres de Burgos habían entregado a Abraham el Barchilón para uso del rey. Unos años antes de 1280 Asensio adquirió una viña extramuros. El otro representante de Burgos, Guillén Trapaz, pertenecía a una de las más poderosas familias de la ciudad —mercaderes y caballeros al mismo tiempo, con extensas propiedades y cargos políticos [34].

Es obvio que centros comerciales de la importancia de Burgos, Vitoria o aun San Sebastián atraían a mercaderes del exterior y de villas circundantes. A finales del siglo XIII y principios del XIV, las condiciones de acceso a los círculos comerciales

---

[33] *Cuentas*, pp. xl, xli, xliii; *Texto*, p. 17; Ruiz, *Sociedad y poder real*, p. 56.

[34] *Cuentas*, xlii; A.M.B., clasif. 2.572 (20-II-1279); A.M.B., clasif. 2.689 (15-II-1281); Archivo Catedral de Burgos (A.C.B.), vol. 49, f. 80 (11-II-1280); Ruiz, *Sociedad y poder real*, p. 196.

mantenían la suficiente fluidez como para permitir el ingreso de dichos mercaderes. En Burgos, que es nuestro mejor ejemplo, algunos de los mercaderes venidos de afuera compartieron sin gran dificultad el poder político y económico de las élites locales. Sus nombres y conexiones, de Carrión, de Frías, de Zamora, etc., nos indican la movilidad de las élites comerciales, aunque su final aceptación se supeditaba a que fuesen capaces de empresas comerciales de envergadura. Los movimientos de mercancía a través de la región, los sostenidos contactos entre los centros urbanos del área y la comunidad de sus intereses eran motivos suficientes para establecer lazos entre las élites mercantiles del norte de Castilla; lazos, debo añadir, que en tiempos difíciles se traducían en alianzas políticas tales como las Hermandades de la época. Sustituyamos la noción de una élite urbana en cada villa por la de una élite comercial regional, pues vecinaje en una ciudad no impedía mantener intereses y aun lealtades al lugar nativo. Para ilustrar este punto basta indicar el ejemplo de Juan Ochoa de Guetaria, mercader de telas en San Sebastián, comerciante de Guetaria, exportador de hierro por Oyarzun, y al mismo tiempo personero y vecino de San Sebastián; o Juan Pérez de Frías, mercader, vecino y caballero de Burgos, pero con propiedades en Frías y afiliación espiritual al Hospital de esa villa.

Debemos resumir con una serie de generalizaciones. Las élites mercantiles del norte de Castilla fueron capaces de integrar mercaderes extranjeros sin perder su preeminencia en los mercados de la región. La vida comercial del norte de Castilla en los siglos XIII y XIV no estaba en manos de comerciantes italianos o de otros extranjeros como era ya el caso en el sur. No existe tampoco evidencia de participación judía o mora en el comercio internacional, ciertamente no en el de Burgos. Pero ya sabemos lo difícil que es superar estereotipos aun cuando no sean ciertos [35]. Estos mercaderes, identificados anteriormente o en algunos de mis trabajos previos, cumplían —en sus respectivas villas— funciones que iban más allá de sus actividades comerciales. Es esa personalidad polifacética del mercader castellano la que creaba una mentalidad distinta a la que emanaba del ámbito rural. Ella les hacía mirar al mundo que les rodeaba, a la dinámica política del reino, y a la cultura de la época en una forma nueva dentro de la manera de pensar del castellano medio en la Baja Edad Media.

II. Los mercaderes del norte de Castilla, y con certeza los de Burgos, derivaban en su mayoría su rango social y su hegemonía política de sus actividades comerciales. Las ganancias del comercio exterior les permitían la adquisición de caballo y armas, y éstas a su vez garantizaban entrada en la Caballería Villana con todos los privilegios económicos y políticos que conllevaba. Nuestros mercaderes, y esto ya lo he demostrado en el caso de Burgos [36], eran al mismo tiempo caballeros, miembros de la milicia municipal, funcionarios de la burocracia real y del gobierno municipal. Estos diferentes aspectos, o podemos casi decir, diferentes personalidades se conjugaban con su creciente interés en la adquisición de propiedades rurales en los

[35] Sobre este tema véase las opiniones de Miguel Angel Ladero Quesada, *El siglo XV en Castilla. Fuentes de renta y política fiscal* (Barcelona, 1982), p. 158 et passim.

[36] Ruiz, *Sociedad y poder real*, cap. VI.

alfoces de sus respectivas villas, con un claro proceso de estratificación social. Cada una de estas facetas de la personalidad pública de los mercaderes del norte de Castilla constituía un paso más hacia la creación de nuevos grupos sociales diferentes no sólo en su rango social, en la ropa que usaban, en cómo se vestían sus mujeres e hijas, o en el despliegue ritual de sus armas y caballos en el alarde anual ante los oficiales del concejo o durante fiestas señaladas. En su juventud podemos encontrar a algunos de estos comerciantes en San Sebastián, en uno de los Cuatro Puertos, en Inglaterra, o en Flandes. Unos años más tarde, los documentos de la época nos los revelan como miembros del concejo de la ciudad, o al servicio del rey. Paralelo a estas funciones administrativas, los vemos también como compradores de tierras alrededor de la ciudad o casas dentro de la cerca. Esto lo subrayamos pues los documentos nos muestran en ciertos casos una determinación racional explícita de crear un dominio bien integrado, o de invertir en propiedades que ofreciesen buenas ganancias. Tal es el caso de las familias Sarracín y Bonifaz, pero también de mercaderes de poca monta tales como Pedro Pérez quien adquirió un buen número de viñedos en el área de Burgos, o de Miguel Pérez en Oter de los Herreros, cerca de Segovia[37].

En muchos sentidos nuestros mercaderes, quienes por lo general eran al mismo tiempo caballeros, propietarios de fincas en las inmediaciones de la ciudad y gozaban de casi un monopolio absoluto de los cargos públicos, eran ya a principios del siglo XIV casi indistinguibles de la pequeña nobleza. Podemos añadir que en ciudades castellanas, villas como Soria, Sepúlveda o Segovia, villas sin una orientación mercantil y donde la oligarquía derivaba sus rentas de la agricultura o de la trashumancia, la aristocratización ocurrió antes que en Burgos.

Visualicemos los aspectos más sobresalientes de la vida de estos mercaderes. Ellos nos servirán de pistas para trazar el proceso que los lleva a distanciarse de otros grupos sociales dentro de la ciudad. Al mismo tiempo, las tensiones y conflictos sociales que dicho proceso conllevó, nos señalan el desarrollo de un tipo de mentalidad a medio camino entre la manera de pensar del mercader y la del noble. Si regresamos al Burgos de finales del siglo XIII, y contemplamos algunos de estos mercaderes caballeros, podremos ver que cuando no estaban de viaje en el extranjero regresaban de sus fincas a sus casas en la ciudad al final de la cosecha, alrededor de la fiesta de San Miguel. Los privilegios de Alfonso X a los caballeros villanos y las descripciones que nos ofrecen los documentos de la época nos muestran que la élite urbana compartía su tiempo entre la ciudad y el campo, y que sus residencias en la ciudad eran las «casas mayores». Dichas casas eran de construcción diferente a las de otros grupos sociales, y en Burgos, Valladolid, Avila y otras villas de la región estaban localizadas en barrios donde —en el caso de Burgos, en las calles de Sanct Llorente, Armas, San Esteban, Huerto del Rey— sólo vivían caballeros, mercaderes y oficiales del concejo. A estas casas mayores, los caballeros transportaban el trigo, la cebada, el vino cosechado en sus tierras para llenar sus graneros. También debemos aña-

[37] *Ibid.*, p. 169. Para las actividades de Miguel Pérez véase el excelente trabajo de Miguel Santamaría Lancho, *La gestión económica del cabildo de Segovia*, en preparación.

dir que los transportaban dentro de los muros de la ciudad libre de impuestos, tasas que por lo general tenían que pagar otros grupos urbanos menos afortunados[38].

Nos encontramos, por lo tanto, ante un grupo, una élite mecantil, manejadora del comercio a larga distancia, con residencias urbanas capaces en el caso de algunas en Burgos de alojar a la familia real, y con extensas fincas en el alfoz; un grupo que repartía su tiempo entre el campo y la ciudad, con provisiones y sustento asegurados para todo el año, en un período, principios del siglo XIV, en que la hambruna y la carestía amenazaban la fábrica social de la sociedad castellana. Con sus grandes casas, sus numerosos sirvientes, sus contactos con el exterior, los hijos de los mercaderes-caballeros participaban de una cultura que era ya en esta época inaccesible al resto de la población urbana. Ora como culminación de estudios universitarios —los maestres que aparecen con frecuencia en la documentación burgalesa o el abogado Ruy Pérez, miembro de la Real Hermandad en 1338—, ora como recompensa por años de servicio a la corona —tal como fue el caso de Blasco Blázquez, juez del rey en su madurez, canónigo y deán de Avila en su senectud— encontramos a estos mercaderes-caballeros, sobre todo en Burgos, no sólo en control de la vida política de la ciudad sino también de su vida eclesiástica. La mayor parte de los canónigos y beneficiados en Burgos y otras villas de Castilla eran miembros de estas familias de mercaderes y caballeros. Esto significó acceso a los beneficios económicos que se derivaban de una posición eclesiástica, así como a los intereses intelectuales y modo de vida del clero. Al mismo tiempo se introducía un elemento secular y caballeresco en la vida eclesiástica de la época. En Burgos, durante este período, la posición de deán del cabildo, los más importantes arciprestazgos y jugosos beneficios eran casi siempre reservados para miembros de las dos grandes familias de la ciudad, los Sarracín y los Bonifaz[39].

Por un lado, los mercaderes con su visión de un mundo más allá de los muros de Burgos o de las costas del mar Cantábrico, conocían y se relacionaban con extranjeros, estaban obligados a entenderse más o menos con gentes que hablaban otras lenguas, y a acudir a las cortes de príncipes y dignatarios extranjeros. Andrés Pérez de Castrojeriz es sólo uno de muchos ejemplos de este tipo de mercader: con casa y negocios en Burgos, mercader y legado del rey de Inglaterra y residente en Albión por muchos años[40]. Sus experiencias de un mundo distinto por necesidad le aportaban una visión única en sus relaciones sociales dentro del ámbito de la ciudad, una visión inspirada en parte por modelos extranjeros, pero definida por las condiciones peculiares de la vida urbana del norte de Castilla. Esta mentalidad cosmopolita —que por otro lado correspondía perfectamente a una ciudad como Burgos, que gracias al camino de Santiago y a la presencia frecuente de la corte estaba abierta al exterior— emerge con claridad en los testamentos y donaciones de algunos de estos

---

38 *Memorial histórico español*, I, // XLIII, XLIV, XLV, LXXXIII, CII et passim.

39 Sobre Blasco Blázquez véase, Angel Barrios García, *Documentación medieval de la catedral de Avila* (Salamanca, 1981), pp. 97-100, 101-103, 105, 109, et passim; A.H.N. Clero, carpeta 24, // 5, 6 20; carpeta 25, // 1-6, 8-11, 16, 17; carpeta 26, // 10, de 1-III-1301 a 3-I-1308. Para los Sarracín y Bonifaz, Ruiz, *Sociedad y poder real*, cap. V.

40 Ruiz, «Mercaderes castellanos», pp. 21-23.

mercaderes y canónigos. En estos textos encontramos menciones de productos exóticos de lugares tan lejanos como la India, libros, paños y una manifiesta devoción a centros espirituales extranjeros. Esta visión peculiar proyectó a muchos de estos mercaderes-caballeros a jugar un papel cada vez más importante en la vida política de Castilla, y a identificar sus propios intereses no sólo con los de su localidad específica sino también con los de la región y el reino. En este sentido, diferentes a la pequeña burguesía o al común que todavía no manejaban el concepto de «nación», es indudable que las élites mercantiles, por razones que crudamente hay que identificar como económicas y egoístas, poseían una percepción embriónica —identificada en todo caso con la figura del rey— de la unidad del reino, que se definía con mayor claridad en su posición contraria a la violencia de los que Moreta Velayos ha descrito con acierto como malhechores feudales [41].

Al mismo tiempo, sus intereses comerciales en Burgos, en Vitoria y en los puertos del norte contrastaban con su rápida asimilación al estado nobilario, con sus inversiones en propiedades rurales y a veces el consiguiente abandono de sus actividades mercantiles. Con una nueva consciencia de clase, este período marca el lento proceso de transformación por el que una nobleza de dinero se convierte en una nobleza de sangre, marcado por el énfasis de estos caballeros-mercaderes en formas de vestir, despliegue de armas, ritos de hermandades semi-caballerescas y religiosas, nuevos intereses culturales y la exclusividad social. Las reglas de la cofradía del Santísimo y Santiago, con su énfasis en los «buenos», en la propiedad de caballo y armas y la descripción de cómo ir a bofardear, son una indicación clara de su nuevo espíritu de clase, de su creciente sentido de nobleza. Así mismo las alianzas matrimoniales entre clanes familiares —tales como la boda entre Teresa Bonifaz y Giralt Prestines en 1345— confirma el proceso por el que la clase mercantil —o sea el grupo dominante en Burgos— tendía a convertirse en un grupo cerrado [42].

Por un lado encontramos una mentalidad mercantil caracterizada por una visión económica que era en ciertos sentidos ajena a la mentalidad medieval típica, una forma de pensar protocapitalista que algunos contemporáneos no cejaban en criticar. Así en la *Danza de la Muerte* el mercader se lamentaba:

> «¿A quién dexaré todas mis riquesas
> E mercadurias que traygo en la mar?
> Con muchos traspasos e mas sotilesas
> Gané lo que tengo en cada lugar.»

Y la muerte le responde:

> «De oy mas non curedes de pasar an Flandes
> Estad aquí quedo e yredes ver
> La tienda que traigo de buuas y landres
> De graçia las do non las quero bender.» [43]

El estereotipo del mercader que obtiene su fortuna mediante engaños y sutilezas es similar en otras partes de Europa donde mercaderes, aun sin las aspiraciones nobiliarias de los de Castilla, trataron al final de sus días de remediar los errores de su profesión mediante donaciones piadosas. Pero en Castilla y en Burgos donde actitudes nobilirias mitigaban el espíritu emprendedor de los mercaderes, esta tensión entre lo político, lo económico, lo espiritual y lo caballeresco se resolvía a veces en una síntesis mental no ajena al espíritu del medioevo, pero que hoy resulta difícil de explicar en términos psicológicos. En el caso de Burgos y otras villas del norte de Castilla las tensiones internas se resolvieron en la mayoría de los casos por la aristocratización masiva de estos grupos mercantiles. Mientras que en el resto de Europa occidental dicho proceso ocurrió sólo en casos aislados y esporádicamente, en las ciudades del norte de Castilla la transformación de élites urbanas en grupos nobiliarios, que comienza en Avila, Soria y Valladolid ya a finales del siglo XII, culmina a finales del XIV con un movimiento irreversible que se extiende por toda la región. El espíritu caballeresco y religioso y espíritu mercantil conforman una mentalidad contradictoria. Por un lado se participa en, podemos decir que se explota a, la estructura eclesiástica de la ciudad y paradójicamente al final de la vida prevalece el espírtu de la época a través de donaciones piadosas.

En Burgos la familia Sarracín, mercaderes, grandes propietarios, caballeros, alcaldes y eclesiásticos, dedicaron gran parte de su caudal a mantener el Hospital de San Lucas para auxilio de los pobres. Ese fue el caso también de la familia de los Blázquez en Avila o de Juan Pérez de Frías, mercader, vecino de Burgos, morador en la cal de Sanct Llorente, miembro de la Real Hermandad, con lazos espirituales y propiedades en Frías, quien en 1350 donó importantes propiedades al Hospital de esa ciudad[44].

Podemos poner punto final a esta ponencia con un comentario historiográfico. Fue quizás el éxito de la burguesía castellana y no su debilidad lo que llevó en siglos posteriores a una serie de deficiencias estructurales fatales para la historia de Castilla. Es este período en que la tensión entre sus aspiraciones económicas y nobiliarias marcan el inicio de un nuevo sentido de consciencia social y de un mentalidad de grupo urbano y noble el que Fernando de Rojas nos muestra con colores sombríos 150 años más tarde. Pero en los siglos XIII y XIV todavía se hace difícil aceptar la visión estrecha de una Castilla gentil, mística y guerrera. Gentil, Castilla siempre ha sido, mística y guerrera también; pero al mismo tiempo en la Baja Edad Media, Burgos y otras ciudades del norte de Castilla eran centros de comercio, susceptibles a nuevas ideas, prestas a cambiar. Una visión de la historia de Burgos no siempre heroica, pero que pienso mucho más ajustada a la realidad y lo que nos muestran las fuentes.

---

41 Ladero Quesada, pp. 65-75; Salustiano Moreta Velayos, *Malhechores-feudales: Violencia, antagonismo y alianzas de clases en Castilla, siglos XIII-XIV* (Madrid, 1978).

42 *Texto*, p. 6; A.H.N. Clero, carpeta 201 // 2 (20-VII-1345).

43 *Poetas castellanos anteriores al siglo XV* (Biblioteca de Autores Españoles, vol. LVII, Madrid, 1966), p. 382.

44 Ruiz, *Sociedad y poder real*, cap. V; A.H.N. Clero, carpeta 227 // 13b (14-II-1350).

IV

Una nota sobre la estructura y relaciones fiscales del Burgos bajomedieval

Entre los problemas todavía por estudiar con detalle en el amplio campo de la historia castellana en la baja Edad Media, ocupa un lugar importante el estimar los ingresos y gastos de la administración real. Aunque existen una relación de las «Cuentas y gastos» para el reinado de Sancho IV, publicado por Mercedes Gaibrois de Ballesteros, y un padrón de encabezamientos y servicios de judíos para el año 1290, publicado por Amador de los Ríos, estos documentos o no han sido examinados exhaustivamente, o no nos proporcionan toda la información necesaria [1]. Es indudablc que no sabemos con certeza a cuanto ascendían los ingresos reales, ni tenemos tampoco un presupuesto de la monarquía castellana para los siglos XIII y principios del XIV. Esta omisión es aún más penosa cuando la comparamos con la información fiscal con que contamos para otros reinos medievales de Europa occidental [2]. Tal información es esencial para un mejor entendimiento de la política económica, o en muchos casos falta de ella, de los reyes de Castilla. En tiempos de crisis y dificultades económicas, como lo fueron las postrimerías del siglo XIII y la primera mitad del siglo XIV [3], la corona padecía de una crónica deficiencia fiscal como se evidencia en los continuos abusos de los agentes del fisco real [4].

[1] Mercedes GAIBROIS DE BALLESTEROS: *Historia del reinado de Sancho IV de Castilla,* 3 vols. Madrid, 1922-28; José AMADOR DE LOS RÍOS: *Historia social, política y religiosa de los judíos de España y Portugal,* 3 vols. Madrid, 1876.

[2] Véase, por ejemplo, Marcel PACAUT: *Louis VII et son royaume* (París, 1964); John F. BENTON: «The revenue of Louis VII», en *Speculum,* 42 (1967), pp. 84-91.

[3] Sobre la crisis castellana, véase Julio VALDEÓN BARUQUE: «Aspectos de la crisis castellana en la primera mitad del siglo XIV», en *Hispania,* 111 (1969), pp. 5-24; T. F. RUIZ: «Expansión et changement: la conquête de Séville et la société castillane (1248-1350)», en *Annales E. S. C.,* núm. 3 (junio, 1979, pp. 548-65.

[4] Sobre este tema, véase el reciente libro de Salustiano MORETA VELAYOS:

Estudios en memoria del Profesor D. Salvador de Moxó, II. U. C. M. 1982 (387-398)

Lo más probable es que la documentación que nos permita resolver este misterio, o no existe, o sólo existe en condiciones tan fragmentarias que impiden una conclusión feliz a nuestras investigaciones.

Sin embargo, si nos trazamos una meta más modesta, quizá podríamos obtener algunos resultados que nos ofrezcan una idea, todavía vaga e imprecisa es menester precisar, de las posibilidades económicas de la corona castellana. Me refiero en esta instancia a la contribución financiera que los centros urbanos de Castilla y León aportaban al tesoro real, así como su resistencia a las exigencias fiscales de los reyes castellanos. También aquí hemos de lamentar la escasez de fuentes documentales y de estudios especializados sobre el tema, sobre todo para el período anterior al año 1350, pues para un período posterior tenemos estudios como el de A. Collantes de Terán sobre Sevilla, que aunque no discute el problema de impuestos en detalle, nos muestra una meticulosa cantidad de estadísticas, ya de por sí prometedoras [5]. Este tipo de estudios nos daría una idea real de las fuentes de ingresos con que contaba el fisco castellano y las dificultades que los reyes de Castilla tenían que afrontar en su gestión económica.

No hay que enfatizar en estas páginas lo que ya bien sabemos, o sea, que las ciudades de Castilla jugaron un papel importante en la sociedad y economía del reino, y de las ciudades de Castilla la Vieja, la más importante por su potencial económico y también por la cantidad de documentos que han sobrevivido el paso del tiempo fue, sin duda, Burgos [6].

¿Qué podemos decir de las contribuciones de Burgos al erario real y de sus relaciones fiscales con la corona? Y, por lo tanto, ¿cuáles eran los ingresos de la ciudad? Para las rentas y gastos de la ciudad de Burgos en el período posterior a 1350, contamos ya con valiosas aportaciones. Bajo la dirección del profesor Julio Valdeón, Bonachía Hernando ha examinado el concejo burgalés a finales del siglo XIV, incluyendo en uno de sus capítulos valiosa información acerca del tema que nos preocupa. Asimismo, Hilario Casado, en su estudio de las rentas urbanas del cabildo catedralicio de Burgos, también bajo la dirección de Julio Valdeón, nos permite obtener una visión parcial de la estructura económica de la ciudad. Para el siglo XVI, la tesis doctoral de Paul Hiltpold, a punto de ser leída en la Universidad de

---

Malhechores-feudales: violencia, antagonismos y alianzas de clases en Castilla (siglos XIII-XIV). Madrid, 1978.

[5] Antonio Collantes de Terán: *Sevilla en la Baja Edad Media: La ciudad y sus hombres.* Sevilla, 1977.

[6] Sobre Burgos, véase Teófilo F. Ruiz: *Sociedad y poder real en Castilla,* Barcelona, 1981; J. A. Bonachía Hernando: *El concejo de Burgos en la Baja Edad Media (1345-1426).* Valladolid, 1978.

Texas, contiene una detallada relación de los ingresos de la ciudad, así como de sus relaciones con la hacienda real. Esperemos que su pronta publicación llene una laguna más de la historia burgalesa.

Para el período antes del año 1350 he tratado, como será evidente en las páginas que siguen, de reunir el mayor número posible de datos relativos a la estructura financiera de la ciudad y de sus relaciones con los reyes de Castilla a finales del siglo XIII y principios del XIV. Aunque, como se verá, nuestra información es bastante incompleta, estos documentos nos muestran sobre todo la constante tensión entre la ciudad y el rey en sus esfuerzos por controlar los escasos recursos fiscales. Como con anterioridad ya he examinado en detalles los conflictos jurisdiccionales entre el concejo y otras entidades y corporaciones eclesiásticas [7], así como las complicadas relaciones entre el concejo y la corona [8]; por lo tanto, estas páginas sirven como un complemento a mis estudios anteriores.

I. Mucho antes de 1248, los reyes castellanos habían eximido a la ciudad de Burgos del pago de la anubda y la fonsadera [9], aunque estos privilegios no tenían, en realidad, nada de particular, y eran por lo general similares a los privilegios concedidos a otras ciudades y corporaciones eclesiásticas. Si bien la corona otorgaba estos privilegios de exención con bastante frecuencia, sus agentes fiscales los respetaban pocas veces. En 1266, Alfonso X ordenó a los recaudadores de impuestos que devolvieran las contribuciones que habían obtenido ilegalmente de los ciudadanos de Burgos [10]. Estas frecuentes violaciones de los privilegios fiscales de Burgos y de otras ciudades castellanas, así como la costumbre bastante frecuente de exigir arbitrariamente una cantidad superior a las tasas que habían sido convenidas de antemano entre el rey y la ciudad, llevaron a continuas protestas del concejo. La principal razón de este conflicto fue, sin duda, la crítica y crónica carencia de fondos de Alfonso el Sabio, y trajeron consecuentemente, y como respuesta a sus demandas, una amplia resistencia a las imposiciones reales; tópico que ya ha sido estudiado por O'Callaghan [11]. Burgos, como es natural, participó de lleno en estos problemas.

---

[7] Ruiz: *Sociedad y poder real*, cap. IV.

[8] Ruiz: «The Transformation of the Castilian Municipalities: The case of Burgos (1248-1350)», en *Past & Present*, 77 (1977), pp. 22-29.

[9] Tomás Muñoz y Romero: *Colección de fueros municipales y cartas pueblas de Castilla, León...* Madrid, 1874, pp. 257 y 266.

[10] Archivo Municipal de Burgos (AMB), clasif. 2694 (20-II-1266).

[11] Véase J. F. O'Callaghan: «The Cortes and Royal Taxation During the Reign of Alfonso X of Castile», en *Traditio*, 37 (1971), pp. 379-398; A. Ballesteros: «Burgos y la rebelión del infante Don Sancho», en *Boletín de la Real Academia de la Historia*, 119 (1946), pp. 93-194.

El concejo burgalés, junto con otros concejos del reino, accedió en las Cortes de Burgos (1269) al pago de un servicio. El concejo lo otorgó «de su buena voluntad», pero como recompensa a esta «buena voluntad», y más probable como resultado de negociaciones previas entre el rey y los concejos castellanos, el monarca prometió poner término al control sobre los precios que había sido establecido en las Cortes de Jerez el año anterior y estabilizar la moneda. Los concejos municipales, dominados ya en esa época por oligarquías mercantiles, sobre todo el de Burgos, es obvio que exigieron estas medidas que afectaban directamente sus intereses económicos. Es más, Alfonso X en una carta al concejo de Burgos, indicó que sus agentes no recaudarían el servicio por más tiempo del que había sido concedido [12].

En 1274, Burgos otorgó al rey otro servicio por dos años, y aunque el documento en cuestión no especifica a cuanto ascendía la contribución, sabemos que era igual a los ingresos devengados por el pago de moneda. Estos dos servicios fueron dedicados a financiar el desdichado «fecho de imperio» de Alfonso X [13]. El rey reconoció a cambio la «gran pobreza» de Burgos, y le aseguró al concejo que no reclamaría los servicios que habían sido concedidos anteriormente [14].

Hemos de notar que a pesar de que Alfonso X obtuvo nuevas contribuciones de la ciudad, la corona encontraba dificultades en recaudarlos. Para recibir nuevos servicios fue necesario cancelar los impuestos todavía sin cobrar.

En 1275 la mayoría de los concejos de Castilla y Extremadura, reunidos en Alcalá de Henares, votaron un tributo de moneda forera por tres años [15]. Aparicio Guillén y John Royz, procuradores del concejo burgalés, se negaron a confirmar esta concesión hasta que hubiesen consultado con el concejo de la ciudad [16]; pero después de un intercambio de cartas entre el concejo y el rey, en las que Alfonso X demandaba el pronto consentimiento a los impuestos, la ciudad claudicó. Dos años más tarde, el rey promulgó nuevas tasas de impuestos para la ciudad y determinó las contribuciones a pagar sobre bienes inmuebles y raíces. Los ciudadanos burgaleses con propiedades urbanas valoradas en 300 mrs., de la moneda nueva debían contribuir con la tasa completa (cantidad que no es especificada en el documento).

---

[12] AMB, clasif. 2684 y 140 (27-XII-1271); Ballesteros: «Burgos y la rebelión...», p. 112; Ruiz: «The Transformation», p. 24.

[13] AMB, clasif. 117 (5-V-1274).

[14] *Ibidem.* «E nos entendiendo la uestra grand pobreza prometimos de uos nunca demandar».

[15] AMB, clasif. 2574 (22-XII-1275); Ballesteros: «Burgos y la rebelión...», pp. 118-119.

[16] Para Aparicio Guillén y John Royz véase T. F. Ruiz: «Prosopografía burgalesa, 1248-1350», en *Boletín de la Institución Fernán González*, 184 (1975), páginas 476-480.

Los que tuvieran bienes inmuebles valorados en 450 mrs. pagaban tasa y media, y así progresivamente [17].

Para el año de 1278 poseemos una serie de documentos bastante extensa sobre el pago de una multa impuesta por el rey a prestamistas burgaleses. Estos documentos nos revelan vívidamente las fricciones entre Alfonso X y la ciudad, así como también entre el rey y su hijo, el Infante don Sancho. Es de notar, al mismo tiempo, las actividades económicas de cambistas y prestamistas cristianos en la ciudad de Burgos y de su franca identificación con las autoridades concejiles. La ya mencionada serie de documentos comienza con una carta del Infante don Sancho, quien en nombre de su padre, ordenó que dos hombres buenos de Burgos acompañasen a los pesquisidores reales investigando el préstamo de dinero a intereses usuarios. Don Sancho pidió, asimismo, el castigo de quienes ponían en peligro sus almas por el «pecado de la Usuria» [18]. Aparte de las preocupaciones espirituales de la época sobre si era lícito o no cobrar intereses y de la rectitud moral de Sancho, algo que no era en realidad característico del Infante, esta transgresión de los cánones eclesiásticos ofrecía una excelente oportunidad para obtener beneficios económicos.

No pasó mucho tiempo antes de que Alfonso X y Sancho se disputasen el derecho a obtener beneficios económicos de las supuestas deficiencias morales de los prestamistas burgaleses: la mayoría de ellos cristianos. El rey impuso una multa de 60.000 mrs. a los prestamistas que cobraban un por ciento de interés superior al nivel que había sido establecido con anterioridad por las Cortes [19]. Contrario a lo que opina Ballesteros, no parece que Alfonso X y Sancho trabajasen al unísono en las recaudaciones de esta multa. Miguel de Sevilla y el abad de San Pedro de Cardeña hicieron las pesquisas y recaudación de la multa para el Infante don Sancho, mientras que Aparicio Guillén y don Çag, el judío de Don Manuel, lo hicieron para el rey [20].

En cierta fecha, que no podemos determinar con exactitud, y por razones que sólo pueden ser atribuídas a la identificación entre los prestamistas y la oligarquía que controlaba el gobierno de la ciudad, el concejo de Burgos se hizo responsable por el pago de la multa. Esto es evidente desde el momento en que el Infante don Sancho aceptó un compromiso con la ciudad mediante el cual, el concejo de Burgos se comprometía a pagar la multa en dos plazos: 40.000 mrs. el 1 de agosto, y los otros 20.000 el día de San Martín, en noviembre. La carta del Infante nos muestra su urgente necesidad de fondos para

[17] AMB, clasif. 2729 (20-VII-1277).
[18] AMB, clasif. 2560 (14-V-1278).
[19] AMB, clasif. 2561 (15-VII-1278); clasif. 2562 (16-VII-1278); Antonio Ballesteros y Beretta: *Alfonso X el Sabio*. Barcelona, 1963, p. 854.
[20] Véase nota anterior. AMB, clasif. 2562 (16-VII-1278).

pagar los estipendios de sus caballeros [21], lo que quizá fue lo que lo impulsó a aceptar este acuerdo con la ciudad. A esta opinión nos lleva la evidencia presente en una carta expedida en Burgos diez días antes (18-VII-1278), en la que el Infante don Sancho demandaba a la ciudad 50 mrs. por el derecho de chancillería y se refería al pasar, al pago y acuerdo sobre la multa de las Usuras [22].

A finales de julio y por segunda vez a principios de agosto, Alfonso X requirió del concejo de Burgos el pronto pago de los 60.000 mrs. de multa a sus agentes, Aparicio Guillén y Simón Raynez, añadiendo que ninguna porción de la dicha multa debía de ser entregada a los representantes de su hijo [23]. El rey envió a Bernardo de Centellas a recaudar 20.000 mrs., suma que él demandaba por el día de San Miguel, pero su emisario no pudo vencer la resistencia concejil [24]. Además, como ya hemos visto, esta suma había sido prometida con antelación a su hijo y rival, el Infante don Sancho. Sin otro recurso que protestar, Alfonso X hizo nuevas demandas por el pago de la multa de las usuras a finales de septiembre, a principios de octubre, y, finalmente, ordenó una investigación de todo el asunto en febrero del año siguiente [25].

Sus esfuerzos ya no tenían sentido, pues para esa fecha el concejo burgalés había cumplido ya las obligaciones concertadas anteriormente con el Infante. El 6 de octubre de 1278, Sancho, respondiendo a una petición de la ciudad de Burgos, que se quejaba de los abusos de los recaudadores de impuestos, ordenó a sus oficiales que cesasen de reclamar el pago de los 60.000 mrs. de multa, pues ya había sido abonado [26]. Tenemos una confirmación adicional de que la ciudad había cumplido sus obligaciones en una carta del Infante don Sancho al concejo de Burgos, en que eximía a la ciudad de pagar 300 mrs. de derechos de chancillería por las «cartas de quitamiento de las Usuras» [27].

Tal era, por lo tanto, la posición de la ciudad que ambos, el rey y el Infante, que en aquel momento se hallaban en conflicto armado sobre la sucesión al trono, le hacían demandas contradictorias al concejo de Burgos. Aunque la ciudad estaba claramente en el campo de Sancho, y como hemos anotado, había contribuido con 60.000 mrs. a su

---

[21] AMB, clasif. 2563 (28-VII-1278); Ballesteros: *Alfonso X...*, p. 854.

[22] AMB, clasif. 2564 (18-VII-1278).

[23] AMB, clasif. 2566 (30-VII-1278); clasif. 2567 (8-VIII-1278).

[24] AMB, clasif. 2912 (14-VIII-1278).

[25] AMB, clasif. 2568 (22-IX-1278); clasif. 2571 (16-X-1278); clasif. 2572 (20-II-1279); Ballesteros: *Alfonso X*, p. 880.

[26] AMB, clasif. 2569 (6-X-1278): «Pesquisidores que eran en ssu logar por mj en rracon delas usuras por sessaenta mill mrs delos dineros blancos dela guerra que me dieron...».

[27] AMB, clasif. 2570 (6-X-1278).

causa, los agentes fiscales del Infante a pesar de esto trataban de recaudar una cantidad mayor de la que el concejo le había otorgado al Infante. Por otro lado, aunque la ciudad apenas había terminado de pagar la pena impuesta por las Usuras, cundo el concejo ya entablaba negociaciones con Yuça Pimientella, uno de los arrendadores de los impuestos reales. El concejo aceptó en principio el pago de seis servicios. Cada uno de estos servicios ascendía a 33.000 mrs. anuales, o sea, la suma que se pagaba por moneda forera. Esta nueva ayuda debía ser abonada por Pascua de Resurrección, y nadie podía ser excusado de estos servicios. A cambio de este tributo, todas las deudas y obligaciones que el concejo tenía todavía pendiente serían canceladas [28]. Sin embargo, después de estas negociaciones iniciales, el concejo de Burgos rehusó cumplir los términos del convenio con Yuça Pimientella. En octubre de 1279, el Infante don Sancho, aunque todavía reclamándole a la ciudad un servicio y medio, le prometió interceder ante su padre [29]. Para este fin, dos representantes del concejo habrían de ir a Sevilla y explicarle al rey las razones por las que la ciudad no podía contribuir a los servicios pormetidos anteriormente. La documentación de finales del año 1279, nos muestra claramente la resistencia del concejo burgalés a pagar estos servicios; pero a pesar de las opiniones expresadas al respecto por Ballesteros y O'Callaghan, la ciudad pagó por lo menos parte de los servicios [30]. Esto lo muestra una misiva del Infante don Sancho dirigida a sus agentes fiscales el 30 de octubre de 1279, en la que les ordenaba regresar a Burgos a recaudar lo que quedaba por percibir del impuesto inicial [31]. Al mismo tiempo, Sancho aseguró al concejo que los representaría ante el rey para impedir que el servicio se convirtiera en un gravamen permanente [32]. Una vez más vemos cómo el Infante se benefició de unos impuestos que habían sido otorgados en principio a su padre. Mientras el rey enviaba protestas frecuentes al concejo, demandando sus impuestos ya Sancho disfrutaba de ellos [33].

Si el Infante recaudaba los impuestos burgaleses, también concedía privilegios. Como es natural, Alfonso X, que no percibía ingresos de la ciudad o por lo menos no tanto como deseaba, negaba la validez de estos privilegios. La conclusión inescapable es que el concejo burgalés no podía oponerse con mucha determinación a las frecuentes

[28] *Memorial histórico español* (MHE), 49 vols. Madrid, 1851-1948, I, pp. 339-41. También F. Cantera Burgos: «Burgos y don Yucef Pimientiella», en *Boletín de la Institución Fernán González*, 118 (1952), pp. 1-4.

[29] AMB, clasif. 2506 (30-X-1279).

[30] Ballesteros: *Alfonso X*, p. 908; O'Callaghan: p. 393, nota 51.

[31] AMB, clasif. 2918 (30-X-1279).

[32] AMB, clasif. 2687 (9-XI-1279).

[33] AMB, clasif. 2767 (9-XI-1279), clasif. 2933 (22-III-1280).

demandas fiscales de la corona castellana. Si resistían algunas de las peticiones de Alfonso X, tenían que doblegarse a las de Sancho. El deseo de resistir o modificar estas demandas se ve claramente en la documentación de la época; pero, en realidad, sin gran éxito. Por ejemplo, en el año de 1282 la ciudad se opuso a que el Infante acuñase nuevas monedas; pero como en otras ocasiones, poco duró su resistencia [34]. Dos años después, a pesar de que Sancho había prometido la remisión de impuestos a los concejos que habían apoyado su causa, sus agentes, Pedro Díaz y Muño Díaz, hacían esfuerzos para recaudar 30.000 de fonsadera en el alfoz de Burgos [35]. Debemos recordar que la ciudad de Burgos estaba excusada de la fonsadera desde el siglo XII.

Aparte del continuo debate en las Cortes sobre impuestos, que es reflejado en sus ordenanzas y cuadernos, la evidencia que posemos de la resistencia del concejo burgalés a las exigencias monetarias de los reyes castellanos disminuye considerablemente; sobre todo después de que Alfonso XI llega a la mayoría de edad. Quizá esto sea porque los documentos que nos muestran conflictos entre la ciudad y el rey han desaparecido o porque el concejo burgalés llegó a un acuerdo con el rey.

Para resumir: aunque a través de su historia Burgos obtuvo exención de muchas de las tasas reales, la ciudad no pudo evitar el pago de servicios extraordinarios y de ayudas financieras. En términos de autonomía fiscal, la ciudad carecía de ella, y no sólo tenía que contender con las presiones de la corona, sino que también la multitud de individuos y corporaciones religiosas exentos de impuestos dejaban poco para la ciudad. Esto nos lleva al segundo problema que deseamos examinar en estas páginas, y esto es, un examen de las fuentes de ingreso de la ciudad para el período antes de 1350.

II. Los ingresos de la ciudad

Es imposible calcular la media anual de ingrcsos del concejo de Burgos a finales del siglo XIII y principios del XIV. Los documentos, aunque mencionan los tipos de impuestos recaudados por la ciudad o los regalos y concesiones por parte del rey, pocas veces incluyen las cantidades recaudadas.

¿Cuáles eran las fuentes de ingresos de que disponía la ciudad? Para empezar, el concejo de Burgos recibía las contribuciones de al-

---

[34] AMB, clasif. 2474 (19-V-1282); clasif. 2475 (4-VI-1282); clasif. 2475 (4-VI-1282); Ballesteros: «Burgos y la rebelión...», pp. 164-165; AMB, clasif. 2477 (6-VI-1282); clasif. 2476 (6-?-1282).

[35] AMB, clasif. 2935 (8-III-1284).

deas y lugares bajo su jurisdicción. En el año 1255, Alfonso X le concedió los lugares de Lara, Barbadillo del Mercado, Villafranca de Montes de Oca y otros pueblos, «con todas sus entradas» [36]. La ciudad, por lo tanto, recaudaba todos los impuestos que habían sido pagados al rey hasta ese momento. Esta relación económica debió de existir más o menos con todas aquellas aldeas del alfoz que se encontraban directamente bajo el control de la ciudad. Ya he mostrado en uno de mis artículos cómo los agentes del rey trataban continuamente de recaudar impuestos en las aldeas bajo la jurisdicción del concejo burgalés, lo que llevó a airadas protestas [37]. Por lo tanto, uno debe asumir que el concejo cobraba derechos e impuestos en esos lugares. La suma a recaudar, sin embargo, no debía de representar una gran cantidad en esa época. Las rentas de Lara y Barbadillo sólo ascendían a 3.000 mrs. al año, en 1299 [38]. Hay que considerar también el escaso potencial económico del alfoz burgalés y su reducida población. Además numerosos lugares dentro del alfoz se hallaban bajo la jurisdicción del monasterio de las Huelgas o del obispo y cabildo de la ciudad. [39].

Otra fuente de ingresos, de por sí nada despreciable, era la propiedad urbana en manos del concejo. En el año 1266 Alfonso otorgó todas las carnicerías de la ciudad al concejo, con la excepción de cuatro bancos que el rey había donado al cabildo catedralicio unos años antes [40]. Tenemos también evidencia de otras propiedades del concejo. Por ejemplo, la ciudad compartía la propiedad de la huerta de Santa Agueda con el cabildo catedralicio [14], y poseía casas y tierras en Burgos y sus inmediaciones [42]. Es probable que estas propiedades eran una fuente de ingresos satisfactoria; pero no era tan importante como la alcabala. Los ingresos de este impuesto (o lo que en esa época era sólo un impuesto sobre ventas locales) habían sido concedidos a la ciudad con el propósito de financiar la construcción de la cerca de la ciudad, y aunque la nobleza fue exenta de contribuir a ella en 1270, la alcabala debió de representar un ingreso considerable para la ciudad [43].

No podemos afirmar a ciencia cierta a cuánto ascendía la recaudación anual de la alcabala. Un documento del año 1313, con mucha

---

[36] MHE, I, p. 68.

[37] RUIZ: «The Transformation», p. 23.

[38] AMB, clasif. 107 (5-III-1299); Antonio BENAVIDES: *Memorias de Fernando IV de Castilla*, 2 vols. (Madrid, 1860), II, pp. 179-180.

[39] RUIZ: *La sociedad y el poder real*, caps. IV y V.

[40] AMB, clasif. 116 (12-IV-1260).

[41] Archivo de la Catedral de Burgos (ACB), vol. 40, f. 212 (16-I-1336).

[42] Archivo Histórico Nacional (AHN). Clero, carpeta 185, núms. 10 y 14 (13-III-1303 y 15-VII-1309).

[43] *Crónica de Alfonso X* en *Crónica de los Reyes de Castilla* (Biblioteca de Autores Españoles, vol. LXVI, Madrid, 1953), pp. 20-21.

probabilidad un acuerdo entre el concejo de Burgos y un arrendador de impuestos, muestra quizá el valor de este impuesto. Don Domingo de Ramos, que fue alcalde de Burgos en 1296, reconoció deber 46.000 mrs. a la ciudad y prometió pagar parte de esta suma a un número considerable de contratistas y deudores de la ciudad [44]. Aunque nada en el documento indica explícitamente que esta cantidad equivalía a la recaudación de la alcabala, hay indicaciones que éste era el caso. El dinero estaba destinado a la construcción de la muralla de la ciudad, y es difícil de explicar que un solo individuo debiese tanto al concejo, a menos que estuviese arrendando el impuesto. Pero la ciudad ni siquiera pudo retener esta valiosa fuente de ingreso, y ya en el año 1345 los ingresos de la alcabala estaban en las manos del rey. Ese mismo año, varios arrendadores de impuestos todavía reclamaban sus derechos a cobrarla, y obtuvieron un decreto de Alfonso XI que les permitió recaudar la alcabala en Burgos; pero sólo del pan y vino vendido en la ciudad [45].

El concejo burgalés también administraba otros impuestos locales. El concejo arrendó los impuestos sobre el vino y el «doblón» (quizá un impuesto cobrado a prestamistas) a Arnalt de Sanchester y a otros hombres buenos en el año 1281. Aunque la suma no se indica en el documento, los impuestos se recaudaban «para pagar pechos al rey» [46].

El 21 de mayo de 1293, Sancho IV concedió a la ciudad el derecho de recaudar y emplear para sí los derechos del portazgo y de la martiniega, excepto por 6.000 mrs. anuales que debían ser abonados al rey o a uno de sus oficiales [47]. La martiniega no representaba gran cosa desde el momento que muchas personas y corporaciones religiosas estaban exentas de este impuesto. El portazgo, considerando el carácter comercial de la ciudad, quizá ya representaba algo más sustancial. A esto debemos añadir las multas impuestas por las cortes municipales; pero para el período antes de 1350, la evidencia no existe. Finalmente, hay que hacer mención de las mercedes reales. Por ejemplo, en el año 1301, Fernando IV donó el lugar de Villafranca de Montes de Oca, perteneciente a Burgos, a uno de sus favoritos, y como compensación el rey otorgó a la ciudad 12.000 mrs. anuales. Este dinero fue asignado al concejo burgalés del servicio anual que la aljama de la ciudad pagaba al rey [48]. Cuarenta y cuatro años más tarde estos

---

[44] AMB, clasif. 652 (19-XII-1313).
[45] AMB, clasif. 2730 (15-V-1345). La alcabala fue concedida a Alfonso XI por las Cortes en 1342.
[46] AMB, clasif. 2925 (12-VII-1281).
[47] AMB, clasif. 157 (21-V-1293).
[48] Anselmo Salva: *Cosas de la vieja Burgos*. Burgos, 1892, p. 105.

12.000 mrs. serían destinados a pagar el salario de los regidores y alcaldes que Alfonso XI impuso en la ciudad [49].

No hay forma tampoco de estimar la contribución media de Burgos a las arcas reales durante el siglo XIII y principios del XIV. Como ya sabemos, la ciudad pagaba al rey 6.000 mrs. del portazgo y de la martiniega. En 1278, el concejo pagó 60.000 mrs. por la multa de las Usuras; pero esto fue una situación excepcional y no puede ser contado como un ingreso normal. En 1284 el servicio representaba una suma de alrededor de 33.000 mrs. anuales [50]; pero los servicios no se recaudaban todos los años, y la ciudad ponía el mayor número de trabas posible para cumplir sus obligaciones [51].

La sisa de Burgos fue calculada en 100.000 mrs. en 1293; pero esta suma representaba el ingreso total del obispado y no de la ciudad [52]. La sisa tampoco se recaudaba anualmente y no puede ser considerada como una fuente de ingreso habitual.

Los ingresos que la ciudad proporcionaba a la corona no eran ni muchos, ni podían ser recaudados con regularidad. Los reyes de Castilla contaban con otros medios de obtener dinero, tales como préstamos obtenidos a la fuerza o bajo presión política. Alfonso XI empleó este medio en 1342, y aunque la ciudad resistió por un tiempo, al final tuvo que aceder a las demandas del rey [53]. En parte, por las numerosas exenciones concedidas a las ciudades, a individuos y a corporaciones, en parte por sus propias dificultades políticas, durante la baja Edad Media los reyes castellanos se vieron obligados a depender de la Mesta y de los judíos como las únicas fuentes de ingreso en las que podían confiar con regularidad. Diferente a otras partes de Europa, donde la corona necesitaba los recursos económicos de los centros urbanos para su gestión administrativa, y, por lo tanto, esta necesidad los llevó a concederles privilegios políticos y representación en parlamentos y asambleas, en Castilla después de 1350, cuando las exportaciones de la lana y los servicios y pagos de los judíos aumentaron considerablemente, vemos una progresiva disminución de la representación urbana en las sesiones de las Cortes o en los órganos de poder real. La disminución de su función económica trajo como consecuencia el declive de su influencia política.

---

49 *Idem.*

50 AMB, clasif. 3082 (29-IX-1284); GAIBROIS DE BALLESTEROS: *Historia del reinado,* III, p. xi.

51 AMB, clasif. 140 (27-IX-1271).

52 GAIBROIS DE BALLESTEROS: *Historia del reinado,* I, p. cxxxvii; BENAVIDES: *Memorias...,* II, pp. 132-134.

53 *Crónica de Alfonso XI,* p. 336.

V

NOTAS PARA EL ESTUDIO DE LA MUJER EN EL AREA DEL BURGOS MEDIEVAL

La historia de la mujer del medievo castellano no ha recibido, como era de esperar, la atención prestada a estos temas en otros países. Las reivindicaciones femeninas no se han aireado públicamente hasta una época reciente, y estas aspiraciones no han sido completamente representadas en los trabajos de búsqueda erudita. Hay, naturalmente, los trabajos de costumbre acerca de reinas importantes, de poderosas abadesas, de santas, de místicas y de figuras literarias; pero hasta hace muy poco no ha habido interés —o muy poco—, en el papel económico y social jugado por la mujer[1]. Existe sin embargo un punto de partida. Heath Dillard en su artículo, «Women in Reconquest Castile: The Fueros de Sepúlveda and Cuenca», nos muestra los amplios derechos legales y de propiedad disfrutados por las mujeres castellanas y leonesas. Estas retenían incluso después del matrimonio, el derecho a tener propiedades y disponer libremente de ellas, si bien ello quedaba restringido por la estructura familiar y las costumbres locales[2]. Esta igualdad en los derechos femeninos en cuanto a la herencia y la posesión, así como a su dote, fue, al parecer, superior a los privilegios disfrutados por sus congéneres en el norte de Europa o en el resto de la Iberia medieval, más específicamente —como nos muestra Dillard— en los

[1] Véase Mercedes Gaibrois de Ballesteros, *María de Molina, tres veces reina* (Madrid, 1967); Claudio Sánchez Albornoz, «La mujer en España hace mil años», en *España y el Islam* (Buenos Aires, 1943), pp. 83-141; Eduardo de Hinojosa, «Sobre la condición de la mujer casada en la esfera del Derecho civil», en *Obras,* 2 volúmenes (Madrid, 1948-1955), I, 345-85; José María Escrivá, *La abadesa de las Huelgas* (Madrid, 1944); Margarita Kelken, *La condición social de la mujer en España* (Barcelona, sin fecha); P. W. Bonli, *La femme dans l'Espagne du Siècle d'Or* (La Haya, 1950). Hay un gran interés en la España actual en temas feministas. El trabajo de Cristina Segura de pronta publicación, promete una nueva visión de este tema.

[2] En Susan Mosher Stuard, ed., *Women in Medieval Society* (Philadelphia, 1977), pp. 71-94.

fueros extensos de Sepúlveda y Cuenca[3]. Aunque el artículo de Dillard nos aporta una excelente introducción al estudio de la mujer castellana del medievo, deja muchas preguntas en blanco en cuanto a cuál fue el papel de la mujer en la vida económica y social cotidiana de la Castilla medieval. Un código legal refleja los ideales de justicia de una sociedad, pero estos ideales no siempre se corresponden con la realidad. Las condiciones reales son con frecuencia distintas a los ideales descritos en la ley. Mejor que un análisis estático de las prerrogativas legales de la mujer, nuestra meta debe ser encontrar algún criterio que nos permita examinar el papel económico y social de la mujer en la Castilla medieval; más específicamente en el área de Burgos[4].

En las páginas que siguen me he concentrado en las mujeres no pertenecientes a la nobleza que, sin embargo, poseían, vendían y/o compraban tierras en la zona de Burgos durante la última parte del siglo XIII y la primera parte del siglo XIV[5]. Además de intentar aportar un porcentaje de mujeres involucradas en transacciones de compra/venta de tierras, espero mostrar, a través de varios ejemplos, algunas de las formas en las que las mujeres participaban en la vida económica y social de la Castilla medieval y que su papel en la economía no difería, con frecuencia, del jugado por los hombres. Hay muchos ejemplos, claro está, de la actividad económica de las clases altas, pero el énfasis de esta ponencia descansa en otra parte: en las mujeres de los grupos sociales menos privilegiados[6].

Entre los documentos del Hospital de Santa María de Frías (Burgos) se incluye un testamento de una tal Sancha Alfonso (1337). Su marido, John Pérez, ya había tomado el hábito religioso en 1341, y quizás antes, cuando marido y mujer aún vivían. El testamento de 1337 es un documento interesante, aun cuando uno queda con el deseo de saber más acerca de Sancha. Después de pedir ser enterrada en Santa María, un monasterio de monjes —aunque no el que su marido había o habría de escoger— legaba sus viñas y las rentas de sus tierras a varios monasterios e iglesias, solicitando a cambio aniversarios y misas: sesenta misas por su madre y hermana y cien por sí misma. Considerables cantidades de dinero fueron también destinadas a

[3] H. DILLARD, pp. 73, 72-89.

[4] Un criterio metodológico es ofrecido por David HERLIHY en su «Land, Family and Women in Continental Europe, 701-1200», en *Women in Medieval Society,* pp. 13-45. Su tratamiento de la Península Ibérica deja mucho que desear. Véase también Natalie Z. DAVIS, «Women's History in Transition: The European Case», *Femenist Studies,* vol. 3, n.° 3-4 (1976), 83-103.

[5] En Burgos durante esos siglos véase Teófilo F. RUIZ, *Sociedad y poder real en Castilla* (Barcelona, 1981).

[6] Hay una multitud de ejemplos de mujeres de la clase nobiliaria comprando y vendiendo tierras en el área de Burgos. Véase por ejemplo Archivo de la Catedral de Burgos (ACB), vol. 36, fol. 182 (3-XII-1275); ACB, vol. 50, p. 1, fol. 49 (17-IX-1285) et passim.

mantener ardiendo lámparas en la iglesia, a velas y a otras finalidades piadosas, demostrando así el profundo interés de Sancha por el bienestar de su alma. Ninguna misa fue ofrecida en sufragio de su padre, marido o cualquier otro pariente masculino. Tampoco limosna alguna fue destinada al monasterio en el que se encontraba su marido. Este es mencionado fugazmente: «Et mando a John Pérez, mi marido 60 mrs.», mezquina suma comparada con sus donaciones a órdenes religiosas y parientes femeninos. Después de doce años, sus tierras debían pasar a sus descendientes inmediatos; los de su carne, y a los parientes de Sancha por parte de madre, excluyendo así a su marido y familia paterna. No sabemos qué buenas razones tendría Sancha Alfonso para sentir tal indiferencia hacia su marido y hacia la familia de su padre, pero no es ése el motivo central de este tema. Su propiedad, y ésta incluía importantes posesiones, era suya. Por ello, no necesitaba requerir ni pedir el consentimiento de su marido, ni de nadie más. Y «si alguno de mis familiares contestara mi testamento, no heredará nada» añadía al final, con tono desafiante[7].

Con la sola excepción del solapado antagonismo hacia su marido y hacia su padre, no hay nada original en este testamento. En la Castilla medieval, la mujer jugó un papel muy activo en el mercado de compra-venta de tierras e inmuebles; con frecuencia comprando y vendiendo, intercambiando y donando tierras con consentimiento marital, pero también por sí sola. La extensa colección documental del archivo catedralicio de Burgos y los documentos pertenecientes a los monasterios de San Agustín y de San Pablo, y los del Hospital del Rey existentes en el Archivo Histórico Nacional (AHN) en Madrid muestran 268 registros de transacciones de tierras e inmuebles en el período comprendido entre 1250 y 1350. Ciento veinte de estas transacciones involucran a parejas o a combinaciones de hermanos y hermanas, padres e hijas y/o madres e hijos. El lenguaje usado en los documentos expone claramente que la propiedad comprada o vendida era compartida por los participantes. Noventa y cinco mujeres aparecen como compradoras o vendedoras de propiedades por sí mismas. En total, más de trescientas mujeres (algunas transacciones incluyen más de una mujer) participaron como propietarias totales o parciales en transacciones de tierras e inmuebles.

Estas cifras requieren una explicación. Nuestro material proviene de los archivos del capítulo catedralicio de Burgos y de los monasterios de la ciudad. Tienen, por lo tanto, tendencia a que aparezcan mayor número de participantes masculinos. Para ser más específico: un gran número de do-

[7] Archivo Histórico Nacional (AHN), Clero, carpeta 227, n.° 1 (18-VI-1337); carpeta 227, n.° 3 (12-VIII-1341).

cumentos incluyen la compra y venta de propiedades por parte de canónigos y monjes que si habrían sido bendecidos con madres y hermanas, no ocurría otro tanto, al menos abiertamente, en lo que a esposas concernía. Intencionalmente, he excluido de estas estadísticas la documentación proveniente del monasterio de las Huelgas, la cual hubiera dado un número desproporcionado de mujeres[8]. Al hacer esta restricción, el número de mujeres participantes en transacciones, tal como se ve en la muestra, se hace aún más significativo. Debe entenderse que las cifras arriba indicadas no constituyen un porcentaje, ya que algunas transacciones comprendían dos o tres mujeres. Por otra parte, el número de mujeres mencionadas en los documentos burgaleses como poseedoras de tierras contiguas o adyacentes es considerablemente más alto que los porcentajes dados por Herlihy para otras partes de Europa[9].

Aparte de la nobleza, el grupo más numeroso de mujeres envueltas en transacciones y por tanto, poseedoras de propiedad, era aquel de las emparentadas por sangre o matrimonio a los funcionarios reales y municipales de Burgos; seguido muy de cerca por mujeres pertenecientes a familias artesanas o relacionadas con el mundo mercantil. Esta distinción se hace totalmente artificial en Burgos, ya que existía una innegable identidad entre ambos grupos[10], pero en aras de la claridad los he examinado por separado. Unos pocos ejemplos serán suficientes: Doña Alda compró un viñedo, una huerta y un terreno en los alrededores de Burgos en 1253. Esta señora era la madre de algunos de los más influyentes miembros de la oligarquía burgalesa a finales del siglo XIII. Casada con Juan Pérez, miembro de la familia Sarracín, y alcalde de Burgos durante la mayor parte de los años entre 1220 y 1250, doña Alda trajo a su alianza matrimonial su propia fortuna, la cual debió ser considerable. Su hijo, Pedro Sarracín, fue deán del capítulo de Burgos, y el propietario más importante de la ciudad. Otros dos hijos, Rodrigo Ibáñez y García Ibáñez, fueron alcaldes de Burgos en la década de 1250 y miembros del concejo de la ciudad[11]. En 1253, su hija (la

[8] Puedo ofrecer un ejemplo de lo que sucedería en el caso de un monasterio de monjas. En este caso sí examinamos las transacciones de Santo Domingo la Real de Madrid, un convento de monjas, entre los años 1259 y 1262. AHN, Clero, carpeta 1354: 21 transacciones. Mujeres solas 5; monjas 19; parejas (hermanos, hermanas, etc.) 7; hombres solos 11. Total femenino 31; total de mujeres solas 24.

[9] D. HERLIHY, pp. 37-42. Porcentajes de mujeres como propietarias de propiedades contiguas es también un método que debe ser usado con recelo y que no nos ofrece respuestas fidedignas. Examinemos de nuevo otro documento de Santo Domingo la Real. AHN, Clero, carpeta 1354, n.° 9 (1-X-1259) en que un cierto Don Esteban y su hija, Olalla, donaban once pedazos de tierra al monasterio. Estas tierras tenían los siguientes vecinos adyacentes: Tierras propiedad de mujeres solas 10; tierras propiedad de hombres 6; tierras del monasterio (femenino) 11; un prado común 2; carreras 4; río 2.

[10] Véase T. F. RUIZ, capítulos 5 y 6.

[11] T. F. RUIZ, «Prosopografía burgalesa, 1250-1350», *Boletín de la Institución Fernán González*, 184 (1975), 471-74.

hija de doña Alda), María Ibáñez adquirió varias casas en la calle de Tenebregosa, una de las principales vías comerciales del Burgos medieval, por 1.080 mrs. Pocos años más tarde, María casó con Juan Pérez de Castro, un funcionario real que servía en Burgos a finales del siglo XIII. La pareja tuvo al menos tres hijos; Pedro Pérez, Ruy Pérez y Juan Pérez, los tres, importantes mercaderes y funcionarios municipales. A la muerte de María, antes de 1290, legó una herencia sustancial a uno de sus hijos. Pedro Pérez recibió propiedades valoradas en 2.200 mrs. Teniendo en cuenta que el testamento no existe, ya que esta información aparece en un contrato de venta, es lógico deducir que sus otros hijos, así como órdenes religiosas hayan sido testados en similar cuantía. Si éste fuera el caso, su fortuna personal debió haber sido considerable[12].

María García era hija de Fernando García, alcalde de Burgos en 1306. En el mismo año, María adquirió derechos de molienda por valor de 400 mrs. Más tarde casó con Ferrand Martínez, funcionario real y municipal en Burgos, residiendo en la calle del Huerto del Rey, uno de los sitios donde tenía su domicilio la oligarquía dominante de la ciudad. María era vecina, es decir, dueña de una casa dentro del recinto amurallado de la ciudad. Al morir su marido y su hija, Sancha García, María testó en favor del monasterio de San Agustín de Burgos las rentas de cinco de sus casas a cambio de una misa diaria que serían cantadas en favor de su alma. Su hijo, Alfonso Ferrández, miembro de la cofradía de caballeros villanos, firmó como testigo, ya que su consentimiento no era requisito para que su madre pudiese disponer de su propiedad[13].

Este derecho indiscutible a la propiedad que disfrutaba la mujer castellana en algunos casos, queda mejor ilustrado en el siguiente ejemplo: Claros Martínez, un caballero villano y mercader de Burgos, quedó viudo con cinco hijas y un hijo. Tres de sus hijas expresaron su deseo de ingresar en un convento. Con este fin, Claros, que poseía una huerta en la ciudad, huerta que pertenecía en común al matrimonio, ofreció vender su parte y la parte que después de la muerte de su esposa, correspondía por completo a sus hijos, para el pago de la dote. Para poder llevar a cabo tal transacción hubo de obtener el consentimiento previo de cada uno de los herederos así

[12] *Ibidem*, p. 475, vol. 49, fol. 4 (15-V-1253); ACB, vol. 50, p. 1, fol. 60 (26-I-1290). 1.080 mrs. es una suma considerable de dinero. La mayoría de las transacciones en la década de 1250 rara vez excedían 100 mrs.

[13] T. F. RUIZ, «The Transformation of the Castilian Municipalities: The Case of Burgos, 1248-1350», *Past & Present*, 77 (1977), 19-20; ACB, vol. 50, p. 2, fol. 156 (23-XII-1337); AHN, Clero, carpeta 177, n.° 4 (24-III-1337); T. F. RUIZ, «Prosopografía», p. 486. 400 mrs. fue una de las sumas más altas pagadas por un viñedo en la región de Burgos entre 1250 y 1350.

como del alcalde de la ciudad: la mitad correspondiente a su mujer no era suya, y, de acuerdo con la ley, no podía disponer de la misma[14].

En Burgos, la oligarquía urbana estaba estrechamente unida por alianzas matrimoniales, mucho más de lo que yo anteriormente estimé[15]. Es más, en las Cortes de Alcalá de Henares (1348), Alfonso XI otorgó a los caballeros villanos el derecho de que sus mujeres llevaran ciertos tipos de paño, los cuales estaban prohibidos al resto de la población femenina de Castilla que no perteneciera a la nobleza[16]. Esta petición originaría probablemente con las esposas e hijas de los caballeros villanos, sirviéndonos como recordatorio de que la consciencia social es, con frecuencia, más fuerte que la solidaridad con el propio sexo. De la misma forma que sus maridos, padres y hermanos, querían ellas también vestir de forma distinta a las mujeres por debajo de su nivel económico y social.

Entre las mujeres relacionadas con el comercio y las ocupaciones artesanales podemos mencionar a doña María y sus hijas, Urraca y Mencia Martínez, las cuales tenían tiendas de pieles en la vecindad de San Gil (Burgos). En 1304 vendieron las mismas por 800 mrs.[17] Otra doña María, de apellido González, vendió una tienda de artículos de cuero en el mismo barrio a su hijo el canónigo John González por 600 mrs.[18] Asimismo encontramos numerosas menciones de panaderas, aunque no es de extrañar, ya que parece ser que el arte de hacer pan era territorio casi reservado a las mujeres en la Castilla medieval[19].

Una mujer, Elvira Pérez, estaba entre más de cien burgaleses que prestaron dinero al concejo de la ciudad con el fin de construir las murallas en 1313. Su préstamo de 1.000 mrs. fue bastante más que la media de sumas prestadas por otras personas en la lista[20]. En términos de riqueza, no obstante, la palma la lleva doña Urraca, viuda de don Vidal, un mercader de paños. Ciudadana de Burgos, con casa en la calle de San Llorente, también residencia de la oligarquía urbana, adquirió viñedos en 1326 por valor de 5.300 mrs.; una suma bastante fuerte a pagar por unos viñedos, teniendo

[14] T. F. Ruiz, «Prosopografía», p. 485; AHN, Clero, carpeta 185, n.° 13 (10-VI-1309).

[15] T. F. Ruiz, «The Transformation», pp. 20-22; AHN, Clero, carpeta 201, n.° 2 (20-VII-1345).

[16] T. F. Ruiz, «The Transformation», p. 19.

[17] ACB, vol. 42, fol. 36 (14-IV-1304). Para mujeres mercaderes y artesanas en otras partes de Europa medieval véase Kärl Michäelsson, *Le livre de la taille de Paris l'an 1297* (Göteborg, 1962); Julia O'Faolain y Lauro Martines, eds. *Not in God's Image. Women in History from the Greeks to the Victorians* (New York, 1973), pp. 154-66.

[18] ACB, vol. 42, fol. 39 (1-III-1330).

[19] Mercedes Gaibrois de Ballesteros, *Historia del reinado de Sancho IV de Castilla,* 3 vols. (Madrid, 1922-28), I, p. XCIV.

[20] Archivo municipal de Burgos, clasif. 652 (19-XII-1313).

en cuenta la época y los precios de otras tierras y viñedos. Diecinueve años más tarde, llevó a efecto unas ventas de tierras por valor de 7.000 mrs.[21]

Actuando junto a sus maridos, o junto a otros parientes masculinos, nos encontramos con mujeres que emparentadas con abogados, carniceros, médicos, etc., compran y venden tierras y casas[22]. Significativamente, la misma indicación de igualdad de derechos de propiedad, se refleja también en los escasos documentos burgaleses que mencionan a judíos y moros. Por ejemplo, Andalla, un tintorero y su mujer Aciense (moros) vendieron casas por valor de 5.000 mrs. a Pedro Mena, alcalde de la ciudad en 1305. En 1286 Juçef Haraçon y su mujer Ledizia (judíos) vendieron partes de un viñedo al deán del capítulo catedralicio por 2.000 mrs[23]. En Avila, donde el número de registros de transacciones entre miembros de las minorías religiosas y cristianos en existencia es mucho mayor que en Burgos, encontramos a mujeres musulmanas y judías que venden propiedades al mismo tiempo o con sus parientes masculinos o por sí solas. Además, hay varios ejemplos de tenderas judías[24]. La evidencia con la que nos encontramos en la ciudad de Burgos no es, de ninguna manera, excepcional, ni refleja las condiciones peculiares de un entorno urbano. Con el fin de ofrecer algún punto de comparación, he revisado la documentación del monasterio de Santa María de Aguilar de Campoo. En los siglos XIII y XIV este monasterio estaba situado en la diócesis de Burgos, aunque Campoo pertenezca hoy a la provincia de Palencia. Emplazado en un rico y fértil valle, la extensa documentación del monasterio nos muestra ciento treinta y cuatro transacciones de tierras en el período comprendido entre 1250 y 1350. Cuarenta y siete de ellas incluyen parejas, madres e hijos, o hermanos y hermanas. Treinta y siete de las transacciones incluían mujeres solas[25].

Las mismas características que aplicáramos a los documentos burgaleses deben ser observados aquí. Más importante aún es la señalada evidencia de la participación femenina en la vida agrícola de Castilla. En un documento carente de fecha —aunque con bastante certeza lo podemos asignar a finales del siglo XIII— aparece una larga lista de campesinos que trabajaban las tierras del monasterio y lo que debían por infurción al mismo. Se cuentan

21 ACB, vol. 49, fol. 4 (18-IX-1326); AHN, Clero, carpeta 201, no. la (27-V-1345). Estas transacciones están entre las de más cuantía por el período que aquí examinamos.

22 ACB, vol. 40, fol. 251 (6-XI-1320); ACB, vol. 37, fol. 20 (5-X-1325); ACB, vol. 37, fol. 24 (27-XII-1336); ACB, vol. 49, fol. 81 (23-IX-1282); ACB, vol. 50, p. 1, fol. 626 (16-II-1262) et passim.

23 ACB, vol. 41, p. 2, fol. 374 (7-IX-1305); ACB, vol. 49, fol. 85 (22-IV-1286).

24 Para Avila véase C. M. AJO G. y SÁINZ DE ZÚÑIGA, *Avila. Fuentes y archivos* (Madrid, 1962), I, pp. 104, 105, 106, 107 et passim. Para Segovia, Miguel SANTAMARÍA LANCHO en su tesina, *La gestión económica del cabildo de Segovia*. Universidad Complutense. Madrid, 1980.

25 AHN, Clero, carpetas 1657 a 1674.

quinientos cincuenta y tres agricultores en tal documento. Al lado de los nombres se pueden ver las cifras debidas. Frecuentemente, estos pagos se hacían en relativamente pequeñas cantidades de especies (trigo, cebada, tocinos, etc.). Unos cuantos hacían pagos adicionales en efectivo y otros pocos trabajaban la tierra a razón de un porcentaje. Noventa y siete de éstos campesinos eran mujeres, o sea, un 17,54 % de la fuerza laboral agrícola, sin contar las mujeres de los hombres arriba apuntados. Estas noventa y siete mujeres tenían la tierra por sí solas, ya que o aparecen como viudas o bien sus hijos —identificados por los matronímicos— aparecían trabajando tierras monásticas en algún otro sitio[26]. Debe haber sido una escena bastante común, el ver mujeres dedicadas al cultivo de la tierra por sí solas. Tenemos también ejemplos en la documentación de Aguilar de Campoo de mujeres que alquilaban tierras ya sea con sus maridos o por sí solas[27]. Además, hombres y mujeres contaban a veces por igual en lo que a trabajo e impuestos concernía en algunas regiones de Castilla. En 1270 los representantes del monasterio de Santa María de Nájera (también parte de la diócesis de Burgos en la Edad Media) y sus vasallos de Covacardiel y Villa Almondar llegaron al acuerdo de establecer una escala de pago por la anubda que se debía al monasterio. Aquellas familias que araban la tierra con dos bueyes u otras bestias cualesquiera pagaban 2 sueldos. Aquellas con un buey o cualquier otra bestia pagaban 1 sueldo. Además, estas familias que poseyeran animales —fueren uno o dos— también tenían que pagar diez «fornazos en parada» (un impuesto, la cantidad no se especifica, que se pagaba por el derecho de hornear el pan en el horno del monasterio) y dos «colodros» (unidad de medida) de vino, amén de un carnero anualmente por cada dos parejas. Las parejas que no tuvieren animales de tiro y, por lo tanto, menos capaces de obtener mejores rendimientos de la tierra, pagaban diez «fornazos de parada» y dos colodros de vino, además de un carnero por cada dos parejas. Los viudos y las viudas, aun cuando tuvieran bueyes, pagaban cinco «fornazos en parada», un colodro de vino y un cordero por cada cuatro de ellos. Esta escala de contribución se mantenía a esos niveles hasta que volvieran a casarse. Puede verse, por lo tanto, que las distinciones no se hacían por el sexo, sino en cuanto a tener una mujer o un marido; es decir, en cuanto a la capacidad de doblar la capacidad de trabajo y, por tanto, la de pago[28].

26 AHN, Clero, carpeta 1665, n.° 1 (sin fecha).

27 Algunos ejemplos pueden verse en AHN, Clero, carpeta 1656, n.° 6 (22-VII-1261); carpeta 1663, n.° 2 (25-VIII-1297); carpeta 1659, n.° 8 (13-X-1271); carpeta 1668, n.° 5 (12-XII-1316); carpeta 1671, n.° 3 (15-II-1334); carpeta 1672, n.° 10 (6-V-1358); et passim.

28 AHN, Clero, carpeta 1032, n.° 4 (10-II-1270); AHN, Codices 105B, fol. 44 (12-XII-1052). En el

No obstante, esta redundante lista de cifras y ejemplos no nos da una indicación clara de cuán difundida era la incidencia de mujeres en posesión de tierras en la Castilla y el Burgos medievales. Antes de 1350, la documentación no nos permite completar un porcentaje estadístico de las mujeres poseedoras de propiedades. Hay, sin embargo, interesantes ejemplos de otras regiones. José M. Bilbao y E. Fernández Pinedo en su artículo, «En torno al problema del poblamiento y la población vascongada en la Edad Media», estudiaron los censos de fuegos de La Guardia, Labraza, Barriobusto y Bernedo —zonas entonces bajo el dominio del rey de Navarra— durante los años 1350, 1366 y 1427. En 1350 La Guardia y caseríos adyacentes tenían 517 fuegos masculinos y 156 femeninos, además de un pequeño número de clérigos, nobles y siervos. En 1350, el 23,58 % de los cabezas de familia, eran mujeres. En 1366, no obstante, este número descendía hasta pasar a ser el 5,70 %, mientras el número de cabeza de familia masculinos se mantenía estable[29]. Los autores atribuyen, lo que consideran un alto y poco frecuente porcentaje de fuegos encabezados por mujeres a la peste, pensando, uno debe asumir que la peste afectaba menos a las mujeres que a los hombres[30]. Esto es difícil de aceptar. En realidad, la meta de Bilbao y Fernández Pinedo no era estudiar el porcentaje de mujeres propietarias; por lo que en este aspecto sus conclusiones no son satisfactorias. En el norte de Europa vemos que A. Chédeville y J. C. Russell han dado diversas cifras del porcentaje de mujeres con propiedades, yendo desde el 8 % en Chartres hasta el 15 % en ciertas regiones de Inglaterra[31].

Si tomamos en cuenta el número de mujeres que participaban en transacciones de tierras e inmuebles en la Castilla medieval, la frecuente mención de mujeres como co-propietarias y la fuerte evidencia de la mujer en labores agrícolas en las tierras de Santa María de Aguilar de Campoo, todo esto me lleva a creer que el número de mujeres dueñas de propiedades en Castilla sobrepasaba con mucho el 15 % señalado por Russell. El sistema legal de Castilla, con sus fuertes componentes romano y local —en los cuales había poca influencia de las costumbres feudales francesas—, sumado a la pobreza demográfica y a las crisis económicas y sociales en las pos-

primitivo acuerdo de 1052, los viudos no recibían los mismos descuentos en sus contribuciones sólo las viudas.

29 José M. Bilbao y E. Fernández Pinedo, «En torno al problema de poblamiento y la población vascongada en la Edad Media», en *III Symposium de historia medieval del señorío de Vizcaya* (Bilbao, 1975), pp. 328-31.

30 *Ibidem*, pp. 329-30.

31 André Chédeville, *Chartres et ses campagnes, XIème-XIIIème siècles* (Paris, 1973), pág. 90 y nota 71; Josiah Cox Russell, *British Medieval Population* (Alburquerque, N. M., 1948), pp. 64-68 y tablas en las pp. 62-63; 4.1.

trimerías del siglo XIII y en el siglo XIV reforzaron probablemente tanto el arrendamiento, como la posesión de tierras por parte de la mujer. Puede que no sea exagerado suponer, que el porcentaje de mujeres en posesión de derechos de propiedad en Castilla, fuese más alto en la Edad Media que en cualquier otro período posterior, incluyendo aún nuestro tiempo. Esto, desde luego, son suposiciones que no pueden sobrevivir la inexorable necesidad de una evidencia que las respalde. Lo que sí queda claro es que la mujer tuvo una participación mucho más importante en la vida económica del medievo castellano y burgalés que lo que habíamos supuesto. Este, como otros temas, aguarda la paciente labor de un historiador.

VI

TWO PATRICIAN FAMILIES IN LATE MEDIEVAL BURGOS: THE SARRACIN AND THE BONIFAZ

Twenty years ago, during my research on the social, economic, and political structures of the city of Burgos in the late thirteenth and early fourteenth centuries, I found numerous references to specific individuals and family groups. It was clear to me then that a few families played a prominent role in the administrative, social and economic life of the city; moreover, their influence often extended to the wider confines of the Castilian realm.[1] My aim here is to present this scattered information about the lives of important Burgalese families in a coherent form, and to indicate how such families came to exercise their power on the affairs of the city.

I. HISTORICAL PRECEDENTS

A brief glance at the most notable individuals and families in late medieval Burgos is a prerequisite for understanding the social and economic life of the city. The extant documents show, unequivocally, the direct relationship between the social and economic status of these families and their control of political life in Burgos. I refer here to the upper segment of the bourgeoisie--those who one may choose to call, for lack of a better term, the patrician elite--dominating Burgos' civic life throughout most of the late Middle Ages.

We should begin with specific questions: Who belonged to this narrow and exclusive hegemonic group? How did these family groups and individuals acquire their influence? There is no need here, of course, to paraphrase the work of previous historians. There are numerous monographs on the origins and development of the bourgeoisie in western Europe and in Castile proper; they trace the general outline of the rise of urban life in the central Middle Ages and the increasing importance of the bourgeoisie in medieval society.[2] In this context, one should acknowledge the labor of local Burgalese historians, such as I. García Rámila, T. López Mata, J. García Saínz de Baranda and others, who toiled for

---

[1] This article was originally published in Spanish in 1974; it was one of the first attempts at a prosopographical study of bourgeois elites in Castile. Since then, several important and more sophisticated studies have appeared, as for example, Angel Barrios García, *Estructuras agrarias y de poder en Castilla. El ejemplo de Avila (1085-1320)*, 2 vols. (Salamanca, 1983-84); María Asenjo, *Segovia. La ciudad y su tierra a fines del medievo* (Segovia, 1986); Adeline Rucquoi, *Valladolid en la edad media*, 2 vols. (Valladolid, 1987).

[2] For the development of the bourgeoisie in medieval Europe see Henri Pirenne, *Les villes et les institutions urbaines*, 3rd ed. (Paris, 1939), I; Jacques Lestocquoy, *Patricians du Moyen Age. Les dynasties bourgeoisies d'Arras du XIe au XVe siècle* (Arras, 1945); also his *Les villes de Flandre et d'Italie sous le gouvernement des patriciens* (Paris, 1952). On Spain see Leopoldo Torres Balbas, et al, *Resumen histórico del urbanismo en España* (Madrid, 1968); Luis García de Valdeavellanos, *Orígenes de la burguesía en la España medieval* (Madrid, 1969).

many years on a variety of topics dealing with the history of Burgos. Their works, often published in the local learned journal, laid the foundations for a more critical approach to these questions.

In referring to the bourgeoisie of Burgos, one is struck by the impreciseness of the term bourgeois in its all-embracing meaning. One must place this construct within a temporal and geographical context, i.e., in the period and in the locality which one is examining--Burgos in the thirteenth and fourteenth centuries. Although we may easily describe the dominant groups of Burgos in this period as members of the bourgeoisie, it would be more accurate, perhaps, to describe them as non-noble knights (*caballeros villanos*). By this, I mean, those town citizens (*villa*) who owned a horse (*caballo*) and weapons and who, therefore, derived a great number of privileges from that condition. Elsewhere in Castile, urban elites, in many respects fulfilling the general description of hegemonic bourgeois groups, nevertheless, derived their income not from trade or artisanal occupations but from the land.[3]

The evidence below shows, incontrovertibly, the privileged position of the non-noble knights and their predominance in the trade and social life of the city. In Burgos and in other urban cities the catalyst for the rise of the *caballería villana* within the city took place shortly after the mid-thirteenth century. On 22 February 1255, Alfonso X granted sweeping tax exemptions to "those who lived in the city of Burgos, those who are now and to come for ever more, and who owned horse and weapons: *lorigas e brafoneras, e escudo e lanza e capiello.*"[4] This privilege, which benefited those Burgalese citizens with horse and weapons, was only a starting point. The following year, on 27 July 1256, the king confirmed the exemption from taxes to the "knights who owned the largest inhabited houses in the town" and added a long list of economic privileges which allowed the non-noble knights to enhance their already well-entrenched social and

---

[3] On the *caballería popular o villana* see Carmela Pescador, "La caballería popular en León y Castilla", *Cuadernos de Historia de España,* XXXXIII-XXXIV (1961), 101-238; XXXV-XXXVI (1962), 56-201; XXXVII-XXXVIII (1963), 88-198; XXXIX-XL (1964), 169-260; Elena Lourie, "A Society Organized for War: Medieval Spain," *Past and Present*, 35 (December, 1966), 54-76; James F. Powers, "The Origins and Development of Municipal Military Service in the Leonese and Castilian Reconquest, 800-1250", *Traditio,* XXVI (1970), 91-111; also his "Townsmen and Soldiers. The Interaction of Urban and Military Organization in the Militias of Medieval Castile," *Speculum*, XLVI (1971); Adriana Bó and María del Carmen Carlé, "Cuando empieza a reservarse a los caballeros el gobierno de las ciudades castellanas," *Cuadernos de Historia de España*, IV (1946), 114-124.

[4] Archivo Municipal de Burgos (AMB), clasif. 138 (22-II-1255).

economic position.[5] The dynamics of this new economic formulation led to changes in the social and political life of the patriciate.

Socially, the non-noble knights articulated their newly acquired privileges through the formation of *cofradías* (confraternities) or brotherhoods of "*caballeros*," such as those of Nuestra Señora de Gamonal and the Real Hermandad. These two brotherhoods, organized in principle for pious and religious aims, brought together the most influential citizens of Burgos. In some respects, the confraternity of Nuestra Señora de Gamonal, founded in 1285, marked just an initial step towards the social consolidation of the *caballería villana.* La Real Hermandad or brotherhood of the Santísimo y Santiago, founded by Alfonso XI in 1338, on the other hand, represents the final chapter in the non-noble knights' rise to undisputed social prominence within the city[6] Politically, the municipal council of Burgos was monopolized by the non-noble knights, or, to be more accurate, by a handful of Burgalese families. This urban patriciate dominated the political life of the city, without any seeming interruption, into the early modern period.

II. THE POLITICAL CONTROL OF THE CITY: SARRACIN AND BONIFAZ

The two most important families in late Medieval Burgos were those of the Sarracín and the Bonifaz, and we should look now in detail at the manner in which they exercised their influence and extended their power.

A. The Sarracín Family

Among the first of the Sarracín to appear prominently in the Burgalese documents, Pedro Sarracín I was *alcalde* (a judicial and executive office) of the city in 1187, 1193, 1196, 1200, 1202, 1207-08, 1210-12, the last year coinciding

---

[5] See AMB clasif. 115 (27-VII-1256). Published in *Monumento histórico español* (hereafter *MHE*), I, 97-100.

[6] These two Burgalese confraternities, their rules and membership lists have been studied by Ismael García Rámila, *Texto cronológico de las tres Reglas por las que, sucesivamente, rigió su vida corporativa la Real Cofradía del "Santísimo y Santiago", de la Ciudad de Burgos* (Burgos, 1970), and Julián García Sainz de Baranda, "Primitiva regla escrita de la Cofradía de Nuestra Señora de Gamonal", *Boletín de la Comisión de Monumentos Artísticos de la Provincia de Burgos,* 65 (1938), 158-64. See also below my "The Transformation of the Castilian Municipalities: The Case of Burgos," in chapter VII of this collection.

with his death.[7] These dates are the only ones for which we have documentary evidence, but one may assume that Pedro Sarracín I served in the municipal council of Burgos far more often than what the extant documents indicate. Besides his frequent participation in the political affairs of the city, Pedro Sarracín owned lands and vineyards in the area of Villatoro, Prado, and Valdecardeña, all of them, villages in the hinterland of Burgos, as well as in the proximity of the mill of Atga in the Burgalese neighborhood of San Juan. These properties were bought jointly with his brother Gonzalo, canon and *sacristán* of the cathedral of Burgos, and with his wife Estefanía Bonifaz (d. 1225).[8] The influence and economic well-being of Pedro Sarracín I and his family, as indicated by their purchase of land, was reflected in their founding the Hospital of San Lucas in the early thirteenth century, a pious establishment with which the family was to be associated for the next century.[9]

Pedro Sarracín and his wife Estefanía Bonifaz had at least six children: three males, Gonzalo Pérez, García Pérez y Juan Pérez and three females, María Pérez, Urraca and Inés.[10] Gonzalo Pérez, who became archdeacon of Valpuesta in the diocese of Burgos and later abbot of Salas, died in 1248.[11] Of García Pérez, the extant documents reveal nothing except his death in 1205, probably as an adolescent.[12] Two of the daughters, María and Inés, married well, one of

---

[7] Amancio Rodríguez López, *El Real monasterio de las Huelgas y el Hospital del Rey*, 2 vols. (Burgos, 1907), I. no. 34, p. 366; no. 36, p. 370; Archivo Catedral de Burgos (ACB) vol. 49, f. 41 (?-X-1195); Rodríguez López, I, no. 36a, p. 370; no. 37 and 37a, pp. 371-372; ACB, vol. 50, p. 2. f. 134 (?-X-1200); Rodríguez López, I, no. 37c and no. 37d, pp. 373-374; no. 37h, pp. 375-376; no. 38a, pp. 377-378; no. 39a. p. 379; no. 39, pp. 378-379; ACB, vol. 50, p. 2. f. 136 (?-VI-1211); vol. 70. no. 83 (1212).

[8] ACB, vol. 49, f. 35 (?-XII-1186); vol. 49, f. 36 (?-V-1192); vol. 49, f. 37 (?-X-1192); vol. 49, f. 40 (?-IX-1193); vol. 49, f. 41 (?-XI-1195); vol. 50, p. 2, f. 134 (?-X-1200); vol. 50, p. 2, f. 135 (1-X-1206).

[9] Luciano Serrano, *El obispado de Burgos y Castilla primitiva desde el siglo V al XIII*, 3 vols. (Madrid, 1935-36), III, 220-21: Serrano confuses Pedro Sarracín I with his grandson, Pedro Sarracín II, the dean of the chapter of Burgos.

[10] Ibid., III, 374; ACB, Vol. 50, p. 1, f. 46 (?-V-1225).

[11] ACB, Vol. 50, p. 2, f. 138 (17-VI-1248); vol. 50, p. 1, f. 46 (?-V-1225).

[12] Serrano, *El obispado*, III, 374.

them to a nobleman. Both of them had properties in and around Burgos.[13]

As for Juan Pérez I, of the six surviving children of Pedro and Estefanía, he was the one to carry on the political career of his father. Juan was *alcalde* in at least 1221, 1222, 1225, 1248 and 1253. Married to doña Alda, their children, Pedro Sarracín II, Rodrigo Ibáñez, Gómez Ibáñez, García Ibáñez and María Ibáñez also occupied important positions in the political, social, and religious life of medieval Burgos. That they did so was directly related to the continuous accumulation of landed property, first by Pedro Sarracín I and, later, by his son, Juan Pérez I.[14]

There is a great deal we know about the six sons and daughters of Juan Pérez I and doña Alda. Pedro Sarracín II was probably born before 1230, since in 1248 he is mentioned in an extant document with the title of master (*maestre*). That same year his brother, García Ibáñez, gave him lands in Villatoro which, at least in the documentary evidence, marked the beginnings of Pedro Sarracín II's long-term investment in that locality.

According to Amancio Blanco Díaz, Pedro Sarracín II was married, taking religious vows only after his wife's early death.[15] I have not found any evidence for this; his title of *maestre* in 1248 already provides testimony to a university training and an early membership in the church. By 1256 Pedro Sarracín had become archdeacon of Palenzuela and, four years later, that of the profitable archdeaconry of Lara.[16] In 1262, he moved to the archdeaconry of Valpuesta, a position which had been held by his uncle Gonzalo. Between 1274 and 1276 he became dean of the cathedral chapter of Burgos. His election must have taken place between these two dates, since, in a transaction of 1274, he is identified as archdeacon of Valpuesta and, in another purchase of 1276, he is already

---

13 María married Sancho Ruiz de Villegas and owned property in the city. Archivo de las Huelgas de Burgos, leg 12, no. 10., leg. 33, no. 1501. Inés married don Lope de Velasco and also owned property in Burgos. AHB, leg 33, no. 1486; ACB, vol. 50, p. 2, f. 142.

14 ACB, vol. 49, f. 46 (?-XI-1221); Rodríguez López, I. no. 44, p. 390., ACB, vol. 50, p. 1, f. 40 (?-V-1225); vol. 49, f. 47 (?-IV-1228); vol. 49, f. 59 (27-V-1248); vol. 49, f. 74 (15-V-1253); vol. 49, f. 89 (1291).

15 ACB, vol. 50, p. 1, f. 43 (29-VI-1248). See Amancio Blanco Díez, "Los Deanes de la Catedral de Burgos", *Boletín de la Comisión...*, 90 (1945), 488-492.

16 ACB, vol. 37, f. 459 (7-VII-1256); vol. 50, p. 1, f. 45 (13-II-1260).

acknowledged as dean of the chapter.[17]

In a little less than twenty years, Pedro Sarracín II rose through the ranks of the chapter's hierarchy, occupying increasingly more profitable positions and finally gaining the deanship. After the bishop, he was the most important and influential ecclesiastic in the diocese of Burgos, the largest and richest in northern Castile. His power and local support must have been considerable. In 1274, he became a serious candidate for the episcopal chair before bowing to the needs of royal policies. As dean, however, he was not unwilling to flex his muscles. In 1278, dean Pedro Sarracín regained control of the Hospital of San Lucas which had been, until then, under the jurisdiction of the monastery of the Trinity in Burgos. He granted a rule to the Hospital and had his rights over the Hospital and his newly drawn rule confirmed by Sancho IV in 1288.[18]

Pedro Sarracín's activities were not limited to the ecclesiastical sphere. His wealth and earthly possessions increased in a course which paralleled his clerical promotions. As his ancestors had done, the dean put a great deal of his energies in the acquisition of lands in the area of Villatoro, in other villages around Burgos, as well as within the city itself.

According to the extant documentation--and one must remember that these are probably only a fraction of the original record--Pedro Sarracín II purchased or exchanged properties in thirty-three occasions between 1248 and 1290. The money invested in these transactions amounted to 30,964 *maravedís* (*mrs.*) 4.*s.* 2*d.*, plus two capes and other properties granted in exchange.[19] Seventeen of these purchases took place before his election as dean, but the monetary investment came to a mere 2,094 *mrs.* After 1276, we find only sixteen transactions, but the property acquired was worth 28,870 *mrs.* This was a

---

17 ACB, vol. 49, f. 48 (11-X-1262); vol. 49, f. 61 (15-IV-1274); vol. 50, p. 2, f. 148 (1276).

18 ACB, vol. 50, p. 1, f. 47 (24-VII-1278); vol. 50, p. 1, f. 48 (1-VII-1279). Confirmation of the Hospital's rule by Sancho IV in ACB, vol. 49, f. 87 (25-IV-1288). Also see Demetrio Mansilla, "Episcopologio de Burgos," *Hispania Sacra*, IV (1951), 17.

19 ACB, vol. 50, p. 2, f. 138 (17-VI-1248); vol. 50, p. 1, f. 43 (29-VI-1248); vol. 50, p. 1, f. 43 (29-VI-1248); vol. 37, f. 459 (7-VII-1256); vol. 50, p. 2, f. 142, (27-VII-1257); vol. 50, p. 1, f. 45 (13-II-1260); vol. 50, p. 1, f. 62b (16-II-1262); vol. 49, f. 48, (II-X-1262); vol. 49, f. 60 (24-III-1265); vol. 49, f. 50 (24-II-1266); vol. 50, p. 2, f. 144, (4-VII-1267); vol. 19, f. 516 (17-VIII-1267); vol. 49, f. 53 (4-XI-1268); vol. 49, f. 101, (22-IX-1269); vol. 49, f. 61, (15-IV-1274); vol. 50, p. 2, f. 148 (31-I-1276); vol. 49, f. 64 (4-II-1280); vol. 49, f. 79 (9-II-1280); vol. 49, f. 78, (11-II-1280); vol. 49, f. 77 (11-V-1280); vol. 49, f. 81 (23-IX-1282); vol. 50, p. 2, f. 145 (?-XI-1283); vol. 50, p. 1, f. 59, (3-XII-1283); vol. 50, p. 2, f. 147, (7-VII-1284); vol. 49, f. 65 (3-VIII-1285); vol. 50, p. 1, f. 49 (17-IX-1285); vol. 49, f. 85, (22-IV-1286); vol. 49, f. 48 (10-VI, 1286); vol. 49, f. 83 (5-X-1286); vol. 49, f. 86 (22-XII-1288); vol. 50, p. 2, f. 149 (26-I-1290).

substantial sum indeed. 30.000 *mrs.* was the equivalent, in fact, of the diocese of Burgos' *fonsadera* (a tax in lieu of military service) annual payment to the king. There is an obvious connection between Pedro Sarracín II's deanship and his activities in the land and real estate market. Yet, the properties were bought for his own and his family's benefit and not for that of the Church of Burgos. At his death, sometime between 1290 and 1291, the bulk of his property was willed to his own relatives.[20]

Pedro Sarracín II's brothers, although not as successful as the dean, also held important positions in the city. His brother, Rodrigo Ibáñez, was *alcade* of Burgos at least in 1259 and 1275. In 1268, he served as procurator of the city to the important gathering or *ayuntamiento* (a partial Cortes) of Jerez and, according to an extant royal document, he is described as *mío ome*, a king's man.[21] This Rodrigo may be the same man named as *monedero* in Burgos in 1279 by the infante don Sancho. We also know that he had at least three sons, Juan García, John Ruiz, Pedro Sarracín III, and a daughter, doña Mayor. We should look briefly at this next generation of the Sarracín family before examining the rest of Juan Pérez's sons. Juan García, Rodrigo's son, married a certain doña Alda (II) in 1275, and she brought a dowry of 2,000 *mrs.* In 1285 Juan sold lands and a house in Villatoro to his brother, Pedro Sarracín III, for 4,050 *mrs.*, and other properties in Temiño for 800 *mrs.* in 1292. He died before 1299 and, in his will, named his brother Pedro Sarracín III as one of the main beneficiaries.[22]

Juan (John) Ruiz, Rodrigo's second son, was a representative of the municipal council of Burgos to Alfonso X's court in 1275 and 1275. The first of these documentary references described him as "John Royz, *fijo de don Rodrigo Ivánez, cavallero*," i.e., a knight or non-noble knight. In 1294, John was *alcalde* of Burgos and *amo* of the Infante don Pedro. That same year he also collected the *fonsadera* for the king in the diocese of Burgos. In 1304, the last extant reference to John Ruiz depicts him as member of the municipal council, holding

---

[20] See the last purchase made by the dean on 26 January 1290 (fn. 19) and his testamentary dispositions in ACB, vol. 49, f. 90 (12-II-1291); vol. 49, f. 94 (15-II-1291); vol. 49, f. 68 (1-III-1291). Simon Ibáñez received 3,500 *mrs.* from his uncle, the dean; Juán Pérez de Castro and Pascual Ochaneret de Castro inherited two houses in the street of Tenebregosa; Pedro Pérez, the son of Juan Pérez de Castro, received 600 *mrs.* in the will of Pedro Sarracín; Amancio Blanco Díez, p. 491, places the dean's death in 1288.

[21] AMB, clasif. 683 (25-IX-1259); clasif. 2574 (22-XII-1275); clasif. 99 (25-III-1268).

[22] ACB. vol. 50, p. 2, f. 150 (5-VI-1291); AMB, clasif. 2922 (18-X-1279); ACB. vol. 49, f. 62 (28-IV-1275); vol. 49, f. 82 (24-VII-1285); vol. 50, p. 2, f. 152 (25-I-1292); vol. 50, p. 1, f. 58 (23-II-1299); vol. 49, f. 69 (12-V-1291).

usufruct rights in the mill of Atga, the most important watermill in the city.[23]

Pedro Sarracín III, the last of the three sons of Rodrigo Ibáñez, followed the path already laid out by his uncle and namesake. In 1285 Pedro was *racionero* of the cathedral of Burgos and six years later a member of the chapter. By 1293, he had also become the warden of the family endowed Hospital of San Lucas.[24] He continued as well his uncle's successful investments in the land and real estate markets in Temiño, Salas de Bureba and Villatoro. Altogether, we have fourteen extant transactions and one exchange of property, totaling an investment of more than 10,000 *mrs.*[25]

The last of Rodrigo's known children was doña Mayor. She is identified in only one document from 1291, as granting power-of-attorney to her brother, Pedro Sarracín, to sell her extensive properties (probably part of her uncle's inheritance) in Burgos, Villatoro, Temiño, Salas de Bureba and Castro del Val.[26]

We must return now to the remaining children of Juan Pérez and to their descendants, although for some of them our information is meager: Gómez Ibáñez, was *alcalde* of Burgos in 1273 and 1288 and owned properties in Villatoro.[27] Of Garcia Ibáñez, probably the oldest of Juan Pérez's son, we have no news, except that his son Fernán García was a member of the municipal council of Burgos in, at least, 1259 and 1268; in the latter year he also served as

---

[23] AMB, clasif. 2574 (22-XII-1275); clasif. 2562 (16-VII-1278); ACB, vol. 36, f. 182 (3-XII-1275); vol. 36, f. 182 (3-XII-1275); vol. 32, f. 277 (13-XII-1276); ACB, vol. 49, f. 1 (5-IX-1285); Mercedes Gaibrois de Ballesteros, *Historia del reinado de Sancho IV de Castilla*, 3 vols (Madrid, 1922-28), I, XLIII; III, CCXC-CCCXCI; ACB, vol. 42, f. 105 (3-V-1301); Antonio Benavides, *Memorias de Fernando IV de Castilla*, 2 vols. (Madrid, 1860), II, 450.

[24] ACB, vol. 49, f. 82 (24-VII-1285), *racionero*: ACB, vol. 49, f. 92 (22-III-1291), *canónigo*: ACB, vol. 49, f. 97b (27-IX-1293).

[25] ACB, vol. 49, f. 82 (24-VII-1285); vol. 49, f. 92 (22-III-1291); vol. 49, f. 91, (14-IV-1291); vol. 49, f. 89 (6-V-1291); vol. 50, p. 2, f. 150 (5-VI_1291); vol. 50, p. 2, f. 152 (25-I-1295); vol. 49, f. 95 (19-X-1292); vol. 50, p. 2, f. 153 (17-XII-1292); vol. 50, p. 2, f. 153 (17-XII-1292); vol. 50, p. 2, f. 151 (23-XII-1292); vol. 50, p. 2, f. 151 (23-XII-1292); vol. 50, p. 2, f. 154 (6-I-1293); vol. 49, f. 97 (7-I-1293); vol. 49, f. 98 (4-II-1293); vol. 49, f. 99 (2-VI-1293); vol. 50, p. 1, f. 64 (4-X-1300).

[26] ACB, vol. 49, f. 69 (12-V-1291).

[27] AMB, clasif. 806 (4-VIII-1273); ACB vol. 50, p. 1, f. 61 (6-II-1288).

procurator to the *ayuntamiento* of Jerez.[28]

María Ibáñez, Juan Pérez I's daughter, married Juan Pérez de Castro, the king's *merino* in Burgos in 1273 and 1293. A merchant as well as a royal official, Juan Pérez de Castro was among the most important merchants in Burgos, buying luxury textiles in Flanders and Brabant.[29] María and Juan Pérez de Castro owned properties in Salas de Bureba, Temiño, Villatoro and Burgos, and in 1291, as part of Pedro Sarracín's will, they inherited two houses in Tenebregosa Street, the commercial center of the city.[30]

The couple had at least three sons who also played significant roles in the economic, social, and political life of the city. Pedro Pérez, probably still as a very young man, traveled to the royal court as a representative of the city in 1278. He was *alcalde* of Burgos in 1293, 1294 and 1313, as well as serving the crown as a collector of the tenth in Laredo, Santander, San Vicente de la Barquera and Castro Urdiales in 1293.[31] In 1299, 1302, and 1303 Pedro Pérez, together with Andrés Pérez de Castrojeriz and other Burgalese merchants, traveled and traded in England under the protection of the English king. He also managed the family property as well as acquiring property of his own in the city and its hinterland.[32]

Of Pedro's other two brothers, there is little one can say. Both Ruy Pérez and Juan Pérez III held minor administrative posts in Burgos in 1293 and 1294. The latter, Juan Pérez III, may have been the same Burgalese merchant trading in Flanders whose ship was pillaged by English pirates in 1321.[33]

At the beginning of the fourteenth century, the Sarracín family ceased to play the leading role in the political and ecclesiastical life of the city. One may assume that they rose to the rank of the nobility and withdrew from city life to their rural holdings or that, as was not unusual, after a few generations the family

---

[28] AMB, clasif. 683 (26-IX-1259); clasif. 99 (25-III-1268).

[29] ACB, vol. 49, f. 75 (12-VII-1273); vol. 43, p. 1, f. 27 (2-X-1293); Gaibrois de Ballesteros, I, XV, VI.

[30] ACB, vol. 50, p. 1, f. 60 (26-I-1290); vol. 50, p. 2, f. 149 (26-I-1290); vol. 49, f. 68 (1-III-1291); vol. 49, f. 89 (2-V-1291); vol. 49, f. 89a (6-V-1291).

[31] A. Ballesteros y Beretta, *Alfonso X, El Sabio* (Barcelona, 1963), p. 856; Gaibrois de Ballesteros, I, VI, XCV and XCI; AMB, clasif. 652 (19-XII-1313).

[32] *Calendar of the Patent Rolls, 1292-1301*, p. 450. See my article "Castilian Merchants in England, 1248-1350." This essay is included in Part II of this collection.

[33] M. Gaibrois de Ballesteros, I. LXIX and LXXIV; Ruiz, "*Castilian Merchants*," below.

died out.[34] In either case, for over a hundred years, the Sarracíns had dominated the municipal council of Burgos, the religious life of the city, and international trade; as leading merchants, royal officials, and non-noble knights, they were as well the most active participants in the market for land in Burgos.

B. The Bonifaz Family.

Linked with the Sarracíns by kinship ties, the Bonifaz clan was the other dominant familial group in the city. Our knowledge of the Bonifaz is far more extensive than that of the Sarracíns, and Burgalese historians have long paid attention to their activities.[35] My task in this section has been to summarize the known information and to add a few references, hitherto unknown.

The founder of the family's fortune and prominence was Ramón Bonifaz, *alcalde* of Burgos in 1243 and so-called first admiral of Castile. To the latter title he had claims because he had recruited and led a fleet of ships from the Bay of Biscay in the final and successful attack against Seville in 1248.[36] Although my concern here is not the activities of Ramón Bonifaz in Andalucía, they give us clues as to the sources of his wealth and economic activities. He was, most probably, a merchant based in Burgos but with commercial ties to Flemish textile centers through the Bay of Biscay ports. Already in 1228, he had purchased, together with his cousin Guiralt Almeric, substantial houses in the cal de Sanct Llorente for the very large sum (especially large in the early thirteenth century) of 6,000 *mrs*. This transaction provides evidence as to the foreign origins of Bonifaz and his cousin, both names being certainly not Castilian. Moreover, the cal or street de Sanct Llorente, a part of the Road to Santiago as it made its way through the city, was also the abode of the most influential non-noble knights of medieval Burgos.[37] According to Nicolás de Goyri, Ramón Bonifaz married more than once. His daughters became nuns, and of his two sons, Luis and Pedro,

---

[34] This transformation of the bourgeoisie into nobility occurred elsewhere in Europe. See Fritz Rörig, *The Medieval Town* (Berkeley, CA., 1971), pp. 122-25.

[35] Teófilo López Mata, *La ciudad y castillo de Burgos* (Burgos, 1949); Guillermo Avila y Díaz-Ubierna, *El primer almirante de Castilla. Don Ramón de Bonifaz y Camargo* (Burgos, 1948); Nicolás de Goyri, *Apuntes para las biografías de algunos burgaleses célebres* (Burgos, 1875).

[36] See also note 35; López Mata, p. 32.

[37] Compare the 6,000 *mrs.* paid for houses with the prices for properties given in previous footnotes. See also ch. XI below.

we only have information for the second. Ramón died in Burgos in 1256.[38]

Pedro Bonifaz I, Ramón's son, was *alcalde* of Burgos in 1263 and 1268 and, as such, he was one of the city representatives at Jerez (1268). In 1279, we find him as an envoy of the city to the court of Alfonso X. During the rebellion of the Infante don Sancho, members of the Bonifaz family sided with the Infante against his father, the king. Pedro Bonifaz I carried a petition of support from the Infante to the municipal council of Burgos. Owner of properties in Sevilla, most probably inherited from his father and obtained during the *Repartimiento* of Sevilla, Pedro was still alive in 1302.[39]

Another member of the family found in the Infante's camp was Remón Bonifaz, probably the son of Pedro Bonifaz I. In 1284, Remón received 1,000 *mrs.* from, by then, king Sancho IV as reparation for his imprisonment in Orbaneja, presumably while in the service of the rebellious Infante. In 1305, his name and that of another member of the family, Rostrán Bonifaz, led the list of members of the confraternity of Our Lady of Gamonal, an important brotherhood of merchants and non-noble knights. In 1313 he was *alcalde* of Burgos.[40]

Another Pedro Bonifaz II, probably a grandson of Ramón and son of Pedro Bonifaz I, was *merino* of Burgos in 1302 and *alcalde* of the city in 1307 and 1309.[41] One more Pedro Bonifaz (III) emerges from the extant documentation as one of the most influential members of the family. In 1325, he was abbot of the monastery of Cervatos and, two years later, *sacristán* and canon of the cathedral chapter of Burgos. In that capacity, he also acted as general vicar of the bishop don García, serving as arbiter and mediator for many disputes between ecclesiastical and secular institutions in the region.[42] By 1333, he had already been elected dean of the cathedral chapter and, that same year, he took charge of

[38] Goyri, pp. 130-137.

[39] AMB, clasif. 1973 (6-VIII-1263); W. Piskorski, *Las Cortes de Castilla en el periodo de tránsito de la Edad Media a la Moderna, 1188-1520* (Barcelona, 1930), p. 54; *MHE*, II, 2-3; AMB, clasif. 2927 (26-3-1282); M. Gaibrois de Ballesteros, I, 15; ACB, vol. 63, f. 57 (3-IX-1302).

[40] AMB, clasif. 2937 (27-XI-1284); J. García Saínz de Baranda, "Primitiva regla," (hereafter "Primitiva regla,") p. 163; AMB, clasif. 652 (19-XII-1313).

[41] ACB, vol. 63, f. 57 (3-IX-1302); T. López Mata, "Ramón Bonifaz," *BCMB*, 105 (1949), 249-250; Ramón Menéndez Pidal, *Documentos linguisticos de España* (Madrid, 1919), pp. 260-61.

[42] ACB, vol. 43, p. 2, f. 4 (5-I-1325); Luciano Serrano, ed., *Fuentes para la historia de Castilla*, 3 vols. (Valladolid, 1096-10), II, 176; ACB, vol. 42, p. 1, f. 128 (3-XI-1327); vol. 29, f. 295 (18-V-1328); vol. 29, f. 295a (8-VI-1328); Serrano, *Fuentes*, II, 140.

the Hospital of San Lucas.[43] One should note, once again, the relation between the rectorship of the Hospital of San Lucas, the holding of important ecclesiastical benefits and the two predominant families in Burgos, the Sarracín and the Bonifaz. In many respects, they constituted one extended familial clan, and the Hospital, about which we do not know as much as we should, was the vehicle for articulating their philantropic activities. It was also an instrument for their exercise of power within the city and its region.

In the case of Pedro Bonifaz III, his life and activities paralleled those of his rèlative and predecessor in the deanship, Pedro Sarracín II. As the former dean had done, Pedro Bonifaz's leadership of the cathedral chapter led to substantial investment in the market for land in Burgos and its territory. Between 1333, when he became dean, to 1350, shortly before his death, he purchased lands and houses on at least seven occasions. The properties, located in the villages of Villariezo, Arcos, Castañares, Castillo del Val, Comparada and Burgos itself, must have been substantial. The dean paid 34,700 *mrs.* for his acquisitions, or almost an average of 5,000 *mrs.* per purchase, the highest in the area of Burgos before 1350.[44]

The grip of the Bonifaz on the life of Burgos was certainly not restricted to the dean. His brother Ramón Bonifaz was *alcalde* of Burgos in 1331, 1334, and 1338. He was one of the first non-noble knights inscribed in the membership lists of the brotherhood of the Real Hermandad, a confraternity established under royal protection in 1338. In 1345, Alfonso XI named him to the *Regimiento*, the newly founded ruling body of the city.[45] Ramón Bonifaz's sons, Remón de Prestinez, Juan López and Pedro Bonifaz IV also belonged to the brotherhood of the Real Hermandad and, like their father, also resided in the cal de Sanct Llorente in Burgos.[46]

Another member of the family, Rostán Bonifaz (perhaps yet another brother), was also named to the *Regimiento* in 1345. Together with his son, Pero Bonifaz V, he belonged to the Real Hermandad and lived in the cal de Sanct Llorente.

---

43 ACB, vol. 50, p. 1, f. 70 (15-IV-1333).

44 ACB, vol 36, f. 650 (23-XI-1334); vol. 36, f. 652 (30-XII-1334); vol. 36, f. 651 (23-VII-1340); vol. 37, f. 245 (4-XII-1340); vol. 50, p. 1, f. 100 (15-I-134?); vol., 43, p. 2, f. 2 (14-V-1347); vol. 44, f. 6 (22-V-1348). For prices see ch. XI below.

45 AMB, clasif. 2200 (27-VI-1331); AMB, clasif. 1783 (2-IV-1334); García Rámila, *Texto cronlógico*, pp. 17-18; AMB, clasif. 154 (9-V-1345).

46 *Texto cronológico*, pp. 17-18.

The Bonifaz were closely related to other influential families in the city: the Prestines, García Camargo, Mathe Pérez de Frías. These familiar links have already been described by Luciano Huidobro Serna, and the appendix to this article expands on the place of these families in Burgalese life and their ties to the Bonifaz.[47] Through intermarriage, commercial and political partnerships, they controlled the life of the city.

We should not conclude without a brief glance at the Prestines, essentially a different name but the same family as the Bonifaz. Their prominence, together with that of the Bonifaz and Sarracín, provides evidence for the existence of a narrow and increasingly closed oligachical group, controlling the life of the city.

Bernalt de Prestines, brother to the dean Pedro Bonifaz III and to Ramón Bonifaz, was also named to the *Regimento* in 1354. Member of the Real Hermandad with residence in the cal de Sanct Llorente, Bernalt was *alcalde* of Burgos in 1350.[48] Another member of the Prestines family was Giralte de Prestines, member of the Real Hermandad, prominent merchant and *alcalde* of Burgos in 1338, as was Ponce de Prestines, member of the Real Hermandad with a house in the cal de Sanct Llorente. There was a Juan Bonifaz, brother to Bernalt de Prestines, the dean Pedro Bonifaz and Ramón and, like all the members of the family, a member as well of the Real Hermandad and resident of the cal de Sanct Llorente. Two other members of the Bonifaz-Prestines family, both named Juan Bonifaz, belonged to the Real Hermandad, one residing in the cal de Armas and the other in the cal de Sanct Llorente.[49]

CONCLUSION

If we add up the García Camargo and the Mathe Pérez de Frías families to the Bonifaz-Prestines, around 17% of the members of the Real Hermandad belonged to one extended family group. Four of the members of the *Regimento*, one quarter of the entire body, also belonged to this family group. Although in the previous pages, I have only examined the participation and influences of the Sarracín and Bonifaz in the economic, political and social life of Burgos, the Appendix shows that, from 1320 on, as far as we can document it, almost all municipal offices were held by non-noble knights, members of the Real

---

[47] *Texto cronológico*, p. 17; AMB, clasif. 154 (9-V-1345).

[48] L. Huidobro Serna, "Nuevos datos sobre el almirante don Ramón Bonifaz and sus descendientes, *BCMB*, 113 (1950), 265; *Texto cronológico*, p. 17; AMB, clasif. 154 (9-V-1345); ACB, vol. 18, f. 265 (9-III-1350).

[49] *Texto cronológico*, pp. 17-18.

Hermandad in 1338. The evidence is unequivocal, the *caballeros villanos*, i.e., those who owned houses in the city, horse and weapons, protected by advantageous royal privileges were able to monopolize civic and ecclesiastical offices in the city. Within this patrician group, the ruling urban elite of Burgos, the Sarracín and the Bonifaz, held a privileged position.

APPENDIX

The purpose of this Appendix is to present a list of those non-noble knights and "good men" who held public office between 1250 and 1350. Two important aspects should be noted: 1) the close relation between mercantile activities and public office. 2) the familial ties linking the patrician class of Burgos.

I. Martín Pérez

He was *alcalde* of Burgos in 1258, 1259 and 1273. As *alcalde,* he witnessed Alfonso X's privilege to the shoemakers of the city in 1259. Martin owned milling rights in Villayuda, which he sold to the chapter from 300 *mrs.* in 1258.

ACB, vol. 70, no. 207 (18-X-1258); AMB clasif. 683 (26-IX-1259); clasif. 806 (25-V-1289).

II. Arnalt de Sanchester

The descendant of one of the foreign merchants settled in Burgos at the end of the twelfth century, Arnalt served in the municipal council of Burgos in, at least, 1259 and 1273. As a procurator of the city, he traveled to Alfonso X's court in 1263 and 1279. In 1281 Arnalt and other "good men" of the city bought the right to farm the taxes on wine and on *moneda.* Married to Isabel Fernández, we have evidence of, at least, two sons, Juan de Sanchester and Lope Pérez, both members of the Real Hermandad (1338). Juan de Sanchester donated his rights in the mill of Atga to the Hospital of San Lucas, which may indicate kinship with the Sarracín and/or Bonifaz family. Other members of the family were Remont de Sanchester (perhaps a brother of Arnalt) and Remont's sons, Curiel Remont, Bernal Remont and John Remont, all three, members of the brotherhoods of our Lady of Gamonal and the Real Hermandad.

Serrano, *El obispado de Burgos,* II, 210-16; AMB clasif. 683 (26-X-1259); clasif. 2908 (6-VIII-1263); ACB, vol. 42, f. 223 (11-IV-1276); AHB leg. 12, no. 384 (10-I-1279); AMB clasif. 2925 (12-VII-1281); ACB, vol. 49, f. 1 (8-XI-1285); AMB clasif. 806 (25-V-1289); ACB, vol. 50, p. 2, f. 151 (23-XII-1292); "Primitiva regla," p. 163; *Texto cronológico,* pp. 16-17.

III. Aparicio Guillén

Also a descendant of a foreign merchant established in Burgos at the end of the twelfth century, Aparicio, a "*cavallero*", represented the council of Burgos at Alfonso X's court in 1263, 1273 and 1275. He was also *alcalde* of the city in that latter date. In 1278, he was one of the collectors of the fine for usurious lending which the king had imposed on the city that year. His relatives and/or descendants, John Guillén and Guillem Fabre, were members of the Real Hermandad 1338 and named to the *Regimiento* in 1345.

AMB clasif. 2908 (6-VII-1263); ACB, vol. 49, f. 75 (12-VII-1273); AMB clasif. 2574 (22-XII-1275); clasif. 2561 (15-VII-1278); clasif. 2563 (28-VII-1278); clasif. 2566 (30-VII-1278); clasif. 2912 (14-VII-1278); clasif. 806 (25-V-1289); "Primitiva regla," p. 163; *Texto cronológico,* pp.16-17.

IV. Johan González

Alcalde of Burgos in 1270 and owner of a garden in the Vega of Burgos, his son was a member of our Lady of Gamonal and also *alcalde* of the city in 1305.

AHN. Clero, carp. 184, no. 4 (20-III-1270).

V. Gil Pérez de Burgos
He was sent by the king as an envoy to the vassals of Don Lope Díaz. (Ballesteros, *Alfonso X*, p. 571.)

VI. Guillén Royz de Burgos
In the service of Alfonso X in 1272. (Ballesteros, p. 548).

VII. Sancho García
Alcalde of Burgos in 1273, a Sancho García, probably the same person, acted as representative of the city council in a dispute with the cathedral chapter over rights in the mill of Vega in 1295. That same year he served as a procurator of the city to Sancho IV's court. He owned a house in the city.

AHB leg. 33, no. 1501 (11-II-1272); ACB, vol. 49, f. 75 (12-VII-1273); AMB clasif. 125 (19-VII-1295); ACB, vol. 42, f. 92 (2-XII-1295).

VIII. Simón Raynez
Simón is an example of promotion within the city through loyal service to the crown, even though he did not belong to the important family networks of Burgos. He began his career as *criado* of doña Berenguela, sister of Alfonso X and Lady of Las Huelgas. In 1273 he was part of the city council of Burgos and he also collected royal taxes. That same year, Simón was named *alcalde apartado* of the Jewish *aljama* of the city. He must have served in that capacity, at least, until 1279 and in 1278 and 1279 and was one of the men assigned by the king to collect the fines on usury. We find him again in 1292 and 1294 as *alcalde* of the city, and as collector of the *fonsadera* in the diocese of Burgos. His son, John Simón, was in the king's service in 1285 and belonged to the brotherhood of Our Lady of Gamonal in 1305.

AMB clasif. 806 (4-VIII-1273); clasif. 4125 (10-VIII-1274); clasif. 2560 (14-V-1278); clasif. 2566 (30-VII-1278); clasif. 2567 (8-VIII-1278); clasif. 2912 (13-VIII-1278); clasif. 2568 (22-IX-1278); clasif. 2919 (2-XI-1279); Gaibrois de Ballesteros, I, XXV and CXLV; III, CCXCVI-XXCVII, CCCXC-CCCXCI.

IX. A document of 1273 list what was probably the entire membership of the city council of Burgos.

AMB, clasif. 806 (4-VIII-1273).
Martín Ibáñez, *alcalde* (see Sarracín family above).
Gómez Ibáñez, *alcalde* (ibid).
Bernal de la Torre, *alcalde*.
Aparicio Guillén, *alcalde* (see III).
Juan Pérez de Carrión, merchant.

Arnalt de Sanchester (see II).
Simón Raynez (see VIII).
Jaime de Valgelada, he owned rights in the mill of San Gil
Bernalt de las Combas.
Antolín Fernández.
Pero Antolínez (see below)
Guy? Ibáñez de Sobresierra
Martín Domínguez
Domingo Pérez
Martin Pérez, (scribe of the council)

X. García Pérez

Another of the *criados* of Doña Berenguela, García Pérez, was also named, together with Simón Raynez, *alcalde* of the *aljama* of Burgos. In 1278, he was *alcalde* of the city, and, fifteen years later, García collected royal taxes in Villadiego.

AMB clasif. 4125 (10-VIII-1274); clasif. 2650 (14-V-1278); Gaibrois de Ballesteros, I, XCII.

XI. Pero Antolínez

Member of the city council in 1273, he was town-crier from 1276 to 1280 with an annual salary of 100 *mrs*.

AMB clasif. 806 (4-VIII-1273); clasif. 2924 (15-IV-1280).

XII. Fernán Pérez

In 1278, Fernán served as representative of the city at the royal court, and in 1293-94 he appeared as one of the men of the Infante don Fernando. Public scribe of Burgos in 1299, the documents describe him as royal scribe in Burgos between 1310 and 1314. In 1304 Fernán Pérez purchased houses in the neighborhood of San Gil in Burgos for 800 *mrs*.

AMB clasif. 2562 (16-VII-1278); Gaibrois de Ballesteros, I, LXIV; Benavides, II, 198-99; ACB, vol. 42 f. 36 (14-IV-1304); Benavides, II, 732-38; Serrano, *Fuentes*, II, 159.

XIII. Juan Fernández

A landholder in Sotrajero, in the city's hinterland, Juan Fernández carried a message from the *concejo* of Burgos to Alfonso X in 1278. Fifteen years later, he was one of the royal agents collecting the tithe on imports at San Vicente de la Barquera. Married to doña Teresa, he died in 1305.

ACB, vol. 49, f. 61 (14-IV-1374); AMB clasif. 2692 (20-IX-1278); ACB, vol. 49, f. 77 (11-V-1280); vol. 32, f. 145 (14-X-1305).

XIV. Ferrand Martínez

The sòn of Alfonso Martínez and brother to Claros Martínez and to Garcia Martínez, Ferrand was one of the royal scribes in Burgos in 1278. In 1293-94, he collected the tithe as a royal agent. Together with his brother García, Ferrand belonged to the brotherhood of Our Lady of Gamonal in 1305. Eight years later, he was the *merino* of the city, while also an important merchant and landholder. Married to María García, he had, as far as the documents show, at least one son, Alfonso Fernández. The latter, together with his mother, donated houses to the monastery of San Agustín in 1337.

Ballesteros, p. 850 (1278); ACB, vol. 42, f. 92 (2-II-1295); AMB clasif. 125 (19-VII-1295); Benavides, II, 450 (9-XI-1304); "Primitiva regla," p. 163; Menéndez Pidal, *Documentos lingüísticos de España*, pp. 260-61; ACB, vol. 48, f. 279 (22-XI-1327); AHN. Clero, carp. 177, no. 4 (24-III-1337); AMB clasif. 652 (19-XII-1313).

XV. Domingo Martínez

A Burgalese merchant trading in England in 1273, he, together with García Ordóñez, served as representative of Burgos to a meeting with the rebellious Infante don Sancho in 1279. A member of Our Lady of Gamonal (1305), he appeared in a long list of citizens owed money by the *concejo* of Burgos in 1313. His son, Diego Martínez de Santo Domingo de Silos, held an important position in the administration of Burgos.

See below chapter IX. Also AMB clasif. 2576 (5-I-1280); "Primitiva regla," p. 163; AMB clasif. 652 (19-XII-1313).

XVI. Asensio García

A royal tax collector in 1279 and 1281, Asensio was one of the representatives of the merchants of Burgos to Alfonso X's court. We also know that he owned a vineyard in the region of Burgos.

AMB clasif. 2572 (20-II-1279); clasif. 2689 (15-II-1281); ACB, vol. 49, f. 80 (11-II-1280).

XVII. Guillén Trapaz

Member of one of the leading Burgalese families, Guillén Trapaz was, with Asensio García, one of the merchants representing the commercial interests of the city in 1281.

AMB clasif. 2689 (15-II-1281).

XVIII. Domingo Pérez

Domingo was the son of Esteban de Castrillo, a former *juez* of doña Berenguela, the Lady of Las Huelgas. He was a member of the city council in 1273 and in 1287 and 1294 appears as a royal messenger. As part of his salary, Domingo received eleven *varas* of cloth. A certain Domingo Pérez, perhaps the same individual, is mentioned in a document of 1294 as a merchant in the Rastro of Burgos, selling lamb and fish to the king's household.

Ballesteros, p. 933 (1281); AMB clasif. 806 (4-VIII-1273); clasif. 2690 (15-II-1281); Gaibrois de Ballesteros, I, LXXIII, XCV, CXXXIX (1294).

XIX. Marín Capero

A citizen (*vecino*) of Burgos, Marín was *alcalde* of the king in the city in 1281. In

1316, he served as arbiter in a dispute between the monastery of Oña and the city council of Frías.

Ballesteros, p. 933; Serrano, *Fuentes*, II, 160 (16-IX-1316).

XX. Miguel Estébanez

Founder of the brotherhood of Our Lady of Gamonal in 1285 and of a hospital for pilgrims in the outskirts of the city, Miguel Estébanez had been a member of the municipal council as early as 1259 and served as *merino* of Burgos in 1281, as well as being treasurer to the Infante don Sancho. Married to doña Ucenda Prestines, Miguel was related to the powerful Prestines-Bonifaz clan. His son, Juan Estébanez, belonged to the Real Hermandad and held important positions in the city administration. The family resided in the exclusive street of Huerto del Rey.

AMB clasif. 683 (26-IX-1259); clasif. 2473 (2-XI-1281); "Primitiva regla," p. 160; L. Huidobro, *Las peregrinaciones jacobeas*, II, 122.

XXI. García Domínguez

Alcalde of Burgos in 1285, García collected royal taxes in Salamanca while a member of Burgos' city council.

Gaibrois de Ballesteros, I, CLXI.

XXII. Alfonso Pérez

He was a royal scribe in Burgos in 1290 and a royal tax collector in 1293-94. A member of the brotherhood of Our Lady of Gamonal, the membership list describes him as the main scribe (*escribano mayor*) of Burgos' city council.

ACB, vol. 50, p. 1, f. 41 (12-V-1290); Gaibrois de Ballesteros, I, XXIV; III, CCLXXX (18-IV-1292), CCXCVI-CCXVII (18-XII-1299); "Primitiva regla," p. 163.

XXIII. Among the documents published by Mercedes Gaibrois de Ballesteros, one finds a large number of Burgalese citizens in the service of the crown. Below is the list of those not mentioned elsewhere in the Appendix (the Roman numerals indicate page references to Gaibrois' book).

J. Martín Ruiz de Burgos (p. LXXIII)
John Pérez de Carrión (p. LXXIV)
Ferrán Gil (p. XCII)
Domingo Díaz (pp. XCII and LXIX)
Simón Remondo (p. XCIV)
John Ferrández (p. CIX)
Matheo García (p. XL)
Alfonso de Formallac (p. XL)
Juan de Morlán (p. XL)
Pedro de la Riba (See chapter II above)
García Matheos (p. LXIX)

XXIV. Alfonso García de Sancta María

Alcalde of the king in 1293 and of Burgos in 1305, Alfonso belonged to the brotherhood of Our Lady of Gamonal.

ACB, vol. 43, p. 1, f. 27 (2-X-1293); "Primitiva regla," p. 163.

XXV. Fernán González de Frías

Collected the *fonsadera* in 1293 and belonged to Our Lady of Gamonal. (For the Frias see below).

XXVI. Lope Pérez

A member of the royal bureaucracy in 1293-94, he served as representative of the city council of Burgos to the royal court in 1295. In 1302 he was *alcalde* of the king and *notario mayor* (main notary) of Castile. Seven years later, he served as *alcalde* of the city and was named to the *Jurado* of the kingdom in 1310. His son was *alcalde* of Burgos, a member of the Real Hermandad and was named to the *Regimiento* by Alfonso XI in 1345.

Gaibrois de Ballesteros, I, CXX; AMB clasif. 125 (19-VII-1295); Benavides, II, 732-38 (13-IV-1310).

XXVII. Domingo Ramos

Alcalde of Burgos in 1296, he owed 46,667 *mrs.* to the city council. This is, perhaps, an indication that he had purchased the farming of city taxes.

Rodríguez López, I, 176 (1296); AMB clasif. 652 (19-XII-1313).

XXVIII. Ruy Domínguez

Alcalde of the city in 1296. (Rodríguez López, I, 176)

XXIX. Pedro López de Fuentecha

Alcalde of Burgos in 1299, he served as arbiter in a dispute between the monasteries of Santo Domingo de Silos and San Pedro de Arlanza. The membership list of the Real Hermandad included a Pero Martínez de Fuentcea and García Martínez de Fuentcea, both residents of the street of Sanct Llorente and probably related to Pedro López.

M. Ferotin, *Recueil des chartes de l'Abbaye de Silos* (Paris, 1897), pp. 292, 315-16; Benavides, II, 198-99; *Texto cronológico*, pp. 16-17.

XXX. Pedro de Mena

He was *alcalde* of Burgos in, at least, 1303 and 1305. In that latter date he purchased houses in the city from Andalla the Moor for the large sum of 5,000 *mrs.* A certain García de Mena, probably a brother, appears in a document of 1313 as a lender of funds to the city.

ACB, vol. 44, f. 2 (31-VIII-1303); vol. 41, p. 2, f. 347 (7-IX-1305); vol. 41, p. 2, f. 374a (7-XII-1305); AMB clasif. 652 (19-XII-1313).

XXXI. Lucas Pérez

Procurator of the city council in 1304, he was the brother of Mayor Pérez and brother-in-law to Claros Martínez (see XIV). He was *alcalde* of Burgos in 1316.

Benavides, II, 436-39; Menéndez Pidal, pp. 260-61; ACB, vol. 44, f. 545 (12-VI-1316).

XXXII. John Mate (Mathe)

Scribe of the council in 1304, he had also been a royal scribe in 1293-94. The son of Diego Mathe, John belonged to the brotherhood of Our Lady of Gamonal. Another John Mathe, perhaps his son, was a member of the Real Hermandad. The Mathe family was closely related to the Bonifaz and Pérez de Frías.

Benavides, II, 436-39; Gaibrois de Ballesteros, I, XXIII; "Primitiva regla," p. 163; *Texto cronológico*, p. 7.

XXXIII. John Simón

The son of Simón Pérez, John was *alcalde* of Burgos in 1305 and a member of Our Lady of Gamonal. ("Primitiva regla," p. 163.)

XXXIV. John González II

He was *alcalde* of the city in 1305, and both, John and his brother, belonged to Our Lady of Gamonal. Earlier, in 1292, he had sold lands in Temiño for 200 *mrs.*

"Primitiva regla," p. 164; ACB, vol. 50, p. 2, f. 153 (17-XII-1292).

XXXV. Sancho Sánchez

Alcalde of the king in 1305 and member of Our Lady of Gamonal. ("Primitiva regla," p. 164.)

XXXVI. Sancho González

The son of Gonzalo Gil, he was *alcalde* of Burgos and a member of the brotherhood of Our Lady of Gamonal in 1305. His brother, Gil González, belonged to the Real Hermandad (1338) and was named to the *Regimiento* in 1345.

Gaibrois de Ballesteros, I, LXXIII; "Primitiva regla," p. 164.

XXXVII. Pernán García

A royal scribe in 1293-94, he was the brother of John González (see XXXIV). Fernán was *alcalde* of Burgos in, at least, 1306 and 1313. His daughter, María García, owned rights in one of the mills in the *alfoz* of Burgos.

Gaibrois de Ballesteros, I, XXXII; "Primitiva regla," p. 163; ACB, vol. 50, p. 2, f. 156 (23-XII-1306).

XXXVIII. Sancho Pérez

A royal scribe and tax collector in 1293-94, Sancho was the son of John Guillén and doña Orpesa. In 1307, he was *fiel* (a low administrative position) of the council of

Burgos.

Gaibrois de Ballesteros, I, XXXIX; Serrano, *Fuentes*, II, 150; AMB clasif. 3145 (1-IX-1307); *Texto cronológico*, p. 17.

XXXIX. Domingo Moro

Married to María Pérez, a member of the Sarracín family, Domingo was named *fiel* in 1307. His name also appeared in the 1313 list of those to whom the city owed money.

AMB clasif. 3145 (1-IX-1307); ACB, vol. 50, p. 1, f. 62b (16-II-1262); AMB clasif. 652 (19-II-1313).

XL. Pedro Alfonso

Alcalde of Burgos in 1309 and procurator of the city to the important meeting of the Hermandad of 1315, Pedro Alfonso was a member of the brotherhood of the Real Hermandad, with residence in the street of Sanct Esteban. In the membership list he is described as *alcalde* of the dowries.

AMB clasif. 100 (29-II-1309); *Cortes*, I, 263; *Texto cronológico*, p. 18.

XLI. Pedro Trapaz

Member of one of the most influential families in Burgos, he served a messenger of the Hermandad of 1315 to the regents of Alfonso XI. (*Crónica de Alfonso XI*, p. 187)

XLII. Pedro García de Frías

One of the representatives of Burgos to the meeting of the Hermandad in 1315, Pedro García de Frías also appears in the 1313 list of those owed money by the city.

Cortes, I, 263; AMB clasif. 652 (19-XI-1313).

XLIII. Juan de Cambranas

He was also one of the Burgalese representatives to the meeting of the Hermandad (1315), and he was in the 1313 list as well. An important merchant, with blood ties to the mercantile family of the Pérez de Carrión, Juan de Cambranas was *alcalde* of Burgos in 1331, member of the Real Hermandad and resident of the Huerto del Rey. A document of 1341 also describes him as *canciller del rey*, and his brother, Simón, held important positions in the administration of Burgos.

Gaibrois de Ballesteros, I, CXL; *Cortes*, I, 263; ACB, vol. 44, f.7 (16-I-1324); AMB clasif. 652 (19-XII-1313); AMB clasif. 2200 (27-VI-1331); *Texto cronológico*, p. 16; ACB, vol. 42, f. 8 (28-IV-1341).

XLIV. Simón Pérez

The son of Joan (John) Mathe, Simón was *alcalde* of Burgos in 1324 and 1338. A member of the Real Hermandad, he resided in the cal de Sanct Esteban.

ACB, vol. 44, f. 7 (16-I-1324); *Texto cronológico,* p. 18.

XLV. Pedro Morlán

The brother of Juan Morlán, he was *alcalde* of Burgos in 1313. Together with his brother, he was listed in the 1313 list of those owed money by the council of Burgos. (AMB clasif. 652, 19-XII-1313).

XLVI. Juan Pérez de Castresana

Alcalde of Burgos in 1324 and 1325, he was still alive in 1330, when his name appears as witness to a document.

ACB, vol. 43, p. 2, f. 5 (17-XII-1324); vol. 43, p. 2, f. 3 (6-VI-1325); Serrano, *Fuentes,* II, 177.

XLVII. García Pérez de Carrión

García and his brother, John Pérez de Carrión, appeared as the most important lenders (5,000 *mrs.*) in the 1313 list. In 1324, he was *merino* of Burgos and five years later he is mentioned as a royal official. A member of the Real Hermandad, García lived in the cal de Sanct Llorente.

AMB clasif. 652 (19-XII-1313);ACB, vol. 30, f. 594 (21-IX-1324); *Cortes,* I, 406; *Texto cronológico,* p. 17.

XLVIII. Pero (Pedro) Sánchez

Alcalde of Burgos in 1331 and member of the brotherhood of the Real Hermandad, Pero Sánchez lived in the cal de Sanct Esteban.

AMB clasif. 2200 (27-VI-1331); *Texto cronológico,* p. 18.

XLIX. Pero (Pedro) Fernández

The son of Ferrán Martínez, Pedro was *alcalde* of Burgos in 1331, belonged to the Real Hermandad (1338) and lived in the street of Huerto del Rey.

AMB clasif. 2200 (27-VI-1331); *Texto cronológico,* p. 16.

L. Alfonso Pérez

He may have been the same Alfonso Pérez who traded in Flanders early in the fourteenth century. The son of Joan Guillém, Alfonso served in the royal bureaucracy, at least, from 1331 to 1334. In 1338, he was a member of the brotherhood of the Real Hermandad and resided in the cal de Sanct Llorente.

Finot, p. 47; AMB clasif. 2200 (27-VI-1331); clasif. 1388 (25-XI-1337); *Texto cronológico,* p. 17.

LI. Juan García

A member of the *Jurado* of the city in 1333 and 1338, Juan was one of the city's representatives during the negotiations to purchase the village of Mazuelo in 1333. He was a member of the Real Hermandad and resided in the Cal de Sanct Llorente.

J. García Saínz de Baranda, *La ciudad de Burgos y su concejo en la Edad Media* (Burgos, 1967), II, 454-56; *Texto cronológico*, p. 17.

LII. Lope Ramírez

The son of Domingo Ramírez, Lope was a *jurado* of Burgos in 1333-34. Together with Juan García, he was one of the Burgalese officials send to negotiate the purchase of Mazuelo. A member of the Real Hermandad he resided in the cal de Sanct Llorente.

La ciudad de Burgos, II, 454-56; *Texto cronológico*, p. 17.

LIII. Ruy Pérez

Perhaps related to the Sarracín family, Ruy was a royal messenger in 1293-94 and a member of Burgos' *Jurado* in 1333 and 1334. On the membership list of the Real Hermandad, he is listed as a lawyer with residence in the cal de Sanct Llorente.

Gaibrois de Ballesteros, I, LXIX; *La ciudad de Burgos*, II, 454-56; ACB, vol. 69, p. 1, f. 116 (22-XII-1335); *Texto cronológico*, p. 17.

LIV. Pedro García de Camargo

Pedro and his brother, García Pérez, appear in the 1313 list of lenders to the city. Members of his family traded in England and Flanders and five of them, including his father, belonged to the mercantile-oriented brotherhood of our Lady of Gamonal. *Alcalde* of Burgos in 1334, 1335 and 1338, Pedro, his brother and a nephew belonged to the Real Hermandad and lived in the street of Huerto de Rey. Other members of the family held important positions in Burgos' city council in the decade after 1350.

See ch. IX below. "Primitiva regla," p. 163; AMB clasif. 652 (19-XII-1313); clasif. 1784 (2-IV-1334); ACB, vol. 40, f. 212 (17-XI-1335); *Texto cronológico*, p. 16; AMB clasif. 152 (18-IV-1366); F. Cantera Burgos, "La judería de Burgos," *Sefarad*, XII (1952), 75.

LV. Alfonso Sánchez

The son of Sancho García, a goldsmith and landholder in the area of Burgos, he was *alcalde* in 1334. A member of the Real Hermandad, he lived in the cal de Sanct Esteban.

AMB clasif. 1784 (2-IV-1334); ACB, vol. 49, f. 3 (10-VIII-1335); *Texto cronológico*, p. 18.

LVI. Joan Estébanez

The son of Miguel Estébanez (see XX) and doña Ucenda Prestines, Joan was *merino* of Burgos in 1334, 1335, and 1338. A member of the Real Hermandad, he resided in the cal de Sanct Esteban.

AMB clasif. 1784 (2-IV-1334); ACB, vol. 40, f. 212 (17-XI-1335); *Texto cronológico*, p. 17.

LVII. Pero (Pedro) Juan

Acting *merino* during Joan Estébanez's absence, Pedro was a member of the Real Hermandad and lived in the cal de Sanct Llorente. (AMB clasif. 1784, 2-IV-1334; *Texto cronológico*, p. 17.)

LVIII. Martín Pérez de Frías

Member of the *Jurado* of the city in 1334, García belonged to the Real Hermandad and lived in the street of Huerto del Rey.

"Primitiva regla," p. 163; AMB clasif. 1784 (2-IV-1334); *Texto cronológico*, p. 18.

LIX. Juan López Gil

Jurado in 1334. (AMB clasif. 1784 (2-IV-1334)

LX. García Fernández del Huerto del Rey

García was the son of Ferrán Martínez and a member of the *Jurado* of Burgos in 1334. He was a member of the Real Hermandad and resided in the street of Huerto del Rey.

AMB clasif. 1784 (2-IV-1334); *Texto cronológico*, p. 16.

LXI. García Fernández

The son of Juan Fernández de Sobresierra and one of the members of the *Jurado* of Burgos, García was a member of the Real Hermandad and lived in the cal de Sanct Llorente.

AMB clasif. 1784 (2-IV-1334); *Texto cronológico*, p. 17.

LXII. García de Soto

Regidor in 1338, he was a member of the Real Hermandad and lived in the cal de Sanct Esteban. (*Texto cronológico*, p. 18.

LXIII. Alfonso Pérez de Villegas

The principal scribe of the council of Burgos in 1338, he belonged to the Real Hermandad and resided in the cal de Sanct Llorente. Alfonso XI named him scribe of the *Regimiento* in 1345 (see next chapter).

LXIV. Giralte de Prestines

A merchant and one of the lenders to the city in 1313, Giralte served as *alcalde* of Burgos in 1338, belonged to the Real Hermandad and lived in the cal de Sanct Esteban.

AMB clasif. 652 (19-XII-1313); Gaibrois de Ballesteros, I, X; *Texto cronológico*, p. 17.

LXV. Simón de Cambranas

A member of Our Lady of Gamonal and of the Real Hermandad, he was *alcalde* of the city in 1338 and resided in the cal de Sanct Esteban. ("Primitiva regla," p. 163; *Texto cronológico*, p. 17)

LXVI. Joan Pérez de Paniagua

A member of the *Jurado* of Burgos in 1338, he belonged to the Real Hermandad and lived in the cal de Sanct Esteban. *Texto cronológico,* p. 18.

LXVII. Juan García, el rico

He was a *regidor* (a member of the *Jurado*) in 1338, belonged to the Real Hermandad and had a house in the cal de Sanct Esteban. *Texto cronológico,* p.18.

LXVIII. Diego González

Treasurer in 1338, Diego was a member of the Real Hermandad and his house was located in the cal de Sanct Esteban.

LXIX. Fernán López de Astriñiga

A royal castellan in 1338, he was a member of the Real Hermandad and lived in the cal de Sanct Esteban.

LXX. Francisco Martínez de Burgos

A *regidor* in 1338, he belonged to the Real Hermandad and resided in cal de Sanct Esteban.

(Reference for nos. LXVIII-LXX is *Texto cronológico,* p. 18.)

VII

THE TRANSFORMATION OF THE CASTILIAN MUNICIPALITIES: THE CASE OF BURGOS 1248-1350*

TRADITIONALLY THE THIRTEENTH AND EARLY FOURTEENTH CENTURIES have been seen as the heyday of municipal liberties, and from this historical perspective the Castilian *concejos* (city councils) have been described as bastions of urban autonomy and democracy.[1] Both interpretations are erroneous. Equally incorrect is the emphasis placed on the cities' involvement through the Cortes and the Hermandades in national politics *vis-à-vis* the crown and the aristocracy.[2] Originating in the creative minds of Golden Age playwrights these concepts emerged as an answer to defeat, as the refuge of idealists. After the victory of Charles I over the *comunero* armies at Villalar in 1521 the troubled centuries which followed the conquest of Seville in 1248 were idealized. The playwrights of the *Siglo de Oro*,[3] Lope de Vega and Calderón de la Barca among others, created the figure of the good *alcalde* (judicial official) standing firm against the abuses of the crown and the nobility.[4] They often placed their works in the medieval past, consciously or unconsciously longing with nostalgia for what they believed to have been an alternative to

* A shorter version of this article was presented to the Columbia University Seminar on Legal and Political Thought in November 1974 and a revised version to the annual meeting of the Society for Spanish and Portuguese Historical Studies in April 1975. This research was supported in part by a grant from the Faculty Research Award Program of the City University of New York. I would like to express my gratitude to Professor Joseph R. Strayer, Professor Elizabeth A. R. Brown and Professor Charles M. Radding for their valuable comments and advice.

[1] The *concejo* is the name given to the administrative and judicial body ruling Castilian as well as other peninsular cities, from roughly the ninth to the mid-fourteenth century. For a discussion of the origins and structure of the medieval *concejo*, see María del Carmen Carlé, *Del concejo medieval castellano-leonés* (Buenos Aires, 1968); José M. Font Rius, "Orígenes del municipio medieval en Cataluña", *Anuario de historia del derecho español*, xvi (1945), pp. 389-529, and xvii (1946), pp. 229-585.

[2] For a critique of this position, see Teofilo F. Ruiz, "Burgos: Society and Royal Power, 1250-1350" (Princeton Univ. Ph.D. thesis, 1973), pp. 227-60.

[3] On this period, see John H. Elliott, *Imperial Spain, 1469-1716* (London, 1963), and his *The Revolt of the Catalans: A Study in the Decline of Spain, 1598-1640* (Cambridge, 1963).

[4] Examples of this attitude can be found in Pedro Calderón de la Barca, "El alcalde de Zalamea", in his *Obras completas*, ed. A. Valbuena Briones (Madrid, 1966); Lope de Vega y Carpio, "Fuenteovejuna", "La estrella de Sevilla" and "El caballero de Olmedo", in *Obras de Lope de Vega*, 15 vols. (Madrid, 1890-1913), ix, x. See also the influential history of Spair by Juan de Mariana, *Historia general de España*, 2 vols. (Madrid, 1623). On the jurisdiction of the *alcalde*, see Carlé, *op. cit.*, pp. 114-17.

the rising despotism of the Habsburgs. Although in reality the crown's centralizing policies were not equally applied throughout Spain, they were effectively carried out in Castile and, thus, most evident to Castilian writers.[5]

Liberal historians of the eighteenth and nineteenth centuries seized upon the idea and used it for their own political aspirations. Floridablanca and Martínez Marina are only the most outstanding of those historians and politicians of the period who viewed the medieval *concejo* as a bulwark against encroaching royal power.[6] It comes as no surprise that the first European liberals meeting in Cadiz in 1812 looked back to the medieval Cortes as a model for their new constitution. In this they were mistaken.

With few exceptions contemporary historians have, unfortunately, accepted this myth. It should be noted, however, that among the supporters of this point of view two different approaches can be distinguished: first, that the municipalities retained a great deal of autonomy until Alfonso XI's imposition of the *Regimiento* on the cities in the late 1340s;[7] secondly, that it was not until the reign of the Catholic Kings that the crown brought to an end urban democracy and autonomy.[8]

How can one challenge this interpretation? What sort of relevant data is available? Although it is true that the rise of the bourgeoisie and the formation of patrician élites have already elicited the interest

[5] On the rule of the Habsburgs in Spain, see note 3 above, and also José A. Maravall, *Estado moderno y mentalidad social, siglos XV a XVII*, 2 vols. (Madrid, 1972); José A. Maravall, *La oposición política bajo los Austrias* (Barcelona, 1972); Antonio Domínguez Ortiz, *Crisis y decadencia de la España de los Austrias* (Barcelona, 1969); Antonio Domínguez Ortiz, *La sociedad española en el siglo XVII* (Madrid, 1963).

[6] See Richard Herr, *The Eighteenth-Century Revolution in Spain* (Princeton, N.J., 1969), ch. 12; Tulio Halperín Donghi, *Tradición política española é ideología revolucionaria* (Buenos Aires, 1961), ch. 5, and p. 163 note.

[7] A brief discussion of the *Regimiento* is provided by Luis García de Valdeavellano, *Curso de historia de las instituciones españolas de los orígenes al final de la edad media* (Madrid, 1968), pp. 548-50.

[8] Rafael Gibert, *El concejo de Madrid* (Madrid, 1949), pp. 123-5; Antonio Ballesteros y Beretta, *Historia de España y su influencia en la historia universal*, 12 vols. in 13 (Barcelona, 1918-58), iii, p. 344; Fernando Soldevila, *Historia de España*, 8 vols. (Barcelona, 1952-9), ii, pp. 88-9; R. Trevor Davies, *The Golden Century of Spain, 1501-1621* (New York, 1965), p. 61. Even such a distinguished historian as Antonio Domínguez Ortiz insists on the democratic nature of the Castilian municipalities: A. Domínguez Ortiz, *The Golden Age of Spain, 1516-1659* (London, 1971), pp. 14-15, where he writes: "Much more important as organs of the community were the townships, although their representative and autonomous character also suffered great changes under the Habsburgs. The great vitality they enjoyed in the Middle Ages was much reduced as the modern age began". The control of municipal offices by the aristocracy in the sixteenth century "put an end to their democratic character". For a different perspective on the democratic nature of Castilian cities, see Luis Suárez Fernández, *Historia de España* (Madrid, 1970), pp. 420-1; García de Valdeavellano, *op. cit.*, pp. 548-9; Joseph F. O'Callaghan, *A History of Medieval Spain* (Ithaca, N.Y., 1975), pp. 447-9.

of renowned historians, these scholars, Pirenne, Lestocquoy and others, have directed their efforts towards Italian and Flemish urban development. They have, however, neglected other areas of medieval western Europe, and northern Castile in particular. The works on the origins and growth of the Castilian bourgeoisie which exist are general accounts which, with few exceptions, fail to promote an understanding of local conditions. They concentrate on the growth of legal institutions rather than on the economic, social and political structure of the urban ruling oligarchy.[9] Therefore they cast little light on the nature of Castilian urban society.

Focusing on the city of Burgos I would like to examine the rise of its urban élite and the interaction of that élite with other groups both within the city itself and within Castile. Since to my knowledge no similar study has yet been undertaken for medieval northern Castile the evidence here presented will serve as the basis for an alternative historical interpretation of Castilian social development. The following account will show that Burgos was neither democratic nor autonomous.

Founded in the 880s as an outpost on the expanding Christian frontier Burgos had become by the twelfth century an important stopping place for pilgrims on their way to Compostella and the unofficial capital of the Castilian realm.[10] Moreover, because of its geographical location, the city was the distribution centre for trade between the Bay of Biscay and the southern half of the kingdom.[11] Throughout most of the thirteenth and fourteenth centuries the kings of Castile and Leon favoured the city with numerous privileges; it was also one of their preferred places of residence, as well as being the place of their burial. Royal decrees were given to Burgos before they were granted to other urban centres of the realm. The city also

[9] For a general if somewhat superficial view of Spanish urban history, see L. Torres Balbas, L. Cervera, L. Chueca *et al.*, *Resumen histórico del urbanismo en España* (Madrid, 1968). Pioneer works in the field are Jaime Vicens Vives, *Historia de España y America social y económica*, 2nd edn. (Barcelona, 1974), ii, pp. 55-87; L. Garcia de Valdeavellano, *Orígenes de la burguesía en la España medieval* (Madrid, 1969), *passim*; Claudio Sánchez Albornoz, *España: un enigma histórico*, 2 vols. (Buenos Aires, 1956), ii, pp. 105-46.

[10] On the road to Compostella and its role in the emergence of Burgos as a trading city, see L. Vázquez de Parga, J. M. Lacarra and J. Uría Ríu, *Las peregrinaciones a Santiago de Compostela*, 3 vols. (Madrid, 1948-9), ii, pp. 181-99. On Burgos in general, see Julián García Sainz de Baranda, *La ciudad de Burgos y su concejo en la edad media*, 2 vols. (Burgos, 1967); Teófilo López Mata, *La ciudad y castillo de Burgos* (Burgos, 1949). See also the many relevant articles published in the *Boletín de la Comisión de Monumentos de la Provincia de Burgos*, now the *Boletín de la Institución Fernán González*.

[11] On the role of Burgos as a trading centre, see T. F. Ruiz, "La estructura económica del área de Burgos", *Boletín de la Institución Fernán González*, no. 186 (1976), pp. 820-3; María del Carmen Carlé, "Mercaderes en Castilla, 1252-1512", *Cuadernos de historia de España*, xxxi-xxxii (1954), pp. 146-328; Manuel Basas Fernández, *El consulado de Burgos en el siglo XVI* (Madrid, 1963), pp. 29-31.

enjoyed the right to cast its vote before all other cities represented at the meetings of the Cortes.[12]

Rather than trace the evolution of municipal administration in Burgos from its foundation, for which there is scant documentary evidence, this inquiry will concentrate on the dynamic changes occurring in the city during the century after the conquest of Seville. Within that period the basic structure of the *concejo* of Burgos and other Castilian cities underwent the radical transformation which will be examined in detail later. The rapid alterations in the structure of the *concejo* were directly related to the ascendance of one particular group within Burgos to the control of the city's resources and political life. The relationship between the crown and a rising bourgeoisie had been transformed by the thirteenth century into a closed partnership between the kings of Castile and the *caballeros villanos* (non-noble knights) of Burgos.

Who were these non-noble knights? References to the *Caballería Villana* can be found as far back as the ninth century, and their contribution to the making of Castile has already been noted in detail elsewhere.[13] As mounted military contingents, the *caballeros villanos* played an important role in the Reconquest, being rewarded for their service to the crown with special privileges. Royal protection led to their eventual control of municipal offices, advantages before the law, and exemption from most taxes.[14] Yet in spite of their rise the non-noble knights remained in a somewhat ambiguous position. On the one hand they shared most of the privileges hitherto reserved for the nobility. On the other hand the *caballeros villanos* were throughout the period the mainstay of the crown against an unruly nobility.

[12] The monastery of Las Huelgas founded by Alfonso VIII served as a palace and burial place for the royal family for most of the century under study. See Amancio Rodríguez López, *El Real Monasterio de las Huelgas y el Hospital del Rey*, 2 vols. (Burgos, 1907). On the right of Burgos to cast the first vote at the meetings of the Cortes, see Manuel Colmeiro, *Introduccion a las Cortes de los antiguos reinos de León y Castilla*, 2 vols. (Madrid, 1883-4), i, p. 281.

[13] There were non-noble knights in both town and country. In this article I refer exclusively to the urban *caballeros villanos*. On the *Caballería Villana*, see Carmela Pescador, "La caballería popular en León y Castilla", *Cuadernos de historia de España*, xxxiii-xxxiv (1961), pp. 101-238, xxxv-xxxvi (1962), pp. 156-201, xxxvii-xxxviii (1963), pp. 88-198, and xxxix-xl (1964), pp. 169-260. See also Elena Lourie, "A Society Organized for War: Medieval Spain", *Past and Present*, no. 35 (Dec. 1966), pp. 54-76; Adriana Bó and M. del C. Carlé, "Cuando empieza a reservarse a los caballeros el gobierno de las ciudades castellanas", *Cuadernos de historia de España*, iv (1946), pp. 114-24. Also valuable are two excellent studies by James F. Powers, "The Origins and Development of Municipal Military Service in the Leonese and Castilian Reconquest", *Traditio*, xxvi (1970), pp. 91-111, and his "Townsmen and Soldiers: The Interaction of Urban and Military Organization in the Militias of Medieval Castile", *Speculum*, xlvi (1971), pp. 641-55. See Powers, "Origins and Development of Municipal Military Service", p. 92.

[14] Pescador, *op. cit.*, xxxv-xxxvi, pp. 89-94, 152-89, and xxxix-xl, pp. 201, 209, 233; Bó and Carlé, *op. cit.*, pp. 120-2.

As a social group they increasingly imitated the aristocracy, eventually gaining admission to its lower ranks by the late fourteenth century.[15] Nevertheless, the magnates (*ricos hombres*) never ceased to stress the humble origins of the non-noble knights, placing them on the same social level as the peasants in the hierarchy of the kingdom.[16]

I

THE *CABALLERIA VILLANA* OF BURGOS

As in the rest of Castile the citizens of Burgos had been pressed into military service by the tenth century and continued to serve throughout the thirteenth and fourteenth centuries. City contingents saw action in the conquest of Seville and, later on, in the campaigns of Alfonso XI against Tarifa and Algeciras.[17] It was the conquest of Seville which had the greatest impact on the institutional structure of Burgos and northern Castile.[18] Because of the increase in the power of the magnates and military orders as the result of their acquisition of extensive holdings in the south, Alfonso X sought closer ties with the non-noble knights of Burgos and the other Castilian and Leonese cities. It is significant that his charters to the non-noble knights came at a time when the Reconquest had for all practical purposes come to an end. The military service which the kings now sought from the cities was aimed at checking the rising power of *ricos hombres*. Further evidence for this new alignment of political forces within Castile can also be found in the sumptuary laws of 1252 and 1258, directed exclusively against magnate profligacy and ostenta-

[15] By the second half of the fourteenth century many of the *caballeros villanos* entered the lower ranks of the nobility. See Sánchez Albornoz, *op. cit.*, ii, p. 53; Carlé, *Del concejo medieval*, p. 69.

[16] See *Siete partidas*, partida II. 10. 3, in *Los codigos españoles concordados y anotados*, ed. M. Rivadeneyra, 12 vols. (Madrid, 1847-51), ii, in which city inhabitants were grouped as artisans or peasants; and also Juan Manuel's low estimation of merchants and artisans in his *Libro de los estados* (Biblioteca de Autores Españoles, li, Madrid, 1860), p. 337, col. 2, and p. 339, col. 1. Alfonso X's charters distinguish between a noble knight (*caballero de linaje*) and a non-noble knight (*caballero ciudadano*): see *Memorial histórico español*, 49 vols. (Madrid, 1851-1948), i, pp. 240, 293, and *passim*.

[17] López Mata, *La ciudad y castillo de Burgos*, pp. 28-9. For the role of the militia of Burgos in the conquest of Seville, see Guillermo Avila y Díaz-Ubierna, *El primer almirante de Castilla: Don Ramón de Bonifaz y Camargo* (Burgos, 1948); *Crónica de Alfonso XI*, p. 357, col. 1, in *Crónica de los reyes de Castilla*, ed. Cayetano Rosell (Biblioteca de Autores Españoles, lxvi, Madrid, 1953). The *Crónica de los reyes de Castilla* includes the chronicles of Alfonso X, Sancho IV, Ferdinand IV and Alfonso XI covering the years between 1252 and 1350. Hereafter they will be cited as the chronicles of each individual king.

[18] The character and extent of the changes undergone by the Castilian-Leonese realm as the result of the opening of the Andalusian region to Christian settlement cannot be discussed here in detail. I have an article on this subject now being considered for publication. See Ruiz, "Burgos: Society and Royal Power", ch. 1.

tion,[19] and in the royal charters of 1255 and 1256 to the non-noble knights of Burgos, later extended to other Castilian cities.[20]

On 22 February 1255 Alfonso X granted exemption from taxes to those citizens of Burgos who owned horses and weapons. The privilege was given to the *caballeros* and their descendants to encourage them to serve the realm better.[21] The following year, on 27 July 1256, the king confirmed the Fuero Real as a local *fuero* (right, privilege) of the city and also defined the status of the non-noble knights.[22] According to the charter of 1256 the *caballeros villanos* had to own horses fit for warfare (worth a minimum of 30 *mrs.* [*maravedís*]) and each to procure a full set of equipment consisting of shield *(escudo)*, spear *(lanza)*, helmet *(capiello de fierro)*, sword *(espada)*, cuirass *(loriga)*, pauldron *(brafoneras)* and doublet *(perpuntes)*. They must also show their horses and weapons to the officials of the *concejo* at least once a year *(alarde)* to maintain their standing as members of the *Caballería Villana* and tax-exempt status.[23] Moreover, the king required the non-noble knights to own and reside in houses within the city walls.[24] The *caballero villano* was a citizen *(vecino)* and, as such, under the jurisdiction of the *concejo*. Thus his status was in sharp contrast to that of the nobility which was, at least in Burgos, exempted from municipal

[19] Archivo municipal de Burgos (hereafter A.M.B.), clasificación 1391 (12 Oct. 1252), printed in Ismael García Rámila, "Ordenamiento de posturas y otros capítulos generales otorgados a la ciudad de Burgos por el rey Alfonso X", *Hispania*, xix (1945), pp. 179-235, xx (1945), pp. 385-439, and xxi (1945), pp. 605-50.

[20] See a list of other cities in Pescador, *op. cit.*, xxxiii-xxxiv, p. 188. Also Archivo municipal de Segovia (hereafter A.M.S.), carpeta III, no. 7 (27 Sept. 1278); charter to the *caballeros* of Peñafiel (19 July 1256): *Memorial histórico español*, i, pp. 89-91; charter to the *caballeros* of Buitrago (23 July 1256); *ibid.*, pp. 93-5; a mention of the *caballeros excusados* of Avila (27 July 1259): *ibid.*, p. 149; and *passim*.

[21] A.M.B., clasif. 138 (22 Feb. 1255).

[22] A.M.B., clasif. 115 (27 July 1256), published in *Memorial histórico español*, i, pp. 97-100. There were important differences between the charter granted to Burgos and those given to Escalona and Segovia: see note 20 above, and *Memorial histórico español*, i, pp. 175-80. On the Fuero Real, see Alfonso García Gallo, *Manual de historia del derecho español*, 2 vols. (Madrid, 1964), i, pp. 392-4.

[23] A.M.B., clasif. 115 (27 July 1256). For the *alarde* (the annual showing of horse and weapons to municipal officials), see Pescador, *op. cit.*, xxxix-xl, pp. 192-5; Antonio Benavides, *Memorias de Fernando IV de Castilla*, 2 vols. (Madrid, 1860), ii, p. 265. Also Real Academia de la História, *Cortes de los antiguos reinos de Leon y Castilla*, 5 vols. (Madrid, 1861-1903; hereafter *Cortes*), i, p. 615, Alcalá de Henares (1348).

[24] This was not the case elsewhere in Castile. In Segovia, for example, well-to-do citizens of the villages "outside the city walls" who belonged to the *comunidad* (community) were included in the royal charters of tax exemption if they owned horse and weapons. See the confirmation by Ferdinand IV of a charter of Sancho IV on 8 March 1282: A.M.S., carpeta V, no. 3.

jurisdiction and taxes and therefore excused from service in the urban militias during the thirteenth and fourteenth centuries.[25]

In the second half of the thirteenth century initial fulfillment of these conditions did not grant *caballero* status for life or continued tax exemption. The non-noble knights came up for review twice a year when their names were placed on the lists of the *Caballería Villana*, eight days before Christmas and eight days before Quinquagesima Sunday.[26] Based on the maintenance of horse and weapons the position of the *caballero villano* was a function of his wealth and economic well-being. If he did not have enough income to maintain both weapons and a horse fit for warfare, the non-noble knight forfeited, at least in the mid-thirteenth century, those benefits granted to him in the royal charters of 1255 and 1256.

In those turbulent times military service was a risky business, often a fatal one. Clearly, without some substantial inducement it would have been difficult to press the *caballeros villanos* into active military service. Horse and weapons represented a sizeable initial investment and a subsequent maintenance cost. In 1256 the non-noble knights of Burgos and later those of other Castilian cities received sweeping economic concessions which more than compensated them for their military service to the crown, since Alfonso X freed their properties in Burgos and elsewhere within the realm from all forms of taxation. Also excused from taxes were the holdings of their servants, if valued under one hundred *mrs.* Added benefits included extended grazing rights for their livestock; furthermore, those serving with the king's host were exempted from *marzadga.*[27] Clearly, these economic advantages encouraged the rise of the non-noble knights to a position of power within Burgos, and by 1255 they were on their way to becoming a distinctive section of the city population. The growing differences between them and the rest of the inhabitants of Burgos had been increasingly evident for many years. The importance of the charters of 1255 and 1256 lies in the manner in which the development of an oligarchy was accelerated by the granting of tax exemption.

[25] A.M.B., clasif. 2508 (8 Aug. 1283). In a letter to the *concejo* of Burgos the Infante Sancho ordered the municipal officials to return to Antolín Fernández, a nobleman, the taxes and services collected from him. According to the Fuero Real the *fijos dalgo* (hidalgos) who lived in the cities were exempted from taxes. See also *Cortes*, i, p. 598, Alcalá de Henares (1348); *Crónica de Alfonso X*, p. 21.

[26] See note 22 above. Other charters granted the non-noble knights a period of four months to replace their horses. See *Memorial histórico español*, i, pp. 175-80.

[27] A.M.B., clasif. 115 (27 July 1256); *Memorial histórico español*, i, p. 315, lists other tax exemptions. *Marzadga* was part of a public tax (*infurción*) paid twice a year. This tax was paid by all the inhabitants of the realm, unless exempted by the king. The *martiniega* was collected on the day of St. Martin and the *marzadga* in the month of March. The income of the *martiniega* was granted to the *concejo* of Burgos in 1293: A.M.B., clasif. 157 (21 May 1293). For medieval Castilian taxes, see García de Valdeavellano, *Curso de historia*, pp. 599-612.

The question of their social origins is still a matter for debate, and in the case of Burgos, the documents do not allow conclusive answers to be given. Most Spanish historians have pointed out the dichotomy of urban development in Castile-Leon, noting that although the cities along the pilgrimage road to Compostella evolved more or less according to the traditional model formulated by Pirenne, with few exceptions towns elsewhere in Castile had a rurally oriented population.[28] Burgos was the mercantile city *par excellence* in northern Castile, and the city's commercial importance prompted a large number of foreign merchants to settle there during the twelfth century.[29] The descendants of these foreign merchants — called Sanchester, Guillén, Giralth, Giraldo, and the like — appear prominently among the non-noble knights of the late thirteenth century. The Bonifaz, the most important of the *caballero villano* families in the first half of the fourteenth century, were also of foreign origin.[30] It is my belief that a significant part of the *Caballería Villana* of Burgos (the most important in terms of influence) can be traced back to the foreign merchants who made Burgos their home in the twelfth century. Moreover, these families retained the trade connections and mercantile interests of their forbears. With the exception of Jews and Mudejars there is no evidence of foreign commercial groups operating in Burgos between 1248 and 1350, a period when Italian merchants (the Genoese above all) were establishing permanent footholds in other Castilian cities.[31] It may not be rash, perhaps, to assume that those foreign merchants who settled in Burgos in the late twelfth century were thereafter able to control long-distance trade, and that they and their descendants excluded any other groups from mercantile activity within the city.

The rest of the non-noble knights were of local origin. They might have been drawn from the large pool of free men, the so-called *omes buenos* (good men) of the town who had enough income to qualify for

[28] García de Valdeavellano, *Orígenes de la burguesía*, chs. 4-5.

[29] Carlé, *Del concejo medieval*, p. 180. For the settlement of foreign merchants in Burgos during the twelfth century, see Luciano Serrano, *El obispado de Burgos y Castilla primitiva desde el siglo V al XIII*, 3 vols. (Madrid, 1935), ii, pp. 210-16; Vázquez de Parga *et al.*, *Las peregrinaciones a Santiago de Compostela*, i, pp. 465-97.

[30] For the Bonifaz, see T. F. Ruiz, "Prosopografía burgalesa, 1248-1350", *Boletín de la Institución Fernán González*, no. 184 (1975), pp. 476-80; T. López Mata, "Ramón Bonifaz", *Boletín de la Comisión de Monumentos de la Provincia de Burgos*, no. 105 (1949), pp. 246-7. None of the local historians have pointed to the relationship between the names of the twelfth-century foreign merchants and the late thirteenth- and early fourteenth-century non-noble knights.

[31] Seville, Cordoba, Jerez and other Castilian cities had colonies of foreign merchants by the second half of the thirteenth century: Sánchez Albornoz, *España: un enigma histórico*, ii, pp. 126-7; Carlé, "Mercaderes en Castilla", pp. 231 ff.; Antonio Ballesteros y Beretta, *Sevilla en el siglo XIII* (Madrid, 1913), pp. 40-9.

caballero status. Historians of medieval Castile have failed however to differentiate, at least for the late thirteenth and early fourteenth century, between *omes buenos* and *caballero villano*, and also clearly to define what is really meant by *omes buenos*. It is true that before and during most of Alfonso X's reign, and sometimes even later, the two terms were employed indiscriminately. In many of the documents of the period they are used synonymously; in others the words denote entirely different groups.[32] After all, the *caballeros villanos* as an entity distinguishable from other members of the urban militia was, to a degree, a new concept. Nevertheless, the available documentary evidence clearly shows a new legal distinction emerging in the late thirteenth century and demonstrates that a final definition of both terms as distinctive from each other had occurred by the early fourteenth.[33]

Beneath the non-noble knights on the social and economic ladder one finds a less privileged social group with mixed characteristics. María del Carmen Carlé has used the term *hombres buenos* (good men) to describe them, a term which I have employed in the previous paragraph although narrowing its meaning to include only those within an urban setting. However, a recent article by E. S. Proctor makes Carlé's definition of *hombres buenos* difficult to accept. In her thoughtful note Evelyn Proctor shows that the term could and did include, according to the context, townsmen, noblemen and ecclesiastics.[34] Nevertheless, we are still left with the problem of describing those people in Burgos who owned property, were above the poverty level, and yet still below the *caballeros villanos*. For want of

[32] For examples of the confused use of the terms *ome bueno* and *caballero ciudadano* or *villano*, see A.M.B., clasif. 1391 (12 Oct. 1252). Note also the following [to the *concejo* of Burgos]: "que me enbiassedes dos cavallos por que avia cosas de fablar con ellos (that they send two non-noble knights for there are things to talk about with them)": A.M.B., clasif. 2574 (22 Dec. 1275). The following year Pedro Bonifaz, a non-noble knight, was described in a royal letter as a "good man": A.M.B., clasif. 2915 (2 Mar. 1276). See also A.M.B., clasif. 2560 (14 May 1278); A.M.B., clasif. 2563 (28 July 1278); Ruiz, "Burgos: Society and Royal Power", pp. 166-8.

[33] "los cavalleros, et los otros omes bonos delas villas et de los Pueblos (the non-noble knights, and the other good men of the villages and the towns)": A.M.B., clasif. 2693 (26 Aug. 1281); Benavides, *Memorias de Fernando IV*, ii, pp. 495-7, 737-8; A.M.B., clasif. 99 (25 Mar. 1268); "las villas mayores enviassen a Sevilla quatro cavallos e seis omes buenos (the large towns send to Seville four non-noble knights and six good men)": A.M.B., clasif. 49 (28 Aug. 1281). Also any superficial reading of the *Libro de las Cortes* will show the differences between the two terms. Further evidence comes from R. Gibert's study of the *concejo* of Madrid. He reports the existence of a body known as the *Junta de Pecheros* (council of tax payers) paralleling the *caballero*-controlled *concejo*. See Gibert, *El concejo de Madrid*, p. 62. There is no evidence surviving of such an institutional structure in Burgos.

[34] See María del Carmen Carlé, "Boni homines y hombres buenos", *Cuadernos de historia de España*, xxxix-xl (1964), pp. 133-68; Evelyn S. Proctor, "The Interpretation of Clause 3 of the Decrees of Leon", *Eng. Hist. Rev.*, lxxxv (1970), pp. 45-53.

a better term they can also be called *pecheros*, a word used in contemporary documents to identify those who paid taxes as opposed to the tax-exempted non-noble knights, nobles and ecclesiastics.

Although the information on the *pecheros* of Burgos is minimal when compared to that available for the non-noble knights, a few general observations can be made. Before the mid-thirteenth century they shared, at least in theory, the same social and political prerogatives enjoyed by the non-noble knights. Among their ranks one would certainly find more artisans than merchants, and they were also generally less well off than the members of the *Caballería Villana*. In Burgos a certain amount of social mobility existed between the two groups. Citizens who were not members of the *Caballería Villana* held some of the municipal offices before the fourteenth century, and a few of them rose to *caballero* rank. In the late 1330s, however, this social fluidity came to an end. The general crisis of Castilian agriculture affecting Burgos as well as the rest of the Castilian realm, together with the large rise in exports of wool, served to improve the economic position of the non-noble knights since most of them were engaged in trade, while at the same time adversely affecting the rest of the population. It was then that the economic advantages of the charters of 1255 and 1256 were strongest felt. This was evident above all in the rise of the *caballeros villanos* of Burgos to economic dominance within the city and the surrounding countryside.

II

THE ECONOMIC STRUCTURE OF THE *CABALLERIA VILLANA* OF BURGOS

If their prominence depended on their wealth, what was its source? The answer lies in trade and, above all, foreign trade. Burgos was the most important centre in Castile for the exchange of goods between the ports of the Bay of Biscay and the South. In addition, as a principal stopping place on the road to Compostella, Burgos profited from the trade of passing pilgrims. Most of the merchants controlling the long-distance trade were non-noble knights. The chronicle of Ferdinand IV, when describing the visit of the queen mother María de Molina to Burgos in 1297, relates that "she went to stay in the street of Sanct Llorente where all the merchants lived...".[35] The chronicle of Alfonso XI provides similar information.[36] In the early fourteenth century all the members of the *Caballería Villana* of Burgos lived on the street of Sanct Llorente and the adjacent streets of Armas, Huerto del Rey and Sanct Esteban.[37] The street

[35] *Crónica de Fernando IV*, p. 108, col. 2.
[36] *Crónica de Alfonso XI*, p. 245, col. 2.
[37] See the rules of the *cofradía* and the portraits of the members in the "Libro de la Real Hermandad o del Santísimo y Santiago": A.M.B.; published in *Texto cronológico de las tres reglas, por las que sucesivamente rigio su vida*

(cont. on p. 13)

of Sanct Llorente was the section of the French Road (road to Compostella) that made its way through the city, and as such it was the main commercial thoroughfare of Burgos.[38] Although it cannot be stated categorically that all the dwellers in these streets were merchants and non-noble knights, the chronicles and other supporting evidence strongly suggest that this was indeed the case.

There are many other indications of the relationship between mercantile activity and membership in the *Caballería Villana.* The three most important families of Burgos — Prestines (Bonifaz), Pérez-Ibáñez (Sarracín) and Trapaz — were actively engaged in mercantile pursuits.[39] They were not alone. The list includes many other prominent non-noble knights — Alfón Martínez, Alfonso Pérez, Asensio García, John Pérez de Carrión, Domingo Martínez, Diego Martínez de Silos and many others.[40] There appears to have been a strong correlation also between commercial activities and tenure of public offices. In most cases merchants based in Burgos conducted their business affairs while engaged in municipal or royal service. Moreover, younger members of these *caballero* families were sent to trade in England or Flanders, and in their later years they remained at home engaged in the administration of the city and local trade.[41] As merchants the non-noble knights of Burgos also received a great number of royal privileges, providing further evidence of the rewards obtained from their close association with the crown.[42]

Nonetheless, merchants did not completely monopolize the *Caballería Villana.* Mingled with them are shopkeepers, retailers, scribes,

(note 37 cont.)
corporativa la Real Cofradía del "Santísimo y Santiago" de la ciudad de Burgos, ed. Ismael García Rámila (Burgos, 1970; hereafter *Texto cronológico*). See also Marqués de Laurencín, "Libro de la cofradía de caballeros de Santiago de la Fuente, fundada por los burgaleses en tiempos de Alfonso XI", *Revista de archivos, bibliotecas y museos,* xii (1905), pp. 1-23, 134-8. I have found no documentary evidence in the rules of 1338 regarding any Santiago de la Fuente.

[38] *Crónica de Alfonso XI,* p. 234, col. 2. For the topography of Burgos, see Ismael García Rámila, "Estudio topográfico-histórico del Burgos de los siglos pasados", *Boletín de la Comisión de Monumentos de la Provincia de Burgos,* nos. 18-19 (1939-40), pp. 261-9, 305-16, 356-66, 398-404; García Sainz de Baranda, *La ciudad de Burgos,* i, pp. 176-329.

[39] T. F. Ruiz, "Castilian Merchants in England, 1248-1350", in W. C. Jordan, B. McNab and T. F. Ruiz (eds.), *Order and Innovation in the Middle Ages: Essays in Honor of Joseph R. Strayer* (Princeton, N.J., 1976), pp. 173-86; Ruiz, "Prosopografía burgalesa", pp. 467-80. See also A.M.B., clasif. 2689 (15 Feb. 1281); Mercedes Gaibrois de Ballesteros, *Historia del reinado de Sancho IV de Castilla,* 3 vols. (Madrid, 1922-8), i, p. v.

[40] Ruiz, "Prosopografía burgalesa", pp. 482-99; Jules Finot, *Etude historique sur les relations commerciales entre la Flandre et l'Espagne au moyen âge* (Paris, 1899), p. 47.

[41] The evidence is not entirely conclusive, and there are a few cases in which the opposite is correct. On the whole, however, the pattern follows the direction already indicated. See Ruiz, "Prosopografía burgalesa", pp. 482-99.

[42] The list of mercantile rights and privileges granted to the city is too extensive to be presented here. A few examples will suffice. García Sainz de

(cont. on p. 14)

tax-farmers and concessionaires, and at least one non-noble knight was engaged in each of the following pursuits: muleteer, salt dealer, scabbard-maker, butcher, woolcloth manufacturer, lawyer and goldsmith.[43] Unfortunately there is neither data as to the size of these businesses nor their volume, but it must have been above that of the mere artisan. Two of these individuals, Martín Martínez, a butcher, and Sancho García, a goldsmith, profited sufficiently from their trades to be able to make sizeable investment in land and real estate.[44]

The non-noble knights had other sources of income besides their trades or businesses. To the income of the *caballero villano* as merchant and manufacturer must be added the income produced by land ownership and employment in royal and municipal administration.[45] Of these aspects the question of land ownership requires particular attention.

TABLE

TRANSACTIONS OF LAND AND REAL ESTATE IN BURGOS 1200-1350*

	1200-49	1250-99	1300-50	Total
Cathedral Chapter	134 (67·7)	4 (4·3)	5 (3·2)	143
Non-Noble Knights	0 (0·0)	66 (67·3)	120 (76·9)	186
Others	64 (32·3)	22 (28·4)	31 (19·9)	117
Total	198	92	156	446

* Note on Sources: The statistics provided here reflect the documents extant at the cathedral archive of Burgos and also, although in less quantity, the municipal and monastic archives of the city and surrounding area. Figures in brackets denote percentages.

(note 42 cont.)
Baranda, *La ciudad de Burgos*, ii, pp. 420-1; A.M.B., clasif. 120 (21 May 1285); Carlé, "Mercaderes en Castilla", p. 224; *Memorial histórico español*, ii, pp. 29-31; A.M.B., clasif. 134 (13 Feb. 1281); A.M.B., clasif. 2689 (15 Feb. 1281), exempting the Burgalese merchants from paying *portadgo*; A.M.B., clasif. 2690 (15 Feb. 1281); A.M.B., clasif. 104 (28 Jan. 1303), in which Ferdinand IV granted to the merchants of Burgos the right to move freely throughout the kingdom with their carts and pack animals; A.M.B., clasif. 103 (7 Apr. 1304); A.M.B., clasif. 100 (28 Feb. 1309); A.M.B., clasif. 96 (28 Nov. 1339), in which Alfonso XI gave to the merchants of Burgos the right to export one work horse per year.

[43] J. García Sainz de Baranda, "Primitiva regla escrita de la cofradía de Nuestra Señora de Gamonal" (hereafter "Primitiva regla"), *Boletín de la Comisión de Monumentos de la Provincia de Burgos*, no. 65 (1938), pp. 163-4; *Texto cronológico*, pp. 16-18; Archivo de la catedral de Burgos (hereafter A.C.B.), vol. 37, fo. 19; A.C.B., vol. 40, fo. 24; A.M.B., clasif. 2925.

[44] See notes 49, 50, 51 and 52 below.

[45] For example, in 1345 the *alcaldes* of Burgos received an annual salary of 2,000 *mrs.* See notes 90 and 91 below.

Land ownership by the non-noble knights follows the general pattern found among patrician élites in other parts of western Europe.[46] Extant documents show the *caballeros villanos* as the most active buyers of land and real estate throughout the late thirteenth and early fourteenth centuries. A rough statistical apparatus is provided in the accompanying Table to illustrate this point.

In the Table buyers and sellers have been grouped according to their social status. Members of the clergy who also belonged to *caballero* families and bought land have been included among the non-noble knights only if their purchases were of a private nature and independent of their ecclesiastical position.[47] Strict differentiation has been made between purchases made for and by the cathedral chapter and those made by individual clergymen. A glance at the Table clearly indicates a change in the economic structure of the city around 1250. Between 1200 and 1250 the cathedral chapter had been the most active buyer of land and real estate. After 1250 the non-noble knights superseded the chapter in this role. It is no coincidence that this change occurred simultaneously with Alfonso X's charters to the *caballeros villanos* in 1255 and 1256. The non-noble knights swiftly put to good use their new economic advantages. Since the servants and farm hands of the *caballeros* were exempted from taxation if their properties did not exceed 100 *mrs.*, one can see that there was now pressure on the *pecheros* and independent farmers to sell their lands to the non-noble knights, and then either to become tenants or to migrate to the new open territory in the south.

The advantageous economic climate for the non-noble knights created by the charters does not entirely explain the dramatic decline in the acquisition of land by the chapter. Nevertheless, by the fourteenth century the *caballeros villanos* had effectively replaced the chapter as the main economic force within the city. One of the reasons for this might be that the non-noble knights not only replaced but actually captured the deanship of the cathedral chapter for the next hundred years.

Interest in the acquisition of land was not restricted to the most prominent families but involved the whole *caballero* social group. Thus, mobility up the social ladder from tax-paying citizen to exempted non-noble knight was often accompanied by investment in land. In Burgos this was not uncommon, and a few examples will illustrate the relationship between landholding and enhanced social status.

Martín Martínez, Pedro Pérez and Sancho García did not belong

[46] *Cambridge Economic History of Europe*, iii (Cambridge, 1963), p. 32.

[47] The records of land transaction clearly state by and for whom the land was bought. Wills and donations also indicate in what capacity the property was held.

to the powerful families dominating the life of Burgos, nor did they enjoy positions of authority within the *concejo*. Yet they rose from their trades into the ranks of the *Caballería Villana*. Their social ascent was paralleled by their purchase of land and real estate. Martín Martínez, a butcher in 1312, invested 10,014 *mrs.* between 1312 and 1346 in lands located in Villalvilla de Burgos (a village some six miles from the city). Between 1322 and 1325 he became a citizen of Burgos, which probably means that he bought a house within the city walls, and in 1338 he joined an exclusive brotherhood of non-noble knights.[48] Pedro Pérez (no relation to the powerful Pérez-Sarracín family) was the majordomus of a certain García Pérez de Carrión, a non-noble knight, important merchant and city official.[49] In the years 1325-6 Pedro Pérez bought eleven vineyards in Madrigal, a town under the jurisdiction of Burgos. By 1322 he had purchased property within the city walls and six years later joined the brotherhood of *caballeros villanos*.[50] Sancho García, a goldsmith, seems to have been wealthier than the other two, even though the documents do not show the extent of his holdings. Between 1310 and 1335 he actively bought large quantities of land, eventually gaining admission to the brotherhood of non-noble knights together with his two sons.[51]

Evidence available in a few other cases points to the presence of social mobility although, as will be seen, by the mid-fourteenth century the non-noble knights were already closing the door to newcomers.

[48] A.C.B., vol. 39, fo. 19 (12 Jan. 1312); A.C.B., vol. 37, fo. 31 (6 Apr. 1315); A.C.B., vol. 37, fo. 88 (12 Sept. 1315); A.C.B., vol. 37, fo. 13 (13 Apr. 1322); "Martín Martínez, carnecero e vecino de Burgos (Martín Martínez, butcher and citizen of Burgos)": A.C.B., vol. 37, fo. 18 (19 June 1325); A.C.B., vol. 37, fo. 20 (5 Oct. 1325); A.C.B., vol. 37, fo. 24 (27 Dec. 1336); A.C.B., vol. 37, fo. 23 (3 Dec. 1337); A.C.B., vol. 37, fo. 29 (25 Aug. 1340); A.C.B., vol. 44, fo. 534 (14 Mar. 1344); A.C.B., vol. 37, fo. 28 (8 Oct. 1346); A.C.B., vol. 37, fo. 22 (10 Oct. 1346); *Texto cronológico*, p. 16.

[49] On García Pérez de Carrión, see Ruiz, "Prosopografía burgalesa", pp. 494-5.

[50] A.C.B., vol. 30, fo. 594 (21 Sept. 1324); A.C.B., vol. 30, fo. 821 (25 Sept. 1324); A.C.B., vol. 30, fo. 584 (23 Oct. 1324); A.C.B., vol. 30, fo. 596 (23 Oct. 1324); "pedro Perez, veçino de Burgos, e amo de Garci perez de Carrion (Pedro Pérez, citizen of Burgos and majordomus of García Pérez de Carrión)": A.C.B., vol. 30, fo. 593 (9 May 1325); A.C.B., vol. 30, fo. 583 (9 May 1325); A.C.B., vol. 30, fo. 583a (19 May 1325); A.C.B., vol. 30, fo. 592 (31 May 1325); A.C.B., vol. 30, fo. 590 (? May 1325); A.C.B., vol. 30, fo. 595 (6 June 1325); A.C.B., vol. 30, fo. 586 (9 Feb. 1326); A.C.B., vol. 42, fo. 7 (5 Feb. 1332); *Texto cronológico*, p. 17.

[51] A.C.B., vol. 40, fo. 24 (28 June 1310); A.C.B., vol. 49, fo. 27 (29 July 1311); A.C.B., vol. 41, pt. 1, fo. 449 (26 Mar. 1319); A.C.B., vol. 43, pt. 2, fo. 17 (27 Mar. 1319); A.C.B., vol. 41, pt. 1, fo. 450 (27 Mar. 1319); A.C.B., vol. 44, fo. 4 (26 May 1319); A.C.B., vol. 40, fo. 253 (5 Dec. 1326); A.C.B., vol. 40, fo. 255 (11 Nov. 1327); A.C.B., vol. 49, fo. 3 (15 July 1335); A.C.B., vol. 49, fo. 3a (10 Aug. 1335); *Texto cronológico*, p. 17.

III

THE SOCIAL WORLD OF THE *CABALLEROS VILLANOS* OF BURGOS

Like the patricians of most other cities in medieval Europe the non-noble knights of Burgos tried to restrict their numbers and to consolidate and preserve their gains. Their growing consciousness of having a distinctive social position led them to form brotherhoods (*cofradías*) which excluded those without horse and weapons. These brotherhoods clearly show the sharp lines of differentiation being drawn between the non-noble knights and other groups within the city.

In the period between 1250 and 1350 two *cofradías* — that of Our Lady of Gamonal, and the Real Hermandad — provided the means for the exclusion of those of lower social standing or economic position. Since the rules of both brotherhoods have survived, they offer valuable information on the social structure of the city. Furthermore, the membership lists provide a convenient census of the *Caballería Villana* of Burgos in the years 1305 and 1338.

The first of these brotherhoods, Our Lady of Gamonal (also known as the brotherhood of non-noble knights), was founded in 1285 by Don Miguel Estevan or Estévanez and his wife Doña Ucenda Prestines.[52] A published copy of the brotherhood rules describes the festivities peculiar to the organization, sets the amount of the admission fee (two *mrs.* and a pound of wax) and establishes procedures for the funerals of members and their families.[53]

In 1305 Our Lady of Gamonal had ninety-nine members with their occupations or trades listed, in most cases, next to their names.[54] Two members of the Bonifaz family headed the membership list. They were followed by representatives of all the important *caballero* families. For many of the *cofrades* there is also concurrent evidence which shows their status as non-noble knights. Moreover, all the *alcaldes* of the city belonged to the brotherhood.[55] However, it cannot be firmly stated that all members were *caballeros villanos*, nor that all the non-noble knights of Burgos had joined the brotherhood. A Johm Fernández de Sovido, described as *criado del alcalde* (servant of the *alcalde*), hardly qualifies as a non-noble knight.[56] Our Lady of Gamonal served also as an instrument for the pursuit of the common mercantile interests of most of the *cofrades*. Many of them were involved in commercial enterprises and later, in the sixteenth

[52] On Don Miguel Estévanez and Doña Ucenda Prestines, see Ruiz, "Prosopografía burgalesa", p. 488.

[53] "Primitiva regla", p. 160.

[54] *Ibid.*, pp. 163-4.

[55] I have presented this evidence in the appendix to my "Prosopografía burgalesa", pp. 482-99. See also "Primitiva regla", pp. 163-4.

[56] "Primitiva regla", p. 164.

century, Our Lady of Gamonal became known as the *cofradía* of merchants.[57]

If Our Lady of Gamonal marked the first attempt to unite the leading elements of the city population, it was still an incomplete step towards social distinction. The final crystallization of the non-noble knights as a social class was achieved through the formation of a new brotherhood, the Real Hermandad or Real Cofradía del Santísimo y Santiago. Founded by Alfonso XI in 1338 the Real Hermandad explicitly excluded those who did not possess fighting horses and weapons, restricting membership to those who had the proper equipment and belonged to the right families.[58]

The name of Real Cofradía del Santísimo y Santiago reveals, I believe, the conscious imitation of the noble military order of Santiago. The beautiful portraits accompanying the rules of the brotherhood show handsome knights dressed with richly ornamented garments showing their families' colours and coats of arms. Even if the rules themselves did not state that the *cofrades* were non-noble knights, the illustrations would show that this was so because possession of horse and weapons within the city implied tax exemption and *caballero* status. They also indicate how close to the nobility the non-noble knights had come by the mid-fourteenth century.[59]

Many of the members of the Real Hermandad had belonged in their youth to the brotherhood of Our Lady of Gamonal. Others were the sons or relatives of the 1305 *cofrades*. Still, the change which took place in the intervening thirty-three years was nothing short of remarkable. By 1338 the members of the Real Hermandad already constituted a ruling élite. Although one could assume that the most powerful citizens of Burgos had joined Our Lady of Gamonal, the gulf between them and those who did not belong to the brotherhood did not appear wide. In 1338 the members of the Real Hermandad stood politically, socially and economically apart from and opposed to other groups within the city.

Alfonso XI founded the brotherhood of the Real Hermandad while he presided over the Ayuntamiento of Burgos in 1338, and the ordinances of that meeting provide the most dramatic evidence of the rise of the non-noble knights within Burgos. Their horses which

[57] Sánchez Albornoz, *España: un enigma histórico*, ii, p. 145; Carlé, "Mercaderes en Castilla", p. 288.

[58] *Texto cronológico*, p. 12.

[59] See the illustrations in Gabriel Jackson, *The Making of Medieval Spain* (New York, 1972). Jackson has mistakenly identified these men as members of the noble military order of Santiago. I would like to thank Don Graziano Diez Sanz, archivist of the Municipal Archive of Burgos, for his continual help and gracious hospitality. For a study of the non-noble knights' coats of arms and the family ties between them, see L. Huidobro y Serna, "Nuevos datos sobre el almirante don Ramón Bonifaz y sus descendientes", *Boletín de la Comisión de Monumentos de la Provincia de Burgos*, no. 113 (1950), pp. 263-9.

in 1256 had been priced at a minimum of thirty *mrs.* were now valued at eight hundred *mrs.*[60] Even considering the rapid inflation of the early fourteenth century, eight hundred *mrs.* represented a very considerable increase, restricting the number of new members to those who were financially privileged. Moreover, those within the municipal contingents who fought on foot were forbidden to wear capes, red or purple cloth, or to use silver-ornamented weapons, these items being reserved henceforth for the non-noble knights and the aristocracy.[61]

Ten years later at the Cortes of Alcalá de Henares in 1348 Alfonso granted further concessions to the ruling élites of the Castilian cities. The wives of the *caballeros villanos* gained the right to wear certain types of cloth which were otherwise banned to the rest of the urban non-noble female population of Castile.[62] Obviously, by 1338 and thereafter the non-noble knights differed from other groups within the city even in the style of their apparel. Although in the sumptuary laws of 1252 and 1258 no mention was made of the non-noble knights,[63] they were prominently named in 1338 and 1348. Unlike the earlier sumptuary regulations the later rules did not restrict the expenses of a specific social group; rather their purpose was to keep the *pecheros* and other citizens below *caballero* rank from imitating the members of the urban oligarchy. Furthermore, in 1348 the Ordenamiento de Alcalá de Henares also prohibited the confiscation of the horses of the *caballeros villanos* because of any outstanding debts, thus guaranteeing their status against financial adversity.[64]

The rules of the Real Hermandad provide additional evidence on the changing relationship of the non-noble knights *vis-à-vis* other groups in Burgos. Admission fees to the brotherhood which had been set at two *mrs.* and a pound of wax for Our Lady of Gamonal in 1305 rose to eighteen *mrs.* and a pound of wax (4 *mrs.*) by 1338. Allowing once again for inflation these higher fees reinforce the impression of the members' increased wealth and power. Although the membership lists of Our Lady of Gamonal made no reference to the *cofrades'* place of residence, those of the Real Hermandad did. All of them lived on the select streets of Huerto del Rey, Sanct Llorente, Armas and Sanct Esteban.[65] This is the area around the

[60] The Ayuntamiento was a meeting of the Cortes which only the procurators of the cities attended. For the prices of horses in 1256 and 1338, see A.M.B., clasif. 115 (27 July 1256); *Cortes*, i, p. 451, Burgos (1338).

[61] *Cortes*, i, p. 455, Burgos (1338).

[62] *Ibid.*, p. 621, Alcalá de Henares (1348).

[63] See Ruiz, "Burgos: Society and Royal Power", ch. 1.

[64] *Cortes*, i, ch. 25, p. 518, Ordenamiento de Alcalá de Henares (1348).

[65] *Texto cronológico*, pp. 16-18. The members were listed by place of residence. Sixteen lived in Huerto del Rey, eighty-eight on the street of Sanct Llorente (the road to Compostella on its way through the city), ten on the street of Armas and fifty-seven on the street of Sanct Esteban.

cathedral and, in the thirteenth and fourteenth centuries, it formed the commercial and religious centre of the city and, thus, the place where the ruling élite of Burgos resided.

Because the king was the founder of the Real Hermandad one can assume that few of the non-noble knights would have failed to join. Should this assumption be correct the membership lists of 1338 offer an almost complete census of the *Caballería Villana* of Burgos. They numbered 171 — almost double the membership of Our Lady of Gamonal. This figure represents about 2 or 3 per cent of what I have estimated to be the total population of Burgos during the period under study (6,500 to 8,000 inhabitants), a percentage similar to that of patrician élites in other medieval cities.[66]

By 1338 the *caballeros villanos* of the city had organized themselves under the king's leadership into a military-religious brotherhood in imitation of the nobility but, because of the political alignment prevailing in Castile, in opposition to the ambitions of the aristocracy. In fact the *Caballería Villana* of Burgos had been strengthening their ties with the kings of Castile throughout the hundred years that followed the conquest of Seville. It is to the political role of the non-noble knights that we must now address ourselves.

IV

POLITICAL POWER AND FAMILY GROUPS

The rise of the non-noble knights of Burgos must be seen in terms of their relationship with other groups challenging them from below, within the city, and from above, in the surrounding countryside. Above all, their privileged position was largely dependent on royal support. Their political power within the city was both the result of their economic and social importance and, paradoxically, the means of preserving this favoured status. It was also a function of their alliance with the crown.

The *caballeros villanos* of Burgos enjoyed a monopoly of municipal offices, but their political control of the city was not shared equally by

[66] Any number given for the population of Burgos between 1248 and 1350 is, as in most medieval demography, the result of little more than a guessing game. The area within the walls (there was almost no urban development outside the walls in the fourteenth century) has been estimated at 45 hectares by L. Torres Balbas, *Algunos aspectos del mudejarismo urbano* (Madrid, 1954), p. 18; and at 54 hectares by J. C. Russell, *Medieval Regions and Their Cities* (London, 1972), p. 189. Russell projected a population of ten thousand although he qualifies this estimate; he also offers two different areas for the city: 54 and 60 hectares. From personal observation and the documentary evidence available for the fourteenth century, showing gardens and empty land within the walls, I have arrived at an inhabited area of 36 hectares. Moreover, part of the land within the walls was taken by the castle, its fortifications and the steep slopes leading to the hill. My own estimate is around 6,500 inhabitants. The population of Burgos in the late thirteenth and early fourteenth centuries must not have exceeded 8,000 inhabitants.

all the members of the *Caballería Villana*. In the years after the conquest of Seville the administration of Burgos fell progressively into the hands of a few influential families, who formed an élite within the élite. In Burgos this development occurred in three stages. First the bourgeoisie wrested control from the community as a whole; then the non-noble knights excluded those who did not own horse and weapons and had not, therefore, obtained tax exemption. Finally with the crown's approval, a few families emerged by the mid-fourteenth century as the dominant force within the city.[67] This development was, of course, a complex process which has been somewhat simplified here and exceptions can be readily provided. For example, the documentary evidence shows that members of the Sarracín family held the position of *alcalde* for most of the late twelfth and the entire thirteenth centuries.[68] In that sense 1248, 1255 or 1256 were not watersheds in the rise of the non-noble knights to political power; yet the conquest of Seville and the subsequent charters to the *caballeros villanos* of Burgos marked their progression to total control of municipal and royal positions within the city. After 1322 all municipal officials, all the members of the *concejo*, and most of the Burgalese citizens serving in the royal administration were non-noble knights. Their political influence was concentrated in the hands of a few families, or to be more explicit in the hands of one large extended family, the Sarracín-Bonifaz-Prestines-García de Camargo and Mathe-Pérez de Frías. They dominated the economic, social, religious and political life of Burgos. Extant documents and their coats of arms, as shown in the book of the Real Hermandad clearly attest to the blood ties and commercial interests uniting them.[69]

Between 1200 and 1350 there is no single year among those which can be documented that did not show at least one member of this family group holding the position of *alcalde*, or of *merino* (he carried out the sentences imposed by the *alcaldes*, recruited the municipal

[67] The transformation of the *concejo* is a rather controversial thesis. I personally doubt the existence of the so-called open *concejo* of the early medieval period so cherished by Spanish historians. See Carlé, *Del concejo medieval*, pp. 33 ff.

[68] Pedro Sarracín I was *alcalde* of Burgos in 1187, 1193, 1195, 1199, 1200, 1202, 1203, 1207, 1210 and 1211. His son, Juan Pérez I, held the position in 1221, 1223, 1225, 1226, 1227, 1228 and 1253. Rodrigo Ibáñez, son of Juan Pérez I, was *alcalde* of Burgos in 1259 and 1275, procurator of the city in 1268 and banker of the Infante Sancho in 1279. Gómez Ibáñez, his brother, was *alcalde* in 1273 and 1288. Pedro Sarracín II, another of Juan Pérez's sons, held the deanship of the cathedral chapter in the second half of the thirteenth century. The list goes on for quite a while. I have already examined their tenure in office and their purchases of land and real estate in my "Prosopografía burgalesa", pp. 467-76.

[69] On the formation of familial clans, see Jacques Heers, *Le clan familial au moyen âge* (Paris, 1974). See Huidobro, "Nuevos datos sobre el almirante don Ramón Bonifaz y sus descendientes", pp. 263-9; Ruiz, "Prosopografía burgalesa", pp. 467-81.

militia and supervised weights and measures within the city), or membership in the municipal council. The group monopolized the deanship of the cathedral chapter with all the economic influence that this implied, as well as the choicest ecclesiastical benefices within Burgos. The two most important landholders during the period under study, Pedro Sarracín II and Pedro Bonifaz III, led their families in the acquisition of extensive estates in and around Burgos.[70] Seventeen per cent of the entire membership of the Real Hermandad belonged to this family group, and four out of the sixteen members of the *Regimiento*[71] also belonged to this powerful ruling clan. This is not to say that they acted as a group, and I have found no indication that they always did so. Nevertheless, the family ties must have been a source of strength.

It should again be indicated that the rise of the non-noble knights to a privileged position within Burgos was paralleled and aided by their dynamic relationship with other elements in Castilian society and, above all, with the crown. In the hundred years that followed the conquest of Seville the kings of Castile made repeated attempts to gain fiscal control of the cities and to transform the institutional structure of Castilian society. This was most evident in Burgos, which served as the prime testing ground for royal policy.

V

BURGOS AND ROYAL POWER

The intervention of the crown in the internal affairs of Burgos took two different forms. First, the kings of Castile took on responsibilities, mainly judicial, reserved or delegated until then to the *concejo*. Secondly, the monarchs sought to change the structure of the city council so that it would be more responsive to their demands.

Beginning with Alfonso X the kings of Castile became more receptive to the complaints and appeals of Burgalese citizens against the judicial decisions of the city *alcaldes*. In 1263 Alfonso X granted to the citizens of Burgos the right to appeal from the ruling of substitute *alcaldes*.[72] Five years later the *concejo* showed its usual indecision by asking the king to clarify the penalties established in the

[70] Documentary evidence has already been provided in Ruiz, "Prosopografía burgalesa", pp. 470-6, and is too extensive to quote here again. Some figures, however, will indicate their power. Between 1248 and 1290 Pedro Sarracín II made thirty-three purchases or exchanges of land for a total investment of 30,964 *mrs.*, 4 *sueldos*, 2 *dineros*. His nephew, Pedro Sarracín III, was involved in eighteen transactions of land and real estate between 1285 and 1291 paying over 12,000 *mrs.* Other members of the family were equally active in land purchase. Pedro Bonifaz III, dean of the cathedral chapter in the first half of the fourteenth century, invested over 34,700 *mrs.* in land and real estate between 1333 and 1350, the year of his death.

[71] See pp. 27, 29-30 below.

[72] A.M.B., clasif. 1973 (6 Aug. 1263), partially though incorrectly edited in Anselmo Salvá, *Cosas de la vieja Burgos* (Burgos, 1892), pp. 13-17.

Fuero Real for obscene language and other offences.[73] Another example of municipal dependence can be found in the king's answer to a petition of the cathedral chapter of Burgos by which Alfonso X prevented the representatives of the city council entering those places under the jurisdiction of the chapter.[74] Also, the appointment of *alcaldes apartados* (special *alcaldes*) to judge criminal and civil cases between Christians and Jews in 1274 was a significant step in undermining the influence of the *concejo* while depriving the municipality of an important source of income.[75] In 1281 the *alcalde del rey* (*alcalde* of the king), a judicial official holding a court at Burgos, was mentioned for the first time in the documents of the period.[76] Although the jurisdiction of these officials was not precisely defined in the extant documents, their presence constituted an obvious check on the municipal authorities. Furthermore, the kings of Castile released prisoners indicted for crimes ranging from murder to breaking and entering, ordered royal officials to interfere in villages belonging to the city, and ruled on property rights and disputed municipal elections in Burgos[77] — and these are just a few examples of the continuous interference of the crown in the affairs of the city.

[73] Alfonso X determined the fine for obscene language, raised to 10 *mrs.* the penalty for slapping someone in the face, and ordered the *concejo* to meet at a specific location rather than in the *alcaldes'* houses: A.M.B., clasif. 99 (25 Mar. 1268). Depositions renewing these measures were granted to the city in 1276 and 1282: A.M.B., clasif. 2915 (2 Mar. 1276); A.M.B., clasif. 2915 (2 May 1282). I owe to Professor Raymond S. Willis my thanks for clarifying the meaning of the obscene term *fide fududincul*, so disturbing to the *concejo* of Burgos: *fi* (son) *de* (of) *foder* (to fornicate) *in* (in) *cul* (anus). See also A.M.B., clasif. 2917 (8 Apr. 1279), where the term is used once again.

[74] A.C.B., vol. 2, pt. 1, fo. 52 (2 Apr. 1274).

[75] The Jewish *aljama* of Burgos appealed to Alfonso X against the abuses of the *concejo* of Burgos. The king answered by naming two *alcaldes apartados*, Simón Ráynez and García Pérez, both having previously served the crown in other capacities, with total responsibility over disputes between Jews and Christians. The *alcaldes apartados* received their powers directly from the king and were totally independent of the *concejo*. See Fritz Baer, *Die Juden im Christlichen Spanien*, 2 vols. (Berlin, 1929-36), ii, p. 57 (7 Mar. 1267); A.M.B., clasif. 4125 (10 Aug. 1274); A.M.B., clasif. 2919 (11 Feb. 1279). For biographical material on Simón Ráynez and García Pérez, see Ruiz, "Prosopografía burgalesa", pp. 484-5.

[76] A. Ballesteros y Beretta, *Alfonso X el sabio* (Barcelona, 1963), p. 933; *Fuentes para la historia de Castilla*, ed. L. Serrano, 3 vols. (Valladolid, 1906-10), iii, p. 160. In all the cases for which there is surviving evidence the position was held by a non-noble knight. For other *alcaldes del rey* in Burgos, see Ruiz, "Prosopografía burgalesa", pp. 482-99.

[77] In 1278 the Infante Sancho ordered the release of a certain Antolín Fernańdez, imprisoned by the *alcaldes* of Burgos on a murder charge. A few days later he also ordered that Gerald Bernal be freed from prison and cleared of the charge of breaking and entering. In 1280 Alfonso X ordered the *concejo* to pay the back salary of Pedro Antolínez, procurator of Burgos. Royal interference in gambling disputes at Castil de Judios in 1285, a disputed election in 1307 decided by Ferdinand IV, and many other examples point to a continuous pattern of royal encroachment. A.M.B., clasif. 2921 (11 Nov. 1279); A.M.B., clasif. 2922 (18 Nov. 1279); A.M.B., clasif. 2924 (15 Apr. 1280); A.M.B., clasif. 2937 (27 Nov. 1284); Gaibrois de Ballesteros, *Historia del reinado de Sancho IV de Castilla*, iii, pp. lii-liii; A.M.B., clasif. 2940 (15 Dec. 1289); A.M.B., clasif. 2696 (28 Mar. 1304).

How did the *concejo* of Burgos controlled by the non-noble knights react to this royal pressure? Its reaction was ambiguous and, at times, altogether contradictory. Although the city representatives to the royal court and to the meetings of the Cortes protested again and again against royal intrusion — this seems to have been widespread, and found echo in other Castilian cities — the *concejo* of Burgos, more often than not, petitioned and welcomed royal intervention. The same attitude can also be found in the fiscal relations between the crown and Burgos. In spite of frequent tax exemptions to the city the crown seldom respected previous privileges.[78] At most, the city was only able to mount a delaying operation, eventually complying with royal demands in financial matters. It must be noted that even though Burgos and other cities acquiesced in the will of the Castilian kings, the exemption of the non-noble knights and religious corporations, together with the exorbitant gifts and grants to monasteries and private individuals, placed great stress on the economic well-being of the realm.[79] It was the inability of the Castilian kings to exploit the resources of the urban centres in an efficient way which drove them to depend on the Mesta and the Jews as the only reliable sources of income.[80]

Royal intervention in the judicial process of the city and its financial structure had a considerable impact on the relations between the crown on the one hand and the *concejo* dominated by the non-noble knights on the other; yet this intervention was not as significant as the tampering by the king and his eventual control of the municipal administration. Having been a city ruled by *fueros* Burgos became after 1255, when the Fuero Real was granted to the city as a local *fuero*, a city ruled by royal law. Alfonso X's attempts to bring the cities under one single code marked the opening move in a programme directed towards the take-over of municipal councils.[81]

[78] The problem of financial relations between the crown and the Castilian municipalities is a difficult and not well understood topic. See Joseph F. O'Callaghan, "The Cortes and Royal Taxation during the Reign of Alfonso X of Castile", *Traditio*, xxxvii (1971), pp. 379-98; Antonio Ballesteros y Beretta, "Burgos y la rebelión del infante Don Sancho", *Boletín de la Real Academia de la História*, cxix (1946), pp. 93-194. For a detailed description of the relations between Burgos and the king on financial matters, see Ruiz, "Burgos: Society and Royal Power", pp. 267-75.

[79] The number of tax exemptions and lavish gifts granted by the kings of Castile to the cathedral of Burgos, the monastery of Las Huelgas and other religious corporations and individuals of the city are too numerous to list here; see Ruiz, "Burgos: Society and Royal Power", ch. 4. A typical donation was that of 60,000 *mrs.* to the monastery of Las Huelgas in 1332: A.C.B., vol. 47, fos. 225-6.

[80] This, like many other topics in Castilian history, deserves further exploration. What consequences did this dependence on the Mesta and the Jews have on the economic development of Castile, and thus of Spain?

[81] On the *fueros* and the Fuero Real, see note 22 above. See also E. N. van Kleffens, *Hispanic Law until the End of the Middle Ages* (Edinburgh, 1968), pp. 288-90.

Another step in the same direction occurred on 26 April 1285 when Sancho IV added a new administrative body to the *concejo*. Up to 1285 the *concejo* had been composed of the *alcaldes*, the *merino*, and the representatives of the parishes, but after Sancho's charter a new institution, the *jurado* (jury), became the dominant body within the city council. According to the edict of 1285 the *jurado* had sole responsibility for farming and collecting taxes, supervised all building projects, including that of the wall, and consulted together with the *concejo* on any decision taken by the city council. Composed of twelve good men and non-noble knights the *jurado* did not supersede the *concejo* but became its main component. Its members conducted inquiries into all cases of murder independently of the *alcaldes*, and only after their investigations had been completed could the *alcaldes* pass judgement. Moreover, the *jurado* regulated prices and enacted local ordinances without the concurrence of the other members of the city council. Although the *jurados* were in theory elected by the *vecinos* (citizens) the king reserved for himself the right of appointing its members whenever he wished or needed to do so.[82] This allowed him greater control over the judicial and financial administration of the city.

After the death of Sancho IV in 1295 the troubled minorities of Ferdinand IV and Alfonso XI provided Burgos and the other cities in Castile with a short respite from royal interference. Yet the weakening of central power inevitably brought to the forefront the twin evils of internal strife and baronial anarchy. The urban centres could not escape this dilemma. The safety and well-being of their ruling oligarchies were best preserved by the rule of a strong king. Because of these hard political facts the cities joined in Hermandades in 1295 and 1315 with the aim of protecting themselves and a weakened crown from the threats and ambitions of the more powerful members of the aristocracy.[83] Although it is true that the period of both these royal minorities witnessed modest gains for the *concejo* of Burgos as it regained, at least temporarily, control over the disputes between Christians and Jews,[84] these gains only lasted until Alfonso XI came

[82] A.M.B., clasif. 2774 (26 Apr. 1285), partially edited in Salvá, *Cosas de la vieja Burgos*, pp. 30-4; confirmed by Alfonso XI: A.M.B., clasif. 2773 (20 Apr. 1332).

[83] This differs somewhat from current interpretations. Nevertheless I believe it to be the only logical explanation of the attitude of the Hermandades towards royal power. I hope to develop this theme at length elsewhere. See L. Suárez Fernández, "Evolución histórica de las hermandades castellanas", *Cuadernos de historia de España*, xvi (1951), pp. 5-78; K. Häbler, "Uber die älteren Hermandades in Kastilien", *Historische Zeitschrift*, liii (1885), pp. 385-401.

[84] In 1293 Sancho IV repealed earlier legislation appointing *alcaldes apartados* for the Moors. This was a minor concession since the Moors, because of their small number and limited economic role in the life of Burgos, had little influence. It was otherwise with the Jews. The *concejo* had to wait until Ferdinand IV's

(cont. on p. 26)

of age in 1322. Alfonso, one of the most effective yet least known rulers of medieval Castile, took immediate steps against the unruly nobility and returned to the traditional royal policy of interference in urban affairs.[85]

In 1327 Alfonso XI ordered the *alcaldes* of the king and a new royal official, the *alguacil* (bailiff), to reside at Burgos on a permanent basis and to hear all the complaints of the citizens against the municipal officials.[86] The question, of course, is who was complaining, and why did the *concejo*, which was after all controlled by the non-noble knights, not only accept royal intervention but ask for it? As the social, political and economic position of the *Caballería Villana* changed within the city, its relationship with other groups was also transformed. With it came rising antagonism between the ruling oligarchy and other sections of the population of Burgos. Signs of unrest and strife appeared in the 1330s and 1340s. The threat to the interests of the non-noble knights was now twofold. First, the long-standing menace of the nobility continued. The nobles and abbots of the surrounding countryside had always opposed the municipal officials' control of small villages around Burgos, and in the mid-fourteenth century some hidalgos began to destroy the vineyards near the city. The city council of Burgos appealed to the king and in 1345 obtained a charter forbidding such abuses.[87] Nevertheless, pressure from above was not, as long as there was a strong central authority, a pressing problem. The real danger came from below.

The growing distinctions between the tax-exempted non-noble knights and the *pecheros* or "good men", as narrowly defined by Carlé, led the *pecheros* to protest against the tax exemption granted to the *Caballería Villana* and against the *caballeros villanos*' duties as collectors of the taxes they themselves did not pay.[88] In Burgos and elsewhere the meetings of the city council became the stage for popular unrest. Fistfights and stoning occurred frequently with disturbances of the public peace spreading throughout the city.

(note 84 cont.)
minority in 1295 to recover jurisdiction over the Jewish *aljama*. However, as soon as Ferdinand IV came of age and regained control of the kingdom, the city lost its short-lived gains. See A.M.B., clasif. 151 (21 May 1293); Benavides, *Memorias de Fernando IV*, ii, pp. 12-13; A.M.B., clasif. 125 (19 July 1295); Benavides, *op. cit.*, ii, p. 396; A.M.B., clasif. 102 (7 Apr. 1304).

85 On Alfonso XI almost nothing has been written. See *Crónica de Alfonso XI*, and the relevant sections in O'Callaghan, *History of Medieval Spain*.

86 A.M.B., clasif. 2697 (18 Aug. 1329), a copy of the 1327 grant (original not extant); confirmed by Alfonso XI in 1336: A.M.B., clasif. 149 (3 June 1336).

87 A.M.B., clasif. 147 (15 May 1345). For further evidence of the municipal antagonism towards the nobility, see *Cortes*, i, p. 177, Medina del Campo (1305); *ibid.*, pp. 449-50, Burgos (1338).

88 For the protests of the *pecheros* against those enjoying tax exemptions — above all, the *caballeros villanos* — see *Cortes*, i, pp. 241-3, Palencia (1313); *ibid.*, pp. 287-8, Burgos (1315); *ibid.*, p. 360, Valladolid (1322); *ibid.*, p. 383, Valladolid (1325).

Descriptions of such events can be read in the royal decree of 25 November 1337 and the severe penalties present in the charter reveal the grave nature of the situation. Alfonso XI laid down that those who drew a sword would lose their hands, while exile from the city for up to two years could be imposed for fistfights, and sixty days in jail for carrying weapons to meetings of the city council.[89] Yet in spite of the measures the violent incidents continued.

On 9 June 1345 Alfonso XI named sixteen non-noble knights to rule the city as a branch of royal government. The action was taken because "to the council come many men to bring discord and obstruction to those things which are ordered and ought to be done for our service and the common good of the city and its vassals". This new municipal institution was known as the *Regimiento*; its members were selected and appointed directly by the king. Its purpose was not to modify the *jurado* or the city council — both of these administrative units were abolished as a result of the establishment of the *Regimiento*. Rather it was to administer the city directly in the name of the king. Together with the two *alcaldes* (four less than had existed in 1338) and the royal *merino*, the *Regimiento* met every Tuesday and Saturday at the tower of Santa María or at the cathedral. At these meetings the members of the newly created administrative body fulfilled all the functions assigned until then to the *concejo*. The *Regimiento* was responsible for all financial matters within the city and its surrounding area *(alfoz)*, the works of the wall, roads, bridges, and the day-to-day administrative and judicial affairs of the city. Moreover, the new ruling body named all the municipal officials within Burgos. The charter even established stiff penalties for those attempting to revive the *concejo*. For their expenses the king allowed a tax of 4,000 *mrs.* to be collected annually within the city; in addition he assigned to the *Regimiento* 12,000 *mrs.* from the tax on the *aljama* (Jewish neighbourhood) of Burgos.[90] All the sixteen citizens of Burgos named to the *Regimiento* were members of the Real Hermandad and, of course, members of the *Caballería Villana*. Four of them, the first four mentioned in the document, belonged to the important Bonifaz-Mathe Pérez de Frías-Camargo family group. The other twelve belonged to prestigious families with mercantile interests and backgrounds in municipal or royal service.[91]

Although the king selected members of the *Caballería Villana* of Burgos to serve in the *Regimiento* he retained other means of control.

[89] A.M.B., clasif. 1388 (25 Nov. 1337).

[90] A.M.B., clasif. 154 (9 May 1345); confirmed by Juan II in 1382: A.M.B., clasif. 1444. A good edition of the document by I. García Rámila is found in *Boletín de la Institución Fernán González*, no. 168 (1967), pp. 435-42.

[91] On the members of the *Regimiento*, see Appendix, pp. 29-32 below.

The two *alcaldes*, Velasco Pérez de Sancthagun (Sahagún) and Velasco García de Valladolid, were neither citizens of Burgos nor members of the Real Hermandad. Their salary of 2,000 *mrs.* per year was, I believe, sufficient in theory to resist the attempts at bribery of the local oligarchs. The *alcaldes* and the royal *merino* were, without a local base, totally dependent on the king and thus constituted a check on any move of the *Regimiento* to act independently of the king.[92]

To summarize, the changes in the institutional structure of the *concejo* of Burgos, and most probably in most of the other Castilian cities,[93] took place within the framework of a rising urban oligarchy. The rapid ascent of the non-noble knights after the tax-exemption charters of 1255 and 1256 from a position of leadership within Burgos to a total monopoly of the economic, political and social life of the city resulted from their close working relationship with the crown. Their changing position *vis-à-vis* other less privileged groups within the city led eventually to open confrontation. By 1345 Burgos had become part of the royal administration. This development occurred with the blessing or, at least, the sympathetic understanding of the non-noble knights. It is therefore incorrect to speak of an alliance between the crown and the cities. Rather, the crucial ties were those which the kings of Castile forged with the ruling urban oligarchies. Royal intervention allowed the *caballeros villanos* to preserve their interests and political power in relation to the rest of the urban population. Although the crown interfered with the political and economic affairs of the city it also provided rewards and order. Members of the *Caballería Villana* of Burgos appeared prominently at the royal court and joined brotherhoods patronized by the king. The city had a special place in the favour of the king,[94] while the royal chancery, often located in Burgos, brought employment and prestige to its citizens. In reality Burgos never had, nor could have had, real independence. Its destiny was closely tied to the health and survival of the monarchy. Under these conditions the *caballeros villanos* made the best possible arrangement for the preservation of their interests. In Burgos the non-noble knights secured social status and economic well-being and sacrificed nothing, since without

[92] A.M.B., clasif. 154 (9 May 1345). In 1350, after Alfonso XI's death, at least one of the members of the *Regimiento* served as *alcalde*; see Appendix, pp. 29-32 below.

[93] A preliminary investigation reveals similar patterns elsewhere; see J. I. Ruiz de la Peña, "Transito del concejo abierto al regimiento en el municipio leonés", in *León y su historia: colección de estudios* (Fuentes y estudios de historia leonesa, i, León, 1969), pp. 301-16; A.M.S., carpeta VII, no. 3, confirmation by Juan I on 5 Nov. 1379; Julio Valdeón Baruque's extraordinary article, "Aspectos de la crisis castellana en la primera mitad del siglo XIV", *Hispania*, no. 111 (1969), pp. 5-24; Julio Valdeón Baruque, *Los conflictos sociales en el reino de Castilla en los siglos XIV y XV* (Madrid, 1975), pp. 73-81.

[94] For employment in the royal service, see Ruiz, "Prosopografía burgalesa", pp. 482-99.

royal backing they would never have risen from the position they originally held. It seems likely that the situation in other Castilian cities was similar.

The kings' effort during the hundred years after the conquest of Seville to impose their authority on the cities was, however, only half successful. The disasters which befell Castile after 1350 — the plague, inflation, civil war and the rise of the Trastamaras — weakened central authority and opened the way for the anarchy of the following years. The patterns of centralization were, nevertheless, not forgotten; they would be resurrected and put to use by Ferdinand and Isabella in their task of organizing Castile as a nation state.

APPENDIX

NON-NOBLE KNIGHTS OF BURGOS NAMED TO THE *REGIMIENTO* 1345

1 *Ramón Bonifaz*. He was *alcalde* of Burgos, at least, in 1331, 1334 and 1338 and a member of the brotherhood of the Real Hermandad. Ramón owned considerable amounts of lands and real estate. His brother, Pedro Bonifaz III, was dean of the cathedral chapter of Burgos, and two other brothers were named to the *Regimiento*. Ramón's sons, Ramón de Prestines, Joan López and Pero Bonifaz IV belonged to the Real Hermandad and lived on the street of Sanct Llorente.[95]

2 *Rostán Bonifaz*. A member of Our Lady of Gamonal in 1305 and of the Real Hermandad, Rostán had been *alcalde* of Burgos in 1311. His son Pero Bonifaz V belonged to the Real Hermandad.[96]

3 *Bernalt de Prestines*. Brother of Ramón, Rostán and the dean Pedro Bonifaz III, Bernalt was *alcalde* of Burgos in 1350 and member of the Real Hermandad. Among his relatives, Giralte of Prestines was an important merchant and *alcalde* of the city in 1338. Ponce de Prestines, a young man, belonged to the Real Hermandad in 1338, and three others with the name Joan Bonifaz, two with residence on the street of Sanct Llorente and the other on the street of Armas, also shared membership in the brotherhood of non-noble knights.[97]

4 *Johan Mathe (Mathe-Pérez de Frías-Bonifaz family)*. Johan Mathe, "fijo de D. Mateo Perez, vezino de Burgos (son of Mateo Pérez, citizen of Burgos)" was the grandson of María Pérez (Sarracín family),

[95] For the Bonifaz, descendants of foreign merchants, and the most powerful family in early fourteenth-century Burgos, see Ruiz, "Prosopografía burgalesa", pp. 476-80.

[96] *Ibid.*

[97] *Ibid.*

his father a cousin of Pedro Sarracín III, dean of the cathedral chapter of Burgos in the second half of the thirteenth century. In 1277 Mateo Pérez was butler of the king *(despensero mayor)* and in documents of 1293-4 he emerges as one of the most important merchants of Burgos. Mateo married a sister of Johan Mathe I from whom our Johan took his name. Johan Mathe II had a brother, García Pérez de Frías, member of Our Lady of Gamonal and of the Real Hermandad, and father of at least three sons, Francisco García de Frías, Ferrán García and Pedro García de Frías. While Johan Mathe II and García Pérez de Frías lived on the street of Sanct Llorente the three brothers resided on the street of Sanct Esteban, probably each at the head of his own household. Returning to Johan Mathe II, he was *alcalde* of Burgos in 1338 and owned a house on the street of Sanct Llorente. Four of his sons, John Mathe III, Pedro Mathe, Pedro Jiménez and Simón Pérez were old enough in 1338 to be members of the Real Hermandad. John lived on the street of Sanct Llorente, Pedro on that of Armas, and the other two on the street of Sanct Esteban. All together, five members of the immediate family appeared in the rolls of Our Lady of Gamonal, thirteen in the lists of the Real Hermandad, a convincing testimony to their influence in the city. A study of the Mathe-Pérez de Frías coat of arms, as shown in the *Libro de la Real Hermandad*, indicates that most of the family members used coats of arms in which the Camargo's wheel and Bonifaz's trimmings were an important part.[98]

5 *Johm Guillén II.* The son of Johm Guillén and Doña Orpesa, he was related to Aparicio Guillén, a descendant of foreign merchants who had settled in Burgos in the late twelfth century, representative of the *concejo* to the royal court in 1263, 1273 and 1275 and *alcalde* of Burgos in 1273. Johm Guillén II was a member of Our Lady of Gamonal and of the Real Hermandad. His brother, Sancho Pérez, was a municipal official in 1307, and another brother, Guillem Fabres, was also named to the *Regimiento.* Together with a third brother, Alfonso Pérez, and a nephew, Johm Guillen III (son of Guillem Fabres), they all belonged to the Real Hermandad.[99]

6 *Guillem Fabres* (see 5 above). *Alcalde* of Burgos in 1338, Alfonso XI named him to the *Regimiento* in 1345. He belonged to Our Lady of Gamonal and to the Real Hermandad. A document of 1313, listing

[98] Gaibrois de Ballesteros, *Historia del reinado de Sancho IV de Castilla*, i, p. cxxvii; "Primitiva regla", p. 163; A.M.B., clasif. 652 (19 Dec. 1313); A.C.B., vol. 50, pt. 1, fo. 43 (9 June 1248); A.C.B., vol. 49, fo. 2 (14 Jan. 1309); *Texto cronológico*, pp. 17-18; A.C.B., vol. 32, fo. 289 (5 June 1302); A.C.B., vol. 42, fo. 223 (15 Dec. 1324); A.C.B., vol. 40, fo. 251 (6 Nov. 1320); Huidobro, "Nuevos datos sobre el almirante Don Ramón Bonifaz y sus descendientes", p. 226; A.M.B., clasif. 154 (9 May 1345).

[99] Ruiz, "Prosopografía burgalesa", p. 483; A.M.B., clasif. 154 (9 May 1345); "Primitiva regla", p. 163; *Texto cronológico*, pp. 16-18.

the important merchants and shopkeepers of the city, describes him as *tendero* (shopkeeper).[100]

7 *Johan Trapaz.* He was probably the son of Guillem Trapaz, representative of the Burgalese merchants to the royal court in 1281, and brother of Pedro Trapaz, official of the Hermandad of 1315. Johan was a member of the Real Hermandad and lived on the street of Sanct Llorente. There were two other members of the Trapaz family in the Real Hermandad, Ferrán Trapaz and Pero Pérez who was married to the daughter of Pedro Trapaz.[101]

8 *Fernán García de Arcelza.* Member of the Real Hermandad, Fernán García de Arcelza owned a house in the street of Sanct Llorente. Another member of the family, Joan García de Arcelza, also belonged to the Real Hermandad and resided on the street of Sanct Esteban.[102]

9 *Diego Martínez de St. Domingo de Silos.* A merchant in Bruges in 1312, Diego Martínez was related to Domingo Martínez de Santo Domingo and Ferrand Martínez, both merchants and municipal officials. Diego and his brother, Gonzalo Martínez, belonged to the Real Hermandad.[103]

10 *Gil González.* His father, Gil González, was a royal official in 1293-4. His brother, Sancho González, was *alcalde* of the city in 1305 and member of Our Lady of Gamonal. Gil was a member of the Real Hermandad and lived on the street of Sanct Llorente.[104]

11 *Miguel García de Gorges.* A member of a family with long-standing mercantile interests, Miguel was a member of the Real Hermandad and lived on the street of Sanct Llorente. His brother, Alfonso García de Gorges, and his three nephews belonged to the Real Hermandad.[105]

12 *Lope Pérez.* His father, Lope Pérez I, was a royal official in 1293-4, a procurator of the *concejo* of Burgos in 1295, *alcalde* of the king in Burgos and notary major of Castile in 1302, *alcalde* of the city in 1309, and member of the *jurado* of the realm in 1310. His son was a member of the Real Hermandad and named to the *Regimiento*

[100] Ruiz, "Prosopografía burgalesa", p. 483; A.M.B., clasif. 652 (19 Dec. 1313); A.M.B., clasif. 154 (9 May 1345); "Primitiva regla", p. 163; *Texto cronológico*, pp. 16-17.

[101] Ruiz, "Prosopografía burgalesa", p. 493; A.M.B., clasif. 154 (9 May 1345); "Primitiva regla", p. 163; *Texto cronológico*, p. 17; A.C.B., vol. 44, fo. 5 (18 Jan. 1324).

[102] A.M.B., clasif. 154 (9 May 1345); *Texto cronológico*, pp. 17-18.

[103] Ruiz, "Prosopografía burgalesa", pp. 486-7; A.M.B., clasif. 154 (9 May 1345); *Texto cronológico*, p. 17.

[104] Ruiz, "Prosopografía burgalesa", p. 492; A.M.B., clasif. 154 (9 May 1345); *Texto cronológico*, p. 17.

[105] A.M.B., clasif. 652 (19 Dec. 1313); A.M.B., clasif. 154 (9 May 1345); *Texto cronológico*, pp. 17-18.

by Alfonso XI. Lope Pérez II was *alcalde* of Burgos in 1334 and 1338.[106]

13 *Simón González.* Simón González owned property, including two vineyards, in Madrigal del Monte. A member of the Real Hermandad with residence on the street of Sanct Esteban, he must have been a money-lender or quite wealthy. Simón lent 94 gold *ecus* to the monastery of Santo Domingo de Silos.[107]

14 *Alfonso Sánchez de Perilla.* A member of Our Lady of Gamonal and the Real Hermandad, Alfonso was *alcalde* of Burgos in 1338. He lived on Huerto del Rey, and his brother, García Sánchez de Perilla, also a member of the Real Hermandad lived on the street of Sanct Llorente.[108]

15 *Gonzalo Gil.* Gonzalo Gil was *cocinero mayor del rey* (cook of the king), which was probably an honorary title rather than his occupation. In 1329 he bought several houses in Burgos for 6,000 *mrs.* He was a member of the Real Hermandad and lived on Huerto del Rey.[109]

16 *Juan Ruiz de San Cristobal (Sanchester).* Member of the Real Hermandad, Juan Ruiz was related to the Sanchester family, active in trade and municipal administration in the late thirteenth century.[110]

[106] Ruiz, "Prosopografía burgalesa", p. 490; A.M.B., clasif. 1784 (2 Apr. 1334); A.M.B., clasif. 154 (9 May 1345); *Texto cronológico*, p. 18.

[107] A.C.B., vol. 30, fo. 585 (20 Mar. 1332); A.C.B., vol. 30, fo. 589 (22 Mar. 1332); A.C.B., vol. 30, fo. 588 (22 Apr. 1333); A.C.B., vol. 30, fo. 587 (23 Apr. 1333); A.M.B., clasif. 154 (9 May 1345); *Texto cronológico*, p. 18; *Recueil des chartes de l'abbaye de Silos*, ed. Marius Férotin (Paris, 1897), p. 418.

[108] "Primitiva regla", p. 163; *Texto cronológico*, pp. 16-18; A.M.B., clasif. 154 (9 May 1345).

[109] A.C.B., vol. 37, fo. 500 (1 Sept. 1329); *Texto cronológico*, p. 16; A.M.B., clasif. 154 (9 May 1345).

[110] Ruiz, "Prosopografía burgalesa", p. 482; *Texto cronológico*, p. 16; A.M.B., clasif. 154 (9 May 1345).

VIII

EXPANSION ET CHANGEMENT : LA CONQUÊTE DE SÉVILLE ET LA SOCIÉTÉ CASTILLANE (1248-1350)

L'expansion territoriale et la confrontation d'une société avec de nouvelles frontières sont des problèmes qui, de longue date, ont attiré l'attention des historiens avant même qu'en 1893 Frederick Jackson Turner ouvrît le débat avec *The significance of the frontier in American history* [1]. Chaque frontière présente ses particularités et chaque nation ou entité politique règle à sa manière les problèmes d'expansion, de population et de repeuplement. Qu'arriverait-il toutefois si un pays ouvrait de nouvelles frontières alors que sa population est en déclin ou stagnante ? Quel fardeau représenterait pour la structure sociale, économique et structurelle d'une nation ou d'un royaume, une expansion prématurée ou se soldant par un échec ? Y a-t-il un rapport entre expansion avortée et crise ? Sans toutefois accorder une importance exagérée à cette dernière question, je voudrais, dans les pages qui suivent, examiner une expansion particulière — l'expansion castillane dans les plaines d'Andalousie au XIIIe siècle et l'impact de ces conquêtes sur la structure économique, sociale et institutionnelle du royaume.

« Le peuple de Castille, écrit don Claudio Sánchez Albornoz, a été pendant des siècles un peuple marqué par un esprit de frontière. » On a vu dans la frontière le catalyseur des libertés castillanes, les racines de la mentalité du Quichotte ainsi que toute une série d'autres caractéristiques qui dépassent le but et les limites de cet article [2]. La Castille mena convenablement son expansion territoriale du IXe au début du XIIIe siècle, mais lorsque l'avance rapide de ses frontières n'alla plus de pair avec une croissance proportionnelle de la population, les institutions existantes se trouvèrent soumises à une grave pression économique, politique et sociale [3]. Au lieu d'être source de libertés, les frontières ont peut-être engendré l'oppression et les crises. En effet, c'est au XIIIe siècle, période d'expansion territoriale rapide, que l'histoire de la Castille, et donc celle de toute l'Espagne, se coula dans un moule dont elle n'est pas encore vraiment sortie.

Ma première proposition est que l'expansion en Andalousie au XIIIe siècle fut une cause majeure de la crise économique, sociale et institutionnelle qui affecta la Castille pour la plus grande partie du siècle qui suivit la chute de Séville en 1248. Ma seconde hypothèse est que ces crises aboutirent à une restructuration économique, sociale et institutionnelle du royaume de Castille, et, dans une large mesure, sont à l'origine de modes de développement dysfonctionnels, ainsi que d'une nouvelle mentalité en Castille et, par la suite, en Espagne. C'est seulement en comprenant les changements qui prirent place entre 1248 et 1350 que l'on peut saisir pleinement la structure sous-jacente de l'histoire espagnole et expliquer certains des traits uniques de son développement.

En 1248, après un court siège, les armées de Ferdinand III (roi de Castille de 1217 à 1252, et de León de 1230 à 1252) placèrent les étendards des châteaux et des lions sur les murs fortifiés de Séville. Les victoires du saint roi sur les *taifas* d'al-Andalus et la conquête de la riche vallée du Guadalquivir n'avaient rien de surprenant. La longue marche de la Reconquête vers la mer, jalonnée par la prise de Tolède en 1085, le triomphe décisif des armées chrétiennes à Las Navas de Tolosa en 1212, et la conquête de Cordoue en 1236, avait finalement apporté en récompense au royaume de Castille et León, la riche plaine andalouse et Séville, capitale opulente et de grande importance stratégique [4]. 1248 est depuis longtemps considéré comme l'un des tournants de la Reconquête et de l'histoire castillane. Dans la deuxième moitié du XIIIe siècle, les Maures cessèrent de jouer un rôle important sur l'échiquier politique de la péninsule Ibérique ; et aux yeux des contemporains, il restait essentiellement à résorber les vestiges affaiblis des royaumes islamiques d'Espagne jadis fiers et puissants. Cependant, au cours des cent années qui suivirent, la Castille fut déchirée par des problèmes internes, et à l'exception d'un bref déploiement d'activité dans les années 1340, aucune incursion importante ne fut faite en territoire maure jusqu'au règne de Ferdinand et d'Isabelle. La Reconquête, qui depuis Las Navas de Tolosa avait pris un formidable élan, cessa brusquement.

Récemment, les historiens espagnols ont jeté une nouvelle lumière sur les conquêtes du milieu du XIIIe siècle. Au lieu de renouveler les tributs à Saint-Ferdinand, aux gloires de la Castille et au triomphe de la Foi, des spécialistes comme García de Cortázar, Julio González, Sánchez Albornoz, Sobrequés Vidal, Ubieto, Valdeón Baruque et Vicens Vives ont attiré l'attention sur les bouleversements démographiques, économiques et sociaux qui ont suivi l'ouverture de l'Andalousie à l'implantation chrétienne. Ces historiens conviennent presque unanimement que l'expansion vers le sud contribua à créer les difficultés qui empoisonnèrent la vie économique et sociale de la Castille [5]. Aucun d'entre eux, cependant, n'est allé au-delà de la simple mention des problèmes engendrés par la conquête de l'Andalousie, ni n'a répondu aux questions implicites soulevées par leurs analyses concernant l'influence générale des conquêtes. En outre, ils ont également omis de souligner l'importance qu'eurent les cent années consécutives à la prise de Séville pour le développement ultérieur de la Castille, donc de ce qui est maintenant l'Espagne.

L'histoire de la Castille à la fin du XIIIe siècle et au début du XIVe a été négligée jusqu'à une date assez récente. Les travaux originaux de Vicens Vives et d'autres ont proposé un exposé global des lignes de force sociales et économiques de la période ; mais en donnant une interprétation trop simplifiée de problèmes complexes, ces études ont en fait entravé le développement d'une recherche plus spécifique. L'histoire politique ne se présente guère mieux. Des quatre rois qui gouvernèrent la Castille, entre 1252 et 1350, deux seulement ont reçu quelque attention, Alphonse X (1252-1284) et Sanche IV (1284-1296), et ce par les soins de deux biographes ayant pour eux des sympathies manifestes, Antonio Ballesteros y Beretta et Mercedes Gaibrois de Ballesteros [6]. Pour Ferdinand IV

(1296-1312), nous possédons une édition de sa chronique et un recueil diplomatique édité par Antonio de Benavides en 1860. Quant à Alphonse XI (1312-1350), un des rois les plus importants et les plus intéressants de la Castille médiévale, il n'a encore fait l'objet d'aucune étude approfondie [7]. Le fait que les historiens aient négligé le développement de la Castille pendant le siècle qui a suivi la chute de Séville rend possible une interprétation nouvelle que les progrès des études économiques et sociales rendent, eux, nécessaires.

I. Une désorganisation démographique et économique

La prise de Séville, apogée de la reconquête de la région andalouse, fut beaucoup plus qu'une simple victoire militaire. La chute de la ville ouvrait à l'implantation des Castillans la vallée du Guadalquivir, riche, bien exploitée, et désormais relativement peu peuplée du fait de la guerre. Pour exploiter ces terres, on eut recours à des journaliers des régions productrices de blé de la Castille du Nord, ce qui eut un effet décisif sur le développement à long terme de l'économie castillane. Il est également important de noter que la distribution des territoires andalous parmi la noblesse castillane augmenta considérablement la puissance de celle-ci vis-à-vis des paysans libres, et tout particulièrement, vis-à-vis de la couronne. Pendant les cent années à venir, le roi allait se voir obligé de rechercher le soutien de la grande bourgeoisie pour maintenir son autorité. Vers 1350, un caractère fondamental des institutions et des traditions politiques est acquis, qui, à quelques variantes près, restera typique de la Castille et de l'Espagne jusqu'à notre époque. Il y eut aussi, bien sûr, d'autres facteurs importants qui influencèrent la transformation de la société castillane après 1248 : des changements climatiques, sans doute, le conflit armé entre Alphonse X et une noblesse frondeuse à la fin des années 1260 et au début des années 1270, ses guerres avec son fils Sanche (le futur Sanche IV) en 1281-1283, et les minorités turbulentes de Ferdinand IV et d'Alphonse XI [8]. Sans ignorer l'impact global de ces événements — qui mériteraient chacun une analyse particulière — je voudrais restreindre mon étude aux conséquences de la conquête de Séville. J'espère pouvoir montrer bientôt comment ces autres éléments influencèrent et modifièrent les conditions créées par l'expansion en Andalousie [9].

La conquête de Séville n'était pas la première annexion territoriale de la Castille. En 1085, après la conquête de Tolède, la Castille accrut sa population d'un nombre considérable de mozarabes (chrétiens ayant adopté la culture musulmane) à sa population [10]. En revanche, les annexions du milieu du XIIIe siècle, bien qu'elles eussent presque doublé le territoire de la Castille, n'amenèrent pas une augmentation importante de population. Après que Las Navas de Tolosa eut donné la suprématie aux chrétiens, la plupart des Maures furent sommairement chassés des villes (Cordoue, 1236 ; Séville, 1248 ; Jaén, 1249), lesquelles furent repeuplées de chrétiens. Qui plus est, après la rébellion mudejare en 1263, les Maures furent également chassés des régions rurales [11]. La couronne de Castille entra en possession de terres riches, mais pratiquement vides, ce qui entraîna un important déplacement de population.

Attirée par ces territoires nouvellement ouverts et par le butin mis à la disposition des conquérants — métaux précieux, maisons et terres que Ferdinand III et surtout Alphonse X distribuèrent aux armées victorieuses — une masse considérable émigra des plaines du nord vers l'Andalousie [12]. Bien que ces hommes représentassent tous les niveaux de la société, ce furent les *ricos hombres* (magnats, appartenant à l'élite de la haute aristocratie), les Ordres militaires (Santiago, Alcantara, Calatrava), ainsi que les établissements monastiques importants et les chapitres cathédraux qui reçurent la part du lion dans la répartition des terres nouvellement acquises [13].

Avec la noblesse vinrent des journaliers, des paysans libres, de petits propriétaires et même des citadins de Vieille-Castille ; tous étaient attirés par les plus hauts salaires offerts dans le sud, par un climat meilleur, et par les nouvelles possibilités économiques créées par l'ouverture à la transhumance des pâturages d'Andalousie. Notons à cette occasion que, bien que la migration annuelle du bétail ait daté de l'époque préromaine, la conquête de l'Andalousie en favorisa le développement et la rendit beaucoup plus profitable. Le décret de 1273 d'Alphonse X organisant la Mesta montre bien les changements survenus dans l'économie castillane et l'échec des efforts de repopulation [14]. Si les plaines du sud s'étaient vues dotées d'une population suffisante et avaient été soumises à une exploitation agricole de grande envergure, il y aurait eu une résistance à la transhumance. Mais l'existence de grands espaces, presque inhabités, facilita leur conversion en pâturages.

La désorganisation démographique et la dépopulation partielle du nord [15] eurent une incidence directe sur la production vivrière. La Castille du Nord était traditionnellement — elle l'est toujours — le grenier à blé de la Péninsule ; dans la deuxième moitié du XIIIe siècle, la production de grain dans les plaines septentrionales diminua à mesure que les champs étaient abandonnés. Cette réduction de la surface arable frappa une région qui souffrait déjà habituellement de maigres récoltes et de mauvaises conditions climatiques. Pénuries et famines en résultèrent [16]. Même si la population avait diminué, des pressions sur la production de grain existante devaient se faire sentir, car l'Andalousie, bien que cultivant le blé et l'orge, avait une économie orientée essentiellement sur la production de vin, d'huile d'olive et de bétail [17]. Après l'expulsion des Maures, le nombre des colons fut insuffisant pour maintenir le même niveau de production ; et comme les techniques agricoles des Maures étaient supérieures à celles des chrétiens, la conquête et sa conséquence — l'expulsion des Maures d'Andalousie — bouleversèrent le schéma habituel d'irrigation, de culture et de récolte. On a aussi des preuves de migration en sens inverse (retour au nord) lorsque les conditions de vie en Andalousie s'avérèrent moins prometteuses qu'on ne se l'imaginait. Les paysans castillans du nord étaient habitués à un certain mode d'agriculture — pratiquement une agriculture de subsistance, concentrée sur la production des seules céréales, complétée par la culture de vignes et de jardins en fonction des besoins liturgiques et alimentaires essentiels. Peut-être s'adaptèrent-ils mal au mode de production du sud, axé sur l'exportation et recourant à des techniques agricoles et travaillant des sols assez différents [18]. Dans le nord, les changements climatiques et les famines du début du XIVe siècle, la croissance des exportations de laine après 1350, et la nouvelle puissance de la guilde de la transhumance, la Mesta, portèrent un coup sérieux à l'agriculture et à la structure économique traditionnelle de la Vieille-Castille [19].

Ces changements brutaux furent désastreux, et les signes de bouleversement économique et social ne tardèrent pas à apparaître. La crise de la production vivrière et les pénuries qui suivirent la chute de Séville contribuèrent à faire monter rapidement le taux d'inflation. Les métaux précieux pris en butin ainsi que la consommation accrue des classes supérieures ont sans doute contribué à la poussée inflationniste. En outre, l'augmentation des salaires, nécessaire pour attirer les paysans en Andalousie, contribua elle aussi à la spirale inflationniste. En Castille, non seulement les prix des produits alimentaires, mais ceux de la plupart des marchandises augmentèrent immédiatement après 1248 à un rythme extrêmement rapide. Les preuves limitées dont nous disposons montrent que le prix du minerai de fer — produit d'exportation d'importance vitale pendant les cent années qui suivirent — passa de 2,5 *maravedis* (mrs) le quintal en 1268 à 12,5 mrs en 1294. Il semble que les régions productrices de fer du golfe de Biscaye aient été également touchées par le déplacement de population vers le sud. Le prix du drap, importé presque exclusivement de Flandre, augmenta de manière spectaculaire. L'*escarlata,* un drap de luxe, se vendait 4 mrs la *vara* (presque l'équivalent d'un mètre) en 1268, et 50 mrs en 1298. On peut donner des exemples semblables pour le drap de qualité plus ordinaire et pour d'autres marchandises [20].

Si les informations dont nous disposons pour la région de Burgos sont représentatives du reste de la Castille — et elles devraient l'être — le prix des maisons, de la terre, des droits de mouture, des vignes et des jardins augmenta considérablement après 1248. Les documents existant dans les archives de la cathédrale de Burgos montrent que 174 transactions immobilières eurent lieu entre 1200 et 1249. Beaucoup d'entre elles concernaient des échanges de terres en plus des paiements en argent, ces derniers montant en moyenne à 99,51 mrs par transaction. Entre 1250 et 1299, le nombre de transactions tomba à 78 — ce déclin étant dû au retrait de l'acheteur actif qu'était auparavant le chapitre de Burgos ; on continua toutefois à échanger les terres dans des proportions en gros semblables à celles des cinquante années précédentes, mais la somme d'argent utilisée dans chaque échange s'éleva en moyenne à 884,35 mrs. Au cours des cinquante et une années qui suivirent, 1300-1350, le nombre des transactions fut de 146 et la somme d'argent impliquée dans chaque échange atteignit en moyenne 1 293,40 mrs [21]. On pourrait voir dans cette évolution la preuve d'une forte demande de terre, donc d'une pression démographique, mais on note, par ailleurs, un déclin général du nombre des transactions. Qui plus est, l'augmentation du prix des maisons et de la terre fut le résultat, du moins dans la région de Burgos, des efforts déployés par l'oligarchie urbaine pour élargir et consolider ses propriétés autour de la ville. Chaque fois qu'une terre était achetée ou vendue, son prix dépendait des possibilités de mise en œuvre qu'elle offrait. Très rares étaient les transactions qui n'incluaient pas, outre la terre, des références à la capacité de production, au matériel agricole, aux maisons et aux paysans qui y travaillaient. C'est la raréfaction de la main-d'œuvre plus que celle de la terre qui constituait le véritable problème.

Si la seconde moitié du XIIIe siècle fut une période difficile, le XIVe n'apporta aucune amélioration. L'information dont nous disposons contient des lacunes, ce qui ne permet pas de présenter des statistiques précises concernant l'évolution des prix. De plus, on doit prendre en considération les conséquences de la Peste noire sur l'ensemble de l'économie après 1348. Les poules qui valaient 5 *dineros* (d) en 1348, se vendaient 16 d en 1351. La *fanega* (unité de mesure équivalent maintenant à un peu plus d'un boisseau et demi) de blé se vendait de 1,5 à 2 mrs en 1293, 20 mrs en 1331-1333, et 25 mrs en 1345, ceci dans une période pourtant antérieure à la peste [22]. Le prix minimum des chevaux de bataille (ceux qu'utilisaient les chevaliers non nobles des villes) passa de 30 mrs en 1256 (les meilleurs chevaux coûtaient 200 mrs) à 800 mrs en 1338 [23]. Cette augmentation du prix des produits alimentaires et des autres marchandises se fit sentir en Castille trente-cinq ans au moins avant l'apparition d'une inflation rapide dans les autres pays occidentaux.

L'effet dévastateur de l'inflation sur le développement économique de la Castille ne laissa guère le choix à la Couronne quant aux mesures qui s'imposaient. Alphonse X tenta d'enrayer l'inflation galopante en imposant un contrôle des prix et des salaires en 1252, 1258 et 1268, mais sa politique fut un échec, et se solda par les véhémentes complaintes des procureurs des villes devant les Cortes [24]. Le malaise général qui affecte la structure fondamentale de la société castillane après la chute de Séville est sensible dans les nombreuses pétitions que les procureurs urbains présentèrent aux rois de Castille aux réunions des Cortes. Les représentants municipaux réclamaient l'exonération d'impôts parce que la terre était pauvre et désertée [25] ; dans bien des cas, par exemple à Santander et à San Vicente de la Barquera, le nombre des citoyens inscrits sur les rôles d'impôt était désormais si réduit que le roi était disposé à abaisser le quota des contribuables *(pecheros)* [26]. La législation antisémite et les pétitions présentées aux Cortes visaient à affaiblir la puissance économique des juifs ; l'annulation des dettes des chrétiens envers ces derniers trahit un ressentiment croissant contre les minorités religieuses pendant cette période de crise [27].

L'altération de la monnaie est un autre signe de la crise castillane. Tout d'abord, en frappant une monnaie affaiblie, la couronne montrait ses difficultés financières et son besoin de capital liquide. En second lieu, bien qu'à court terme la frappe de pièces dévaluées représentât un gain pour le roi, cette politique accentua, à long terme, le déséquilibre économique dans le royaume. Les chroniqueurs contemporains d'Alphonse X réagirent avec colère à la frappe de pièces dévaluées, voyant dans cette pratique l'une des causes principales de l'inflation montante. Sans grand succès, les représentants municipaux aux Cortes ne cessèrent de demander des réformes monétaires et fiscales [28].

Ces crises affectèrent un pays qui n'était en mesure d'en surmonter aucune, même prise séparément, encore moins de les affronter en bloc. La Castille médiévale était un pays sous-développé, au sens où les économistes utilisent le terme aujourd'hui, et ce sous-développement fut accentué par la conquête de Séville [29]. L'expansion en Andalousie, apportant vin, huile d'olive, peaux et autres matières premières exportables, n'encouragea pas la production intérieure de produits finis.

La plupart des historiens des débuts de l'Europe moderne ont décrit et accepté le retard de l'Espagne sans en rechercher les raisons dans son passé. Le sous-développement commercial et industriel de l'Espagne impériale remonte originellement au passé médiéval de la Castille. Dès le XIIᵉ siècle, les royaumes de Castille et de León — tout comme la France et l'Angleterre de l'époque — exportèrent des matières premières et importèrent des produits finis. Vers le milieu du XIIIᵉ siècle, alors que l'Angleterre et la France commençaient à trouver des alternatives économiques, la Castille resta bloquée dans un modèle de sous-développement. Le drap de qualité importé de Flandre causait une prodigieuse hémorragie financière [30], d'autant plus que les importations ne se limitaient pas aux articles de luxe mais incluaient des biens divers, comme des boutons, des hameçons, des chapeaux, des miroirs, des objets religieux, des anneaux, des vases, des dés, des aiguilles, des peignes en os, des cure-dents et des produits alimentaires [31]. Les exportations castillanes étaient essentiellement le minerai de fer, la laine, la peau, l'huile d'olive, le bétail (surtout les chevaux quand leur vente n'était pas interdite par décret royal), exceptionnellement le grain, le cordouan, le vin, le cumin et les amandes [32]. La fragile structure économique de la Castille était évidemment sujette aux crises.

Dans la Castille du Nord, la classe marchande était pour l'essentiel dominée par les descendants de marchands étrangers qui s'étaient établis dans les villes le long de la route de Compostelle à la fin du XIIe siècle. A Séville, les marchands italiens dominèrent le commerce avec l'étranger après 1248 [33]. Comme le gros des marchandises importées consistait en textiles de Flandre, produit extrêmement rentable, l'élite marchande de la Castille septentrionale et les négociants étrangers des villes d'Andalousie n'avaient pas intérêt à fabriquer des produits manufacturés ni à diversifier leur commerce [34]. Leurs profits dérivaient essentiellement de leurs ventes à la haute aristocratie, classe très restreinte et très fortunée. Alors que les marchands français et anglais, soit de leur propre initiative, soit à l'instigation de la Couronne s'assuraient une base solide pour le développement futur de leur commerce — pensons, par exemple, au programme établi par Édouard Ier et Édouard III pour protéger le commerce et encourager les artisans à venir en Angleterre, ou à la confiscation du capital étranger par Philippe le Bel en France —, la bourgeoisie castillane, elle, manquait de l'élément dynamique qui allait bientôt transformer les couches bourgeoises au nord des Pyrénées. Pris au piège de l'étroitesse de leurs propres intérêts, découragés par une politique royale défavorable, les marchands des XVIe et XVIIe siècles répéteront, à peu de chose près, les expériences des marchands du XIIIe et du XIVe siècle.

II. Vers un nouveau régime foncier

La conquête de Séville accéléra la transformation du régime foncier. En distribuant la terre après la conquête de Séville, la Couronne octroya alors systématiquement de larges lots à la haute noblesse et aux Ordres militaires, politique qui avait déjà été pratiquée lors de l'établissement en Estrémadure [35]. Mais les plaines d'Estrémadure n'étaient pas aussi riches que celles d'Andalousie et n'avaient pas le potentiel économique du bassin du Guadalquivir. C'est pourquoi, la mise en place par les chrétiens du système des latifundia en Andalousie, région où existaient, traditionnellement de vastes propriétés remontant à l'époque romaine, eut des répercussions sociales, économiques et politiques immédiates, ce qui ne fut pas le cas en Estrémadure. C'est au milieu du XIIIe siècle qu'est esquissée l'organisation foncière qui, en Andalousie, donnera naissance au prolétariat rural sans terre d'une part, aux vastes propriétés terriennes *(cortijos)* d'autre part, structure qui domine aujourd'hui la vie rurale d'une bonne partie de l'Espagne méridionale.

Bien qu'en Castille septentrionale de grands domaines aient été formés bien avant 1248 [36] un nombre considérable de paysans libres y restaient propriétaires de leurs terres. Ces petits propriétaires avaient joué un rôle important dans la Reconquête et dans l'élaboration de la société castillane. Les sources de Burgos montrent que bon nombre de ces paysans libres vendirent leurs terres après

1248 [37]. Lorsqu'ils les vendirent dans le Nord pour émigrer en Andalousie, comme ce fut le cas à Burgos et dans d'autres secteurs de la Castille septentrionale, ils n'emportèrent pas avec eux leur régime foncier de franc alleu.

Pourquoi ces paysans émigrèrent-ils en Andalousie dans des conditions apparemment défavorables ? Pratiquée à petite échelle, l'agriculture du Nord n'était pas plus rentable au XIIIe siècle qu'elle ne l'est au XXe, en raison d'une topographie et d'un climat difficiles sur les sols généralement pauvres du plateau castillan [38]. Émigrer vers le sud signifiait sans doute rejoindre un prolétariat rural privé de terres ; mais la perspective d'un climat meilleur et de salaires plus élevés compensait la perte de l'indépendance. L'absence d'information concernant la situation réelle en Andalousie encourageait peut-être aussi de faux espoirs. En outre, les chartes d'exemption d'impôts pour les chevaliers non nobles des villes de Castille du Nord comportaient certaines concessions économiques qui pouvaient attirer les petits paysans libres. Elles exemptaient ainsi d'impôts tous les travailleurs agricoles au service de chevaliers non nobles et ne possédant pas de terre d'une valeur supérieure à 100 mrs. Il se peut bien que des gains réels et immédiats, même de courte durée au sud, se soient avérés plus attrayants que la perspective incertaine de gains à long terme au nord.

Quelles qu'en soient les raisons, une redistribution générale de la propriété eut lieu et, sauf le cas des petits propriétaires et à l'exception de quelques particularités de distribution comme dans la région de Jaén, dans la majeure partie de l'Andalousie la terre se retrouva concentrée entre les mains d'un petit nombre de magnats *(ricos hombres),* des Ordres militaires et de divers monastères et chapitres importants [39].

Ce nouveau type d'organisation foncière affecta la Vieille-Castille presqu'autant que l'Andalousie. A la fin du XIIIe et pendant le XIVe siècle, on vit se former dans le nord de vastes domaines [40]. Les magnats étaient les principaux bénéficiaires, mais dans les régions de Burgos, Avila, Ségovie, etc., l'oligarchie urbaine se bâtit également de grosses propriétés rurales au cours du siècle qui suivit la conquête de Séville [41].

III. Les conséquences politiques et institutionnelles

L'acquisition de nouvelles terres dans le *Repartimiento* de Séville et dans toute l'Andalousie eut pour conséquence directe l'augmentation spectaculaire de la fortune des *ricos hombres* et des Ordres militaires que certains de ces magnats contrôlaient également. Cette nouvelle richesse vint aux nobles sous différentes formes : lingots d'or et d'argent, bijoux et objets précieux enlevés aux Maures comme butin ; loyers des maisons et des terres obtenues en partage. La couronne reçut, elle aussi, de ses victoires, quelques bénéfices immédiats [42], mais ils furent éphémères. Possédant de vastes étendues de terres, mais sans la main-d'œuvre nécessaire pour les exploiter ou les défendre, Alphonse X n'eut d'autre recours que de céder la plupart de ces territoires nouvellement conquis aux magnats et aux Ordres militaires, les uns et les autres capables de protéger la terre. Le roi conserva quelques domaines, mais relativement modestes en nombre et en dimensions.

Pourquoi le roi céda-t-il la plus grande partie de la terre au lieu de la garder sous juridiction directe de la couronne ? La politique d'Alphonse X fut très différente de celle de Ferdinand III. Le saint roi n'avait entrepris qu'un *Repartimiento* limité bien qu'il eût disposé pour ce faire de quatre années après la conquête. La plus grande partie des donations en terres eut lieu en 1252, immédiatement après l'accession d'Alphonse X à la royauté. C'est vraisemblablement l'estimation qu'il fit de la situation politique du moment qui poussa le roi à accorder de larges concessions aux magnats. Il avait été hissé sur le pavois par les *ricos hombres*, alors même que son frère Henri avait refusé de reconnaître ses droits sur les trônes de Castille et de León. Les deux royaumes n'avaient été réunis qu'en 1226, et en 1252, une nouvelle séparation de la Castille et du León pouvait ne pas sembler impossible. Ces concessions furent sans doute jugées nécessaires au maintien de la paix [43].

Outre les circonstances politiques, ces donations manifestaient la propension particulière d'Alphonse X aux concessions et aux cadeaux extravagants — qui lui valurent d'ailleurs d'être âprement critiqué par ses contemporains. Comme le suggère la *Crónica de Alfonso X*, le roi surpassa son père en libéralité, cédant la terre par « bonté de cœur », mais aussi pour « s'assurer le service des magnats » [44]. La chronique relate également que les *ricos hombres* s'opposèrent aux présents excessifs faits par Alphonse X au roi du Portugal. Quelles qu'en aient été les motivations, les décisions politiques du roi lors du *Repartimiento* eurent une grande influence sur l'issue de son règne. Parmi les autres aspects malheureux de la politique d'Alphonse X, mentionnons encore sa politique monétaire. Il prit une mesure à courte vue en décidant de frapper, avec le métal précieux pris aux Maures, une quantité limitée de *maravedis* d'argent en 1258 [45]. Mais la quantité de pièces frappées n'était pas suffisante pour subvenir au besoin existant de monnaie saine. Leur seul effet fut peut-être de contribuer à affaiblir encore la monnaie dévaluée émise antérieurement.

Il convient de souligner toutefois que les magnats n'usèrent pas de leur richesse nouvellement acquise à de seules fins politiques. La noblesse castillane était connue comme l'une des aristocraties les plus dépensières d'Europe, et cet argent autorisa de plus grands excès encore. Les magnats en visite à la cour du jeune Ferdinand IV se voyaient allouer par la couronne une pension de 2 000 mrs pour leurs dépenses quotidiennes, somme énorme si l'on considère le coût de la vie en Castille à la fin du XIIIe siècle. En 1293, la Castille importa près d'un million de *maravedis* de drap fin par quatre ports du golfe de Biscaye [46].

Mais cet apport de richesses nouvelles accrut aussi le pouvoir politique de la haute noblesse face à la relative faiblesse du roi. Le tribut *(parias)* que les rois des *taifas* (Cordoue et Séville) avaient à payer à la couronne de Castille diminua énormément. L'auteur anonyme de la chronique d'Alphonse X, critique hostile, se répand en éloges sur l'époque de Ferdinand III où la Castille recevait un tribut annuel de 600 000 mrs, pour se lamenter ensuite sur l'effondrement de ce revenu. Comme il le souligne, ce tribut était tombé, sous Alphonse X, à 250 000 mrs, soit une diminution de 58 %. Les sommes ainsi perdues sur le revenu des terres distribuées dans le *Repartimiento* furent en grande partie récupérées par la noblesse et par les Ordres militaires, qui recueillirent, pour l'essentiel, les profits de la conquête.

La faiblesse économique de la couronne fut aggravée encore par l'ambitieux programme de centralisation et d'extension du pouvoir royal qu'Alphonse X entreprit de manière très inopportune. Le roi prit l'offensive en octroyant le *Fuero Real* (une charte municipale) en guise de *fuero* local à la plupart des villes de

Castille, substituant ainsi aux vestiges fragmentés et peu pratiques du droit coutumier et du système juridique wisigoth (*fueros* en Castille, *Fuero Juzgo* en León), une juridiction uniforme fondée sur le droit romain [47].

Bien que certains historiens, derrière Ballesteros, aient indiqué qu'Alphonse X avait dû retirer le *Fuero Real* sous la pression aristocratique et urbaine, l'exemple de Burgos et d'autres montrent que le *Fuero Real* resta en vigueur dans certaines villes pendant le siècle qui suivit, prouvant ainsi que quelques progrès avaient été réalisés sur le chemin de la centralisation [48]. Alphonse X n'eut pas le même succès avec les *Siete Partidas*, un code juridique qu'il mit en œuvre pour essayer de soumettre l'ensemble du royaume, y compris les magnats, à un système de législation centralisé, renforçant ainsi la position du monarque par rapport aux autres groupes sociaux. Les *Partidas* ne prirent pas force de loi avant 1348, et le programme d'Alphonse X n'aboutit qu'à cristalliser l'opposition d'une noblesse déjà indisposée par l'échec de la politique économique du roi et par sa quête futile de la couronne impériale [49].

L'offensive juridique d'Alphonse X parachevait le programme politique du roi et elle provoqua une âpre lutte avec la haute noblesse. Dans l'état d'anarchie qui résulta de ces querelles entre le roi et la noblesse (1269-1271), Alphonse X dut finalement s'incliner devant les exigences des magnats lors de leur confrontation à Burgos en 1272. Il accepta que Sanche revendique le trône à la place de l'héritier désigné, son petit-fils, l'Infant Ferdinand de la Cerda et fut contraint, par un véritable conflit armé (1281-1283), de confirmer cette concession [50].

Les acquisitions de la noblesse altérèrent donc ses rapports économiques et politiques avec le roi. Jusqu'alors, les rois de Castille et de León avaient bénéficié d'une position différente de celle des rois de France et d'Angleterre. Chefs de la Reconquête, et s'appuyant sur la riche tradition wisigothique, les monarques avaient exercé des droits et des privilèges que leurs homologues nordiques ne purent revendiquer avec succès que bien plus tard [51]. Après la conquête de Séville, toutefois, la supériorité économique et politique de la couronne accusa un net déclin. Ayant besoin d'alliés contre les prétentions des magnats, Alphonse X rechercha le soutien des élites urbaines. C'est ainsi que, dans le conflit qui opposa la couronne et la haute noblesse, les *caballeros villanos* constituèrent le troisième côté d'un triangle politique [52]. Cette relation politique triangulaire avait commencé à prendre forme bien avant 1248, mais la conquête de Séville et la montée de l'influence des magnats définirent clairement les rapports de force entre les trois groupes [53]. La réaction royale à cette transformation politique changeante se fit sentir peu après 1248, lorsque, pour limiter le pouvoir des *ricos hombres*, Alphonse X prit deux décisions clé : il institua une législation somptuaire dirigée contre la haute noblesse, et accorda l'exemption d'impôts et d'autres privilèges aux *caballeros villanos*.

En 1252 et en 1258, le roi promulga de strictes réglementations somptuaires. A la différence de législations semblables de la même époque [54], les décrets d'Alphonse X étaient dirigés exclusivement contre l'aristocratie ; ils avaient été promulgués pour restreindre les excès du train de vie de la noblesse [55]. Quelles étaient les raisons de cette réglementation ? Alphonse X ne s'occupait pas de l'ensemble du royaume — il n'essaya pas d'imposer l'austérité à tout le pays — mais à un groupe spécifique, la haute noblesse. Au milieu du XIIIe siècle, l'apparence de ces nobles vêtus de soie, d'hermine, de brocart d'argent, étaient une offense manifeste à la dignité royale ; c'est pourquoi, cherchant à se placer au-dessus des magnats, le roi réserva la soie et d'autres types d'étoffes à son usage et à celui de sa famille. Néanmoins, ces lois somptuaires n'avaient qu'une valeur limitée — celle d'établir une distinction sociale entre le roi et les magnats ; mais d'autres mesures étaient nécessaires pour contrebalancer le pouvoir politique de la noblesse.

En 1255 et 1256, Alphonse X octroya de nouveaux privilèges aux *caballeros villanos* (les chevaliers non nobles de la ville) de Burgos, et les étendit ensuite aux chevaliers non nobles des autres cités de Castille [56]. Les citoyens qui possédaient des maisons à l'intérieur des murs de la ville, des chevaux de combat et des armes étaient pratiquement exemptés d'impôts. Les droits de pâture et d'autres privilèges spéciaux accordés aux chevaliers non nobles des villes firent de l'octroi royal un moment décisif dans la vie politique, économique et sociale de la plupart des villes castillanes. Bien que les *caballeros villanos* aient reçu de nombreux privilèges royaux depuis le début du XIIe siècle, les concessions de la seconde moitié du XIIIe siècle transformèrent décisivement les rapports entre ces chevaliers non nobles et les autres groupes à l'intérieur des villes [57]. En moins de cinquante ans, les *caballeros villanos,* dont la majorité était engagée dans le commerce lointain, acquirent à Burgos et ailleurs le monopole complet des offices municipaux, achetèrent la plupart des terres autour de la ville, et, à Burgos du moins, prirent le contrôle des bénéfices ecclésiastiques les plus importants [58]. En retour, le roi escomptait, et souvent il obtint, leur soutien militaire contre les magnats, et put accéder aussi aux ressources fiscales des villes [59]. Cette alliance se perpétua efficacement après la mort d'Alphonse X, pendant tout le siècle qui suit la conquête de Séville, et apparaît encore dans les *Hermandades* de 1296 et de 1315. Ce furent des ligues de *Concejos* (conseils municipaux) qui protégèrent la couronne contre les ambitions des magnats dans les périodes de minorité royale. Elles apparaissent comme le résultat concret de cette alliance, puisque la plupart des représentants aux conseils des *Hermandades,* en tout cas tous ceux de Burgos, étaient des chevaliers non nobles [60]. Une autre manifestation des liens étroits qui unissaient désormais le roi et l'oligarchie urbaine fut la fondation par Alphonse XI de la *cofradía* de la Real Hermandad o del Santísimo y Santiago, une confrérie modelée sur l'ordre militaire noble de Santiago, et qui rassemblait tous les *caballeros villanos* de Burgos sous la direction du roi [61]. Il n'est pas étonnant que cette confrérie existe encore à Burgos, et qu'elle inclue, aujourd'hui comme en 1338, les « meilleurs », l'élite dirigeante de la cité.

A cause de la conquête de Séville et de la pression exercée sur la couronne par une haute noblesse puissante, les rois de Castille firent le choix critique de s'allier non avec l'ensemble de la bourgeoisie, comme il a été suggéré par certains auteurs, mais avec la fraction la plus riche et la plus établie socialement de cette bourgeoisie — le groupe étroit, oligarchique des chevaliers non nobles. A mesure que les *caballeros villanos* de Burgos et d'autres centres urbains de Castille acquirent le contrôle de l'administration municipale, ils entrèrent en conflit avec leurs inférieurs sociaux, les *pecheros* (contribuables) ou petite bourgeoisie, qui se virent finalement retirer leur droit électoral. Soumis à la pression exercée d'en bas par ces petits artisans et petits marchands, les chevaliers non nobles se réjouirent de l'ingérence du roi dans les affaires des villes. Ceci eut pour conséquence la transformation structurelle des institutions municipales. En ce qui concerne Burgos, j'ai commenté ailleurs les documents illustrant ces changements ; des explications semblables peuvent être fournies pour les autres villes de Castille. Les rois commencèrent par s'approprier l'autorité judiciaire réservée au conseil municipal. En même temps, ils s'immiscèrent dans les institutions municipales. En 1255, Alphonse XI assujettit la plupart des villes de Castille et de León à la couronne en imposant le *Fuero Real* comme législation locale, et, dans les années qui suivirent, il plaça des officiers royaux à Burgos et dans d'autres localités. En quelques décennies, avec le soutien ou l'approbation tacite de l'élite locale, la couronne prit en main l'administration des municipalités.

Lorsque, dans les années trente et quarante du XIVe siècle, de violents conflits éclatèrent dans les rues de Burgos, de León, de Ségovie, etc., entre les *caballeros villanos* et la petite bourgeoisie, ceux-là requirent l'intervention royale. Alphonse X répondit en mettant à la tête de la ville un corps d'officiers royaux, le *Regimiento*, qui était dominé par les chevaliers non nobles [62]. Ils s'assurèrent ainsi le soutien royal dans leur lutte pour la préservation de leurs intérêts de caste.

La conquête de Séville changea donc les rapports entre le roi et la noblesse et aboutit finalement à la formation d'élites patriciennes dans la plupart des villes castillanes. D'une part, l'alliance entre les *caballeros villanos* et la couronne était dirigée contre les magnats ; d'autre part, menacés d'en bas, les *caballeros villanos* recherchaient la protection royale pour leurs privilèges sociaux, économiques et politiques nouvellement acquis. Ils sacrifiaient donc volontiers ce qui restait d'autonomie municipale, une autonomie longtemps chère aux élites urbaines, mais qui n'existait déjà plus à la fin du XIIIe siècle, en échange d'un contrôle permanent sur les autres groupes sociaux à l'intérieur des villes. L'histoire des cent années qui suivirent la chute de Séville doit être envisagée en fonction de cette relation triangulaire entre la couronne, les magnats et les *caballeros villanos*, dans laquelle le roi et l'élite urbaine s'unirent contre la haute noblesse et la petite bourgeoisie.

Il est commun parmi les historiens de l'Espagne du XVIe et du XVIIe siècle de considérer que de l'échec du développement d'une bourgeoisie dynamique dans la Castille médiévale résulte un affaiblissement ultérieur du royaume ; mais cette théorie va à l'encontre de l'évidence. En fait, la bourgeoisie était trop florissante, et vers la fin des années 1350, ces *caballeros villanos* abandonnèrent les villes et le commerce, et entrèrent dans les rangs de la petite noblesse castillane. Une nouvelle bourgeoisie dut donc se former dans une phase que les changements radicaux survenus dans la structure économique de la Castille après 1350 rendaient la plus défavorable. La croissance d'une classe moyenne vigoureuse fut, jusqu'à un certain point, amoindrie et ralentie jusqu'à une époque récente.

Aux problèmes discutés ci-dessus, ajoutons encore une fois tous les facteurs mentionnés précédemment : l'anarchie dans les campagnes, les guerres civiles et la violence causées par deux minorités royales. Plus que la France ou l'Angleterre, la Castille fut affligée par une désastreuse série de minorités et victime d'une noblesse rapace, généralement peu disposée à accepter un compromis ou à considérer les problèmes en termes nationaux [63]. Cet antagonisme entre le roi et la noblesse bloquait toute tentative de réforme. Vers le milieu du XIVe siècle, Alphonse XI, qui avait fait preuve d'une remarquable habileté à soumettre la noblesse comme les élites urbaines, tomba victime de la Peste noire pendant le siège de Gibraltar. Les épidémies, l'élargissement de la guerre de Cent Ans à la Castille et la révolution de Trastámara, une réaction baroniale qui conduisit à un changement de dynastie en 1369, tous ces événements constituèrent un fardeau supplémentaire pour la société castillane [64]

Ainsi, le futur développement de la Castille, de l'Espagne, s'enferma dans une organisation économique, sociale et institutionnelle arriérée. Une expansion prématurée entraîna l'hypertrophie d'un régime foncier spécifique, la grande propriété terrienne, qui prévaut encore de nos jours en Castille méridionale, dans la majeure partie de l'Espagne et en Amérique du Sud [65]. Ce type de propriété se fixa et suscita une haute noblesse qui fut capable de sauvegarder ses privilèges plus sûrement qu'aucun de ses homologues de l'Europe occidentale. Il est vrai que les tendances autoritaires et centralisatrices de Ferdinand et d'Isabelle ainsi que de leurs descendants Habsbourg, à la fin du XVe et au XVIe siècle, enlevèrent à la noblesse beaucoup de son pouvoir politique, mais les magnats castillans n'en conservèrent pas moins l'essentiel de leur fortune [66], et leurs héritiers jouissent encore d'une influence considérable dans l'Espagne contemporaine. L'expansion castillane en Andalousie favorisa également le développement excessif des élites marchandes. Il faut ajouter qu'après l'intégration de ces élites patriciennes à la noblesse, le vide fut comblé par les *conversos,* victimes de la haine raciale. La Castille et plus tard l'Espagne furent modelées dans une large mesure par l'expansion en Andalousie au XIIIe siècle. L'expérience devait être encore réitérée dans des circonstances différentes lorsque la Castille conquit l'Amérique.

« Castilla que haces a los hombres y los desgastas », écrit un chroniqueur du XVe siècle. Mais la Castille, qui créa des hommes pour les perdre ensuite dans des aventures don quichottesques bien que nécessaires, a aussi créé l'Espagne et lui a donné sa structure durable. Maintenant que le vent du changement a fini par souffler sur ce pays unique et déconcertant, la Castille, l'Espagne seront-elles capables de se dégager, une fois pour toutes, du tragique héritage imposé par la conquête de Séville ?

NOTES

Une version plus succincte de cet article a été présentée à la réunion de l'Academy of American research historians sur l'Espagne médiévale à Kalamazoo, Michigan (mai, 1975), et elle bénéficia des commentaires des professeurs Joseph F. O'Callaghan, James F. Powers et Mel Preusser. J'ai pu compléter ma recherche pendant les étés 1975 et 1976 grâce à une bourse du Faculty Research Award Program de l'Université de la ville de New York. Mais surtout, j'ai une éternelle dette de reconnaissance envers les professeurs Joseph R. Strayer, Elizabeth A. R. Brown, Charles M. Radding, Philip Dawson, Barbara et Stanley Stein pour leurs suggestions et leur soutien.

1. Voir Frederick JACKSON TURNER, *The frontier in American history,* New York, 1920.

2. Claudio SÁNCHEZ ALBORNOZ, « The frontier and Castilian liberties », dans *The New World looks at its history,* A. R. LEWIS et F. F. MCGANN eds, Austin, Texas, 1963, p. 45 ; également Américo CASTRO, *La realidad histórica de España,* Mexico, 1954.

3. Voir Charles J. BISHKO, « The Castilian as plainsman : the medieval ranching frontier in La Mancha and Extremadura », dans *The New World looks at its history,* pp. 47-69 ; C. SÁNCHEZ ALBORNOZ, *Despoblación y repoblación del valle del Duero,* Buenos Aires, 1966. Voir le compte rendu par Pierre PONSOT du livre de SÁNCHEZ ALBORNOZ dans *Annales E.S.C.,* 25, n° 2, 1970, p. 391.

4. Pour une présentation de la période précédant la conquête de Séville et du siècle qui la suivit, voir *Crónicas de los reyes de Castilla,* I, Madrid, Biblioteca de autores españoles (BAE), LXVI, Madrid, 1953 — ci-dessous citées sous le titre de *Crónica.* Les *Crónicas* comprennent celles d'Alphonse X, de Sanche IV, de Ferdinand IV et d'Alphonse XI. Voir également Luis GARCÍA DE VALDEAVELLANO, *Curso de historia de las instituciones españolas desde su origen hasta el final de la edad media,* Madrid, 1968, pp. 221-628 et bibliographie. Voir aussi la note 5.

5. Voir C. SÁNCHEZ ALBORNOZ, *España. Un enigma histórico,* 2 vols, Buenos Aires, 1956, II, pp. 123-124 ; J. VICENS VIVES, *An economic history of Spain,* Princeton, N. J., 1969, pp. 161-162 ; S. SOBREQUÉS VIDAL, « La epoca del patriciado urbano », dans VICENS VIVES ed., *Historia de España e América social y económica,* 2ᵉ éd., Barcelone, 1971, II, pp. 8-12 ; Jose A. García DE CORTÁZAR, *La epoca medieval,* « Historia de España Alfaguara », II, Madrid, 1970, pp. 295-299 ; Julio VALDEÓN BARUQUE, *El reino de Castilla en la edad media,* Bilbao, 1968, pp. 61-81 ; et également « Aspectos de la crisis castellana en la primera mitad del siglo XIV », *Hispania,* 111, 1969, pp. 5-24 ; « La crisis del siglo XIV en Castilla : revisión del problema », *Revista de la Universidad de Madrid,* 79, 1972 ; Luis SUÁREZ FERNÁNDEZ, *Historia de España,* Madrid, 1970, pp. 295-299. Et aussi Antonio UBIETO ARTETA, *Ciclos económicos en la edad media española,* Valence, 1969, pp. 134-135 et *passim ;* Angus MACKAY, *Spain in the Middle Ages ; from frontier to empire, 1000-1500,* Londres, 1977, pp. 2-4, 17, 41 ss. MACKAY examine les problèmes de repopulation à une période beaucoup plus ancienne dans la région du Tage et plus tard dans la région de Séville.

6. Antonio BALLESTEROS Y BERETTA, *Alfonso X. El Sabio,* Barcelone, 1963 ; Mercedes GAIBROIS DE BALLESTEROS, *Historia del reinado de Sancho IV de Castilla,* 3 vols, Madrid, 1922-1928.

7. En Espagne, ce sont les historiens du droit nationalistes qui ont dominé l'historiographie du pays. Cette situation a heureusement changé. Voir la note 5, et J. GAUTIER-DALCHÉ, « L'histoire castillane dans la première moitié du XIVᵉ siècle », dans *La investigación de la historia hispánica del siglo XIV. Problemas y cuestiones,* Barcelone, 1973, pp. 239-252.

8. VALDEÓN BARUQUE, « Aspectos de la crisis castellan », p. 8. Pour la rébellion de Sanche et des nobles, voir plus bas.

9. On peut trouver un abondant matériau étayant certaines des idées avancées ici, dans plusieurs de mes articles. Voir T. F. RUIZ, « Prosopografía burgalesa, 1248-1350 », *Boletín de la institución Fernán González,* 185, 1975, pp. 467-499 ; « Castilian merchants in England, 1248-1350 », dans *Order and innovation in the Middle Ages. Essays in honor of Joseph R. Strayer,* W. C. JORDAN, B. MCNAB, et T. F. RUIZ eds., Princeton, N.J., 1976, pp. 173-185 ; « La estructura económica del área de Burgos », *Boletín de la institución Fernán Gonzáles,* 186, 1976, pp. 819-830. Et surtout mon article « The transformation of the Castilian Municipalities : the case of Burgos, 1248-1350 », *Past and Present,* 77, 1977, pp. 3-33. Ajoutons que les recherches en cours sur les régions de Ségovie, Avila et du golfe de Biscaye appuient les conclusions avancées dans cet article.

10. Sur les *Mozarabes* de Tolède, voir Reyna PASTOR DE TOGNERI, « Problèmes d'assimilation d'une minorité : les Mozarabes de Tolède (de 1085 à la fin du XIIIᵉ siècle) », *Annales, E.S.C.,* 25, nº 2, 1970, pp. 351-390.

11. Manuel GONZÁLEZ JIMÉNEZ, *La repoblación de la zona de Sevilla durante el siglo XIV. Estudio y documentación,* Séville, 1975, pp. 23-26. Sur la rébellion Mudejare, voir BALLESTEROS Y BERETTA, *Alfonso X,* chap. 9.

12. Garcia DE CORTÁZAR, pp. 200-201 ; SOBREQUÉS VIDAL, pp. 9-14 ; Nicolás CABRILLANA, « Los despoblados en Castilla la Vieja », *Hispania,* 120, 1972, p. 22. Cent *hidalgos* et deux cents 'anciens' chrétiens, quittèrent avec leurs familles les villes de Santander, Castro Urdiales, Laredo et San Vicente de la Barquera (toutes dans la région du golfe de Biscaye) pour s'installer à Cadix en 1266 : Biblioteca Menéndez Pelayo, Fondos Modernos, Ms. 219, vol. II, pp. 12-15. On peut trouver des exemples individuels ou des références à des familles ayant émigré dans le sud parmi les documents des archives épiscopales de Burgos, Avila et autres, mais surtout dans les documents publiés par Julio GONZÁLEZ dans son *Repartimiento de Sevilla,* 2 vols, Madrid, 1951.

13. A la fin du XIIIᵉ siècle, le terme de *ricos hombres* (magnats) n'était pas aussi clairement défini que ne le seront par la suite *títulos* ou *grandes* à partir de la fin du XIVᵉ siècle. Les *ricos hombres* étaient ceux qui avaient soussigné des chartes royales ; c'était aussi le terme utilisé pour désigner les nobles de la première catégorie, qui formaient la couche supérieure de la noblesse. Certains d'entre eux, par consanguinité ou par alliance, avaient des liens de parenté avec la dynastie au pouvoir. Voir *ricos hombres* dans *Diccionario de historia de España,* 3 vols, 2ᵉ éd., Madrid, 1969, III, p. 481 ; Salvador DE MOXÓ, « De la nobleza vieja a la nobleza nueva. La transformación

nobiliaria en la Baja Edad Media », *Cuadernos de historia*, 3, 1969, pp. 1-210. Pour les documents du *repartimiento* touchant à cette question, voir GONZÁLEZ, *Repartimiento de Sevilla*, vol. II. Pour le point de vue de González, cf. I, pp. 227-231 ; *Crónica de Alfonso X*, p. 4.

14. Sur les salaires, voir María del Carmen CARLÉ, « El precio de la vida en Castilla del rey Sabio al Emplazado », *Cuadernos de historia de España*, 15, 1951, pp. 132-156 ; *Cortes de los antiguos reinos de León y Castilla*, Madrid, 1861, I, Jerez, 1268, pp. 72-78. Cité plus bas sous le titre de *Cortes*.

15. GONZÁLEZ, *Repartimiento*, pp. 16-17 ; GONZÁLEZ JIMÉNEZ, p. 10 ; CABRILLANA, pp. 21-22.

16. Au sujet des difficultés à produire des céréales en quantité suffisante dans la région de la Vieille Castille, et des structures de la production agricole, voir Jesús GARCÍA FERNÁNDEZ, « Champs ouverts et champs clôturés en Vieille Castille », *Annales E.S.C.*, 20, nº 4, 1965, pp. 696-699. Je ne partage évidemment pas son point de vue sur les pressions démographiques au début du XIVᵉ siècle (p. 706). Voir Salustiano MORETA VELAYOS, *El monasterio de San Pedro de Cardeña*, Salamanca, 1971, p. 209. Sur les disettes : *Crónica de Alfonso X*, p. 6 ; *Crónica de Fernando IV*, p. 119. Pour les conditions climatiques, voir FLOREZ, *España sagrada : theátro geográphico-histórico de la Iglesia de España*, Madrid, 1761, XVIII, p. 374.

17. Salvador RODRÍGUEZ BECERRA, *Etnografía de la vivienda : el Aljarafe de Sevilla*, Séville, 1973, p. 51.

18. Sur l'échec des tentatives de repopulation, voir GONZÁLEZ JIMÉNEZ, pp. 22-25.

19. La Mesta a été tenue responsable de la faiblesse de l'agriculture castillane. Il reste que l'extension de la transhumance, après 1248, et l'augmentation des exportations de laine, après 1350, étaient venus remplir le vide créé par l'écroulement de l'agriculture du Nord. Sur la crise du début du XIVᵉ siècle, voir l'excellent article de VALDEÓN BARUQUE, « Aspectos de la crisis castellana ».

20. CARLÉ, « El precio de la vida », pp. 142-56 ; et aussi son article « Mercaderes en Castilla, 1252-1512 », *Cuadernos de historia de España*, 21-22, 1954, pp. 318-328. Pour l'importance du fer et du drap dans l'ensemble du commerce castillan, voir RUIZ, « Castilian merchants », pp. 175, 182.

21. Sur le rang social des personnes impliquées dans ces transactions, voir RUIZ, « The transformation of the Castilian Municipalities », pp. 12-16. Également ma « Prosopografía burgalesa », p. 470 ss.

22. CARLÉ, « Mercaderes en Castilla », pp. 318-328 ; VALDEÓN BARUQUE, « Aspectos de la crisis castellana », p. 19.

23. Archivo municipal de Burgos (AMB) clasif. 115 (25-VII-1256) ; *Cortes*, I, Burgos, 1338, p. 451.

24. Sur les contrôles des prix, voir Ismael GARCÍA RÁMILA, « Ordenamiento de posturas y otros capítulos generales otorgados a la ciudad de Burgos por el rey Alfonso X », *Hispania*, 19, 20, 21, 1945, pp. 179-235, 385-439, 605-650 ; *Cortes*, I, Jerez, 1268, pp. 64-85 ; *Crónica de Alfonso X*, p. 6 ; BALLESTEROS Y BERETTA, *Alfonso X*, pp. 167-169.

25. Pour les requêtes municipales demandant des exemptions d'impôts en raison des conditions économiques, voir *Cortes*, I, Palencia, 1286, p. 95 ; Haro, 1288, pp. 102-103 ; Valladolid, 1293, pp. 110-111 ; Valladolid, 1298, p. 138 ; Burgos, 1301, p. 149 ; Valladolid, 1307, p. 191 ; Valladolid, 1312, pp. 217-218 ; Palencia, 1313, p. 236 ; Carrión, 1317, p. 307 ; Valladolid, 1325, p. 387 ; Madrid, 1329, p. 420 ; Madrid, 1339, p. 460 ; Burgos, 1345, p. 488 ; León, 1349, p. 636. Voir également VALDEÓN BARUQUE, « Aspectos de la crisis castellana », pp. 5-24.

26. Biblioteca Menéndez Pelayo. Fondos modernos, Ms. 219, I, fº 276, fºˢ 387-389, 390-391.

27. Sur la législation antisémite, voir *Cortes*, I, Valladolid, 1258, p. 60 ; Jerez, 1268, pp. 80-81 ; Valladolid, 1293, pp. 114, 127 ; Valladolid, 1299, p. 144 ; Valladolid, 1307, p. 195 ; Palencia, 1313, pp. 227-230 ; Burgos, 1315, pp. 280-282, 284-285 ; Carrión, 1317, p. 312 ; Medina del Campo, 1318, p. 334 ; Valladolid, 1322, pp. 352-356 ; Valladolid, 1325, pp. 378-379 ; Valladolid, 1329, pp. 418-419, 421-422 ; Madrid, 1339, pp. 464-465 ; Burgos, 1345, p. 486 ; Alcalá de Henares, 1348, pp. 598-599, 613.

28. *Cortes*, I, Valladolid, 1297, p. 135 ; Burgos, 1303, pp. 165-169 ; Alcalá de Henares, 1348, p. 607. Voir *Crónica de Alfonso X*, p. 14 : « E en este tiempo, por el mudamiento de estas monedas, encarescieron todas las cosas en los regnos de Castilla e de León, e pujaron muy grandes cuantías ». Les métaux précieux sortirent du pays en dépit des ordonnances royales interdisant l'exportation des lingots et de la monnaie. Vers le milieu du XIVᵉ siècle, le déficit de la balance commerciale

s'ajoutant à la faiblesse de la monnaie, on fut amené à utiliser des pièces étrangères en Castille. Voir *Cortes*, I, Jerez, 1268, p. 71 ; Ordenamiento de Alcalá de Henares, 1348, p. 607 ; *Crónica de Alfonso XI*, p. 230.

29. Cette idée n'est pas nouvelle ; malheureusement, je n'ai pas pu remonter à sa source, à savoir le livre de Antonio Bermúdez Cañete, *La decadencia económica de España en el XVI. Ensayo de una interpretaction*, Madrid, 1924, cité dans Jose Larraz López, *La época del mercantilismo en Castilla, 1500-1700*, 2e éd., Madrid, 1943, pp. 100-101.

30. Miguel Gual Camarena, « El commercio de telas en el siglo xiii hispano », *Anuario de historia económica y social*, I, 1968, pp. 85-106 ; Charles Verlinden, *El comercio de paños flamencos y brabanzones en Espana durante los siglos XIII y XIV*, Madrid, 1952.

31. Gaibrois de Ballesteros, *Historia del reinada*, I, apéndice documental. « Cuentas y gastos del rey don Sancho IV », pp. iii-clxxiv ; *Cortes*, I, Jerez, 1268, pp. 64-85 ; Américo Castro, « Unos aranceles de aduana del siglo xiii », *Revista de filología española*, I, 1921, pp. 1-29, 325-356 ; 9, 1922, pp. 266-276 ; 10, 1923, pp. 113-136.

32. Ruiz, « Castilian merchants », pp. 181-183.

33. Sur la question de l'établissement des marchands étrangers dans les villes jalonnant la route de Compostelle, voir L. García de Valdeavellano, *Orígenes de la burguesía en la España medieval*, Madrid, 1969, pp. 125-127, 157-164. Pour les marchands étrangers dans la région de Séville, voir A. Ballesteros y Beretta, *Sevilla en el siglo XIII*, Madrid, 1913, pp. 40-49 ; Ramón Carande, *Sevilla, fortaleza y mercado*, 2e éd., Séville, 1975, pp. 70-84 ; Carlé, « Mercaderes en Castilla », pp. 231 ss.

34. Au sujet de l'orientation vers le commerce des élites urbaines de la Castille du Nord, voir Ruiz, « The transformation of the Castilian Municipalities », pp. 12-13.

35. Julio González, « La Extremadura castellana al mediar del siglo xiii », *Hispania*, 127, 1974, pp. 265-424. Pour les différents types d'implantation et le *Repartimiento*, voir l'article non publié de Mel Preusser, « Innovations of the *Reconquista* : Alfonso VIII's success », présenté à la dixième conférence d'Études médiévales à Kalamazoo, Michigan, 1975.

36. Sur l'existence des grands domaines en Castille du Nord, voir J. A. García de Cortázar, *El dominio del monasterio de San Millán de la Cogolla (siglo X al XIII). Introducción a la historia rural de Castilla altomedieval*, Salamanque, 1969 ; Julio Puyol y Alonso, *El abadengo de Sahagún. Contribución al estudio del feudalismo en España*, Madrid, 1915.

37. Sur la question de la libre concession des terres, voir Sánchez Albornoz, *Despoblación y repoblación del valle del Duero* ; sur la vente de leur propriété par les paysans libres de la région de Burgos, voir Ruiz, « The transformation of the Castilian Municipalities », pp. 13-14. Également García de Cortázar, *El dominio del monasterio de San Millán*, p. 334.

38. Cabrillana, « Los despoblados en Castilla la Vieja », *Hispania*, 19, 1971, pp. 507-508, 511, 516-517. Cabrillana fait état de taux de rendement descendant jusqu'à 2/1 à Avila vers la fin du xixe siècle.

39. Vicens Vives, *An economic history*, pp. 161-162 ; Salvador de Moxó, « El señorio, legado medieval », *Cuadernos de historia* (Anexos de Hispania), I, 1967, pp. 105-118.

40. Sobrequés Vidal, p. 56.

41. Ruiz, « Prosopografía burgalesa », pp. 470-480 ; Archivo histórico nacional, Clero, carpetas, 21-25.

42. Les rois avaient droit à un cinquième de tout le butin sans compter les propriétés qu'ils réclamèrent sans autre forme de procès dans le *Repartimiento*. Voir García de Valdeavellano, *Curso de historia*, p. 609.

43. Ballesteros y Beretta, *Alfonso X*, p. 54.

44. *Crónica de Alfonso X*, p. 4.

45. Octavio Gil Farrés, *Historia de la moneda española*, Madrid, 1959, pp. 203-204. Quel était le rapport entre les acquisitions de métal précieux, pendant la conquête de Séville et la frappe de pièces d'or et d'argent dans les autres parties de l'Europe occidentale peu après 1248 ? La question mérite qu'on l'étudie de près.

46. Gual Camarena, « El comercio de telas », pp. 91-97 ; Gautier-Dalché, p. 247 ; voir plus bas pour les lois somptuaires reflétant les excès de costume et de bouche au milieu du xiiie siècle.

47. Sur les *fueros*, voir Alfonso García Gallo, *Manual de historia del Derecho Español*, 2 vols, Madrid, 1971, I, p. 379 ss.

48. Le *Fuero Real* fut octroyé à Burgos en 1256, mentionné par Alphonse X en 1274 et en 1279, lorsqu'il prononça un jugement contre des citoyens de Burgos en vertu du *Fuero Real*, confirmé par Sanche IV en 1285, et par Ferdinand en 1297 et en 1302 : AMB, clasif. 115 (27-vii-1256) ; *Cortes*, I, p. 94 ; AMB, clasif. 2917 (8-iv-1279) ; AMB, clasif. 119, et aussi *Cortes*, I, Valladolid, 1293, p. 108 ; Antonio Benavides, *Memorias de Fernando IV de Castilla*, 2 vols, Madrid, 1860, II, pp. 316-322. Le *Fuero Real* fut donné à Ségovie par Alphonse X en 1256, et confirmé par Alphonse XI en 1341 : Archivo municipal de Segovia, carpeta III, nº 1 (22-ix-1256) ; AMS, carpeta VI, nº 5 (20-ii-1341). Les petites villes comme Belorado rejetèrent le *Fuero Real* et revinrent à leur ancien *Fuero*. Voir Flor Blanco García, *Belorado en la edad media*, Madrid, 1973, p. 127.

49. Sur les *Siete Partidas*, voir A. García Gallo, I, pp. 390-406. Sur l'agitation dans les villes, voir *Crónica de Alfonso X*, p. 7 ; sur l'aventure impériale, voir Joseph F. O'Callaghan, *A history of medieval Spain*, Ithaca, N. Y., 1975, pp. 358-381. Sur la rébellion de la noblesse, voir Ballesteros y Beretta, *Alfonso X*, pp. 491, 517-534.

50. Pour l'histoire politique de cette période, cf. notes 4 et 5. Sur la révolte de Sanche : A. Ballesteros y Beretta, « Burgos y la rebelión del Infante don Sancho », *Boletín de la Real academia de la historia*, 119, 1946, pp. 93-194.

51. Garcia de Valdeavellano, *Curso de historia*, pp. 440-449 ; Joaquín Gimeno Casalduero, *La imagen del monarca en la Castilla del siglo XIV*, Madrid, n.d., pp. 26-45.

52. Les *caballeros villanos* existaient sur tout le territoire de Castille depuis le xᵉ siècle, où ils sont mentionnés dans le *Fuero* de Castrogeriz (924). Sur les origines et le rôle des chevaliers non nobles dans la vie politique de la Castille, voir Carmela Pescador, « La caballería popular en León y Castilla », *Cuadernos de historia de España*, 33-34, 1961, pp. 101-238 ; 35-36, 1962, pp. 56-201 ; 37-38, 1963, pp. 88-198 ; 39-40, 1964, pp. 169-260.

53. J'évoque ici le problème de la représentation municipale dans la Castille médiévale et de la montée des *hombres buenos* (hommes bons) et des *caballeros villanos* dans les villes de Castille et de León. Voir Gaines Post, « Roman Law and early representation in Spain and Italy, 1150-1250 », *Studies in medieval legal thought*, Princeton, N. J., 1964, pp. 61-90 ; Joseph F. O'Callaghan, « The Beginnings of the Cortes of Leon-Castile », *American historical review*, 74, juin 1969, 1503-1537 ; Adriana Bó et María del Carmen Carlé, « Cuando empieza a reservarse a los caballeros el gobierno de las ciudades castellanas », *Cuadernos de historia de España*, 4, 1946, 114-124.

54. Sur les lois somptuaires au milieu du xivᵉ siècle, voir *Cortes*, I, Burgos, 1338, p. 451 ; *Cortes*, Madrid, 1863, II, Valladolid, 1351, pp. 14-15, 91 ss.

55. AMB, clasif. 1391 (12-x-1252).

56. AMB, clasif. 138 (22-ii-1255) ; AMB, clasif. 115 (27-vii-1256) ; AMS, carpeta 3, nº 7 (27-ix-1278). Également Pescador, « La caballería popular », 33-34, 1961, p. 188.

57. Pour une étude exhaustive des chartes et de leur impact, voir Ruiz, « The transformation of the Castilian Municipalities », pp. 8-10.

58. Ruiz, « Prosopografía burgalesa », pp. 470-480 ; et aussi mon article « The transformation of the Castilian Municipalities », pp. 20-22.

59. A combien s'élevait en moyenne la contribution de la ville de Burgos au revenu de la couronne ? Quelle était la contribution des autres centres urbains ? Tous ces éléments nous sont inconnus. Contrairement à la France ou à l'Angleterre, nous ne disposons pour les villes de Castille d'aucune statistique sérieuse. Selon ma propre estimation, la contribution de la ville de Burgos ne devait pas dépasser en moyenne la somme annuelle de 50 000 mrs entre 1248 et 1350. Il y avait quelques exceptions ; en 1278 par exemple, la ville paya 60 000 mrs à cause d'amendes frappant les usuriers. Voir Ruiz, « Burgos. Society and royal power, 1250-1350 », Diss. Princeton Univ. 1973, pp. 274-275. Pour l'aide militaire, voir *Cortes*, I, Cuadernos de Hermandad, 1315, pp. 247-472.

60. Il faut souligner que de nombreuses villes s'élevèrent contre Alphonse X, mais uniquement pour soutenir Sanche IV. Voir Ballesteros y Beretta, « Burgos y la rebelión del Infante don Sancho », pp. 93-194. Sur les Hermandades, voir Luis Suárez Fernandez, « Evolución histórica de las Hermandades castellanas », *Cuadernos de historia de España*, 16, 1952, pp. 5-78. Les représentants de Burgos aux Hermandades étaient des *caballeros villanos*. Voir Ruiz, « Prosopografía burgalesa », pp. 481-499.

61. Ruiz, « The transformation of the Castilian Municipalities », pp. 17-20.

62. AMB, clasif. 154 (9-v-1345) ; Ruiz, « The transformation of the Castilian Municipalities », pp. 27-28.

63. Cabrillana, « Los despoblados en Castilla la Vieja », p. 25.

64. Voir Valdeón Baruque, « Aspectos de la crisis castellana », pp. 5-24 ; et aussi son *Enrique II de Castilla. La guerra civil y la consolidación del régimen, 1366-1371*, Valladolid, 1966.

65. Voir Stanley et Barbara Stein, *The colonial heritage of Latin America. Essays on economic dependence in perspective*, New York, 1970.

66. John H. Elliott, *Imperial Spain, 1469-1716*, Londres, 1970, p. 34.

IX

Castilian Merchants in England, 1248-1350

The history of the commercial relations between Castile and England in the thirteenth and early fourteenth centuries has not received sufficient study. Although general works on the history of trade and economic histories of England and Castile point to these relations, they do not examine them in detail.[1] For example, L. F. Salzman's English Trade in the Middle Ages includes a substantial number of references which show Castilian merchants actively trading in England,[2] but his book fails to clarify how important this commercial activity was.

In addition to the secondary works mentioned above, we must consider the wealth of information available in English public records. The considerable data present in the published materials, above all in the Calendars of the Patent, Close, and Fine Rolls, deserve to be brought to the attention of English and Castilian historians. This paper, using the Calendars as its main source, will examine these data and relate them to similar Castilian material, the bulk of which remains unpublished.[3] The purpose of the following pages is to encourage further study of some of the issues and problems, rather than to essay an exhaustive study of Castilian-English trade.

Questions should be raised as to the nature of these commercial relations, who was involved in the trade, and the role of Castilian merchants in the overall pattern of English trade during the years between 1248 and 1350.

Why these two dates? The chronological limits chosen are marked by major historical events which ushered in great changes in both societies. The capture of Seville in 1248 brought about a radical transformation of Castile's political, economic, and social structure. The Christian advance into Andalusia led to the final and complete opening of the Straits of Gibraltar to the trade between northern Europe and the Mediterranean. It also signaled the beginnings of an uneasy peace between Castile and Al-Ándalus which lasted for almost the next hundred years.[4] With the end of the campaign, the maritime towns of the Bay of Biscay, which had been active in the siege of Seville, turned their energy to trade.[5] At the other extreme of the chronological boundary, the mid-fourteenth century witnessed the crowning of a new king, Peter I, the plague, and renewed economic and political upheaval.[6] Moreover, the rise of the Castilian wool trade after 1350 radically altered the pattern of trade with England and the rest of western Europe.[7]

In England, the mid-thirteenth century marked the end of the Anglo-French conflict with the conclusion of the treaty of Paris in 1259. Prince Edward's marriage to Eleanor, Alfonso X's sister, at Las Huelgas (Burgos) in 1255 initiated a period of fairly good relations between Castile and England. The mid-fourteenth century found England at war with France, in the midst of the plague, and still bound to Castile by dynastic ties.[8]

The century between the conquest of Seville and the coming of the plague was not a single epoch in the history of trade. Between these dates there were events and changes which were critical in shaping the relations between the two kingdoms. The Anglo-French war of 1294-1303 was such an event.[9] Sancho IV and Philip the Fair had signed a peace agreement at Bayonne in 1290 which held the promise of an understanding on the claims of the Infantes de la Cerda.[10] With Sancho IV's death in 1295, the peace between Castile and France came to an end; prince Henry (Enrique), regent for the child king Ferdinand IV, sided with England in the conflict against France.[11] This new Anglo-Castilian alliance opened new opportunities for trade between the two countries. It is not a coincidence that grants to Castilian merchants increased dramatically after 1300.

Though the chronological framework spans a little over a hundred years, the period between 1248 and the last years of the thirteenth century has to be considered as a preparatory stage. The events of 1248 did not bring about an immediate increase in the volume of trade. Castilian merchants had visited northern markets before, but the number of their visits did not rise to significant levels until the end of the century. By then, the events and changes mentioned above, as well as the favorable policies of Edward I toward foreign merchants and his marriage with Eleanor, lured Castilian merchants to England in ever-increasing numbers. Even if trade between the two kingdoms did not reach important proportions in the late thirteenth century, the foundations for a greater volume of exchange were laid during those years.

As the volume of trade rose, it was not evenly distributed throughout the Castilian kingdom. The greater part of the Castilian goods exported to England were shipped from the ports of the Bay of Biscay. There are some mentions of Galician merchants in English records (there was a regular maritime route to the ports of El Ferrol and La Corunna for the pilgrims to Compostela)[12] and of merchants from Seville,[13] but both areas did not constitute, in my own rough estimate, even five percent of those entries in the Calendar of the Patent, Close, and Fine Rolls dealing with Castilian merchants or trade. Most of the Castilian merchants visiting and trading in England came from the towns of the Bay of Biscay and the interior cities of Burgos, Medina del Pumar, Vitoria, and Tolosa. This area of northern Castile formed a commercial and geographical unit, with Burgos as distribution center for the north-south trade.[14] The region also had ties which went beyond geography and commerce. In times of trouble, the Bay of Biscay towns joined with the interior cities in defensive leagues or brotherhoods (Hermandades) designed to protect their economic and political well-being.[15]

The main towns trading with and providing ships in which to carry goods to England were Santander, Bermeo, San Sebastián, Lequeitio, Guetaria, Portugalete, Laredo, Bilbao (after 1300), Plencia, Fuenterrabía, Castro Urdiales, and the interior cities already mentioned.[16]

It is only by drawing attention to the commercial relations between Castile and Flanders that we can properly understand the nature of Castilian trade with England and other countries. England was not the main trading partner of Castile during most of the period under study or afterward. That position was reserved for Flanders, which supplied most of the finished goods, mainly fine cloth, bought in great quantities by the spendthrift Castilian nobility. In one year alone, 1293-1294, Castile imported close to one million maravedises worth of cloth from Flanders and smaller quantities from Brabant and northern France,[17] and cloth was not the only item imported. A varied assortment of finished goods such as buttons, fish hooks, hats, mirrors, religious articles, rings, vases, dice, needles, bone combs, and toothpicks found their way to Castile from Flanders and other foreign markets.[18]

Castilian trade with England can be seen as a triangular trade. England became a stopping-point for Castilian merchants on their way to northern markets, who could sell their goods in England or exchange them for English merchandise.[19] If their cargo could not be sold, the merchants proceeded to other markets with the authorization of the English crown. In 1337, for example, Sanceius Ferandi de Frias (Sancho Fernández de Frías) brought "fifteen tuns of honey, one thousand salt hides of Seville, dry and salted, and eight pipes of grain to Sandwich." Because he could not sell his goods, he was given permission to take his cargo to Brabant or Hainault in a ship of Zeeland or Spain.[20] The same year Domingo Pérez and Peter Nicholas of Spain came to England in the "ship of St Mary of Santander in Spain with a cargo of honey, hides, fells, cinnamon and fat." Unable to sell their goods, they were granted leave to depart for Brabant and Zeeland.[21] These examples are but a few of the many instances in which Castilian merchants reached markets in the Low Countries by way of England.[22]

England was not only a convenient station on the way to Flanders, Brabant, and northern France, but also a market for Castilian goods. Though as a market it could not compare with Flanders or Champagne, it attracted a fair number of Castilian merchants, considering that trade relations between the two countries were often hampered by many incidents of piracy and attacks on the high seas. Sailors from Castro Urdiales, Santander, and other ports on the Bay of Biscay were particularly active pirates throughout the period under study, but with the increase in the volume of trade and good relations between the two kingdoms, reports of piracy and complaints against Castilian seamen decreased.[23] Let us now consider the amount and nature of these commercial relations.

Between 1248 and 1350 there was rarely a year in which Castilian merchants did not visit England. A glance at the Calendars of the

Patent, Close, and Fine Rolls will attest to their continuous presence in England, to which they came under two different types of royal safeguards. First, they were included in general privileges granted to foreign merchants by the English kings. In 1309, 1311, 1316, 1322, 1338, 1340, and 1341 the English crown confirmed and expanded the policies of the Statute of Merchants of 1283 and the Carta Mercatoria of 1303.[24] Obviously, Castilian merchants also profited from the three Edwards' desire to attract and protect foreign merchants.

Second, after 1300 the crown frequently granted privileges of safeguard directly to Castilian merchants. For example, in 1315 Edward II wrote to Alfonso XI, king of Castile and Leon, promising that all the merchants from Castile "will be protected from demands of Arnold of Sanct Martino, citizen of Bayonne."[25] Merchants from San Sebastian received safe-conducts for one year to trade in England in 1337.[26] The same year Edward III promised Alfonso XI that he would give preference to Castilian merchants if they avoided going to Flanders, renewing his offer the following year.[27] In 1345 the English king issued two additional charters protecting Castilian merchants.[28]

But these general privileges were not so important as the individual safe-conducts granted by the English kings. Between 1248 and 1350 they reached into the hundreds, the majority of them coming after 1300. These safe-conducts to individuals or small groups of three or four merchants guaranteed protection for periods ranging from a few months to five years.[29] They covered merchants selling their goods at port-side, traveling throughout the land to sell their wares, and visiting the fairs of St. Giles and St. Ives.[30] Royal justice also protected them, if not always successfully, from attacks by the local population.[31] Let us consider now some of the most important Castilian merchants trading in England.

Andrew Peres de Castro Xeriz (Andrés Pérez de Castrogeriz), merchant of Burgos, was the most prominent of the Castilian traders doing business in England between 1248 and 1350. Born in Castrogeriz (38 kilometers west of Burgos), he settled in Burgos and achieved a high social and economic position in the city.[32] His first recorded voyage to England apparently occurred in 1299, when a royal privilege gave protection for two years to Peter Peres (Pedro Pérez) and Andrés Pérez de Castrogeriz, merchants of Burgos. They came with their men and merchandise in English ships, and by royal grant they were exempted from an "arrest called 'la Mark' which the king lately granted to be made for the men of the duchy of Aquitaine."[33] Their safe-conduct was renewed for two years in 1301 and 1303 at the request of Edward, the king's son.[34]

After 1303 Andrés Pérez de Castrogeriz's name appeared alone in royal grants, as Pedro Pérez ceased to trade in England.[35] Andrés received further safe-conducts in 1308, 1312, and 1314, each privilege extending for two years.[36] In 1315, 1317, 1321, and 1323 the privileges covered periods of three years, allowing the Burgalese merchant "to come within the realm with his men and wares to trade."[37] By 1325 Andrés had gained special protection from Edward II. One of his men, John de la Pays, went to Gascony "on the business of the king's merchant Andrew Peres de Castro Soryz of Burgos in Spain."[38]

While an active merchant in England, he also served the Castilian crown as envoy and representative in the negotiations for the wedding of Alfonso XI and Eleanor.[39] As merchant of Burgos, the unofficial capital of Castile, Andrés' ties with the Castilian court and his long residence in England made him an ideal envoy for matters involving both courts. While employed by his native Castile, he also worked for his adopted land, and even though it might have proved difficult to serve two masters at the same time, at least Andrés served Edward well. In 1325, prior to his participation in the negotiations for the royal wedding, Andrés Pérez received a procuration from the king of England to arrange a loan in Spain or "neighbouring places." The loan was for six thousand pounds, and Andrés was "to pledge the king's goods" as security and make provisions for its repayment within the realm.[40]

The engagement of foreign merchants in missions of this sort was rather common, and many Castilian merchants performed such duties for the English crown. In 1336 Andrés traveled to Castile accompanied by Gunsalvus Goderitz (Gonzalo Gutiérrez ?) and carried one thousand marks sterling of Edward's money to buy destrier-horses and bring them back to England.[41] He never completed his task, dying in Spain while on business of the king of England. Edward II demanded restitution of his thousand silver marks from Alfonso XI, the concejo (municipal council) of Burgos, the executors of Andrés' will, and Gunsalvus Goderitz. His claims seemed to have been successful, because the next year Arnald Garcia of Saint John, another Castilian serving Edward II, returned to England with the horses.[42]

Another important Castilian merchant was Ferrand Mangoun (Mangeon). Ferrand and Peter Loupez (López) Mangeon, probably a relative, accompanied Peter de Galiciano abroad on the affairs of the English king.[43] In 1331 Ferrand Mangeon and John de Sagassola (Zaragoza), "merchants of Spain, put in their places Peter Gardeche to prosecute the execution of a recognisance for sixty pounds made to them in chancery by John Peche, knight, and Nicholas his son."[44] The courts failed to provide a swift decision, and three years later the two merchants were still pleading their case.[45] In 1337 Ferrand and an English merchant, Richard Lacer, gave security to the authorities of London "that they will not take elsewhere than to Middleburgh in Seland (Zeeland) lasts and ox hides which they had a royal licence to export there."[46]

The following year Ferrand Mangeon received protection and safe-conduct for one year for himself, his men, and his servants while trading in the counties of Warwick and Leicester, and elsewhere in the kingdom.[47] By then, Ferrand must have been well on his way to settling permanently in England and had probably married an Englishwoman. As much can be inferred from a donation by John de Harewell, who in 1338 alienated in mortmain "67 s. 2¾ d. of rent in Heule to a chaplain to celebrate divine service daily in the chapel of St Mary the Virgin...in honor of the said Virgin" for the good health of Ferrand Mangeon and his wife Margaret (not a Castilian name) and for their souls after death.[48] Late that year Ferrand Mangeon, "citizen of London," lent £50 to the prior and convent of Andover, diocese of Winchester.[49]

Lupus Johannis (Lope Juánez), a merchant of Bermeo in Biscay and master of the ship St. Saviour of Bermeo, received protection and safe-conduct from the king of England in 1345 while going to Spain to trade with English goods.[50] In 1346 he was carrying "fish and other things" from Spain to Flanders when his ship was attacked and robbed by English subjects. Lope, under the protection and safeguard of the king, brought his complaints to the English courts.[51] A document shows that a few months later he had obtained a license "at the request of the king's daughter Joan" to buy and export one thousand quarters of wheat to Spain.[52]

Other Castilian merchants also made good use of royal favor. In 1276 Peter de Mundenard received a grant for five years at the instance of Eleanor, the king's consort, exempting his goods from litigation which did not directly involve him. The privilege allowed him to remain in the kingdom and trade there under the protection of the king.[53] Queen Eleanor had been brought up at Burgos, and she sought goods imported by Castilian merchants from her native land.[54]

Finally, let us consider the members of the Frías family. Politically and economically one of the most influential families of Burgos, they traded in England between 1309 and 1346.[55] Their commercial activities were not restricted to England but also included Flanders and northern France.[56]

The first member of the family mentioned in English documents was Fernando Gonsalvi (Fernán González) de Frías. In 1309 he carried a letter from Edward II to Ferdinand IV in which the English king complained of the many acts of piracy committed by men from the Bay of Biscay. Fernán, a citizen of Burgos, was a member of the brotherhood of Our Lady of Gamonal in Burgos. This religious fraternity counted among its members all the municipal officials, important urban knights, and merchants of the city.[57] His membership in the oligarchy of Burgos did not seem to interfere with his service to the English crown.

In 1312 Diego González de Frías and his son, John González de Frías, received protection for one year while "coming into the realm with their wares." The elder de Frías returned again "with his men and wares" in 1320. Both merchants were influential citizens of Burgos and members of the brotherhood of Our Lady of Gamonal.[58]

Another member of the family, Andrew (Andrés) Pérez de Frías, went to England with his men and wares in 1315, receiving royal protection while trading throughout the realm. On leaving England, Andrés commissioned Benedict de Gounceales (González) to act as his attorney for one year.[59] Andrés, like other Castilian merchants, left unfinished business or ongoing commercial operations while he continued his voyages to and from other markets in Flanders, Brabant, and northern France.

In 1337 Sanctius Ferrandi (Sancho Fernández) de Frías was granted a licence to take fifteen tuns of honey, one thousand salt hides of Seville, and eight pipes of corn to Brabant.[60] His relative, Ferrandi Martínez de Frías, merchant of Burgos, received protection and safe-conduct to trade in England until Whitsunday of 1337;[61] his safe-conduct and those of other Burgalese merchants were extended soon after until Easter, 1338.[62] That same year John Ruiz de Frías carried hides from England to Brabant, and in 1346 John Fernández de Frías transported in a Castilian ship six hundred quarters of English wheat for Edward's armies operating in Gascony in 1346.[63]

The next problem concerns the type of goods traded between the two countries. This is a question which Salzman has partially answered, but some aspects of the nature of this trade require elaboration.

Among the items England imported from Castile, two had strategic importance--horses and iron. The first of these two items presents difficulties because the trade of horses from the Iberian peninsula has not been fully investigated.[64] Castilian horses played an important role in medieval warfare and were highly valued in countries north of the Pyrenees; therefore the Castilian crown was careful to keep this important commodity under strict supervision. To this end long-standing royal decrees and ordinances of the Cortes forbade the export of horses throughout most of the thirteenth and fourteenth centuries.[65] Added to their military value, there was an economic factor, as the price of horses rose to almost prohibitive levels by the late 1330's.[66] Since Castilian merchants seldom enjoyed the right to export good horses out of Castile,[67] they served as mediators between the courts of England and Castile. Negotiations for the purchase of horses were carried out by envoys of the English crown, usually Castilian merchants in the service of England, sent directly to Castile or other countries.

On at least thirteen occasions during the period under study, Castilian merchants or English envoys traveled to Castile to buy horses for the English kings. Some examples will illustrate the importance of this trade. In 1282 Edward I assigned one thousand pounds tournois to acquire an undetermined number of horses in Aragon and Spain (Castile).[68] William de Tholosa (Tolosa in Biscay), merchant and envoy of the king of England, visited Castile to purchase horses in 1309, 1312, 1313 and 1314.[69] As we have already seen, Andrés Pérez de Castrogeriz and Gonzalo Gutiérrez performed similar service for England in 1331.

Iron was another strategic item of trade. Most of the Castilian iron came from the area of Bilbao in Biscay, one of the "two main European sources of high quality iron."[70] Salzman has already pointed out the importance and volume of this trade, offering revealing examples. Other instances of iron exported to England from the Bay of Biscay can be cited.[71] In sheer quantity, iron was the main Castilian export until the rise of the wool trade.[72]

Other goods imported by England from Castile during the thirteenth and early fourteenth centuries were tallow, rice, quicksilver, alum, honey, almonds, figs, dates, other types of fruit, liquorice, leather, skins, dishes, fells, cumin, armours, and, of course, wine--mainly sweet wines, which were the third most important item among those exported by Castile.[73] There are also a few references to wheat, but it seems to have been imported to England only during the 1317 famine when the country was forced to import grain.[74]

Trade means exchange, and this leads to the question, what did England export to Castile? This is a puzzling problem, and the correct answer is nothing or close to nothing. Indeed, the few entries in English records indicating permission to export and actual exporting of grain to Castile cluster around the mid-fourteenth century, a period of agricultural crisis and famine in Castile.[75] Even fewer entries show export of wool to Seville. Castile did not need wool, and most of the importing was done by Genoese merchants based in Seville. The final destination of this wool was probably Italy.[76]

If the Castilian merchants did not take back English goods to Spain, what then was the nature of their commercial relations? It is evident from the entries in the Patent and Close Rolls that Castilian merchants carried English goods to Flanders, Brabant, Hainault, French ports, Gascony, and Italy. These goods they exchanged for cloth or other merchandise in northern ports to take back to Castile. More important in terms of the overall pattern of English trade with Flanders, Brabant, France, and Gascony, they served as carriers of English goods to those ports. Although there are numerous examples of Castilian merchants engaged in this carrying trade throughout the period under study,[77] the evidence is overwhelming for the year 1337 and the early part of 1338. With the outbreak of the war between England and France, Flanders sided with the French. Edward III, tied to Castile by dynastic and military alliances, made every effort to attract Castilian merchants to England while barring them from their traditional Flemish markets, and was successful.

At the beginning of hostilities, with the English ships engaged in the watch on the Channel, Castilian merchants and ships, almost all from the Bay of Biscay or northern Castile, increased their participation in English trade. They continued to bring Castilian products to England while carrying a greater share of English goods to Brabant, Hainault, Zeeland, Gascony, and Italy. Their presence in England reached record numbers in 1337 and early 1338. More than one hundred Castilian merchants and forty of their ships visited England in less than fifteen months, and these figures do not totally reflect the real volume of trade during that time-span.[78]

Above all, their role as carriers of at least part of the English wool exports to Italy deserves a closer look. Diagus Lopes de Arbo Lanchia, Lopes Sanches de Bassurco, and their fellow merchants of Bilbao received protection for one year in 1337 to "trade in Gascony, Brabant, Ireland and other lands friendly to England, and passing to and from Lombardy and their own ports."[79] The same day Sebastian of Nordyncho of San Sebastian, master of la Seint John, and other merchants of San Sebastian received the same protection. Two days afterward, on November 20, 1337, Sebastian of Nordyncho hired his ship to merchants of the Bardi society who were sending six hundred sacks of wool to Lombardy. La Seint Johan carried three hundred sacks, and Martin Inaignes de Fraro's ship la Seinte Marie de Bermeo took the rest.[80] The Bardi also exported another three hundred sacks of English wool to Lombardy in two Castilian ships, la Seinte Marie and la Seinte Katerine;[81] the same year merchants of the Peruzzi society hired John Amour of Santander and his ship la Katerine of Spain to carry wool from Southampton to Lombardy.[82]

Castile also served as a stopping-point or base for Italian merchants. Several royal privileges of protection were granted to Italian merchants in 1338 to trade in England, Gascony, Brabant, Ireland, and other lands friendly to the king and to return "to Spain and their own parts."[83] One of these royal grants gave safe-conduct for one year to John Bussyns, merchant of Piacenza "going to Wynchelse and other places to recover goods and merchandise lately put on board a ship of Spain which have been carried away by men of Wynchelse."[84]

Castilian contributions to Anglo-Italian trade were not limited to 1337 and 1338. In 1353 a Castilian ship with a Genoese merchant as its master received protection from the king of England to take Genoese goods from Seville to Flanders.[85] The same year, Martín de Laparada of Santander hired his ship to Genoese merchants taking English wool to Genoa, and Ferrandus Sanchos de Arrieta, master of the Seinte Marie la Rose of Castro Urdiales carried goods of Genoese merchants from Seville to Flanders under an English safe-conduct.[86]

Why did the Castilian ships take on this role in 1337? Several reasons should be considered. The war between England and France decreased England's ability to supply its markets while augmenting the need for Castilian ships--after all, a friendly ally. The war itself affected the overland route through Gascony, making the voyage through the Straits of Gibraltar a more acceptable option.[87] Finally, the growth of an Anglo-Castilian-Italian trade was determined largely by the increased influence of Italian merchants in Seville.[88] It must be stressed, nevertheless, that, in addition to these economic considerations, the structure of Anglo-Castilian trade was shaped by the political and dynastic alliances of the two kingdoms. Castile's economic interests lay in Flanders and not in England. With the rise of the Trastamaras in Castile in 1368, Henry II, who had captured the crown with French support, abandoned the long-lived alliance with England.

To summarize, Castilian trade with England, although not so important as Castilian trade with Flanders, was important enough to influence

English commercial life. Above all, the part played by Castilian traders in the first years of the Hundred Years' War, as carriers of English goods to foreign markets--especially to Italy--deserves further study, for the promise of the Bay of Biscay ports as a center of international trade was never realized.

Notes

[1]On trade see M. M. Postan and E. E. Rich, eds., Trade and Industry in the Middle Ages in Cambridge Economic History of Europe, II (Cambridge, 1952); E. Lipson, The Economic History of England, 12th ed., 3 vols. (London: Black, 1961), I, chs. 6, 10; M. M. Postan, Medieval Trade and Finance (Cambridge, 1973); Louis F. Salzman, English Trade in the Middle Ages (Oxford, 1931); Jules Finot, Étude historique sur les relations commerciales entre la Flandre et L'Espagne au Moyen Age (Paris, 1899), pp. 43, 59; Santos Madrazo Madrazo, Las dos Españas. Burguesía y nobleza (Madrid, 1969), pp. 73-86; María del Carmen Carlé, "Mercaderes en Castilla, 1252-1512," Cuadernos de Historia de España, XXI-XXII (1954), 237-242; Charles Verlinden, El comercio de paños flamencos y brabanzones en España durante los siglos XIII y XIV (Madrid, 1952); Verlinden, "The Rise of Spanish Trade in the Middle Ages," The Economic History Review, X (1940), 44-59; Verlinden, "Contribution a l'étude de l'expansion commerciale de la draperie flammande dans la péninsule ibérique au XIII siècle," Revue du Nord, XIII (1936), 5-20.

[2]The documents in the Calendar of the Patent Rolls (C.P.R.), Close Rolls (C.C.R.), and Fine Rolls (C.F.R.) often refer to Spain, Aragon, and Catalonia in the same sentence, with Spain being synonymous with Castile. See below.

[3]One of the limitations of the Calendars is that they consist only of royal documents.

[4]For a general background of Castilian history see Antonio Ballesteros y Beretta, Historia de España y su influencia en la historia universal, 12 vols. (Barcelona, 1918-58), III; Claudio Sánchez Albornoz, España: Un enigma histórico, 2 vols., 3d ed. (Buenos Aires, 1973); Jaime Vicens Vives, Manual de historia económica de España (Barcelona, 1959), ch. 3; also Vicens Vives, ed., Historia social y económica de España y America, 5 vols. in 6 (Barcelona: 1957-59), II, 8-162, 184-222. For English merchants settling in Castile in the late twelfth century see Luciano Serrano, El obispado de Burgos y Castilla primitiva desde el siglo V al XIII, 3 vols. (Madrid, 1935-36), II, 210-216. Also Yves Renouard, "Les voies de communication entre pays de la Méditerranée et pays de l'Atlantique au Moyen Age," Études d'histoire medievale, 2 vols. (Paris: S.E.V.P.E.N., 1968), II, 720. "Ce n'est qu'au XIIIe siècle et surtout après la reconquête de Carthagène (1245) et de Seville (1248) par les chrétiens qu'un courant régulier de navigation commerciale s'etablit d'une mer dans l'autre." Robert S. Lopez, The Commercial Revolution of the Middle Ages, 950-1350 (Englewood Cliffs, N.J., 1971), pp. 144-145.

[5]For the role of the Bay of Biscay fleet in the conquest of Seville see Guillermo Ávila y Díaz-Ubierna, El primer almirante de Castilla. Don Ramón de Bonifaz y Camargo (Burgos, 1948).

[6]Ramón Menéndez Pidal, ed., Historia de España, 17 vols. to date

(Madrid, 1935 ff.), XIV (1966), pp. xv-201; Julio Valdeón Baruque, "Aspectos de la crisis castellana en la primera mitad del siglo XIV," Hispania, XXIX (1969), 5-24.

[7]For the Mesta see Julius Klein, The Mesta. A Study in Spanish Economic History, 1273-1836 (Cambridge, Mass., 1920).

[8]The treaty of Paris in 1259 settled the long standing disputes with France. Maurice Powicke, The Thirteenth Century, 1216-1307 (Oxford, England: Clarendon Press, 1953), pp. 119-128. On Lord Edward's protection of foreign merchants, Powicke, p. 619; for the period up to 1350, May McKisack, The Fourteenth Century, 1307-1399 (Oxford, England: Clarendon Press, 1959). Both Powicke and McKisack rarely mention Castilian merchants in England. For merchants in England after 1350 see Alice Beardwood, Alien Merchants in England, 1350 to 1377. Their legal and economic position (Cambridge, Mass., 1931).

[9]Powicke, pp. 644-719.

[10]Ballesteros y Beretta, III, p. 33. On the Infantes de la Cerda see A. Ballesteros y Beretta, Alfonso X. El Sabio (Barcelona, 1963).

[11]Letter from Edward I thanking Don Enrique, regent of Castile, for his offer of military aid in Gascony in Thomas Rymer, ed., Foedera, conventiones, literae... (London, 1705), II, pp. 687-88.

[12]C.P.R., 1292-1301 (London, 1895), p. 203 (9-16-1296), safe-conduct to merchants and sailors from Pontevedra, Noya, and Bayona in Galicia coming to England to trade. For the pilgrimage to Compostella see Luis Vázquez de Parga et al., Las peregrinaciones a Santiago de Compostela, 3 vols. (Madrid, 1948-49), I, 77-79.

[13]C.P.R., 1334-1338 (London, 1895), p. 554 (11-18-1337); p. 571 (1-3-1338); p. 546 (11-2-1337); C.C.R., 1349-54 (London, 1906), p. 537 (4-8-1353); C.P.R., 1350-1354 (London, 1907), p. 396 (1-30-1353).

[14]See T. F. Ruiz, "Burgos. Society and Royal Power, 1250-1350," unpubl. Ph.D. diss., Princeton, 1973, ch. II.

[15]Luis Suárez Fernández, "Evolución histórica de las hermandades castellanas," Cuadernos de Historia de España, XVI (1951), 22-23.

[16]See below for references to these towns. In English documents these names often appear under different form, e.g., Vermeu for Bermeo, Font Araby for Fuenterrabía, Plasencia for Plencia, etc.

[17]Miguel Gual Camarena, "El comercio de telas en el siglo XIII hispano," Anuario de Historia Económica y Social, Ano I (1968), 91-97; Verlinden, El comercio de paños....

[18]See Mercedes Gaibrois de Ballesteros, Historia del reinado de Sancho IV de Castilla, 3 vols. (Madrid, 1922-28), I, Apéndice documental, "Cuentas y gastos del Rey Don Sancho IV."; Cortes de los

antiguos reinos de León y Castilla, 5 vols. (Madrid: Real Academia de la Historia, 1861-63), I, Jerez (1268), pp. 64-85.

[19]See below for the role of Castilian merchants as carriers of English goods.

[20]C.C.R., 1333-37 (London, 1898), p. 644 (1-23-1337); also same entry in C.F.R., 1337-47 (London, 1915), p. 5 (1-30-1337).

[21]C.C.R., 1337-39 (London, 1900), p. 85 (7-12-1337); C.P.R., 1334-38, p. 525 (9-25-1337).

[22]Other examples: C.F.R., 1337-47, p. 5 (1-28-1337); C.P.R., 1292-1301, p. 234 (2-17-1297); C.P.R., 1338-40 (London, 1898), p. 5 (2-6-1338); C.P.R., 1327-30 (London, 1891), p. 250 (3-5-1328); C.P.R., 1338-40, p. 373 (1339); C.C.R., 1349-54, pp. 470-71 (3-9-1351); pp. 578-80 (1-14-1353).

[23]Cases of piracy or complaints against seamen from the Bay of Biscay. Some examples: C.P.R., 1281-92 (London, 1893), p. 509 (10-18-1292); C.C.R., 1296-1302 (London, 1906), p. 98 (4-1-1297); C.P.R., 1301-07 (London, 1908), pp. 460-61 (7-28-1306), a truce between Bayonne, Castro Urdiales, Laredo and Santander; C.P.R., 1307-13 (London, 1892), p. 124 (8-8-1308), a merchant of Southampton robbed of his wines by Spaniards on the high seas while he traveled from Gascony to England. Ibid., p. 243 (10-1-1309), merchants of Southampton complained that their ship had been robbed by Spaniards off the coast of Brittany; C.C.R., 1307-13 (London, 1892), p. 383 (11-12-1311); pp. 488-89 (11-4-1312); C.C.R., 1313-18 (London, 1893), pp. 38-39 (1-22-1314); p. 580 (12-7-1317); C.C.R., 1330-33 (London, 1898), p. 138 (3-28-1330); p. 401 (8-26-1331); C.C.R., 1333-37 (London, 1898), p. 106 (4-24-1333), protests to Alfonso XI of piratical acts by ships from Santander off the Isle of Wight; C.C.R., 1339-41 (London, 1901), p. 512 (8-20-1340); C.C.R., 1341-43 (London, 1902), pp. 265-66 (7-26-1341); C.C.R., 1343-46 (London, 1904), p. 219 (6-4-1343); p. 231 (9-2-1343); p. 549 (2-4-1345); C.C.R., 1346-49 (London, 1905), p. 79 (6-25-1346).

[24]Salzman, pp. 103, 161; C.C.R., 1307-13, p. 112 (5-20-1309); p. 342 (2-18-1311); C.C.R., 1313-18, p. 425 (7-16-1316); C.C.R., 1330-33, p. 556 (4-13-1332); C.C.R., 1337-39, p. 379 (1-25-1338); C.P.R., 1338-40, p. 464 (4-12-1340); C.P.R., 1340-43 (London, 1900), p. 172 (4-15-1341).

[25]C.C.R., 1313-18, pp. 231-232 (5-28-1315); other examples: C.P.R., 1292-1301, p. 234 (2-17-1297); C.P.R., 1321-24 (London, 1900), p. 175 (7-13-1322); C.P.R., 1324-27 (London, 1904), p. 16 (8-23-1324); C.C.R., 1337-39, p. 282 (1-8-1338); C.C.R., 1339-41, p. 625 (9-1-1340).

[26]C.P.R., 1334-38, p. 537 (10-8-1337).

[27]C.C.R., 1337-39, pp. 125, 143 (3-18-1337); p. 282 (1-8-1338).

[28]C.C.R., 1343-46, pp. 552-553 (3-10-1345); p. 589 (6-22-1345).

[29]Peter de Mundenar received a safe-conduct for five years in 1276 (see below). Gauselin Angevini and other Spanish merchants were granted license until Easter to take their goods to Brabant, Holland, and Zeeland. C.P.R., 1338-40, p. 5 (2-6-1338). A year was the most common period of time granted in the royal safe-conducts.

[30]See below and Salzman, pp. 14, 153.

[31]Some examples: C.P.R., 1301-07, p. 547 (5-5-1307), John de Ispannia and other Spanish merchants were robbed of most of their goods when their ship was wrecked in the coast of Cornwall. C.P.R., 1307-13 (London, 1894), p. 422 (9-28-1311); C.C.R., 1307-13, p. 527 (4-24-1313); C.P.R., 1313-17 (London, 1898), p. 144 (4-8-1314); C.P.R., 1317-21 (London, 1901), p. 481 (3-6-1320); pp. 605-06 (4-30-1321); C.P.R., 1334-38, p. 140 (3-25-1335); p. 367 (11-8-1336); p. 367 (11-8-1336).

[32]In 1313 Andrés Pérez de Castrogeriz was listed among the most predominent citizens of Burgos. He had lent 1,000 maravedises to the concejo of Burgos for the building of the city walls. Archivo Municipal de Burgos (AMB) clasif. 652 (12-19-1313).

[33]C.P.R., 1292-1301, p. 450 (11-2-1299).

[34]C.P.R., 1301-07, p. 7 (12-30-1301); p. 165 (11-9-1303).

[35]Pedro Pérez was alcalde of Burgos (the most important judicial position in Castilian cities in the late thirteenth century) in 1293, 1294, and 1313. He was also collector of custom duties in Laredo, Santander, San Vicente de la Barquera, and Castro Urdiales. He was a member of the Sarracín family, the most important family of Burgos in the thirteenth century, and nephew of the dean of Burgos' cathedral chapter. M. Gaibrois de Ballesteros, I, pp. vi, xcv and cxi; AMB clasif. 652 (12-19-1313); Archivo Catedral de Burgos (ACB), vol. 49, f. 68 (3-1-1291).

[36]C.P.R., 1307-13, p. 139 (10-1-1308); p. 451 (4-4-1312); C.P.R., 1313-17, p. 116 (5-17-1314).

[37]Ibid., p. 299 (6-11-1315); C.P.R., 1317-21, p. 2 (7-11-1317); p. 559 (1-30-1321); C.P.R., 1321-24, p. 266 (3-21-1323).

[38]Ibid., p. 2 (7-8-1324).

[39]On the matter of the negotiations for the wedding see C.C.R., 1323-27 (London, 1898), pp. 254-255, 334, 344-346, 351 (1325). Another entry in 1325 shows that Andrew Petri de Castro Xeriz put in his place James de Ispannia to prosecute a recognisance for 16 l. made to him in chancery by Robert de Killesey. C.P.R., 1324-27, p. 84 (1-26-1325).

[40]C.P.R., 1324-27, p. 93 (2-16-1325).

[41]C.C.R., 1330-33, p. 423 (12-29-1331). "To Alfonso, king of Castile, whereas the late king caused 1,000 marks sterling to be paid to Andrew

de Peritz de Castro Suriz burgess of Burgos (Burgh), and Gunsalvus Goderitz to buy destrier-horses in Spain...."

[42]Ibid., p. 423. Communication to Alfonso XI, the heirs and executors of Andrés Pérez's will and the concejo of Burgos. Also C.P.R., 1330-34 (London, 1893), p. 230 (12-29-1331). Arnald Garcia returned with the horses. C.P.R., 1330-34, p. 364 (10-26-1332).

[43]C.P.R., 1324-27, p. 181 (10-12-1325).

[44]C.C.R., 1330-33 (London, 1898), p. 391 (10-15-1331).

[45]C.C.R., 1333-37, p. 308 (4-6-1334).

[46]C.F.R., 1337-47, p. 5 (1-28-1337).

[47]C.P.R., 1338-40, p. 23 (2-27-1338).

[48]Ibid., p. 10 (2-20-1338).

[49]C.C.R., 1337-39 (London, 1900), p. 539 (10-10-1338). Another entry on Ferrand Mangeon C.C.R., 1343-46, p. 127 (7-14-1343).

[50]C.P.R., 1343-45 (London, 1902), p. 545 (8-28-1345).

[51]C.P.R., 1345-48 (London, 1903), p. 55 (2-15-1346).

[52]Ibid., pp. 201, 213.

[53]C.P.R., 1272-81 (London, 1901), p. 184 (12-8-1276). Extended for five more years in 1285, C.P.R., 1281-92, p. 149 (1-1-1285).

[54]Salzman, pp. 412-413. "Gonzalo Martinez was sent to Portsmouth to buy fruits from a Spanish ship for Queen Eleanor (Dec. 1289), he bought a frail of figs of Seville, a frail of raisins, a bale of dates, 230 pomegranates, but only 15 lemons (pom-cedrin) and 7 oranges."

[55]Although the English documents do not show their family ties, there is enough evidence in the municipal and cathedral archives of Burgos to verify their relationship. Gaibrois de Ballesteros, I, p. cxxvii; AMB clasif. 652 (12-19-1313); ACB vol. 50, p. 1, f. 43 (6-29-1248); ACB vol. 49, f. 2 (1-14-1309); ACB vol. 32, f. 289 (6-5-1302); ACB vol. 42, f. 223 (12-15-1324); ACB vol. 40, f. 251 (11-6-1320).

[56]Finot, p. 47.

[57]C.C.R., 1307-13, p. 230 (8-17-1309). On the brotherhood of Our Lady of Gamonal Julían García Sainz de Baranda, "Primitiva regla escrita de la cofradía de Nuestra Señora de Gamonal," Boletín de la Comision de Monumentos Artísticos e Histtóricos de Burgos, 65 (1939), 158-164.

[58]C.P.R., 1307-13, p. 486 (8-17-1312); C.P.R., 1317-21, p. 440 (4-20-1320).

[59]C.P.R., 1313-17, pp. 300, 368 (6-12 and 11-4-1315).

[60]C.C.R., 1333-37, p. 644 (1-23-1337); C.F.R., 1337-47, p. 5 (1-30-1337).

[61]C.P.R., 1334-38, p. 546 (11-2-1337).

[62]Ibid., p. 572 (1-3-1338).

[63]C.C.R., 1337-39, p. 342 (3-12-1338); p. 346 (4-7-1338); C.P.R., 1345-48 (London, 1903), p. 206 (11-8-1346).

[64]Y. Renouard, "Un sujet de recherches: l'exportation de chevaux de la péninsule ibérique en France et en Angleterre au Moyen Age," Études..., II, pp. 1113-20.

[65]Ban on exports of horses, Cortes..., I, Valladolid (1258), #12, p. 57; Jerez (1268), #14, p. 71; Haro (1288), #24, p. 105; Valladolid (1307), #25, p. 194; Valladolid (1312), #74, 75, p. 215; Palencia (1313), #17, p. 225; Burgos (1315), #17, pp. 277-278; Valladolid (1322), #43, 44, pp. 348-349; Madrid (1339), #14, pp. 465-466; León (1349), #27, pp. 635-636.

[66]The horses used by the urban knights, i.e., horses fit for warfare, set at a minimum price of 30 mrs. in 1256 (the best horse at 200 mrs.) went up to a minimum of 800 mrs. in 1338. AMB clasif. 115 (7-25-1256); Cortes..., I, Burgos (1338), #18, p. 451.

[67]Grant to Burgalese merchants to take one rocín (work horse) out of Castile. AMB clasif. 96 (11-28-1339). "...por les ffaser merced touiemos lo por bien. E mandamos alos mercaderes dela dicha Ciubdat que ffueren ffuera del nuestro Senorio como dicho es que puedan levar ssendo rrocines...."

[68]C.P.R., 1281-92, p. 11 (2-11-1282).

[69]C.P.R., 1307-13, p. 204 (1-11-1309); p. 437 (3-4-1312); p. 557 (3-15-1313); C.P.R., 1313-17, p. 162 (4-1-1314).

[70]Postan, p. 172.

[71]Salzman, pp. 409-410. Also C.C.R., 1288-96, p. 365 (8-21-1294), goods arrested from three Spanish merchants, including 1,500 quintals of iron. C.P.R., 1307-13, pp. 246-247 (11-16-1309), Martin Moygnez, merchant of Castro Urdiales, "being on a voyage to England in a ship laden with iron and other goods," wrecked on the coast off the Isle of Wight. C.P.R., 1340-43, p. 364 (11-26-1341), three great ships freighted with iron of Spain and other goods attacked by citizens of Southampton. C.C.R., 1346-49 (London, 1905), p. 213 (5-7-1347).

[72]A simple look at the Bay of Biscay custom accounts for 1293-94 will bear this out. See Gaibrois de Ballesteros, I, "Apéndice documental."

[73]Salzman, pp. 14, 254, 264, 372, 381-383, 401, 409-418. Also C.C.R., 1288-1296, p. 365 (8-21-1294); C.C.R., 1333-37, p. 118 (6-6-1333); C.C.R., 1337-39, p. 85 (7-12-1337); C.P.R., 1334-38, p. 367 (11-8-1336); C.P.R., 1350-54, p. 442 (5-10-1353); C.P.R., 1334-38, p. 443 (3-17-1337).

[74]C.C.R., 1313-18, p. 452 (1-31-1317); p. 580 (12-7-1317). "To the rulers or keepers of the realm of Spain. Request that they will permit the servants of Anthony Pessaigno of Genoa, knight, to buy and provide up to 1,000 rased bushels (rasura) of wheat in that realm...." Also Renée Doehaerd, Les relations commerciales entre Gênes, La Belgique et L'Outremont (Bruxelles, 1941), pp. 225-226.

[75]See J. Valdeón Baruque, op. cit. Also C.P.R., 1330-34, pp. 419, 487 (1333); p. 542 (1334); C.P.R., 1345-48, p. 58 (3-18-1346).

[76]C.P.R., 1334-38, p. 546 (11-2-1337); C.C.R., 1349-54, p. 537 (4-18-1353).

[77]See above. Also C.C.R., 1288-96, pp. 324-325 (7-15-1293); C.P.R., 1292-1301, p. 376 (3-7-1298); C.P.R., 1292-1301, p. 590 (4-25-1301); C.P.R., 1321-24, p. 371 (7-15-1323); Registres du Trésor des chartes, 2 vols. to date (Paris, 1966), II, part 1, #505 (6-?-1317), #1266 (3-8-1317), #1977 (12-?-1318), #2186 (1-?-1319).

[78]This represents only figures from the Calendar of the Patent, Close, and Fine Rolls. The numbers of ships and merchants going from Castile to England were probably higher in 1337 and early 1338.

[79]C.P.R., 1334-38, p. 554 (11-18-1337). The same day Arnald Tolosan and his fellow merchants of the city of Seville received the same protection as did Diagus Lopes de Arbo Lanchia.

[80]C.P.R., 1334-38, p. 554 (11-18-1337); p. 554 (11-30-1337); ibid.

[81]Ibid., p. 529 (9-28-1337). Protection and safe-conduct granted to Michael Leure. He brought a cargo of merchandise to Southampton in his ship la Seinte Katerine of San Sebastian. Ibid., p. 539 (10-8-1337); ibid., p. 537 (10-8-1337), protection and safe-conduct to Peter Viellardel, William Peres, and Hugh de Mayork, masters of la Seinte Marie. Their ship had been hired by Dinus Forcetti and other merchants of the Bardi society to carry English wool to Lombardy.

[82]C.P.R., 1334-38, p. 543 (11-2-1337).

[83]C.P.R., 1338-40, p. 3 (1-26-1338); p. 4 (2-9-1338); p. 19 (2-20-1338); p. 23 (2-27-1338). These grants covered merchants from Chieri, Piacenza and Asti.

[84] _Ibid._, p. 1 (1-26-1338).

[85] C.P.R., 1350-54 (London, 1907), p. 396 (1-30-1353).

[86] _Ibid._, p. 472 (6-20-1353); p. 442 (5-10-1353).

[87] See Doehaerd, pp. 223-224; Alfred Doren, _Die florentier Wollentuchindustrie vom 14. bis zum 16. Jahrhundert_ (1901; rpt. Aalen, 1969), p. 107; A. Deroisy, "Les routes terrestres des laines anglaises vers la Lombardy," _Revue du Nord_, 25 (1939), 40-60.

[88] A. Ballesteros y Beretta, _Sevilla en el siglo XIII_ (Madrid, 1913), pp. 43-49; Carlé, pp. 230-248.

X

UNE NOTE SUR LA VIE RURALE DANS LA RÉGION D'AGUILAR DE CAMPÓO

Au cours des deux dernières décennies, de grands pas en avant ont été faits vers une meilleure connaissance de la vie rurale dans la Castille du bas Moyen Age. Des travaux et des études récemment publiés par des étudiants et des thèses soutenues dans les Universités espagnoles et autres fournissent, par l'examen des conditions locales spécifiques, les données de base pour un débat général sur l'agriculture et les techniques agricoles en Vieille Castille durant le bas Moyen Age (1). Il s'agit là d'une vaste entreprise pour les historiens de la Castille médiévale dans la mesure où les travaux classiques sur l'agriculture médiévale et la vie rurale ignorent totalement la Castille ou ne s'occupent que superficiellement de cette région (2). L'excellent travail sur les histoires rurales de l'Angleterre, de la France, des Pays-Bas et d'autres pays de l'Europe du Nord ne fait que souligner le manque de liens qui existe entre notre connaissance de la

---

J'ai pu compléter ma recherche grâce à une bourse de l'A.C.L.S. et du Faculty Research Award Program de l'Université de la ville de New York.

1. Parmi les plus importants travaux dans ce domaine, citons ceux de José A. García de Cortazar, *El dominio del monasterio de San Millán de la Cogolla (siglos X a XIII). Introducción a la historia rural de Castilla altomedieval* (Salamanca, 1969) "La economía rural medieval : un esquema de análisis histórico de base regional," *I Jornadas de metodología aplicada a las ciencas históricas (Santiago de Compostela, 1973)*, vol. I, tema 3.1 ; C. Estepa Díaz, "El dominio de San Isidro de León según el Becerro de 1313," in *León y su historia,* III (León, 1975) ; Jean Gautier-Dalché, "Le domaine du monastère de Santo Toribio de Liébana : formation, structure et modes d'exploitation," *Anuario de Estudios Medievales, 2* (1965), 63-117 ; Salustiano Moreta Velayos, *El monasterio de San Pedro de Cardeña. Historia de un dominio monástico castellano (902-1338)* (Salamanca, 1971) ; *Rentas monásticas en Castilla ; problemas de método* (Salamanca, 1974) ; Miguel Santamaría Lancho est actuellement en train d'achever une première étude d'évaluation des biens du chapître de Segovie et sa structure économique sous la direction du Professeur Ladero Quesada. Un travail similaire est entrain d'être réalisé à l'Université de Valladolid sur les régions d'Avila et de Burgos (le travail de Hilario Casado) sous la direction du Professeur Valdeón Baruque. Pour une excellente introduction à la période en discussion voir Julio Valdeón Baruque et al, *Feudalismo y consolidación de los pueblos hispánicos (siglos XI-XIV)* in Manuel Tuñón de Lara, ed., *Historia de España* (Barcelona, 1980), IV, 11-197.

2. Voir par exemple B.H. Slicher van Bath, *The Agrarian History of Western Europe. AD 500-1850,* trans. by Olive Ordish (London, 1963) ; Georges Duby, *L'économie rurale et la vie des campagnes dans l'Occident médiéval (France, Angleterre, Empire), neuvième - quinzième siècles,* 2 vols. (Paris, 1962) ; Wihelm Abel, *Agricultural Fluctuations in Europe. From the thirteenth to the twentieth century,* trans. Olive Ordish (London, 1980).

Castille et celle des autres régions (3). Ceci ne doit cependant pas être considéré comme une critique envers ces études générales qui traitent des conditions rurales dans l'histoire médiévale. Elles restent des guides valables qui nous permettent d'effectuer des comparaisons, mais dans la mesure où l'histoire rurale de la Castille médiévale reste encore à écrire, elles ne peuvent être, au mieux, que des points de départ.

Il y a malheureusement une tendance à extrapoler à partir des exemples anglais et français et à supposer que des conditions semblables existaient en Castille. En fait, cette approche n'est pas nécessairement incorrecte puisque les conditions rurales étaient à peu près uniformes d'un bout à l'autre de l'Occident médiéval et que les distinctions s'opèrent principalement entre les types méditerranéen et septentrional d'agriculture (4). L'histoire rurale de la Castille présente néanmoins assez de particularités pour mériter un examen approfondi, analyse qui doit cependant obligatoirement débuter par l'étude de régions déterminées avant d'aboutir à des conclusions relatives à la nature et à la structure de l'histoire rurale médiévale castillane.

Le professeur Jean Gautier Dalché, pionnier dans plus d'un domaine de l'histoire de la Castille, a déjà signalé quelques uns des problèmes de l'histoire de la Castille au bas Moyen Age qui appellent une recherche plus approfondie (5). La contribution qui suit, rédigée en son honneur, suit par conséquent la ligne directrice générale déjà indiquée par le professeur Gautier Dalché. J'aimerais exposer quelques unes des conclusions préliminaires de mes recherches actuelles dans le domaine de l'histoire rurale de la Vieille Castille et, ici plus précisément, dans la région de Campóo. En raison des limites d'espace, j'ai réduit mon enquête à l'examen d'un seul document. Il s'agit d'un *apeo* ou inventaire des contributions dues au monastère de Santa María de Aguilar de Campóo par les paysans qui tenaient des terres du monastère. Ce document date probablement de la seconde moitié du XIIIe siècle et mon étude de cette source ne prétend en aucun cas être un traitement exhaustif des informations qui y sont contenues (6). On peut cependant obtenir, même sans réaliser un examen approfondi du document, une vue partielle de la production agricole et de la vie rurale dans la région d'Aguilar de Campóo.

Le monastère de Santa María de Aguilar de Campóo, monastère masculin de l'ordre des Prémontrés, fut fondé au XIIe siècle et était déjà, aux XIIIe et début du XIVe siècles, une entité économique considérable. Situé dans la *villa* d'Aguilar de Campóo (actuellement dans la province de Palencia), le monastère dépendait, pen-

---

3. Quelques-uns de ces exemples sont : Marc Bloch, *Les caractères originaux de l'histoire rurale française*, 2e éd., 2 vols. (Paris, 1952 et 1956) ; Georges Duby, *La société aux XIe et XIIe siècles dans la région mâconnaise* (Paris, 1953) ; E.A. Kominsky, *Studies in the Agrarian History of England in the Thirteenth Century* (Oxford, 1956) ; Joseph R. Strayer, *The Royal Domain in the Bailliage of Rouen* (Princeton, 1936) ; "Economic Conditions in the County of Beaumont-le-Roger, 1261-1313", dans *Medieval Statecraft and the Perspectives of History*, eds, J.F. Benton et T.N. Bisson (Princeton, N.J., 1971) et de nombreux articles et monographies de Slicher van Bath sur l'agriculture dans les Pays-Bas.

4. Une distinction déjà montrée par Ferdinand Braudel, *La Méditerranée et le monde méditerranéen à l'époque de Philippe II*, 2e éd., 2 vols. *(Paris, 1966)*, 1, partie 2.

5. Des travaux d'exploration dans plusieurs domaines de l'histoire castillane sont son *Historia urbana de León y Castilla en la Edad Media (siglos IX-XIII)* (Madrid, 1979) ; sa collaboration avec Ch. E. Dufourcq sur l'*Histoire économique et sociale de l'Espagne chrétienne au Moyen Age* (Paris, 1976) et "L'histoire castillane dans la première moitié du XIVe siècle", *Anuario de Estudios Medievales*, 7 (1970-71).

6. Archivo histórico nacional (AHN). Clero. Carpeta 1665, no. 1(dix-sept folios).

dant le Moyen Age, de la juridiction de l'évêque de Burgos. Aguilar de Campóo se trouve sur la route qui relie Reinosa et les ports septentrionaux du golfe de Biscaye à Palencia et à Valladolid, route commerciale très usitée au Moyen Age. La petite ville et le monastère occupaient une vallée le long du cours du Pisuerga dans une région agricole relativement riche par rapport aux normes castillanes (7).

L'*apeo* que je vais étudier dans les pages suivantes est conservé à l'Archivo Histórico Nacional (A.H.N.) de Madrid, Section de Clero, Carpeta 1665, nº 1. Ce n'est pas l'unique *apeo* de propriétés qui existe parmi les archives de Santa María. Des inventaires des possessions monastiques se trouvent aussi dans A.H.N., Clero, Carpeta 1664, nº 8, 10, 12, 13, 15, 16, 20 et Carpeta 1665, nº 2 (le nº 20 est un *apeo* des proriétés du comte *don* García), mais, contrairement au nº 1 de la Carpeta 1665, ils ne contiennent pas de liste détaillée des contributions payées au monastère, ne sont pas aussi complets ou sont, dans certains cas, illisibles. En analysant cet *apeo* on ne peut évidemment obtenir qu'une vue partielle de l'ensemble des possessions du monastère qui, comme le montre l'abondante documentation des XIIIe et XIVe siècles, étaient très étendues. Néanmoins, bien que les renseignements ne soient pas complets, cet *apeo* nous fournit une information intéressante sur la vie rurale et la production agricole sur les terres de Santa María de Aguilar de Campóo.

Cinq cent cinquante-trois paysans sont inscrits en total dans le document avec les redevances qu'ils doivent au monastère pour l'*infurción* (taxe de reconnaissance du *dominium* de Santa María sur la terre) (8), redevance qui est soigneusement notée à côté de leurs noms. Vingt lignes environ du document ne sont pas lisibles et doivent probablement contenir les noms d'autres paysans et leurs redevances. Quatre-vingt dix-sept des paysans dont les noms peuvent être lus sont des femmes. Elles tenaient les terres du monastère par elles-mêmes puisque quelques unes d'entre elles sont décrites comme veuves ou ont des enfants (repérables par leurs matronymes ou par des références explicites dans le texte) qui sont inscrits comme travaillant des terres du monastères ailleurs, dans le même village ou des localités proches (9). Les 97 femmes représentent 17,54 % de l'ensemble des paysans inscrits dans cet *apeo*, pourcentage important quand on le compare avec les moyennes obtenues dans d'autres régions de l'Europe médiévale pour le nombre de femmes tenant des propriétés rurales. La quantité de céréales payée par ces femmes au monastère entre tout à fait dans les normes et il n'y a rien qui prouve, dans cet *apeo*, que les femmes aient constitué une sous-classe au sein de la population paysanne. Si l'on considère le montant moyen de leurs contributions, on doit conclure que la taille de leurs tenures ne différait pas foncièrement de celle du reste des paysans. La présence d'un grand nombre de femmes s'adonnant aux

---

7. Concernant Aguilar de Campóo et le monastère voir : Luciano Huidobro Serna, *Breve historia de la muy noble villa de Aguilar de Campóo* (Palencia, 1980), une réédition du travail qui parut pour la première fois en 1954. Ainsi que, bien que ne traitant pas directement de la région de Campóo voir Angel Vaca Lorenzo, "La estructura económica de la Tierra de Campos a mediados del siglo XIV", *Publicaciones de la Institución "Tello Téllez de Meneses"*, 39 (1977), 229-399 ; 42 (1979), 203-387.

8. Pour une description et une discussion des taxes et redevances payées en Castille, voir Ramón Sánchez de Ocaña, *Contribuciones e impuestos en León y Castilla durante la Edad Media* (Madrid, 1896) ; Luis García de Valdeavellano, *Curso de historia de las instituciones españolas desde su origen hasta el final de la Edad Media* (Madrid, 1968), pp. 599-612.

9. Par exemple, AHN. Clero, Carp. 1665, no. 1, f. 1 "el de mari pedros la muger de fangundo con sus hijos" ; "el de la suegra" ; el de domingo hijo de dona benita" ; f. 2 "el de la madre de marcos" ; "el de la mujer de ferrando de felecha" ; f. 3 "el de mujer de domingo yllano el ferrero" *et passim*.

travaux agricoles en Castille n'est pas surprenante dans la mesure où on les trouve aussi dans les rangs des marchands et des artisans dans les villes de la Castille du bas Moyen Age. Il est ainsi démontré qu'un document concernant des terres monastiques au XIIIe siècle s'avère être un exemple notable des larges possibilités de recherche pour l'histoire des femmes en Castille et dans d'autres royaumes au Moyen Age(10).

Si hommes et femmes payaient des contributions à peu près équivalentes au monastère, de quelle sorte de contributions s'agissait-il ? Les paiements s'effectuaient vraisemblablement en nature, soit exclusivement en grains, soit en grains et une pièce de lard ou de viande, et, dans quelques cas, en grains, en lard et petites sommes d'argent. On ne trouve que rarement des paiements exclusivement en espèces. L'*apeo* indique la quantité des grains payée au monastère par 330 paysans. 167 autres paysans versaient un pourcentage (*al tanto*) de leur récolte, quoique le document n'indique pas la quantité que cela représentait. Cinquante cinq *solares* sont mentionnés et pour dix-huit d'entre eux il y a une nette évidence qu'ils n'étaient pas cultivés (*yermos*), mais la situation des trente-sept autres n'est pas très claire. Bien que dix-huit *solares* sur plus de cinq cents représentent une proportion négligeable, leur présence dans l'*apeo* révèle peut-être un changement des conditions rurales dans la région de Campóo. Ces unités agricoles avaient été exploitées jusqu'à une période voisine de celle de la rédaction de l'*apeo* et étaient encore comptées parmi les propriétés monastiques soumises à la taxe. Le fait qu'elles ne fussent plus exploitées, ajouté au nombre de femmes et de membres d'une même famille qui travaillaient sur divers lopins de terres, révèle, à mon avis, une raréfaction de la main-d'œuvre agricole durant la seconde moitié du XIIIe siècle. J'ai déjà étudié ailleurs les problèmes démographiques auxquels fut confrontée la Vieille Castille après le milieu du XIIIe siècle, et le témoignage de l'*apeo* et d'autres documents concernant la région de Campóo semble confirmer l'abandon progressif des campagnes de la Vieille Castille(11).

Soixante-quatorze paysans payaient leurs redevances au monastère en grains et en argent, et dix payaient une part spécifique ou la totalité de l'*infurción* en espèces, en nature, ou en espèces et en nature, et il n'y a qu'un cas où le mode de paiement soit clairement spécifié (*infurción* de 5 *solidii*). En additionnant les divers types de contribuables on atteint un nombre plus élevé que celui de l'ensemble des paysans inscrits dans le document car j'ai choisi de mettre en valeur les différentes manières dont l'*infurción* était payée au monastère. Les contributions en lard (*tocino*) et/ou en viande (*carne*) étaient souvent formulées en argent.

Le monastère collectait l'*infurción* en grains et/ou en argent en quantités qui étaient relativement uniformes dans l'ensemble du domaine. Les contribuables les plus

---

10. Mon article, "Una nota para el estudio de la mujer en el área del Burgos medieval", *I Congreso de Historia de Castilla y León*, Valladolid. 1-3 décembre 1982, traite de plusieurs de ces sujets. Pour l'Europe médiévale du Nord, A. Chédeville et J.C. Russel donnent des pourcentages quant aux possessions et aux tenures des femmes, pourcentages qui s'échelonnent amplement de 8 % à 23 % suivant l'endroit examiné et aussi, il semblerait, du statut social des femmes. Voir André Chédeville, *Chartres et ses campagnes, XIe-XIIIe siècles* (Paris, 1973), p. 90, ainsi que p. 71 ; Josiah C. Russel, *British Medieval Population* (Alburquerque, N.M., 1948) pp. 64-68 et les tables aux pages 62, 63. Heath Dillard est sur le point de terminer une monographie concernant l'histoire des femmes en Castille. Ceci sera une importante contribution dans ce domaine.

11. Voir T.F. Ruiz, *Sociedad y poder real en Castilla* (Barcelona, 1981), ch. 1 ; J. Valdeón Baruque, "Aspectos de la crisis castellana en la primera mitad del siglo XIV, "*Hispania*, 111 (1969), 5-24. En particulier AHN. Clero. Carp. 1670, no. 8 (22-I-1331) qui donne une indication claire sur les problèmes démographiques dans la région de Campóo avant la Peste Noire.

importants inscrits dans l'*apeo* étaient un certain *don* Ague (?) et le *solar* de Domingo Estevañez ; chacun d'eux payait deux *moyos* de pain. Entre ces deux contribuables, dix-neuf *solares* sont incrits dans la liste pour lesquels aucun paiement n'est mentionné, mais l'utilisation de *don* et *doña* pour trois de ces dix-neuf tenanciers (signe d'un certain "standing" social rarement utilisé dans ce document) révèle l'aisance économique de ce groupe. Il est probable que la plupart d'entre eux ou tous aient payé la même quantité de grains au monastère pour l'*infurción*. En marge de la page où sont inscrits ces paysans se trouve une petite inscription qui indique les délais de paiement pour les tenanciers du monastère à Lomilla. "Celui qui possède deux paires de bœufs donne quatre *moyos* en deux fois (deux de froment et deux d'orge). Celui qui possède une paire de bœufs donne deux *moyos* en deux fois (un de froment, un d'orge). Celui qui possède un bœuf paie un *moyo* en deux fois, et celui qui possède un feu (*ficiera fumo*) deux *quartos* en deux fois" (12). Dans le *Becerro de las Behetrías*, recensement des *behetrías* et des droits royaux, ecclésiastiques et seigneuriaux en Vieille Castille rédigé sur ordre du roi au milieu du XIVe siècle, Lomilla "*logar*" ou lieu de la *Merindad* de Campóo, appartenait par moitié à l'abbé de Santa María de Aguilar de Campóo et à l'abbesse de Las Huelgas de Burgos. Les habitants de Lomilla payaient au roi *moneda* et *servicios* en 1351 mais étaient exemptés de *fonsadera*, *martiniega* et *yantar* (13). Le *Becerro* n'utilise plus les deux paires de bœufs comme critère pour l'*infurción*, mais les paysans qui possédaient une paire de bœufs devaient trois *fanegas* (1,58 boisseaux) et huit *celemines* de céréales (mi-orge, mi-froment). Ceux qui ne possédaient qu'un bœuf n'en payaient que la moitié pour l'*infurción*. Les veuves et les paysans sans bœufs ne devaient au monastère que onze *celemines*. Dans l'*apeo*, le témoignage interne du document prouve qu'un *moyo* équivalait à peu près à 20 *celemines*. Deux *moyos* (une *fanega* comprend 12 *celemines*) correspondent approximativement à la quantité due par les paysans de Lomilla possédant une paire de bœufs au milieu du XIVe siècle, selon le *Becerro*. Dans l'*apeo* de Santa María de la fin du XIIIe siècle, les redevances en grains sont indiquées selon les mesures des diverses localités ("a la medida de Aguilar", "a la medida de Villadiego"), ce qui rend impossible le calcul précis de la quantité de céréales collectée par le monastère.

Vers la fin du XIIIe siècle, aucun des habitants de Lomilla qui tenaient des terres du monastère ne possédait deux paires de bœufs, bien qu'il semble possible que certains en aient eu dans un passé proche. En 1352, posséder deux paires de bœufs n'était pas même envisageable. L'appauvrissement de la région de Campóo, et probablement d'autres régions de Castille, est ici mis en évidence. De plus, si l'on applique le critère de deux *moyos* d'*infurción* par paire de bœufs, quelques uns seulement parmi les plus de cinq cents paysans inscrits dans le document possédaient une paire de bœufs, et peu d'entre eux également avaient un seul bœuf à la fin du XIIIe siècle. La contribution la plus fréquemment rencontrée dans l'*apeo* pour l'*infurción* est de dix *eminas* ou dix *celemines*, ce qui correspond aux deux *quartos* ou onze *celemines* payés à Lomilla par les paysans qui ne possédaient pas de bœufs, dans l'*apeo* comme dans le *Becerro*. Nous nous trouvons ici en face d'une population de petits tenanciers (y compris les plus prospères d'entre eux) possédant quelques animaux domestiques. Il n'y a aucune mention de

---

12. AHN. Clero. 1665, no. 1, f. 12.

13. Voir la nouvelle et excellente édition du Becerro. Gonzalo Martínez Díez, ed., *Libro Becerro de las Behetrías*, 3 vols. (Léón, 1981), I, 425. Pour les taxes, voir note 8.

14. AHN. Clero. 1665, no. 1, f. 6, 8, 11, 12, 15 donne des indications sur les types de mesures employés. Celle d'Aguilar était la préférée.

chevaux de trait, comme l'on pouvait d'ailleurs s'y attendre. L'*apeo* et la documentation qui l'accompagne pour la région de Campóo font implicitement apparaître le retard de l'agriculture en Vieille Castille et le manque de techniques et d'outillage agricole en comparaison avec d'autres régions de l'Europe septentrionale au Moyen Age (15).

La plus petite contribution relevée dans l'*apeo* est celle d'un certain Pedro Yuánez, un "solariego de Rebilla" (16). Son *infurción* n'atteint que trois *sextos* (*sextario*). Il est suivi dans la liste par Ladrón Yuánez, probablement un de ses parents, dont la redevance est de deux *quartos*. Trois *sextos* représentent environ 1,5 *celemines*, une quantité négligeable. Ceci pose le problème du pourcentage de la production totale de chaque tenure individuelle que représentent ces contributions. Les réponses à ce problème resteront, je le crains, dans le domaine des hypothèses. Quelques indications dans le texte affirment qu'au moins certains paysans donnaient le quart ("dan la quarta"), mais rien ne permet de supposer qu'il en était ainsi pour l'ensemble de l'*apeo* (17). En fait, à l'exception d'une seule indication d'une *infurción* d'un montant de 5 *solidii*, rien dans ce document ou dans d'autres documents en provenance de Santa María de Aguilar de Campóo ne permet de connaître le montant ou le pourcentage que représentait cette redevance. Moreta Velayos cite l'édition par J.J. Garcia González du *Libro de las Cuentas de 1338* comme preuve que les terres proches du monastère de San Zoilo de Carrión (à faible distance d'Aguilar) "étaient données au cinquième ou au quart". García de Valdeavellano décrit les paiements de l'*infurción* comme "un montant variable suivant l'endroit, allant du quart de la production au dixième" (18). De toutes façons, qu'elle atteigne le quart, le cinquième ou le dixième, l'*infurción* n'était pas la seule redevance due par les paysans. Sur la base du pourcentage d'un quart, ce qui semble le plus probable, les tenanciers les plus prospères de l'*apeo* auraient produit une récolte annuelle moyenne d'environ 16 *fanegas*. Il est probable que la moitié de cette récolte passait en redevances et en semence, il ne restait donc à notre paysan prospère que 8 *fanegas* qui, au taux actuel, représentent 12,64 boisseaux ou 758,40 livres de céréales (334,11 kg) par an. La comparaison avec les études d'Abel sur la production annuelle de certains paysans anglais tenanciers d'une demie *virgate* offre un résultat défavorable (19).

Dans la mesure ou la Vieille Castille, avec son assolement biennal, ses techniques agricoles arriérées, son sol et son climat défavorables, ne peut être comparée à l'Angleterre ou à la France, mes conclusions hypothétiques ne sont peut-être pas déraisonnables. Il convient de rappeler ici qu'il s'agit d'hypothèses qui intéressent ceux qui payaient le montant le plus élevé pour l'*infurción*, et que la majorité des paysans inscrits dans l'*apeo* n'en payait à peine que la moitié. Une grande partie des tenanciers de Santa María de Aguilar n'obtenait visiblement que des récoltes qui les laissaient à la limite ou en dessous du seuil de subsistance (20). Comment cela s'explique-t-il ? Nous

15. Il n'y a pas de bons inventaires sur l'outillage de l'agriculture dans les documents existants concernant Santa María, mais on peut trouver des contrats de location détaillés avec la description des outils et des appareils dans les documents de San Andrés del Arroyo, un monastère proche. Voir AHN. Clero 1732, no. 5 (19-XII-1300). Ainsi que Slicher van Bath, pp. 183-89.

16. Pour *solariego*, voir García de Valdeavellano, p. 351.

17. AHN. Clero 1665, no. 1, f. 9 "dan la quarta". Il y a aussi mention des diezmos (f. 5) et du 1/4 et du 1/2 paiement de l'*infurción*.

18. Moreta Velayos, *Rentas monásticas*, p. 85 ; García de Valdeavellano, p. 25.

19. Abel, p. 32.

20. Idem ; Slicher van Bath, pp. 21-22, 41-45.

avons déjà signalé plus haut l'existence de frères, fils, filles, mères, pères et autres parents travaillant différents lopins de terres du monastère. "Marina Gonzálvez, la cabezuda" payait par exemple dix *eminas* d'*infurción*. Elle était suivie dans la liste par sa sœur qui devait la même quantité de céréales. Les dix *eminas* de redevance pour l'*infurción* de Gonzalo Domingo étaient complétées par une contribution similaire de son beau-frère. Nombreux sont les exemples de ce genre tout au long de l'*apeo*, ce qui laisserait croire que des individus ou des familles exploitaient deux ou trois petites tenures en communauté afin de survivre. Pedro Yuánez, mentionné comme étant redevable de la plus basse contribution, est peut-être le même Pedro Yuánez qui tenait des terres du monastère à Villanueva del Rio et payait six *eminas* de seigle à Santa María.

L'*apeo* révèle que bon nombre de tenanciers avaient également d'autres occupations. Le travail de la terre était donc complété par un revenu obtenu ailleurs. Huit *solares* étaient tenus par les abbés de petites maisons monastiques autour de Campóo ; deux autres *solares* se trouvaient entre les mains de gros propriétaires. Nous pouvons supposer que ces dix *solares*, et d'autres probablement, étaient entre les mains de tenanciers absents et étaient travaillés par certains des paysans inscrits dans l'*apeo* en échange d'un salaire ou d'une partie de la récolte. Ce témoignage illustre aussi la diversité des métiers et de l'activité artisanale dans la région. Huit forgerons, trois tanneurs, deux bouchers, un ménestrel, un meunier, un sonneur de cloches, un enseignant, un sacristain, un peintre et un collecteur d'impôts sont mentionnés dans le document. En outre, une femme désignée comme "la caballera", probablement la femme d'un *caballero villano* ou d'un chevalier, est inclue dans la liste. Il y en a probablement d'autres dans la liste qui peuvent être considérés comme travailleurs agricoles à mi-temps, ce qui expliquerait en partie l'excessive fragmentation des terres de Santa María de Aguilar. Beaucoup de ces individus devaient jouir de l'usufruit de la terre qui était probablement travaillée par quelqu'un d'autre. Une ressource supplémentaire provenant du commerce ou d'un travail agricole représentait la différence entre la vie et la mort.

Surprenant est également le petit rôle que jouent les paiements en espèces dans cet *apeo* particulier. Ils atteignent en tout et pour tout 24 *maravedies*, 46 *ss.* et 294,5 *dineros*. Je me suis abstenu de convertir les *solidii* et les *dineros* en *maravedies* puisque, à l'instar de celle des mesures, la valeur de la monnaie à la fin du XIIIe siècle est sujette à des fluctuations incontrôlées. Il y a de plus cinq paiements d'*infurciones* complètes (obtenues par addition de fractions de celles-ci) qui étaient certainement effectués en espèces (une *infurción* de 5 *ss*). En outre, la valeur du lard (*tocino*) et de la viande (*carne*) est souvent exprimée en termes monétaires : dix *tocinos* à 2 *ss.* l'un, un à 1/3 de maravédi, trois à 1/4 de maravedi, un à 1 *s.* . Les pièces de viande sont exprimées suivant diverses valeurs : cinq morceaux à 6 *d.*, un de 18 *d.* et un de 1*s.*.

L'écrasante prépondérance des redevances en nature par rapport aux contributions en espèces reflète peut-être la structure économique d'une époque antérieure, conservée par la tradition jusqu'au XIIIe siècle et au-delà. A partir du milieu du XIIIe siècle, cependant, chaque fois que le monastère passera un contrat de location, le paiement en espèces sera généralement stipulé. Les montants de quelques uns de ces baux dépassent facilement, pour chacun des cas, le montant total collecté des paysans inscrits dans l'*apeo*. En 1265 par exemple, le monastère loua sa maison (*casa*) de San Salvador de Cuestar avec les terres, etc., à Pedro Martin, archiprêtre de *Ffrexnos* (Fresnos), et à son neveu pour 300 maravédis. L'année suivante, le monastère donna à bail la "*heredad*" de Castrillo de Riopisuerga pour 202 maravédis et sept *moyos* de pain (3 de froment, 2 d'orge et 2 de seigle) par an (21).

21. AHN. Clero. 1658, no. 15 (27-V-1265) ; no. 18 (17-VIII-1266).

Au problème des espèces de céréales qui étaient plantées et de leur proportion, aucune réponse concluante ne peut être donnée. La plupart des documents ne spécifient pas la sorte de céréales qui était utilisée pour les redevances du monastère. Celles qui ont pu être déterminées sont les suivantes : 59 *quartos* et 24 *moyos* furent remis au monastère moitié en orge et l'autre moitié en froment (22) ; 13 *quartos* et 1 *moyo* furent versés en orge exclusivement ; 8 *moyos*, 5 *quartos*, 6 *eminas* et 3 *sexterces* de seigle sont également inscrits dans l'*apeo*. Des treize mentions de redevances payées en seigle, deux seulement indiquent une autre sorte de céréales, l'une du froment, l'autre du froment et de l'orge. Le plus grand nombre de redevances comprend de l'orge et du froment dans des proportions de l'ordre de 4:3, 3:2, 2:1, 3 1/3 : 1 2/3 jusqu'à 6:4 et d'autres combinaisons dans lesquelles la quantité de chaque céréale due par les paysans était exprimée en mesures différentes. Mari Miguez de Barzenilla paya, par exemple, au monastère une *infurción* d'"un *quarto* d'orge et un *sextero* de froment". A partir des informations limitées dont nous disposons et en rappelant que la majorité des mentions ne spécifie pas la sorte de céréales qui était cultivée, nous pouvons tenter quelques remarques. Sur les terres de Santa María de Aguilar de Campóo, l'orge est la céréale la plus cultivée, suivie du froment et, en moindre part, du seigle. Pour autant que nous ayons pu le constater, il n'y a aucune redevance d'*infurción* exprimée en froment seulement, quoique nous ayons des exemples de contributions semblables en orge ou en seigle. Ici encore l'absence de toute mention d'avoine ou de chevaux parmi les animaux domestiques confirme l'utilisation exclusive des bœufs et probablement des vaches pour les labours. En même temps, les fréquentes références au lard par rapport au bœuf montre la dépendance vis-à-vis du porc comme source de viande (23).

Il y a d'autres aspects de la vie rurale dans la région de Campóo, ainsi que des témoignages du déclin des tenures de Santa María vers le milieu du XIVe siècle qui mériteraient une étude plus approfondie et que les limites spatiales de cet article ne me permettent pas d'aborder. On peut les apprécier en effectuant une comparaison rigoureuse entre l'*apeo* et le *Becerro de las Behetrías*. Un bref coup d'œil sur les sources permet de constater que le nombre des paysans contribuables qui restait dans de nombreux villages mentionnés dans l'*apeo* avait dramatiquement baissé vers 1351/52, même si nous tenons compte de la peste. En outre, au milieu du XIVe siècle, le monastère partageait le *dominium* sur plusieurs de ces villages avec d'autres entités ecclésiastiques ou des nobles, alors qu'à la fin du XIIIe siècle Santa María détenait l'exclusivité des droits seigneuriaux dans beaucoup de ces mêmes villages. Ce sont de sinistres rappels des conditions économiques qui vont en s'aggravant dans la région de Campóo et dans la vie économique du monastère (24).

Le rôle de l'argent, une analyse prosopographique de l'*apeo* et l'étude de cette source dans le contexte de l'abondante documentation de la région sont quelques uns des thèmes sur lesquels je poursuis actuellement des recherches détaillées. Pour cette première étude, cependant, et pour la suite, je ne fais que suivre la voie si remarquablement tracée par le professeur Jean Gautier Dalché.

---

22. Chaque inscription ne spécifiait pas que c'était moitié blé moitié orge mais il est clair, provenant du témoignage interne de l'*apeo*, que tel était le cas.

23. Autant le travail de Santamaría Lancho que celui de Vaca Lorenzo montrent les mêmes et quasi similaires proportions entre le blé, l'orge et le seigle.

24. En 1352, dans beaucoup de villages, le nombre des payeurs de taxes a été réduit à un ou deux individus. Dans quelques cas, les villages ont été désertés et ont cessé d'être comptés comme des unités taxables.

XI

LA FORMAZIONE
DEL MERCATO DELLA TERRA
NELLA CASTIGLIA DEL BASSO MEDIOEVO

Nella ricca documentazione relativa alla Castiglia del basso medioevo sopravvivono, in mezzo a decreti dei re e a descrizioni delle azioni dei grandi, centinaia di contratti di acquisto e di affitto della terra: anzi, la maggior parte dei documenti riguardanti la storia della Castiglia settentrionale porta alla luce l'attività economica di persone relativamente prive di potere, che attraverso le loro transazioni vengono alla ribalta della storia una volta, due volte, raramente di più, per poi sparire per sempre dalla nostra vista.

Che cosa ci rivelano queste transazioni di terra e di altri tipi di proprietà sulla struttura della società castigliana? Che cosa ci dicono della condizione economica e sociale di coloro che vendevano le loro piccole proprietà, e di coloro che investivano in proprietà rurali nelle campagne della Castiglia?

L'esistenza di questa documentazione, che ci riporta fino all'inizio dell'XI secolo, è tanto più notevole in quanto ciò che è rimasto è senza dubbio una piccola parte del totale di transazioni effettuate nel basso medioevo nella Castiglia settentrionale. A differenza di altre parti d'Europa, come per esempio l'Inghilterra, dove i registri signorili costituiscono una fonte straordinaria per lo studio dei trasferimenti di proprietà nelle aree rurali, o la Catalogna o l'Italia, dove l'introduzione della pratica notarile ha garantito anche in tempi remoti la sopravvivenza di una documentazione sia secolare sia ecclesiastica, nella Castiglia settentrionale questa documentazione deriva quasi esclusivamente dagli archivi ecclesiastici. Le fonti disponibili registrano quindi in larga misura l'acquisizione di proprietà da parte della chiesa o

* *Traduzione dall'inglese di Mario Trucchi*

la terra che nel corso del tempo sia passata nelle mani di monasteri, capitoli o chiese, mentre sono andate perdute per lo storico quelle transazioni di terra o di immobili in cui non intervenivano preti o istituzioni ecclesiastiche [1]. Dobbiamo inoltre presumere che tutta una serie di transazioni, quelle tra i più poveri, non sia stata registrata perché probabilmente consistenti in accordi orali, strette di mano o baci, giuramenti e scambi di pegni simboleggianti l'oggetto della transazione in presenza di testimoni: molte piccole compravendite sono così sfuggite alla registrazione, per motivi che possono andare dal costo della stesura dei documenti alla riluttanza a entrare nel mondo della parola scritta. Questi accordi informali continuano naturalmente a far parte del sistema di scambi economici anche oggi e anche nelle società sviluppate, ma come storici possiamo esaminare solo di rado e solo di sfuggita queste transazioni o le persone che vi partecipano, per cui bisogna tenere ben presente che quando parliamo del mercato contadino della terra non sempre abbiamo davanti agli occhi l'intero spettro della società: come sempre, solo la storia di coloro che hanno messo per iscritto o le cui attività sono state registrate può essere raccontata per intero.

La documentazione che ci rimane, per quanto incompleta, offre un panorama molto variegato dell'attività economica e della vita della Castiglia settentrionale, sia in campagna sia in città [2]. In questo saggio intendo concentrare la mia attenzione su queste transazioni nel loro aspetto fondamentale, quello di scambi di proprietà, e occuparmi di una questione, quella del mercato contadino della terra, che è stata studiata dettagliatamente per l'Inghilterra medievale, ma non per la Castiglia. Due sono le difficoltà. Innanzitutto la documentazione per la Castiglia, per quanto consistente, non è paragonabile ai registri dei *manors* inglesi né per quantità né per precisione. Sui trasferimenti di terra in Inghilterra siamo in grado di scoprire più di quanto possiamo sperare di scoprire in altre parti del mondo occidentale del medioevo, mentre le registrazioni di transazioni terriere nella Castiglia settentrionale in genere non precisano le dimensioni, e a volte nemmeno la natura, degli appezzamenti acquistati: espressioni come «*todo lo que tengo*» o «*todo lo que me pertenece*» (tutto quello che ho) o semplicemente *heredad* o *heredamiento*, che si trovano in molte transazioni, non ci consentono di calcolare il prezzo unitario della terra nel tempo né l'estensione che viene acquistata o venduta [3]. Riguardo all'estensione spesso l'unico indizio di cui disponiamo è il prezzo, e non è certo un indizio affidabile: dobbiamo supporre che lo scambio di grosse somme corrisponda a terreni altrettanto grandi e viceversa, ma il prezzo della terra dipendeva ovviamente dalla sua ubicazione, dal momento in cui veniva ceduta, oltre che dall'inflazione, dal clima e da altri fattori, senza contare la diversità di prezzo tra vigne, campi di lino e campi di grano. La seconda difficoltà che incontriamo nello studio del mercato contadino della terra nella Castiglia settentrionale (e del resto anche altrove) è di natura teorica. Non c'è bisogno di passare in rassegna in questa sede il ricco dibattito, vivo soprattutto tra gli storici inglesi, sulla questione se sia esistito un vero «mercato» della terra nel senso che il termine ha nell'economia moderna, «la compravendita di terra in cambio di denaro su scala abbastanza grande da costituire qualcosa di simile a un "mercato" nel senso che a questo termine danno gli economisti» [4], e in che modo l'esistenza o meno di questo mercato influisca sulla nostra comprensione delle strutture della società medievale.

Zvi Razi ha riassunto questo dibattito in modo chiaro e conciso, anche se per portarlo a sostegno della sua concezione dell'argomento. Da una parte un gruppo di storici guidati da J. Ambrose Raftis e la Toronto School of Medieval Studies ritiene che le conseguenze della peste, declino demografico e stagnazione economica, abbiano provocato un indebolimento dei legami comunitari per cui «gli interessi privati e indipendenti presero il sopravvento su quelli dei gruppi». Facendo propria questa concezione, Alan MacFarlane ritiene che il mercato della terra riveli l'esistenza di «contadini individualisti che perseguivano un sistema di produzione quasi capitalistico» e sostiene, andando ben oltre Raftis e il suo gruppo, che «la comunità di villaggio non è mai esistita» [5]: assistiamo quindi, almeno in Inghilterra, al tramonto dell'ordine «feudale» e alla nascita di un sistema moderno rappresentato soprattutto da un «interessato» e aggressivo trasferimento di terra in cambio di denaro. Razi e altri hanno messo alla prova e respinto questa interpretazione mostrando, come ha fatto Razi per Halesowen, che molti cosiddetti scambi di mercato erano in realtà transazioni interfamiliari o quanto meno tra vicini stretti, così mettendo in dubbio l'immagine di un contadino medievale inglese impegnato a vendere e comprare terra in un mercato libero [6]. Il tipo di ricostruzione della storia della famiglia attuato da Razi difficilmente potrebbe essere applicato ad altre parti d'Europa, e nemmeno all'Inghilterra di prima del 1400, ma possiamo ammettere che se la documentazione esistente ce lo consentisse scopriremmo probabilmente molti più scambi interfamiliari di quelli che troviamo nelle nostre fonti [7].

Nel contesto della vita economica della Castiglia settentrionale entrambe le spiegazioni si rivelano molto insoddisfacenti. Il dibattito inglese implica, sia pure con numerose limitazioni, che l'esistenza di un mercato contadino della terra escluda un modello capace di spiegare in modo preciso e definitivo la vita dei contadini, il loro rapporto con la terra e, soprattutto, con i padroni: un mercato contadino della terra «quasi capitalistico» mina le basi ideologiche delle strutture «feudali» e signorili elaborate in tutti questi anni di dibattiti storici e ideologici. Nello stesso modo, se il «mercato della terra» si rivela essere non un vero «mercato» ma più che altro una serie di transazioni tra parenti o tra vicini appare evidente la permanenza di strutture comunitari al di là delle trasformazioni e dei cambiamenti economici della società del basso medioevo. In questa discussione si tende tuttavia a sottovalutare il fatto che entrambe le posizioni possono essere in parte corrette. Inoltre, almeno nella Castiglia settentrionale, quello che è vero per i compratori non sempre è vero per i venditori. E ancora, ignoriamo le peculiarità che si riscontrano spostandosi da un luogo all'altro. Il fatto di trovare tra i contadini segni di indipendenza, di avidità, di volontà di accrescere i propri possessi non comporta necessariamente un completo rovesciamento della tradizione comunitaria. In effetti il recente libro di Ruth Behar ha mostrato in modo conclusivo che entrambi i modelli di vita rurale sono sopravvissuti fino al recente passato e tuttora sopravvivono, in un rapporto alquanto difficile, nei villaggi spagnoli [8]. Manca inoltre dalla discussione inglese l'interazione tra città e campagna. È chiaro che nella Castiglia settentrionale come nelle altre regioni dell'Occidente il cosiddetto mercato contadino della terra non può essere studiato isolatamente: i cittadini, come acquirenti e come affittuari di terra coltivabile nei *contados (alfoces)* delle città castigliane del nord, ebbero un ruolo di grande importanza nella formazione di un «mercato» della terra. Inoltre il loro intervento creava il presupposto per scambi economici tra persone che non si conoscevano, al di fuori quindi dei modelli di transazione interfamiliare o tra vicini stretti [9].

Se volgiamo la nostra attenzione alla situazione della Castiglia settentrionale vera e propria troviamo schemi di coltivazione della terra e rapporti contadino-padrone assai diversi da quelli comunemente accettati per la maggior parte dell'Europa settentrionale del medioevo. Recentemente un gruppo di giovani storici spagnoli ha risuscitato la vecchia ed esausta controversia sull'esistenza o meno del «feudalesimo» (inteso qui come uno degli stadi canonici dello sviluppo marxiano) nella Castiglia medievale. Per incominciare, come ha già rilevato in modo convincente la mia collega Elizabeth A. R. Brown, l'uso di questi «ismi» è il frutto di un rigido schematismo. Per quanto riguarda la Castiglia in particolare, Peter Linehan ha già ridimensionato, con erudizione e intelligenza, questi tentativi di ricostruire il passato in modo da adattarlo a schemi ideologici precostituiti [10]. Non intendiamo dilungarci qui su tali questioni metodologiche e ideologiche, ma semplicemente mettere in rilievo il fatto che ben di rado le fonti giustificano interamente modelli statici di organizzazione economica e sociale.

1. IL MERCATO CONTADINO DELLA TERRA NELLA CASTIGLIA DEL BASSO MEDIOEVO

La mia tesi nelle pagine che seguono, basata sulla documentazione esistente, è che è sbagliato prendere in esame le transazioni di terra e di immobili allo scopo di adattarle a modelli preconcetti di strutture di sviluppo economico. Dobbiamo quindi parlare dei contadini che vendevano la loro terra senza ricorrere alla camicia di Nesso dei modelli «feudali» o semicapitalistici. In Castiglia, ma lo stesso vale anche nel resto dell'Occidente, i contadini erano economicamente, socialmente e politicamente oppressi, costretti a tutta una serie di obblighi e di doveri la cui varia natura dipendeva da diversi fattori. Ma i contadini della Castiglia settentrionale alla fine del medioevo non erano così vincolati alla terra da non potersene separare. In una regione molto meno «signorile» di quanto possiamo essere disposti ad ammettere, anche i contadini che non avevano nessun potere vendevano e affittavano terra: alcuni di loro anzi vendettero piccoli appezzamenti che avrebbero a malapena potuto mantenerli, ma la documentazione ce li mostra come attori economici consapevoli e autonomi. E in Castiglia non c'è una magica linea di confine tra un periodo in cui i contadini non compravano e non vendevano terra e la nascita, quasi Venere dalla spuma del mare, di un mercato della terra, come è stato sostenuto per l'Inghilterra [11] ma, come vedremo più oltre, per quanto indietro risale la documentazione ci mostra sempre contadini che comprano e vendono: la transazione da quelli che si potrebbero chiamare scambi tradizionali o non economici a transazioni più «moderne» o di mercato fu assai più sfumata di quanto non abbiano rilevato certi studiosi inglesi, e non dipese solo dall'aumento del numero di transazioni. Inoltre quando i contadini compravano o, molto più spesso, vendevano terra lo facevano come se l'avessero in allodio. L'acquisto di proprietà rurali spesso comportava certi obblighi nei confonti della corona sotto forma di tasse territoriali, e a volte anche nei confronti dei signori ecclesiastici. Eppure non si trova quasi mai nessuna traccia nel linguaggio delle fonti disponibili che possa far pensare ad altro che a un mercato di proprietà allodiali, né esiste alcun indizio che i contadini chiedessero l'autorizzazione del signore per disporre della loro proprietà [12]. Resta da fare ancora una precisazione. La regione di cui ci occupiamo non era zona di frontiera. Si era organizzata già nel IX secolo, e nel periodo di cui ci occupiamo in queste pagine non poteva più essere propriamente considerata una frontiera con l'Islam già da quattrocento anni. Benché la frontiera abbia influito sulla formazione di un mercato della terra, non possiamo però considerare la Castiglia settentrionale un'eccezione, ché anzi non si vedono grandi differenze dal resto dell'Occidente medievale, il che ne fa un ottimo campo di studio per verificare se sia esistito o meno un «mercato» della terra e quale sia stata la sua natura.

Le accluse tabelle 1 e 2 mostrano il numero e lo schema di transazioni di terra e di immobili nella Castiglia settentrionale tra il 1240 e il 1360, così come le zone da cui provengono i documenti. La regione qui presa in esame coincide più o meno con il regno storico della Vecchia Castiglia, compresa tra il golfo di Biscaglia a nord e le Sierras centrali a sud e confinante a est con la Navarra e a ovest con il regno di León, anche se nelle tabelle abbiamo incluso anche la documentazione relativa a Salamanca. I confini cronologici sono stati scelti perché più o meno coincidono con date importanti nella storia della regione. Nel 1236 le armi cristiane conquistarono Cordoba ed erano già pronte ad assediare e infine (1248) conquistare Siviglia, così portando sotto il dominio cristiano gran parte dell'Andalusia. Il 1360 è un decennio dopo che la peste nera aveva spazzato quasi tutta la penisola, e quindi il limite di questa inchiesta avrebbe dovuto essere esattamente la metà del secolo, ma ho allargato i limiti fino a includere gli anni immediatamente successivi alla peste per vedere se a dieci anni di distanza se ne risentivano gli effetti, e se

TABELLA 1. *Transazioni di terra e di immobili, 1240-1360*

	1240-1299	1300-1360	Totale
Numero di transazioni	673	460	1133

	Acquirenti	*Venditori*
A – *Ecclesiastici*		
Istituzioni	453	32
Individui		
a) Maschi	309	57
b) Femmine	2	19
B – *Secolari*		
a) Maschi	267	423
b) Femmine (da sole)	47	144
c) Coppie	78	259
d) Famiglie	12	126
e) Gruppi	3	16
f) Consigli Comunali	3	6
g) Sconosciuti	7	9

Numero di transazioni in cui è esplicitamente dichiarato che sono effettuate per dividere un'eredità	37
Numero di transazioni in cui è esplicitamente dichiarato che sono effettuate tra parenti	16

Proprietà trasferite nella Castiglia settentrionale in base all'ubicazione, al tipo di proprietà e al prezzo, 1240-1360

C – *Ubicazione della proprietà*	
a) Rurale	799
b) Urbana	334
Totale	1133

D – *Tipo di proprietà*	
a) Proprietà agraria [1]	217
b) Terra [2]	416
c) Vigne	154
d) Mulini o diritti di macinazione	68
e) Orti	58
f) Prati e pascoli	25
g) Altro (comprende campi di lino, bacini da pesca, granai, fiumi, piccionaie, frutteti, arnie, ecc.)	32
h) Case (comprende negozi, magazzini, ecc.) [3]	229

E – *Gamma dei prezzi (in maravedies) / Numero di transazioni* [4]

0-50 *mrs.*	301	401-500 *mrs.*	43
51-100 *mrs.*	123	501-1000 *mrs.*	64
101-200 *mrs.*	119	1000-5000 *mrs.*	119
201-300 *mrs.*	85	5000 *mrs.* e oltre	32
301-400 *mrs.*	65	Sconosciuti	66

Note:

[1] Questa categoria comprende designazioni generiche come *heredades*, *algos*, «tutto ciò che ho», ecc. Nella maggior parte dei casi la voce principale è la terra, ma accompagnata da una serie di annessi che sono quelli che si trovano abitualmente nelle proprietà rurali medievali.

[2] Questo gruppo comprende sia la terra da sola, sia la terra unita a non più di due altri tipi di proprietà, cioè vigne, orti, ecc.

[3] La maggior parte delle transazioni riguardanti case non specificano il numero delle case. Spesso i documenti usano il termine *casas*. In gran parte erano urbane, ma le cifre comprendono anche case di villaggio.

[4] Il valore del *maravedi* fluttuò enormemente per tutta la fine del XIII secolo e nel XIV. Quanto al potere d'acquisto potrà essere utile sapere che nel 1268 nella Castiglia settentrionale un contadino guadagnava 6 *mrs.* all'anno, più cibo e vestiti. Nel 1294 il medico di corte guadagnava 10 *mrs.* al giorno. Vedi M. del Carmen Carlé, *El precio de la vida en Castilla del Rey Sabio al Emplazado*, in «Cuadernos de historia de España», XV (1951), pp. 32-156.

Tabella 2. *Distribuzione geografica e fonti per le tabelle 1-4*

Località	Anni		Totale
	1240-1299	1300-1360	
Ávila (cattedrale e monasteri)	40	100	140
Burgos (cattedrale)	86	140	226
Burgos (monasteri urbani e rurali, documenti nell'AHN)	29	53	82
Cañas-Santa María de Nájera (Rioja)	7	3	10
Covarrubias (Burgos)	3	4	7
Las Huelgas (Burgos)	112	3	115
Chiese collegiate, Lograno-Albelda (Rioja)	13	16	29
Osma (cattedrale)	–	1	1
Nuestra Señora, Beneviveri (Palencia)	19	–	19
Salamanca (cattedrale)	125	11	136
San Andrés de Arroyo (Palencia)	6	9	15
Santo Domingo de Silos	11	7	18
San Juan de Burgos	8	6	14
Santa María la Real, Aguilar de Campóo (Palencia)	61	37	98
San Salvador de El Moral	3	1	4
San Salvador de Oña	98	22	120
Santo Toribio de Liebana (Santander)	6	4	10
San Zoilo de Carrión	2	1	3
Segovia (cattedrale e monasteri)	24	38	62
Siguenza (cattedrale)	10	4	14
Valladolid	10	—	10
	673	460	1133

Fonti:
Ávila fino al 1299, A. Barrios García, *Documentación medieval de Ávila* (cfr. note); 1300-60, AHN, *Clero*, carps. 23-30. Burgos (cattedrale), Archivo catedral de Burgos.

Cfr. anche i documenti pubblicati in *Fuentes medievales castellano-leonesas*, voll. 13, 14, 16 e 17.
Burgos (monasteri), AHN, *Clero*, carps. 169-71, 174, 177, 184-86, 198-201, 225-27, 232-34, 239-43, 250-51, 354-56, 380-83.
Cañas e Santa María de Nájera, AHN, *Clero*, carps. 1024-25, 1031-33; AHN, *Codice* 106B.
Covarrubias, L. SERRANO, *Fuentes para la historia de Castilla*, 3 voll., Valladolid 1907-10.
Las Huelgas (Burgos), *Fuentes medievales castellano-leonesas*, voll. 30, 31; A. RODRÍGUEZ LÓPEZ, *El real monasterio de Las Huelgas y el Hospital del Rey* (cfr. note).
Logroño-Albelda, E. SAÍNZ RIPA, *Colleción diplomática de las colegiatas de Albelda y Logroño (924-1399)*, I, Logroño, 1981.
Nuestra Señora, Beneviveri, AHN, *Clero*, carp. 1693.
Osma, J. LOPERRÁEZ CORBALÁN, *Descripción histórica del obispado de Osma*, 3 voll., Madrid 1788.
Salamanca 1240-1300, J. L. MARTÍN, *Documentos de los archivos catedralicio y diocesano de Salamanca (siglos XII-XIII)*, Salamanca 1977. 1300-60, AHN, *Clero*, carps. 1886-88.
San Andrés de Arroyo, AHN, *Clero*, carps. 1731-35.
Santo Domingo de Silos, M. FEROTIN, *Recueil des chartes de l'abbeye de Silos*, Paris 1897.
San Juan de Burgos, *Fuentes medievales castellano-leonesas*, 1.
Santa María la Real de Aguilar de Campóo, AHN, *Códice* 994B; *Clero*, carps. 1657-74.
San Salvador de El Moral, SERRANO, *Fuentes* cit.
San Salvador de Oña, fino al 1284 J. DEL ÁLAMO, *Colección diplomática de San Salvador de Oña, 802-1284*, 2 voll., Madrid 1950; *Fuentes medievales castellano-leonesas*, 3. 1284-1360, AHN, *Clero*, carps. 297-313.
Santo Toribio de Liebana, L. SÁNCHEZ BELDA, *Cartulario de Santo Toribio de Liebana*, Madrid 1948.
San Zoilo de Carrión, AHN, *Clero*, carps. 1703-04.
Segovia (cattedrale, monasteri), AHN, *Códices*, 104B, 247B; *Clero*, carps. 1955-60, 1962-63, e i documenti contenuti nel libro, di prossima pubblicazione, di M. Santamaría.
Siguenza, T. MINGUELLA, *Historia de la diocesis de Siguenza y de sus obispos*, 3 voll., Madrid 1910-13.
Valladolid, fino al 1300, M. MAÑUECO VILLALOBOS, *Documentos de la iglesia colegial de Santa Maria la Mayor de Valladolid*, I, Valladolid 1917.

sì quali. Bisogna dire che la documentazione sulle conseguenze della peste è ben poca cosa: di quel periodo ci restano solo alcune transazioni non particolarmente diverse in natura da quelle anteriori al 1350, e se qualcosa si può dedurre dalle fonti è che negli anni '50 i trasferimenti di terra e di immobili subirono una drastica riduzione, anche se occorre notare che una tendenza verso il basso dell'attività economica era già osservabile alla fine degli anni '30 e negli anni '40 [13].

Le tabelle richiedono qualche spiegazione. Acquirenti e venditori sono stati divisi in base alla loro appartenenza allo stato ecclesiastico o secolare e, tra gli appartenenti alla prima categoria, ho operato una distinzione tra le istituzioni e gli individui. Riflettendo l'origine ecclesiastica della documentazione, il grosso degli acquisti risulta effettuato in primo luogo da istituzioni religiose e poi da membri del clero, in stragrande maggioranza canonici, e poi i diaconi dei capitoli delle cattedrali di Ávila, Burgos, Salamanca e Segovia, e anche membri del clero secolare. Queste acquisizioni individuali erano tuttavia chiaramente effettuate a titolo personale e non istituzionale, per il profitto economico e sociale degli acquirenti e delle loro famiglie, anche se a volte parte della proprietà finiva per passare alla chiesa tramite donazioni o testamenti. Nel caso per esempio di Blasco Blázquez (vedi sotto) quasi metà degli acquisti furono effettuati quando era ufficiale del re e laico: dopo essere entrato nella chiesa egli continuò ad acquistare proprietà rurale in due villaggi nei pressi di Ávila esattamente come aveva fatto prima.

Categorie come famiglie e gruppi non erano sempre uniformi, e quasi sempre compaiono come venditori. Le famiglie erano molto spesso composte da una vedova con i suoi figli che vendeva proprietà: nel 1329, per fare solo un esempio, Doña Juana insieme con i figli e le figlie vendette gli Algos di Castellanillo per 300 *maravedies (mrs.)* a mastro Sancho, prebendario della cattedrale di Ávila. Non era però insolito neanche l'altro caso, quello di un vedovo con i figli come venditore: nel 1305 un uomo e i suoi tre figli adulti vendettero terra al monastero di San Salvador de Oña per 700 *mrs*. In questi e in altri casi analoghi, compresi quei gruppi di persone che a prima vista non sembrano avere rapporti di parentela, ci troviamo probabilmente di fronte a casi di divisione di proprietà ereditata, anche se la cosa non è dichiarata esplicitamente nei documenti [14]. In tutta la Castiglia le eredità erano divisibili, e molte vendite senz'altro testimoniano il ricorso alla conversione della proprietà in denaro, riconosciuta come il modo più semplice e più equo di dividere un'eredità. I riferimenti diretti a vendite effettuate con questo scopo sono relativamente pochi, ma l'esigenza di disporre della proprietà di coloro che erano morti intestati, specialmente nelle zone rurali, deve aver rappresentato un'importante spinta a vendere. Abbiamo molti esempi di intere serie di transazioni intese o a dividere un'eredità o a rimettere insieme una proprietà dispersa dai termini del testamento. Il 9 maggio 1299 quattordici persone diverse vendettero diritti di macinatura al monastero di Santa María la Real di Aguilar del Campóo in dieci diverse transazioni tutte effettuate nello stesso giorno, e le registrazioni degli acquisti mostrano che buona parte dei venditori erano parenti di sangue (fratelli, sorelle, nipoti, ecc.) e probabilmente tutti e quattordici appartenevano allo stesso gruppo familiare: tutti vendevano diritti di macinatura nello stesso mulino (vicino allo *huço*) evidentemente per sistemare un'eredità. D'altra parte gli acquisti effettuati da Pedro Sarracín III, e altri analoghi avvenuti in seguito, avevano lo scopo di ricostituire la proprietà che era stata di suo zio Gonzalo Pérez, dispersa alla sua morte [15].

Tra i laici gli uomini, da soli o in gruppo, acquistavano terra più spesso delle donne, in un rapporto di quasi 6 a 1, mentre per quanto riguarda le vendite il rapporto, pur restando il numero globale di uomini impegnati nella vendita di terra superiore a quello delle donne, scendeva a 3 a 1: naturalmente includendo i membri del clero il rapporto è molto più alto per quanto riguarda gli acquisti, 12 a 1, mentre resta di 3 a 1 tra i venditori. Le coppie in quanto tali sono incluse nella tavola solo quando i termini del documento rendono esplicito che sia il marito sia la moglie più o meno condividessero la responsabilità economica di ciò che veniva venduto o acquistato, per cui se aggiungiamo il numero delle donne sposate a quello di quante vendevano in proprio, senza partecipazione maschile, riscontriamo un notevole livello di presenza femminile nelle transazioni di terra e di immobili. Per quanto riguarda ebrei e mori, in quei casi in cui sono citati nella documentazione (in proporzione schiacciante nelle transazioni relative a proprietà urbane) i loro acquisti erano fondamentalmente simili a quelli dei cristiani. Dobbiamo inoltre tener presente che, se è vero che molte piccole transazioni non furono mai registrate o non ci sono pervenute, il numero delle donne impegnate in transazioni economiche doveva essere più alto. Considerando gli schemi di distribuzione della proprietà tra uomini e donne nella Castiglia medievale, possiamo prevedere di trovare più donne nel settore della piccola proprietà o della piccola locazione, e così è nella tabella 4 [16].

C'è ancora un punto che richiede qualche precisazione. Come si è visto, Razi sostiene che molte delle transazioni terriere di Halesowen furono concluse tra parenti o tra vicini stretti. Per la Castiglia la documentazione esistente mostra il contrario: la maggior parte degli acquirenti erano istituzioni ecclesiastiche o membri del clero, oppure persone esterne alla comunità, in genere abitanti delle città vicine. Anche quando gli acquirenti erano abitanti del luogo troviamo prove che i loro acquisti erano spesso non un semplice scambio tra parenti o tra amici ma un razionale tentativo di accumulare proprietà. Così avviene per Miguel Peres, studiato dettagliatamente da Miguel Santamaría Lancho. Miguel Peres era un *vecino* e *morador* (cittadino e abitante) di Oter de Herreros, un villaggio nella diocesi di Segovia, che troviamo presente in 14 diverse transazioni avvenute tra il 30 ottobre 1341 e il 24 novembre 1358 come acquirente, da solo o con la moglie Doña Ines o con altri nove uomini, come nel caso dell'ultima transazione pervenutaci, di terre, vigne, campi di lino, di una casa e di altre proprietà rurali. Le quattordici transazioni comprendevano numerosi appezzamenti sparsi intorno al villaggio di Oter de Herreros: per esempio il 13 aprile 1347 acquistò in un'unica transazione 12 appezzamenti di terra, un campo di lino e un pascolo, quasi tutti di piccole dimensioni e sparpagliati in tutta la zona. Come era prevedibile in un piccolo villaggio, alcuni dei venditori erano legati da parentela tra loro e probabilmente anche con Miguel [17]. Il punto naturalmente non è tanto sapere se venditori e acquirenti erano parenti, quanto di sapere quale era lo scopo delle transazioni, e in questo caso particolare non c'è dubbio che le motivazioni non fossero semplicemente quelle di procurarsi altra terra per un erede, di dividere un'eredità o di aiutare un parente bisognoso, bensì si tratta chiaramente di un investimento: molto probabilmente questi acquisti migliorarono la posizione sociale di Miguel Peres nel villaggio e certamente anche la sua posizione economica.

Per quanto riguarda l'oggetto delle transazioni, la maggior parte delle vendite e degli acquisti riguarda la terra. Per terra intendiamo terra da cereali già coltivata ma anche, come a volte riferiscono i documenti, semplicemente adatta ad essere coltivata. L'agricoltura nella Castiglia settentrionale medievale, come anche in altre zone dell'Occidente, ben di rado era un'attività specializzata o esclusiva, incentrata su una sola produzione, e spesso quando si vendeva della terra nella transazione erano inclusi anche pascoli, campi di lino (dove la geografia e il clima lo permettevano), prati, ecc. Siamo qui di fronte alla tendenza e spesso alla necessità per il contadino medievale di produrre la massima varietà possibile di prodotti: nonostante la crescita nella regione del commercio e dell'interdipendenza economica, i contadini castigliani del XIII e del XIV secolo difficilmente avrebbero osato dipendere da un solo prodotto. Vi sono innumerevoli esempi di transazioni in cui, pur essendo indubbiamente la terra la voce principale, erano inclusi anche altri tipi di proprietà agricola: per lo più troviamo transazioni in cui tutta una serie di proprietà sono indicate con le formule «*heredamientos*» (letteralmente eredità o terra tenuta in allodio, ma nel contesto castigliano anche *tierras de pan llevar*, terre da cereali) o *todo lo que tengo* (tutto quello che ho). Il 28 agosto 1284 Blasco Martín, le sue due figlie e i mariti di queste vendettero a Blasco Blázquez «*todo quanto herediamento*» possedevano a Serranos de Avianos. In questo caso particolare la proprietà non è descritta in dettaglio, per quanto si possa presumere con sicurezza di che tipo fosse per analogia con altre transazioni nello stesso villaggio. Nel maggio 1242 Fernando Díaz de Cerezo e sua moglie Doña Endolza vendettero la loro *heredad*, terre cerealicole, vigne, case rurali, *solares* (proprietà tenuta in allodio) abitati e non abitati, orti, mulini, pascoli, acque, alberi, boschi, compresi tutti i diritti e ciò che vi si trovava, per 500 *mrs*. al monastero di Las Huelgas di Burgos. Moltissime transazioni comprese nella tabella 1 ripetono quasi parola per parola il linguaggio rispettivo dei due documenti citati, cioè il termine *heredad* è usato senza ulteriori precisazioni oppure precisato. A volte però le somme pagate appaiono in contraddizione con la descrizione dei beni venduti: nel 1249 cinque fratelli burgalesi effettuarono tre distinti acquisti nel villaggio di Villamorica, in tutti e tre i casi acquistando terra, servi, vigne, case, *solares*, orti, mulini, prati, ecc., ma il prezzo delle prime due transazioni, 15 *mrs*. e 40 *mrs*., non ha una reale corrispondenza con il valore di ciò che veniva acquistato [18]. La terra costava dunque così poco? L'acquisto comportava pagamenti occulti che a noi sfuggono? Oppure il linguaggio delle transazioni altro non era spesso che una vuota formula?

Se passiamo agli altri tipi di proprietà oggetto di transazione nella Castiglia settentrionale, vediamo che dopo la terra i più trattati erano le vigne e i mulini (o meglio i diritti di macinatura) e, in misura minore, gli orti. Vigne e mulini erano chiaramente acquistati e scambiati, molto più della terra, in vista di un ritorno finanziario: benché si acquistassero e vendessero vigne quasi dappertutto in Castiglia, in quelle regioni che erano più adatte alla viticoltura, per esempio la Rioja, la netta preferenza per le vigne come oggetto di scambio rivela l'esistenza di un attivo sottomercato del vino, senza contare il fatto che, dove i confini sono indicati, le vigne risultano ubicate vicino alle strade, a riprova del fatto che la produzione era destinata al mercato. Sotto questo punto di vista è indicativo l'investimento di Pedro Peres, che era cittadino di Burgos. Tra il 1324 e il 1326 Pedro acquistò sei vigne, sei appezzamenti di terra (di dimensioni non precisate) e una casa nel villaggio di Madrigal del Monte, spendendo in tutto la modesta somma di 713 *mrs.* La vigna più costosa fu venduta per 90 *mrs.*, e in una delle transazioni sei uomini gli vendettero una vigna per la miseria di 38 *mrs.*, mentre per la terra il prezzo più alto pagato fu di 123 *mrs.* e la casa costò 22 *mrs.* Abbiamo qui il caso di un cittadino che investe in un villaggio non poi così vicino alla città, e che, come risulta dalla documentazione, in seguito rivende nello stesso villaggio parte della proprietà con profitto, un cittadino che inoltre, come abbiamo visto, acquistava vigne e terre come mezzo di promozione sociale a Burgos. I documenti in genere non ci consentono di seguire i trasferimenti di proprietà attraverso diverse transazioni, ma Pedro Peres non fu l'unico a comprare e poi rivendere con profitto [19]. Per quanto riguarda i mulini la documentazione mostra senza ombra di dubbio l'esistenza di un attivo mercato di diritti di macinazione o di usufrutto con tendenza a una progressiva concentrazione dei diritti sui mulini nelle mani di potenti corporazioni locali, soprattutto capitoli, a partire dalla fine del XII secolo. Anche gli affitti dei mulini mostrano grandi fluttuazioni, dovute al mutamento della situazione economica e tali da smentire la tradizionale concezione di una politica economica rigida e conservatrice. Al contrario, nel XIII e nel XIV secolo i capitoli delle cattedrali castigliane consentirono, o furono costretti, ad abbassare i canoni di affitto quando le condizioni economiche lo richiedevano: così avvenne senz'altro nel 1314, quando il maltempo e la guerra civile congiurarono a peggiorare la situazione economica, e ancora nel 1344, che fu un anno di grande difficoltà nella Castiglia settentrionale, e molto più nel 1350, dopo la peste [20]. Ho lasciato per ultime le case (in genere urbane) perché l'argomento dell'articolo è soprattutto la compravendita di terra. Nella Castiglia settentrionale esisteva un attivo mercato di beni immobili urbani, così come di orti, granai, ecc., compresi entro la cinta urbana, che spesso avevano prezzi quattro o più volte superiori a quelli degli stessi beni ubicati in campagna. In queste transazioni assunsero un ruolo di rilievo dopo il 1200 i capitoli delle cattedrali e i monasteri urbani alla ricerca di proventi da affitto all'interno delle città, poi imitati e infine superati dall'aristocrazia urbana e dagli abitanti più intraprendenti, che cercavano di comprare case entro le mura per rivendicare il loro diritto alla cittadinanza (*vecinaje*) [21].

2. COMPRATORI URBANI: INDIVIDUI E CORPORAZIONI ECCLESIASTICHE

Dobbiamo ora passare dalla trattazione generale degli scambi di terra agli esempi specifici, che possono aiutarci meglio a chiarire la natura del mercato della terra nella Castiglia medievale ma anche, ciò che è ben più importante, i motivi per cui contadini e cittadini nel medioevo acquistavano e vendevano terra. La nostra principale fonte di informazione è rappresentata da coloro che effettuarono un certo numero di acquisti in un certo lasso di tempo e in una determinata località e che, per quanto possiamo ricavare dai documenti, lo fecero per migliorare la loro posizione economica. In questo senso il rapporto economico tra città e campagna è di importanza fondamentale. Se lasciamo da parte per un momento le corporazioni ecclesiastiche, la maggior parte delle transazioni elencate nella tabella 1 furono effettuate da un piccolo numero di individui. Si trattava di laici o di membri del clero, e le loro acquisizioni avevano chiaramente lo scopo di incrementare la loro ricchezza, di costituire una proprietà familiare – in alcuni casi un patrimonio o un'assegnazione – che ne migliorasse la posizione sociale nella città, o, in alcuni casi, di fare una donazione benefica degna del donatore. A parte una notevole eccezione, tutti quelli che comparivano come acquirenti nel cosiddetto «mercato contadino della terra» erano cittadini, e anche Miguel Peres, che è l'eccezione, potrebbe essere stato o un agente di interessi segoviani o egli stesso un «cittadino» (*vecino*) sia di Segovia sia di Oter de Herreros. Vale la pena di ribadire questo punto: negli acquisti di terra e di proprietà rurale nei villaggi della Castiglia settentrionale troviamo alcuni contadini benestanti, quelli che Moxó ha appropriatamente definito «*campesinos hacendados*» (contadini con terra), ma, a parte l'eccezione che abbiamo citato, in genere abbiamo solo qualche accenno di transazioni che rivelino un loro ruolo di acquirenti nel mercato della terra, mentre abbiamo prove documentarie sicure delle acquisizioni effettuate da abitanti delle città. Non bisogna però dedurne che esistesse una dicotomia netta tra città e campagna, ché nella Castiglia settentrionale, come si è già osservato, non esisteva quasi distinzione tra le due: le oligarchie urbane, i canonici, persino i ceti medi delle città, quasi senza eccezione, avevano proprietà nelle campagne intorno alle città castigliane, derivavano una parte spesso maggioritaria del loro reddito dagli affitti rurali e vivevano nelle loro tenute almeno per una parte dell'anno, spesso dalla festa di S. Giovanni fino a quella di S. Michele, al culmine del ciclo agricolo. Ho già mostrato in altra sede come l'investimento in proprietà rurali fosse un aspetto importante della vita economica e sociale dell'aristocrazia burgalese: a Burgos questo valeva non solo per le due famiglie dominanti della città ma anche per persone di rango inferiore, e ad Ávila, dove l'élite al potere non era così impegnata nel commercio come quella di Burgos, gli acquisti di terre e la costituzione di patrimoni rurali era ancor più importante [22].

Sotto questo punto di vista il caso di Blasco Blázquez è significativo, in quanto ci permette di esaminare il tentativo da parte di un solo uomo di acquisire più terra possibile in una località specifica della campagna di Ávila. Membro del *linaje* di Blasco Jimeno, una delle prime famiglie di Ávila, Blasco Blázquez fu giudice del re ad Ávila almeno dal 1283 fino al 1289, arcidiacono della cattedrale di Ávila dal 1297 al 1303 e decano del capitolo tra il 1303 e il 1307. Ci restano 50 transazioni in cui lui o suoi agenti compaiono come acquirenti in un lasso di tempo compreso tra il 1284 e il 1302, transazioni che riguardano tutte l'acquisto di proprietà rurali o nel villaggio di Serranos de Avianos o nella frazione di Cornejuelos, due località che secondo Barrios García confinavano con il possedimento di Blasco di San Adrian. È chiaro che queste cinquanta transazioni rappresentano solo una parte di un'attività ben più ampia di Blasco nell'acquisto di terre in questi due villaggi e in altre parti della regione di Ávila. Notiamo ancora che gran parte della terra acquistata a Serranos de Avianos fu lasciata in eredità, donata o venduta al capitolo, non senza quello che sembra un buon profitto per la sorella di Blasco [23].

La tabella 3 ci mostra la gamma dei prezzi e i tipi di proprietà che venivano acquistati e, soprattutto, ci permette di prendere in esame tutta una serie di venditori che non erano potenti proprietari terrieri. È chiaro che ci troviamo di fronte a contadini medi che spesso vendevano quel poco di terra che possedevano: tutti scambiavano terra o altri tipi di proprietà rurale con denaro in termini che, gioverà ripeterlo, ce li mostrano nelle vesti di attori economici indipendenti e consapevoli. Alcuni dei venditori presenti nella tabella hanno apparentemente venduto tutto ciò che avevano, spesso per dividere un'eredità, il che può servire in parte a spiegare il numero di famiglie o di gruppi (probabilmente comprendenti anche i congiunti) che appaiono nell'atto di vendere. In due casi questo è esplicito: Menga Andrés, vedova di

Gil Blázquez, vendette a Blasco tutto ciò che lei e i suoi fratelli avevano ereditato dalla madre a Cornejuelos (campi di cereali misti, orti, mulini, pascoli e diritti di pascolo nel villaggio) per 33 *mrs.* nel 1301, e nello stesso anno Doña Juana, per conto dei suoi fratelli e sorelle, gli vendette proprietà nello stesso villaggio per 600 *mrs.* Come mostra la tabella, una buona parte dei venditori si libera di tutta la terra posseduta in ciascuno dei due vil-

TABELLA 3. *Acquisti effettuati da Blasco Blázquez a Serranos de Avianos e Cornejuelos, 1284-1302*

Acquisti a Serranos de Avianos			25
Acquisti a Cornejuelos			25
Totale			50
Venditori:			
Numero totale degli individui citati come venditori			96[1]
Numero totale degli uomini			56
Numero totale delle donne			40
Uomini da soli			20
Donne da sole			3
Coppie			15
Famiglie/Gruppi			12
Numero delle transazioni in cui la formulazione indica che i venditori cedevano tutto ciò che possedevano nella località			26
Numero di volte in cui i venditori sono designati con l'appellativo *don* o *doña*			9[2]
Gamma dei prezzi nelle transazioni			
0-50 *mrs.*	7	301-400 *mrs.*	7
51-100 *mrs.*	11	401-500 *mrs.*	0
101-200 *mrs.*	12	501-600 *mrs.*	2
201-300 *mrs.*	10	Sconosciuto	1
Tipo di proprietà venduta			
a) Proprietà agraria (vedi tabella 1)			40
b) Terra (vedi tabella 1)			6
c) Mulini/ diritti di macinatura			1
d) Orti			3
e) Terra da pascolo			1
f) Coppie di buoi			1
g) Diritti di pascolo sulle terre comuni			2

Note: [1] Due transazioni si riferiscono a fratelli e sorelle, il cui numero non è precisato dai documenti.
[2] Anche molti dei parenti dei venditori sono tuttavia citati come *don* o *doña*.

laggi. Disponevano di proprietà altrove? Acquistarono proprietà nella stessa località con il ricavato della vendita? O le formule «*todo heredamiento*» o «*todo lo que tengo*» sono ingannevoli? In effetti nel 1299 Domingo Sancho e sua moglie Andariezo vendettero «tutto ciò che avevano» a Serranos de Avianos per 100 *mrs.*, eppure due anni dopo la stessa coppia vendette a Blasco Blázquez per 60 *mrs.* due case con un'aia nello stesso villaggio [24].

Le registrazioni delle transazioni ci forniscono inoltre qualche informazione su chi erano i venditori: l'uso di *don* o di *doña* per indicare alcuni di essi o i loro parenti dimostra che avevano un certo rango all'interno del villaggio; l'uso di termini come *heredad* così come la vendita di diritti di pascolo indica che la terra era tenuta in allodio con pochi o nessuno dei cosiddetti obblighi «feudali» o signorili; inoltre buona parte dei venditori erano *vecinos* (cittadini dei villaggi) con tutti i diritti di usare i pascoli compresi nei villaggi stessi [25].

Se passiamo alle istituzioni come compratori, il modello è in realtà simile. Per motivi di spazio, le informazioni possono essere date in modo più economico nella tabella 4. In alto abbiamo gli acquisti effettuati dal monastero femminile di Las Huelgas di Burgos e dai suoi agenti in un periodo di tre decenni nel villaggio di Frausillas nei pressi di Dueñas [26]. Quello che distingue queste transazioni da altre esaminate in altre parti di questo articolo è il prezzo uniformemente basso pagato dal monastero, oltre all'uniformità di ciò che viene comprato, solo terra: forse ci troviamo finalmente di fronte al livello più basso di proprietari terrieri nella gerarchia economica e sociale dei contadini. Eppure anche qui sono evidenti segni di stratificazione sociale nell'uso degli appellativi *don* e *doña*. A Frausillas le suore di Las Huelgas decisero consapevolmente di creare una tenuta abbastanza unitaria: insieme con numerosi altri acquisti in quattro frazioni vicine, abbiamo una parziale visione della formazione di una proprietà di dimensioni consistenti attraverso la ridefinizione dei confini nell'arco di trent'anni.

Tra coloro che hanno venduto terra a Frausillas solo alcuni lo hanno fatto più di una volta. Interpolando da alcuni dei pochi documenti in cui è precisata la quantità di terra venduta, possiamo constatare l'abisso che separa, almeno in questo caso particolare, i venditori dagli acquirenti. Si può valutare a 2 *sueldos* il valore dell'*obrada* di terra (la quantità di terra che si può arare in un giorno, più o meno tra le 46 e le 53 *areas*): se questo è il prezzo, con un calcolo approssimativo possiamo calcolare che la maggior parte degli appezzamenti messi in vendita non superasse mediamente le 12 *obradas*, un'estensione non sufficiente a mantenere una famiglia. Prendendo in considerazione le necessità del convento di Las Huelgas, non è difficile capire perché le monache acquistassero terra. Nella Castiglia settentrionale esisteva nel XIII secolo una tendenza generale a unificare le tenute agricole e ad aumentare gli affitti rurali e urbani, ma in un certo

Tabella 4. *Acquisti effettuati dal monastero di Las Huelgas (Burgos) a Frausillas (Dueñas), 1229-1262*

Numero totale delle transazioni			53
Venditori			
Numero totale dei contadini citati come venditori			108
Uomini			65
Donne			43
Famiglie/Gruppi			14
Coppie			20
Uomini			19
Donne			4
Tipo di proprietà venduta			
Esclusivamente terra			
Gamma dei prezzi			
0-5 *mrs.*	43	5-10 *mrs.*	10
Cifra massima pagata per la terra:		9 *mrs.*	
Cifra minima pagata per la terra:		4 *ss.*	
Prezzo medio per transazione:		3 *mrs.*	
Numero di contadini che vendono terra più di una volta:			
Contadini che vendono due volte:			4
Contadini che vendono 3 volte:			1
Numero di volte in cui è usato l'appellativo *don* o *doña*			
Don	30		
Doña	34		
Confini della proprietà venduta a Las Huelgas			
Terra appartenente ad altri contadini			71
Di questa, terra appartenente a Juan Adrian			9
Monte (terreno boscoso e incolto)			100
Carrera (strade, sentieri)			22
Terra appartenente a Las Huelgas			13
Terra appartenente ad altra istituzione ecclesiastica			5
Vigna			1

senso questo schema di acquisizioni non differiva molto dagli acquisti del periodo precedente. Che così stiano le cose basta a dimostrarcelo una semplice occhiata alle registrazioni di transazioni di terra conservate nella cattedrale di Burgos per il periodo fino al 1240 (cfr. tabella 5).

TABELLA 5. *Numero di transazioni conservate nell'archivio della cattedrale di Burgos per il periodo 1000-1360*

1000-1099	1100-1199	1200-1240	1240-1299	1300-1360
5	83	133	86	140

La differenza era sotto molti aspetti qualitativa, e dipendeva dal luogo e dal tempo dell'acquisto e, soprattutto, dalla persona che all'acquisto procedeva. Prima del 1200, almeno a Burgos, troviamo molti acquirenti diversi, ma ben pochi comprano più di una manciata di proprietà; manca inoltre la netta connotazione urbana che caratterizza le transazioni successive. Dopo il 1200, e certamente dopo il 1240, il ruolo decisivo dell'aristocrazia urbana nel mercato della terra determina quella netta transizione che Jacques Le Goff, in un diverso contesto, appropriatamente definisce transizione «dal cielo alla terra». Assistiamo in questo periodo a un duplice processo: innanzitutto, dal 1200 in poi le oligarchie urbane castigliane monopolizzano importanti benefici nei capitoli delle cattedrali e dei collegi, per poi volgere a proprio favore le rendite ecclesiastiche, un processo che nella Castiglia settentrionale si riflette molto chiaramente nel diverso schema di acquisizioni, che passa dagli acquisti ad opera dei capitoli ad acquisti ad opera di membri dei capitoli. In secondo luogo gli abitanti delle città, spesso con denaro guadagnato con il grande commercio o con l'allevamento, prendono a costituire grandi proprietà nelle campagne circostanti. La nascita di una nuova mentalità urbana in concomitanza con la pratica mercantile, che nella Castiglia settentrionale si può far risalire alla fine dell'XI secolo, prende a interagire, molto nettamente dopo il 1200, con i più tradizionali modelli rurali di organizzazione e di mentalità economica [27].

3. LA FORMAZIONE DI UN MERCATO DELLA TERRA

Se possiamo avanzare ipotesi assai attendibili sui motivi per cui i monasteri e/o gli individui acquistavano proprietà, resta da chiarire perché i contadini vendevano la loro terra. Che cosa facevano poi? Purtroppo i dati necessari a rispondere a questa domanda non sempre ci sono pervenuti, e nessuna spiegazione appare da sola del tutto soddisfacente. La risposta più facile è che i contadini castigliani abbiano venduto la loro terra perché avevano l'opportunità di emigrare nel meridione. Questa spiegazione appare estremamente attendibile per il periodo compreso tra la vittoria cristiana di Las Navas de Tolosa nel 1212 e gli anni successivi alla conquista definitiva di gran parte dell'Andalusia, dopo il 1250, quando la regione fu aperta alla colonizzazione cristiana. I *repartimientos* di Siviglia, Jerez, Murcia e Cadice (le registrazioni della distribuzione delle proprietà dei mori ai nuovi colonizzatori cristiani) mostrano l'origine geografica di coloro che ricevettero terra e immobili nella zona, in gran parte provenienti dalla meseta settentrionale. Oltre ai vantaggi climatici, nel meridione il prezzo della terra era notevolmente basso, mentre i salari rurali erano e restavano più alti che nella Castiglia settentrionale. Nondimeno numerose transazioni di terra e di immobili furono effettuate nel settentrione prima del 1212, un periodo in cui la frontiera cristiano-musulmana era notevolmente stabile, e continuarono dopo gli anni '60 quando l'attrazione dell'Andalusia cominciò a venir meno o quando di fatto presero a verificarsi casi di migrazione in senso inverso [28]. L'attrazione della frontiera non può essere la sola spiegazione: deve esserci una serie di altre ragioni per cui i contadini hanno venduto le loro proprietà. Molte di queste ragioni sono già state esaminate dagli storici a proposito del mercato della terra in Inghilterra, o sono implicite in quanto abbiamo detto prima: l'esigenza di dividere un'eredità, le difficoltà economiche, l'impossibilità per i contadini di opporsi agli acquisti predatori di un potente come Blasco Blázquez o di un'istituzione ecclesiastica. È un fatto che in alcune transazioni è detto esplicitamente che la vendita viene effettuata allo scopo di pagare un debito con un usuraio ebreo, ed è chiaro che alla fine del XIII secolo e all'inizio del XIV molti contadini dei villaggi di tutta la regione dovevano contrarre forti debiti, e che le loro terre erano vendute su ordine delle autorità per pagarli: sotto molti aspetti anche questo è uno dei modi in cui avveniva l'interazione tra città e campagna, certo non a favore di quest'ultima [29]. Ma questi non sono gli unici fattori, ché altri vennero alla ribalta alla fine degli anni '50 e nella seconda metà del secolo. A questo proposito nei decreti reali rivolti ai cavalieri non nobili della Castiglia (estesi poco dopo il 1256 anche ai canonici e agli ecclesiastici) troviamo notevoli concessioni economiche che possono aver stimolato le transazioni terriere. Coloro che servivano o lavoravano (braccianti) per cavalieri urbani non nobili e per canonici potevano possedere terra esente da tasse fino a un valore di 100 *mrs.* Ci troviamo di fronte a settori contadini che stavano diventando affittuari delle oligarchie urbane ed ecclesiastiche in ascesa e nello stesso tempo mantenevano proprietà di valore inferiore a 100 *mrs.*? Dopotutto alla fine del XIII secolo con questa somma si acquistava abbastanza terra da mantenere comodamente una famiglia e anche di più, come si deduce dalla gamma di prezzi inclusa nella tabella 1. Inoltre col procedere del XIV secolo il livello di violenza politica crebbe fino a diventare un grave motivo di dissesto della vita agricola [30]. Non è quindi assurdo supporre che molti contadini abbiano venduto la loro terra o almeno parte di essa per ottenere non solo l'esenzione dalle tasse ma anche la protezione di un monastero o di un membro della guardia a cavallo della città vicina. La documentazione di cui disponiamo è marginale rispetto al problema, ma indica molto nettamente l'esistenza di un meccanismo per cui i contadini vendevano la loro terra ma vi restavano come affittuari. In effetti non esiste altra spiegazione, in quanto in Castiglia non c'era quell'eccedenza demografica che alla fine del XIII secolo caratterizzava la Francia o l'Inghilterra, e questo conferisce un carattere totalmente diverso al mercato contadino della terra in Castiglia. Se prendiamo attentamente in esame gli acquisti effettuati dal monastero di Las Huelgas a Frausillas notiamo che il terreno arabile acquistato era molto spesso circondato da *montes*, appezzamenti boscosi e incolti, e la corrispondente documentazione relativa a Segovia mostra che in Castiglia doveva esserci abbondanza di terra ma probabilmente non abbastanza braccia per coltivarla tutta: questo è vero fino al 1300 e lo è ancora di più in seguito. Nella Castiglia settentrionale quindi non c'era alcuna pressione sulle terre marginali, ma semmai scarsità di manodopera. Inoltre c'era nello stesso periodo penuria di attrezzi agricoli e di animali da lavoro, il che può contribuire a spiegare la volontà dei contadini di vendere la terra per poi restarvi come affittuari in modo da avere accesso a buoi e attrezzi agricoli [31]. Perché mai i monasteri o le oligarchie urbane avrebbero acquistato terra se non ci fosse stato nessuno a coltivarla?

Il rafforzamento dei diritti signorili sulla proprietà rurale e urbana nella Castiglia del basso medioevo presenta notevoli parallelismi con analoghi sviluppi avvenuti in altre parti d'Europa, benché tale rafforzamento non sia stato, per quanto possiamo dedurre dai documenti, opera di signori ma di abitanti non nobili delle città. In Castiglia c'è comunque la stessa reazione che si verifica in altre parti dell'Occidente al declino dei redditi derivanti da affitti e all'aumento del costo del lavoro. I meccanismi che portarono a questo processo sono però assai diversi e non sempre facili da definire: per esempio non abbiamo abbastanza dati sui braccianti giornalieri e sul loro ruolo nella produzione agricola, se non quanto basta per osservare che a loro era affidata la maggior parte dei lavori agricoli nei monasteri benedettini della Castiglia settentrionale. Possiamo inoltre supporre che questi braccianti possedessero anche terra propria, forse non abbastanza da mantenere la famiglia o da renderli indipendenti, ma comunque qualcosa che potevano dire loro. Così in Castiglia i legami personali tra contadini e proprietari e tra i contadini stessi non escludevano l'esistenza di un numero considerevole di contadini che o possedevano terra o la tenevano in affitto perpetuo a condizioni almeno in teoria meno vincolanti di quelle praticate in altre parti dell'Europa settentrionale; il che non significa naturalmente che il livello di sfruttamento o di vera e propria estorsione subita dai contadini fosse inferiore a quello del nord. Nella prima metà del XIV secolo, quando gli affitti terrieri presero a diminuire in tutto il territorio (una diminuzione che è dimostrata molto chiaramente dal fatto che la corona accettò una drastica riduzione del numero degli iscritti nelle liste fiscali), il re e i proprietari sia laici sia ecclesiastici si trovarono con molta meno gente di prima a cui imporre tasse o estorsioni, senza contare il fatto che sia la situazione economica sia gli usi radicati non permettevano di aumentare i contributi per compensare le perdite. In questa lotta per il reddito la corona e i signori esigevano denaro in tutti i modi possibili, dall'appropriazione diretta di terre monastiche ai prestiti forzosi al furto vero e proprio [32].

In questo contesto cosa possiamo dedurre dalle transazioni di terra o di immobili? La documentazione indica un deciso processo di passaggio della proprietà rurale e urbana dalle mani dei più deboli e più poveri a quelle dei più ricchi: contrariamente alle fonti inglesi, che riflettono forse una fase precedente di questo processo per quanto riguarda il villaggio, quelle della Castiglia settentrionale mostrano molto chiaramente una concentrazione di terra nelle mani di pochi potenti, ma a differenza di altre parti d'Europa, questi cambi di proprietà non ebbero luogo nel contesto di un aumento di popolazione, della cosiddetta pressione malthusiana. Le distinzioni economiche e sociali che stavano emergendo all'interno delle comunità rurali castigliane – e i conflitti erano aggravati dall'ingresso della piccola nobiltà rurale e del clero nei consigli comunali – provocarono sempre più forti tensioni sociali, a cui si aggiungeva l'aggravarsi del divario economico tra gli acquirenti cittadini e i venditori rurali, un divario che spesso sfociava nella violenza. Non intendo far mia la tesi di Brenner, che spiega lo sviluppo economico europeo nel basso medioevo esclusivamente in termini di rapporti di classe, ma certo non possiamo ignorare che si tratta di un fattore importante del mutamento avvenuto in quel periodo nella Castiglia settentrionale e della formazione di un mercato della terra. Nel nostro caso specifico il passaggio della proprietà dal basso verso l'alto era molto spesso il modo in cui l'oligarchia urbana e i canonici e i diaconi dei capitoli delle cattedrali trasformavano i loro profitti commerciali o le loro rendite ecclesiastiche in proprietà terriere e, potremmo aggiungere, in proprietà terriere poco costose. Né la cosa deve sorprenderci: fin dove arriva la documentazione abbiamo sempre tracce di questo movimento della proprietà dal basso verso l'alto, anche se non si tratta, bisogna precisare, di un processo uniforme e immutabile, e anzi i contadini, specialmente in tempi difficili, possono essere stati consenzienti. Eppure attraverso il prestito, vitalizio o limitato a un determinato numero di anni (è una questione che non può essere trattata in questa sede per mancanza di spazio), la terra era ridistribuita ai contadini a condizioni non diverse da quelle di cui usufruivano quando della terra erano proprietari. Questo passaggio dalla frammentazione della terra alla concentrazione e poi di nuovo alla frammentazione, come abbiamo osservato, è stato uno schema ricorrente nei villaggi della Castiglia e del León fino a tempi molto recenti [33].

Esisteva un mercato contadino della terra? I contadini vendevano, e a volte compravano? Sì, ed erano molti a farlo, se è vera la mia tesi che ciò che ci è pervenuto è solo una piccola parte di un ben più ampio sistema di scambi. Ma questo cosiddetto mercato contadino della terra ben poco ci aiuta a scoprire se il capitalismo fosse o no dietro l'angolo, o se, avendo la possibilità di esaminare più a fondo la documentazione, si scoprirebbe che i caratteri tradizionali di vita rurale erano cambiati ben poco. Sempre dominati dall'avidità e dal bisogno, dal dovere familiare e dal timor di Dio, acquirenti e venditori di terra e di immobili continuarono a soddisfare le esigenze molto terrene e comuni della vita quotidiana. Sono caratteri che a volte possono inserirsi molto bene in un quadro di sviluppo, ma più spesso non sopportano categorizzazioni di questo tipo: nella Castiglia settentrionale del basso medioevo le transazioni di terra e di immobili riflettevano il momento e la peculiare situazione del regno, e ci danno un'idea della mentalità e del tipo di organizzazione economica e sociale che a quel tempo permetteva ai potenti di dominare i deboli.

Non sto naturalmente dicendo nulla di nuovo: non meno di questo, e molto meglio, ha già detto Angus MacKay. L'intrusione del capitale mercantile e della mentalità urbana nel mondo rurale non segnò la nascita del capitalismo ma solo un cambiamento del modo in cui gli abitanti delle città, laici o ecclesiastici che fossero, traevano vantaggio economico dalla terra [34]. Nelle pagine precedenti ho mostrato che la documentazione indica l'esistenza nella Castiglia settentrionale di un mercato della terra e degli immobili, e che questo mercato fu caratterizzato dall'intrusione di mentalità e pratiche economiche urbane nel mondo rurale: la lenta interazione dei due fattori fu un processo lungo e continuo, non risolto nella Castiglia settentrionale fino a pochi anni fa, e tuttora esistente e osservabile in molte parti del mondo.

NOTE AL TESTO

[1] Fino al XIV secolo il grosso della documentazione disponibile per la Castiglia settentrionale fu conservata negli archivi delle cattedrali e dei monasteri. Buona parte di queste raccolte si trova attualmente nell'Archivo histórico nacional (d'ora in poi AHN), sección *Clero*, a Madrid. La stessa logica interna di queste fonti mostra che sono molto spesso incomplete. Vedi T. F. Ruiz, *Sociedad y poder real en Castilla*, Barcelona 1981, p. 84 (d'ora in poi citato come *Sociedad y poder real*). Anche le raccolte di documenti relativi alle grandi case nobiliari iniziano ad avere consistenza dopo il 1350. Vedi P. Martínez Sopena, *El estado señorial de Medina de Rioseco bajo el almirante Alfonso Enríquez (1389-1430)*, Valladolid 1977, pp. 54-83; S. De Moxó, *De la nobleza vieja a la nobleza nueva*, in *Cuadernos de historia. Anejos de Hispania*, III, Madrid 1964. Vedi anche sotto, nota 4, per la documentazione non registrata.

[2] Sto attualmente rivedendo una lunga monografia sulla società della Castiglia settentrionale nel basso medioevo, dal titolo provvisorio *Patterns of Development in Northern Castile in the Late Middle Ages*, in cui utilizzo i documenti delle transazioni terriere per ricostruire la vita di villaggio, le dimensioni delle proprietà, i rendi-

menti, i metodi di coltivazione, ecc., nonché il rapporto tra città e campagna. Per l'uso delle transazioni ai fini della ricostruzione della storia della famiglia vedi il mio *The Transformation of the Castilian Municipalities: The Case of Burgos*, in «Past and Present», 77 (1977), pp. 3-33; e *Los Sarracin y los Bonifaz. Dos linajes patricios de Burgos, 1248-1350*, in *Sociedad y poder real*, cap. 5.

[3] Vedi per esempio AHN, *Clero*, carpeta (carp.) 24, n. 16 (9.V.1301) in cui Blasco Blázquez (vedi sotto) acquistò «todo cuanto hay salvo tierra con su pan» a Serranos de Avianos (nei pressi di Ávila) per 400 *maravedies (mrs.)*. Anche AHN, *Clero*, carp. 27, n. 3 (29.IV.1317) in cui Gómez Gil, arciprete di Ávila, acquista *heredamientos* a San Miguel de Serrazuelos (regione di Ávila) per 120 *mrs*. Per analoghe vendite di *heredades* a Oña (a nord di Burgos) vedi AHN, *Clero*, carp. 297, n. 12 (18.VII.1285); carp. 297, n. 21 (14.II.1286); per *todo lo que tengo*, carp. 301, n. 6 (27.VI.1292) e *passim*. *Heredad* significa proprietà in completo possesso. Vedi *Heredad* in *Diccionario de historia de España*, 3 voll., Madrid 1952, I, 1337. Per *heredad* nell'altro significato di terra cerealicola vedi sotto.

[4] Uno dei più recenti contributi al dibattito è *The Peasant Land Market in Medieval England*, a cura di P. D. A. Harvey, Oxford 1984, e in particolare l'introduzione di Harvey, pp. 1-28. Vedi anche p. 22 per le sue argomentazioni relative alle transazioni non registrate. Anche P. R. HYAMS, *The Origins of a Peasant Land Market in England*, in «Economic History Review», 23 (1970), p. 19; Z. RAZI, *Family, Land and the Village Community in Later Medieval England*, in «Past and Present», 93 (1981), pp. 3-36; E. KING, *Peterborough Abbey, 1086-1360. A Study in the Land Market*, Cambridge 1973, pp. 55-62, 168 ss. A causa della natura della documentazione castigliana questo articolo non è incentrato sulle transazioni tra contadini di rango economico e sociale più o meno uguale, anche se alcune transazioni di questo tipo sono prese in esame, ma piuttosto su quelle in cui persone notevolmente benestanti comprano da persone più povere.

[5] RAZI, *Family, Land and the Village Community* cit., pp. 3-4, 29; e anche, dello stesso autore, *Life, Marriage and Death in a Medieval Parish: Economy, Society and Demography in Halesowen, 1270-1400*, Cambridge 1980.

[6] Vedi sopra, nota 5. Per la tesi opposta vedi J. A. RAFTIS, *Tenure and Mobility. Studies in the Social History of the Medieval English Village*, Toronto 1974; A. MACFARLANE, *The Origin of the English Individualism: The Family, Property and Social Transaction*, Oxford 1978. Devo ancora mettere in rilievo il fatto che buona parte di queste discussioni vertono sull'impatto della Morte Nera sulla società rurale. Gran parte della documentazione usata in questo articolo risale a prima del 1350, e almeno in parte una delle mie obiezioni è che in Castiglia importanti trasformazioni si erano già verificate negli anni precedenti la peste. Ad attirare per prima la mia attenzione su questa questione e sui suoi aspetti comparativi è stata la stimolante comunicazione di G. LEVI, *The Market for Land; England, Colonial America, India and a Village in Piedmont in the XVIIth Century*, presentata al Social Science Seminar all'Institute for Advanced Study, Princeton, aprile 1984.

[7] Solo di rado la documentazione castigliana fornisce indicazioni di parentela. Tuttavia, come vedremo più oltre, la maggior parte delle transazioni castigliane *non* avvennero tra parenti o tra amici intimi.

[8] R. BEHAR, *Santa Maria del Monte. The Presence of the Past in a Spanish Village*, Princeton 1986, pp. 189-285.

[9] Solo ora la questione del rapporto tra città e campagna nella Castiglia medievale riceve l'attenzione degli storici. Si tratta di una delle questioni prese in esame nel mio libro di prossima pubblicazione. Un'opera pionieristica sull'argomento è l'eccellente articolo di A. MACKAY, *Ciudad y campo en la Europa medieval*, in «Studia histórica», II (1984), 2, pp. 27-53; C. ESTEPA DIEZ, *El alfoz y las relaciones*

campociudad en Castilla y León durante los siglos XII y XIII, in «Studia histórica», II (1984), 2, pp. 7-26. Anche J. Langton, G. Hoppe, *Town and Country in the Development of Early Modern Western Europe* (Historical Geography Research Series), 11, nov. 1983.

[10] E. A. R. Brown, *The Tyranny of a Construct: Feudalism and Historians of Medieval Europe*, in «American Historical Review», 79 (1974), pp. 1063-88; P. Linehan, *The Toledo Forgeries*, Antiquary Prize Essay, Denis Hay Seminar in Medieval and Renaissance History. Università di Edinburgo, gennaio 1986, e *La reconquista de Toledo y la supuesta feudalización de Castilla*, dattiloscritto. Voglio ringraziare qui il professor Linehan che mi ha permesso di esaminare entrambi i saggi prima della pubblicazione.

[11] Per la tesi relativa alla formazione di un mercato della terra in Inghilterra alla fine del XII secolo o all'inizio del XIII, in corrispondenza di «un brusco cambiamento dell'atteggiamento della famiglia nei confronti delle sue proprietà», vedi King, *Peterborough Abbey* cit., pp. 61 ss., 168 ss.; Harvey, *op. cit.*, pp. 12, 27. L'intera discussione non può prescindere quanto meno dal riconoscimento dei problemi posti da R. Brenner, *Agrarian Class Structure and Economic Development in Pre-Industrial Europe*, in «Past and Present», 70 (1976), pp. 30-75 e dal dibattito che ne seguì su «Past and Present», 78, 79, 80 e 97. Vedi sotto.

[12] Le restrizioni più comuni si trovano spesso negli affitti terrieri vitalizi. I monaci proprietari ammettevano implicitamente che in futuro la terra o il diritto d'affitto potessero essere venduti, e chiedevano che la terra non venisse alienata né venduta o affittata a nobili o a persone esentate dalle tasse. Vedi per esempio AHN, *Clero*, carp. 1658, n. 15 (27.V.1267); carp. 1733, n. 2 (20.XI.1321); carp. 1033, n. 5 (20.XII.1323); carp. 1025, n. 15 (24.II.1328).

[13] Sulla scarsità della documentazione per il decennio successivo alla peste, così come per i due decenni precedenti, vedi T. F. Ruiz, *From Love to Ritual: Feeding and Clothing the Poor in Late Medieval Castle*, di prossima pubblicazione. Il generale rallentamento delle transazioni negli anni '30 e '40 del XIV secolo appare evidente dagli esempi che seguono, tratti dalla cattedrale di Burgos e dal monastero di Santa Maria la Real de Aguilar de Campóo.

	numero di transazioni	decenni
Burgos	41	1320-29
	30	1330-39
	28	1340-49
	4	1350-59
Aguilar de Campóo	10	1320-29
	9	1330-39
	2	1340-49
	1	1350-59

[14] AHN, *Clero*, carp. 27, n. 16 (24.III.1329); carp. 305, n. 10 (17.VII.1305).

[15] Sulle eredità divisibili vedi L. K. Berkner, F. F. Mendels, *Inheritance Systems, Family Structures, and Demographic Patterns in Western Europe, 1700-1900*, in *Historical Studies of Changing Fertility*, a cura di C. Tilly, Princeton 1978, pp. 209-33; *Household and Family in Past Time*, a cura di P. Laslett e R. Wall, Cambridge 1972; R. Behar, D. Frye, *Property, Progeny and Emotion: Family History in a*

Leonese Village, di prossima pubblicazione su «Journal of Family History». Vedi anche esempi in AHN, *Clero*, carp. 1663, n. 4 (9.V.1299); Archivo catedral de Burgos (ACB), vol. 50, f. 152 (25.I.1292); vol. 49, f. 96 (28.XII.1292); vol. 49, f. 98 (4.II.1293) e *passim*.

[16] Sulle donne come acquirenti e come affittuarie e per riferimenti alle minoranze vedi T. F. Ruiz, *Notas para el estudio de la mujer en el área del Burgos medieval*, in *El pasado historico de Castilla y León. Ier Congreso de Historia de Castilla y León*, 3 voll., Burgos 1983, I, pp. 419-28; sulle donne in Castiglia vedi l'eccellente libro di H. Dillard, *Daughters of the Reconquest. Women in Castilian Town Society, 1100-1300*, Cambridge 1984.

[17] Sebbene io abbia trascritto tutte le registrazioni di queste transazioni all'Archivo histórico nacional di Madrid, l'analisi di questi scambi viene dall'opera di prossima pubblicazione dedicata da Miguel Santamaría Lancho alle politiche economiche del capitolo della cattedrale di Segovia. Voglio ringraziare il professor Santamaría per il suo aiuto e la sua gentilezza.

[18] A. Barrios García, *Documentación medieval de la catedral de Ávila*, Salamanca 1981, § 116, pp. 103-104 (d'ora in poi citato come *DM*). Per Blásco Blazquez vedi sotto. Anche J. M. Lizoaín Garrido, *Documentación del monasterio de Las Huelgas de Burgos (1231-1262)*, in *Fuentes medievales castellano-leonesas*, 31, Burgos 1981, pp. 115-16, 186-90.

[19] Su Pedro Peres vedi il mio *The Transformation of the Castilian Municipalities* cit., p. 16, n. 50. Per un esempio di vendita per profitto vedi AHN, *Clero*, carp. 1959, n. 5 (20.XII.1337). Nel 1337 Llorente Yuanez e sua moglie vendettero parte di una casa a Segovia al capitolo della cattedrale per 280 *mrs.*: in origine la casa era costata solo 130 *mrs.*

[20] Vedi il mio *Patterns of Development*, in corso di pubblicazione, cap. IV. Sui mulini Ruiz, *Sociedad y poder real*, cap. III; A. Rucquoi, *Molino et aceñas au coeur de la Castille septentrionale (XIe-XVe siècles)*, in *Les Espagnes médiévales. Aspects économiques et soçiaux. Mélanges offerts à Jean Gautier-Dalché*, Nice 1983, pp. 107-22; J. Gautier-Dalché, *Moulin à eau, seigneurie, communauté rurale dans le nord de l'Espagne* (IXe-XIIe siècles), in *Etudes de civilisation médiévale, mélanges E.R. Labande*, Poitiers 1974. Vedi ACB, *Cuadernos de contabilidad*. Un esempio della fluttuazione della rendita dell'affitto del mulino di Villayuda (di proprietà del capitolo) sarà qui sufficiente.

1277	101 *mrs.*, 4 *sueldos*, 4 *dineros*
1279	103 *mrs.*
1280	60 *mrs.*
1282	212 *mrs.*, 2 *ss.*, 9 *ds.*
1314	168 *mrs.*, 51/2 *ss.*
1325	380 *mrs.*
1344	310 *mrs.*
1350	200 *mrs.* da portare a 230 l'anno successivo.

[21] Per quanto riguarda il possesso di proprietà urbana da parte dei capitoli di cattedrale a Burgos vedi ACB, *Cuadernos de contabilidad*, che mostrano come il capitolo possedesse una grande quantità di case all'interno delle mura cittadine e precisano gli affitti che ne ricavava. Anche H. Casado Alonso, *La propiedad eclesiástica en la ciudad de Burgos en el siglo XV: el cabildo catedralicio*, Valladolid 1980, pp. 97-137. Per Ávila, *DM*, pp. 223-32, 416-48. Per i diritti di *Vecinaje* vedi il mio *Patterns of Development*, in prossima pubblicazione, e *The Transformation of the Castilian Municipalities* cit., pp. 11-20.

[22] Vedi S. De Moxó, *Campesinos hacendados leoneses en el siglo XIV*, in *León medieval*, León 1978, pp. 165-98. Per le restrizioni agli abitanti delle città residenti

in campagna vedi il *fuero* di Trevino in *Monumento histórico español* (d'ora in poi *MHE*), 49 voll., Madrid 1851-1948, I, xxiii-xxiv e *passim*. Vedi anche i miei *The Transformation of the Castilian Municipalities* cit., e *Patterns of Development*, in corso di stampa, contenente una lunga discussione dell'interazione tra città e campagna. Per Ávila vedi sotto.

[23] Vedi A. Barrios García, *Estructuras agrarias y de poder en Castilla. El ejemplo de Ávila (1085-1320)*, 2 voll., Salamanca 1983-84, II, pp. 135-51, 147, n. 37. Vedi la tavola e *DM*, p. 215. In un elenco delle proprietà del capitolo di Ávila c'è anche la registrazione di una proprietà di Blasco Blázquez, che aveva ceduto al capitolo le sue terre di Serranos de Avianos, Cornejuelos e El Villar: benché sappiamo che per acquistare proprietà nelle prime due località egli aveva speso 10.831 *mrs.*, pure la sorella, Maria Blázquez, accettò di pagare al capitolo 30.000 *mrs.* per quelle proprietà più El Villar.

[24] AHN, *Clero*, carp. 24, n. 18 (9.V.1301); n. 19 (9.V.1301); *DM*, 178; AHN, *Clero*, carp. 24, n. 5 (1.III.1301).

[25] Questo risulta chiaro da almeno due delle transazioni in cui vennero venduti integralmente i diritti di accesso ai pascoli del villaggio. AHN, *Clero*, carp. 24, n. 18 (9.V.1301); carp. 25, n. 2 (12.VI.1301).

[26] Su Las Huelgas vedi A. Rodríguez López, *El real monasterio de Las Huelgas y el Hospital del Rey*, 2 voll., Burgos 1907.

[27] La frase «du ciel à la terre» è tratta dalla relazione di Jacques Le Goff alla Society of Fellows, Columbia University, nella sessione primaverile del 1985. Vedi anche il mio *From Love to Ritual*, di prossima pubblicazione, per un'ampia trattazione di questo cambiamento.

[28] Vedi J. González, *Repartimento de Sevilla*, 2 voll., Madrid 1951; M. González Jiménez, A. González Gómez, *El libro del repartimento de Jerez de la Frontera. Estudio y edición*, Cadice 1980, pp. XLVI-XLIX; J. Torres Fontes, *Repartimiento de Murcia*, Madrid 1968; T. F. Ruiz, *Expansion et changement: la conquête de Seville et la société castillane (1248-1350)*, in «Annales E.S.C.», 3, 1979, pp. 550-55; M. González Jiménez, *La repoblación de la zona de Sevilla durante el siglo XIV*, Sevilla 1975, pp. 22-25.

[29] Alcuni esempi di vendite di terra effettuate per pagare debiti contratti con ebrei sono di Aguilar de Campóo: AHN, *Clero*, carp. 1667, n. 12 (26.II.1315); nell'area di Logrono: *Colección diplomatica de las colegiatas de Albelda y Lograno*, a cura di Sainz Ripa, § 93, p. 183; a Oña: del Alamo, *Coleccion diplomatica de San Salvador de Oña*, II, § 552, pp. 669-70; da Rioseco: AHN, *Clero*, carp. 354, n. 5 (2.XII.1285), n. 6 (12.I.1290), n. 7 (19.II.1290), n. 9 (7.XII.1292); da La Vid: AHN, *Clero*, carp. 383, n. 10 (14.X.1347) e *passim*.

[30] Sulla violenza politica vedi il mio *Expansion et changement* cit., e anche J. Valdeón Baruque, *Aspectos de la crisis castellana en la primera mitad del siglo XIV*, in «Hispania», 111 (1969), pp. 5-24, e il mio *Patterns of Development*, di prossima pubblicazione. Sui decreti di Alfonso X destinati ai cavalieri urbani non nobili e agli ecclesiastici vedi Ruiz, *The Tranformation of the Castilian Municipalities* cit., e MHE, I, § XLIII, XLIV, XLV, LXVIII, CII e *passim*.

[31] Sui confini a Frausillas vedi la tabella 4. Per Segovia vedi l'importante libro di A. García Sanz et al., *Propriedades del cabildo segoviano, sistemas de cultivo y modos de explotación de la tierra a fines del siglo XIII*, Salamanca 1981, pp. 65-68, 87-106. La scarsità di attrezzi agricoli è rivelata da una serie di accordi di affitto, stilati con molta cura e molto particolareggiati, stipulati dalle monache di San Andres del Arroyo tra il 1300 e il 1332. AHN, *Clero*, carp. 1732, n. 5 (19.XII.1300), n. 7 (31.X.1306), n. 9 (22.VII.1310), n. 14 (19.X.1315), n. 15 (12.I.1318); carp. 1733, n. 2 (20.XI.1321), n. 20 (28.III.1332); carp. 1734, n. 1 (16.IV.1332). Nel 1334 un contadi-

no vendette la sua terra al monastero di San Andres del Arroyo e ne divenne il *vasallo solariego*. Vedi anche un altro esempio in cui la terra viene venduta e poi ripresa in affitto in I. Oceja Gonzalo, *Documentación del monasterio de San Salvador de Oña (1032-1284)*, in *Fuentes medievales castellano-leonesas*, 3, Burgos, 1983, p. 64.

[32] Vedi per esempio AHN, *Clero*, carp. 1667, n. 9 (13.IV.1315); carp. 1033, n. 1 (15.IV.1315) e *passim*, dove Alfonso XI e/o i suoi reggenti accettano di diminuire il numero dei contribuenti compresi negli elenchi fiscali. Nel 1316 John Ferrandez bruciò e saccheggiò il villaggio di Ribafrecha in modo così grave che i contadini sopravvissuti emigrarono, e per questo i monaci di Santa María de Nájera chiesero una moratoria fiscale di dieci anni, ottenendone da Alfonso XI (o dai suoi reggenti) una di sette: vedi AHN, *Codices*, 105B, 125-127v. La minaccia continuò a incombere sui poveri abitanti dei villaggi fino alla fine degli anni '30. Nel 1283, quando l'infante Don Sancho confiscò la proprietà di Juan García de Covarrubias, ordinò a uno dei suoi uomini a Covarrubias di scegliere i dodici uomini più ricchi della città e di costringerli ad acquistare la proprietà. L. Serrano, *Fuentes para la historia de Castilla*, 3 voll., Valladolid 1906-10, II, pp. 126-27.

[33] Vedi la monografia in via di pubblicazione, dove prendo in esame oltre cinquecento accordi d'affitto collegandoli all'acquisto e alla vendita di terra nella Castiglia del basso medioevo.

[34] MacKay, *op. cit.*, pp. 52-53.

XII

Oligarchy and Royal Power: The Castilian Cortes and the Castilian Crisis 1248-1350

Long before representative assemblies came into being north of the Pyrenees, the urban procurators of Castile made their way acoss the endless plain of their kingdom to protest, to plead and often to bow to the wishes of their lord and king at the meetings of the Cortes. Yet, in spite of their long tradition and the fact that for many years scholars have studied and debated about the origins of the Cortes, there have been no attempts at using the *cuadernos* of the medieval Cortes (the published proceedings) as an useful source to understand the complex relationship between the representatives of the Castilian cities and the crown. Furthermore, with a few notable exceptions, historians of medieval Castile have also failed to see the petitions which the urban procurators presented to the king at their meetings for what they are: a clear graph of the problems affecting the realm from the late thirteenth century onwards.[1]

Spanish historians have long argued about the origins and functions of the Cortes. Francisco Martínez Marina, a liberal priest and supporter of the 1812 constitutional movement at the Cortes of Cadiz, traced their origins to the great church councils during the Visigothic period. He described the Cortes as representative assemblies acting as a check on royal power and sharing legislative functions with the king.[2] For Manuel Colmeiro, the Cortes also had their origins in the Visigothic councils, but he saw the institution as a mere consultive body, submissive to the king's will.[3] Vladimir Piskorski, in his monograph, *Las cortes de Castilla en el período de la edad media a la moderna (1188-1520),* adopted a compromise position. The Cortes, according to Piskorski, came into being both from the surviving political and social institutions of the Visigothic monarchy and from new elements in the feudal milieu of León and Castile.[4] Claudio Sánchez Albornoz saw the urban purchase of money rights (*moneda,* a tax) from the king by the urban centers as the catalyst for the establishment of the Cortes.[5] These are only a few examples of an exhausting and by now dated debate summarized to a large extent by L. García de Valdeavellano, in his *Curso de historia de las instituciones españolas.*[6]

Before 1188 one can only speak of the curia regis or council of noblemen and high clergy assisting the king in the government of the realm, but with the admission of the non-noble representatives of the cities to the council, the Cortes came into being. Beginning with the Cortes of León (1188), the procurators of some Leonese cities began to attend the meetings of the Cortes. In Castile urban representation occurred shortly afterwards. Urban procurators

Professor Teofilo F. Ruiz, Department of History, Brooklyn College, City University of New York, Brooklyn, New York 11210, U.S.A.

[1]The ordinances of the Cortes have been used to illustrate the political, economic and institutional crisis of the late thirteenth and fourteenth century by Julio Valdeón Baruque, *Los conflictos sociales en el reino de Castilla en los siglos XIV y XV* (Madrid, 1975); 'Aspectos de la crisis castellana en las primera mitad del diglo XIV', *Hispania,* 111 (1969), 5-24; 'La crisis del siglo XIV en Castilla; Revisión del problema', *Revista de la Universidad de Madrid,* 79 (1972), 161-83; Teofilo F. Ruiz, 'Expansion et changement; La conquête de Séville et la société castillane (1248-1350)', *Annales E.S.C.* 34 year (May-June 1979), 548-65; Salustiano Moreta Velayos, *Malhechores-feudales: violencia, antagonismos y alianzas de clases en Castilla, siglos XIII-XIV* (Madrid, 1978). Since the preparation of this article, Professor E. Proctor's excellent book on the Castilian and Leonese curia has become available. It is the best introduction to the subject.

[2]Francisco Martínez Marina, *Teoría de las Cortes,* 2 vols. (Madrid, 1813), I, pp. 8-15, II, pp. 199-297.

[3]Manuel Colmeiro, *Introducción a las Cortes de los antiguos reinos de León y Castilla,* 2 vols. (Madrid, 1883), I, pp. 4-7, 45.

[4]Vladimir Piskorski, *Las Cortes de Castilla en el período de transito de la Edad Media a la Moderna* (1188-1520), first published in Russian in 1877, translated from a German translation by C. Sánchez Albornoz (Barcelona, 1930), p. 7.

[5]Claudio Sánchez Albornoz, 'La primitiva organisación monetaria de León y Castilla', in *Estudios sobre las instituciones medievales españolas* (Mexico, 1965), pp. 474-75.

[6]See Luis García de Valdeavellano, *Curso de historia de las instituciones españoles (Madrid, 1968), pp. 463-77;* also Alfonso García Gallo, *Manual de historia del derecho español,* 2 vols. (Madrid, 1964), I, pp. 805-08; R. B. Merriman, 'The Cortes of the Spanish Kingdoms in the later Middle Ages', *American Historial Review,* 16 (1911), 476-95.

might have attended meetings of the Cortes as early as 1202.[7] After their admission they became the key to the crown's financial policy. They voted on, and more important, collected and some times paid taxes to the crown. In theory each city granted its procurator powers to answer and vote only on issues previously submitted to them by the king. If a new matter was to consider, the procurators had to seek the opinion of the *concejos* (city council).[8] In practice the urban procurators presented to the king a list of petitions which he granted or denied according to his own political needs. It is important, therefore, to realize the role played by the king. He called the Cortes into session, and his presence gave legal force to the meetings.[9]

Piskorski accounts for fifty-seven meetings of the Cortes between 1250 and 1350. Colmeiro identified forty-six Cortes and five *ayuntamientos* (meetings in which one or two of the estates were not present) for the same period.[10] The *Libro de las Cortes,* published by the Real Academia de la Historia, only includes the ordinances of twenty-nine Cortes for those years. Regardless of the exact number of meetings, the kings of Castile met often with the three estates of the kingdom. Troubled times made for frequent meetings. The period from 1295 to 1302 which encompassed part of María de Molina's turbulent regency witnessed at least ten meetings. Periods of relative stability made for infrequent Cortes. Alfonso XI's control of the kingdom after 1325 was reflected in the absence of session of the Cortes between 1329 and 1339. Clearly, the king had no need or desire to call them into session.

At the meetings of the Cortes the urban procurators of Castile and León submitted petitions to the king. After they were granted or denied by the crown, the petitions were sent, if approved, to the *concejos* of the realm and became part of the ordinances of the cities. These ordinances were often granted separately to each estate and even to each kingdom. Such was the case at the Cortes of Medina del Campo (1305) when María de Molina, regent for her son Fernando IV, granted different ordinances to the concejos of Castile and Extremadura. At the Cortes of Valladolid (1295) one ordinance was enacted for the municipalities of the realm and another for the prelates and clergy.

I do not intend to make a detailed study of the institutional origins of the Cortes. Here, it will suffice to raise two important questions. First, what was the nature of the relationship between the monarch and the representative assemblies or Cortes? Second, how did the Cortes reflect and react to the social, economic and institutional crises affecting Castile after 1248? Clearly, these representative assemblies were not very representative, a point which, although it is hard to deny considering the evidence, has never been popular with Spanish institutional historians.[11] Professor Strayer's description of the evolution of representative assemblies in England and France fully applies to Castile; thus, his comments on this matter serve as a good introduction to our discussion:

> 'A representative assembly was a tool of government, just as a court was. And just as subjects learned how to use courts to obstruct government actions, so they learned how to use assemblies. These meetings, where important men of all classes came together were convenient occasions for voicing grievances, for demanding investigations and reforms.'[12]

[7]See Gaines Post, 'Roman Law and Early Representation in Spain and Italy, 1150-1250', in *Studies in Medieval Legal Thought* (Princeton, 1964), pp. 70-79; Joseph O'Callaghan, 'The Beginnings of the Cortes of Leon-Castile', in *American Historical Review,* 74 (1969), 1503-37. Professor O'Callaghan has been working on different aspects of the Cortes in the last few years. His work is beginning to fill the blank spaces in our knowledge of the workings of the Cortes.

[8]Piskorski, pp. 56-58.

[9]Ibid., p. 78. The *omes buenos et caballeros delas cibdades* attending the Cortes were under the king's peace while in session and in their travelling to and fro the Cortes. See *Cortes de los antiguos reinos de León y Castilla,* vol. I (Madrid, 1861), p. 163, Medina del Campo (1302). Hereafter *Cortes, I.*

[10]Piskorski, p. 78; Colmeiro studies the number indicated above.

[11]On this see Richard Herr, *The Eighteenth Century Revolution in Spain* (Princeton, N.J., 1969), pp. 341-47; Tulio Halperin Donghi, *Tradición política española e ideología revolucionaria* (Buenos Aires, 1961), chapter V and p. 161 fn.

[12]Joseph R, Strayer, *On the Medieval Origins of the Modern State* Princeton, N.J., 1970), p.67.

We do not really know how many cities sent procurators to the meetings of the Cortes. Before the late fifteenth century when the Catholic Kings limited the right of representation to just eighteen cities,[13] the number of those in attendance probably varied from meeting to meeting. The important Cortes of 1315 which met in Burgos to approve the charter of an *Hermandad* or league of lesser nobles *(hijosdalgo)* and the cities of the kingdoms of Castile, León, Toledo and Extremadura against baronial excesses drew representatives from one hundred and one cities and towns.[14] This probably represents the high point of attendance. From Castile proper and the Bay of Biscay area, only fifty urban centers sent their men to Burgos. Among the places sending procurators one finds some, such as Salinas de Anaña, which were there because they produced a vital commodity (in this particularly case salt), or were stopping places along an important trade route (Belorado, Oña), or a mighty fortress (Coca, Olmedo), or a significant maritime, mercantile locality (Laredo, Castro Urdiales,), or finally, an important urban center in its own right such as Burgos, Segovia and Ávila.

Altogether there were two hundred procurators present at the Cortes of Burgos 1315. Of these around ninety representatives came from Old Castile and the Basque area. Most of the representatives of Ávila (which sent the largest group, 16), Segovia and Burgos were members of the ruling patrician elites of their respective cities. In the case of Soria, a distinction was made between the respresentatives of the urban oligarchy of the town (four of them) and those from the *común* (two), i.e. from the taxpaying, by now often disfranchised group known in Castile as *pecheros* (those who paid taxes). Certainly, it may not be exaggerated to assume that the majority of the urban procurators were members of the Castilian urban oligarchy, the so-called *caballeros villanos* or non-noble knights.[15]

In 1315 the kingdom stood at the crossroads. Two opposing noble factions struggled for control of the regency. Alfonso XI, barely three years old, was a pawn to the passions of the aristocracy. Lawlessness and violence ruled the countryside, threatened the trade, the security and economic well-being of the urban centers. The lesser nobility and the Castilian upper bourgeoisie joined in a kingdom-wide alliance to protect themselves and their king, and to check the excesses of the magnates. The Cortes of 1315 probably represents, as pointed out before, the peak of participation during the medieval period. Yet, what and who was represented? Most of those present were non-noble knights *(caballeros villanos)*, themselves exempt from most taxes. Therefore, these procurators represented the particular interests of a few urban centers and, usually, the interests of one specific social group, the urban oligarchy. Their petitions to the king at the meetings of the Cortes reflect, above all, their desire to control the collection of taxes and their fierce antogonism to the nobility.[16] Obviously, these representatives also voiced the wish of most segments of Castilian society of a peaceful and well

[13]John H. Elliott, *Imperial Spain 1469-1716* (London, 1970), p.93.

[14]*Cortes*, I (Burgos, 1315), pp. 247-72.

[15]Ibid., pp. 263-71; T. F. Ruiz, 'Prosopografía burgalesa, 1248-1350', *Boletín de la Institución Fernán González*, 184 (1975), 467-99; for the representatives of Sevogia see Diego de Colmenares, *Historia de la insigne ciudad de Segovia y compendio de las historias de Castilla*, 2 vols. (Segovia, 1969), I, pp. 449, 466; for Ávila and the social standing and family connections of those representing the city in the Cortes of Burgos see C. M. Ajo G. y Saínz de Zuñiga, *Ávila I. Fuentes y archivos*, 2 vols. (Madrid, 1962), I, p. 105; Luis de Ariz, *Historia de las grandezas de la ciudad de Ávila* (Alcalá de Henares, 1607), p. 13; Archivo Histórico Nacional (hereafter AHN). Clero, carpeta 24, no. 3 (5-I-1300); carpeta 25, no. 3 (13-VIII-1301); carpeta 26, no. 3 (28-VII-1305); no. 5 (25-XII-1305) *et passim*.

[16]For examples of the urban procurators' petitions to the king on the right to collect taxes and limit the farming of taxes see *Cortes* I, Madrid (1329), p. 428: 'Otrossi alo que me pidieron por mercet que tenga por bien delos non echar nin mandar paga pecho dessafforado ninguno especdial nin general en toda la mi tierra ssin asset llamados primera miente a cortes, a esto respondo quelo tengo por bien'. Also *Cortes*, I, Madrid (1329), p. 435; Palençia (1286), p. 97; Haro (1288), p. 104; Valladolid (1293), p. 110; Valladolid (1295), p.131; (1299). p. 142; Burgos (1301), p. 149; Medina del Campo (1307), p. 191; Palençia (1313), p. 224; Palençia (1313), p. 239; Burgos (1315), pp. 275-76; Carrión (1317), p. 305; Medina del Campo (1318), pp. 332-33; Valladolid (1322), p. 342; Valladolid (1325), p. 383; Madrid (1339), p. 469; Alcalá de Henares (1345), p. 481. For protests against the nobility see *Cortes*, I, Palençia (1313), pp. 241-43; Burgos (1315), pp. 287-88; Carrión (1317), p. 300; Valladolid (1322), p. 338 *et passim*.

ordered realm. To this end they requested in session after session of the Cortes royal action on four broad areas: 1) economic policy and taxation; 2) justice; 3) administrative reforms; 4) control and segregation of religious minorities. It is not necessary to delve into these matters here, since the widespread desire for reform and justice, the hatred of Jews, and in Spain, of Moors, and the continuous demands to limit the amount of taxes to be paid and the conditions under which they were to be collected were not peculiar to Castile.[17]

What can be said of Castile without much doubt is that what bound the king and the urban oligarchies together was a great deal stronger than what separated them. When the kings of Castile were able to rule effectively, which was not often in the period between 1248 and 1350, the urban procurators protested the excesses of royal officials, pleaded for greater participation in the administration of the realm and sought a diminished role for the Jews.[18] One must remember, as mentioned earlier, that when the king had a good grip on the country, he could and often did dispense with the Cortes. Yet, when the kind was weak as some portions of Alfonso X's reign (1252-85), or a minor (minorities of Ferdinand IV and Alfonso XI), then the urban oligarchs had to shore up the monarchy and sacrifice their wealth and often their lives for the safe keep and preservation of royal institutions.[19] The bond which tied crown and patriciate in the Cortes, as it did in individual cities,[20] was hatred and mistrust of the nobility. The petitions of the urban procurators are filled with their complaints against the excesses of the nobility, against their violence and rapacity, against their threat to the stability of the realm and royal institutions.[21] An energetic and active king meant reduced representation, more fiscal demands, arbitrary behaviour by royal officials. It also meant some curtailment on the criminal activities of the magnates and their retinues. Above all, a strong royal power brought the peace necessary for the conduct of trade, the main source of income for the urban oligarchs.

There were, however, other factors. The language of the *cuadernos* of the Cortes and the events taking place in many Castilian cities provide a revealing glimpse at the growing confrontation between the oligarchy and the recently disfranchised segments of the urban population.[22] The specter of revolution haunted the mid-fourteenth century and Castile was no exception.[23] Subservience to the king in the Cortes, especially to a king such as Alfonso XI after 1325, and in the cities, as I have already shown elsewhere, brought royal protection against the threats of the nobility and the aspirations of the lower classes.

Thus, between 1248 and 1350 the meetings of the Cortes allied the urban patriciate and the crown in the mutual protection of royal institutions and narrow oligarchical interests. One must add that in the one hundred years after the mid-thirteenth century and even afterwards, the urban centers of Castile shared the greater burden in this alliance and that again and again they were forced to rally to defend and protect the crown from its own incompetence and the ambitions of others.[24]

[17]For a detailed discussion of these matters see T. F. Ruiz, 'Burgos. Society and Royal Power, 1250-1350', (Unpublished Diss. Princeton University, 1973, pp. 223-60.

[18]Protests against royal officials are numerous. See *Cortes*, I, Madrid (1329), pp. 402-06, p. 432; Madrid (1339), p. 467; Alcalá de Henares (1345), pp. 477-48; Burgos (1345), pp. 485-86; León (1349), p. 629. Ordinances against religious minorities were enacted in every session of the Cortes between 1248 and 1350. They are far too numerous to cite here. These measures sought to segregate Jews and Moors both economically and socially.

[19]This was done through the formation of *Hermandades* or leagues of cities in 1296 and 1315. See Luis Suárez Fernández, 'Evolución histórica de las Hermandades castellanas', *Cuadernos de historia de Espana*, 16 (1951), 5-78; K. Habler. 'Uber die älteren Hermandades in Kastilien', *Historische Zeitshrift*, 53 (1885), pp. 385-401.

[20]For the alliance between the crown and the urban centers at the local level see T. F. Ruiz, 'The Transformation of the Castilian Municipalities. the Case of Burgos, 1248-1350', *Past & Present*, 77 (1977), 3-33.

[21]See note 16 above and Moreta Velayos, *Malechores-feudales.*

[22]*Cortes*, I, Palencia (1313). p. 243; Burgos (1315), p. 388; Valladolid (1322), p. 360; Ruiz, 'The Transformation', pp. 26-27.

[23]Valdeón Baruque, *Los conflictos socialas*, pp. 15-139.

[24]See above fn. 19. Not everyone agrees with this interpretation of the alliance between the crown and the urban oligarchies in Castile. I discuss this topic in detail in my article, 'Expansion et changement'.

This relationship was forced upon king and oligarchy partly by the series of catastrophes plaguing Castile shortly after 1248 and extending through the next century and a half.[25] This was a veritable Time of Troubles, but unlike Muscovy, the period of crises extended far more than thirteen years. The crises were manifold and they are clearly revealed in the petitions found in the *cuadernos* of the Cortes. Some of the problems were man made and others, such as the Plague and bad weather, simply added to the difficulties. The king and the Cortes tried to find remedy to some of these economic and political disasters but were seldom successful in their attempts.

The debilitating economic crisis began shortly after the mid-thirteenth century and brought a rapid rate of inflation and a shortage of goods. In 1252, 1258 and at the *Ayuntamiento* of Jerez (1268) Alfonso X and the Cortes imposed price controls on a wide range of goods and on wages, forbade the export of livestock, grain and wine and tried to establish a ceiling on interests rates.[26] In 1288 at the Cortes of Haro, Sancho IV agreed to a general tax reform (it was never carried out) and to banning the export of some items.[27] Similar measures in the following decades point to an unmitigated rate of inflation, to the continuation of the abuses of royal officials and the burden of taxation, to the failure of attempts to control exports.[28] More relevant to us are the numerous petitions presented to the king by the urban procurators after 1300, in which they requested remission of taxes because the land was poor or barren.[29] The royal concessions allowing a reduction in the number of taxpayers inscribed in the tax rolls, the villages and hamlets which were deserted in the early fourteenth century, the frequent and noisy protests of peasants against the fiscal demands of their secular and ecclesiastical lords speak to us vividly of the demographic dislocations, of the rapid erosion of the tax base and of a deep structural crisis. It comes as no surprise then, that while the king granted widespread tax relief to the urban centers and was often willing to reduce the number of tax payers in specific localities, royal officials, faced with mounting costs, their salaries often in arrears, disregarded these royal concessions and extorted by force payment in specie and in kind from suffering communities and religious institutions.[30] The frequency of individual protests and the comforting royal responses do not mask the violence of official demands and the fact that they went on unimpeded for most of the first half of the fourteenth century. Above all, the *cuadernos* of the Cortes reflect a time of violence, of near anarchy. Moreta Velayos in a recent book has described the nature of this violence as being essentially aristocratic. Looking, however, through ideologically tinted glasses, he paints a picture with only shades of white and black, the class excesses of the aristocratic rich against the rural poor.[31] Yet, if we look carefully at the petitions presented at the meetings of the Cortes and at the many documents of the period, most of the protests came from the oligarchical, mercantile, ruling elites of the Castilian cities. Of course, poor peasants suffered the abuses and excesses of a nobility which found its profession in war and looting, but those with something to lose, status, merchandise, estates in the countryside around the cities, were the ones who felt most vividly the scourge of magnate

[25]See fn. 1. above.

[26]Ismael García Rámila, 'Ordenamiento de posturas y otros capítulos generales otorgados a la ciudad de Burgos por el rey Alfonso X', *Hispania,* 19 (1945), 179-235; 20 (1945), 385-439; 21 (1945), 605-50; *Cortes,* I, Valladolid (1258), pp. 56.57; Jerez (1268), pp. 65.78.

[27]*Cortes,* I, Haro (1288), pp. 103-05.

[28]Ruiz, 'Burgos. Society and Royal Power', pp. 223-46.

[29]*Cortes,* I Palencia (1286), p. 95; Haro (1288), pp. 102-03; Valladolid (1293), pp. 110-11; 138; Burgos (1301), p. 149, Valladolid (1307), pp. 187-91; Valladolid (1312), pp. 216-18; Palencia (1313), p. 236; Carrión (1317), p. 307; Valladolid (1325), p. 387; Madrid (1329), p. 420; Madrid (1339), p. 460; Burgos (1345), p. 488; León (1349), p. 636.

[30]Ruiz, 'Expansion et changement', p. 553; Valdeón Baruque, 'Aspectos de la crisis castellana', pp. 5-23; examples of individual protests against the abuses of the nobilitiy and of royal officials AHN. Clero. carpeta 169, no. 3 (28-V-1288); no. 4 (20-XII-1289); carpeta 171, no. 9 (25-III-1309); no. 10 (18-IV-1326); no. 12 (18-IV-1338); carpeta 174 no. 17 (12-XII-1331); no. 19 (12-III-1312); carpeta 225 no. 2 (9-V-1288); carpeta 233 no. 6 (28-XII-1295), and hundreds of other examples from every corner of Castile.

[31]Moreta Velayos, *Malechores-feudales,* pp. 67-68 *et passim.*

violence. Yet, these oligarchs were themselves not innocent of exploitation and violence against those below them in the social ladder. Unlike the poor, however, whose voices went unheard, theirs were heard at the Cortes and in the royal chambers. Engaged in a death struggle against the upper nobility, the oligarchical urban elites found ready allies among the lower nobility, with which they had been mingling for several decades, among the great monastic houses of Castile and, above all, in the crown.[32] The demands of royal officials although annoying could be somewhat overlooked, for indeed most of the urban procurators to the Cortes were employed at one time or another as royal officials.[33] In this capacity they profited greatly from collecting taxes they have voted for but did not usually pay. The nobility, on the other hand, was something different. It had to be controlled, if not by the king then by any other means.

The civil war of 1365 and the baronnial reaction of the late fourteenth century and early fifteenth weakened the influence of the urban procurators to the Cortes and the institution itself. After 1365 the urban oligarchies bided their time until the Catholic Kings during the 'Days of Wrath' paid once and for all the accumulated debt of magnate violence and extortion. As the criminal noblemen hung and turned slowly in the wind, the oligarchs enjoyed their long awaited revenge, their long hoped for peace. In gaining it, however, they lost their reason for existence and any semblance of real participation in the decisions of government. Their own turn came at Villalar when the army of the Comuneros was slaughtered by the forces of Charles I. As their noble counterparts, the urban ruling elites had no choice but to become also servants of the new raising and despotic state.

One further point ought to be made which may help us make some distinctions between the development of representative institutions in Castile and those same institutions elsewhere. Unlike England or France where sooner or later the crown had to go to the representative assemblies for consent to taxation, or for emergency funds,[34] the Castilian kings had important sources of income totally independent of the consent of their subjects. One was, of course, the booty of the Reconquest, replaced in the sixteenth century by the fifth of the silver and gold from the New World. The second source was the income from the *Mesta* and the wool trade, and finally the huge taxes paid by the Jews until 1492. Thus, the crown of Castile had to depend less on the willingness and loyalty of its subjects on financial matters than its northern counterparts. The Castilian kings, therefore, had also to share less in the task of ruling the realm.

To summarize briefly some of the ideas explored throughout this paper. Although the Cortes fulfilled an important economic role, it was secondary to the political task of neutralizing or eliminating the power of the high nobility. The representative institutions of Castile in the High Middle Ages essentially represented the interests of the crown and of a narrow urban oligarchy. Sometimes those interests coincided with those of the entire realm, but more often than not their decisions were aimed at curtailing the aristocracy and preserving the prerogatives of the crown and the urban oligarchs. At the same time, the ordinances of the Cortes reflect the serious crises affecting the kingdom during the hundred years after the conquest of Seville. However, since the attempts at reforms were often partial and aimed at the protection of narrow interests, they seldom, worked.

Finally, the relative financial independence of the Castilian crown and the need of the urban representatives for a strong king weakened the development of representative institutions in Castile. Their growth and attempts to reach some workable constitutional arrangement were

[32]Ruiz, 'The Transformation of the Castilian Municipalities', pp. 25-30. *Cortes,* I, Burgos (1315). Carta de Hermandad.
[33]Ruiz, 'Prosopografía burgalesa', pp. 482-99.
[34]See Joseph R. Strayer, 'Consent to Taxation under Philip the Fair', in Strayer and Taylor, *Studies in Early French Taxation* (Cambridge, Mass., 1939); also his 'The Statute of York and the Community of the Realm', in *Medieval Statecraft and the Perspectives of History,* John F. Benton, Thomas N. Bisson, eds. (Princeton, N. J., 1971), pp. 266-90; John H. Elliott, *Imperial Spain,* p. 92 already has pointed out the independence of the Castilian crown in financial matters in the late fifteenth century and afterwards.

truncated in the thirteenth and fourteenth centuries and any surviving hope extinguished, for all practical purposes, at Villalar. Thus, as it had often happened to poor Castile, having been among the first to sit at the table of representation, its portion was meager, its stay was short.

XIII

Unsacred Monarchy: The Kings of Castile in the Late Middle Ages

In the year of Our Lord 1332, Alfonso XI (1312–50), by the grace of God king of Castile, León, Galicia, Seville, Córdoba, Murcia, Jaén, the Algarve, and lord of Molina, came to the monastery of Las Huelgas in Burgos to be anointed with holy oil and crowned. While preparations for the ceremonies were completed, the king traveled along the pilgrimage road to Santiago de Compostela. There, on the main altar of the cathedral, he was knighted by the mechanical arm of a statue of St. James, the Apostle and Patron of Spain. A few days afterward upon his return to Burgos, Alfonso XI was anointed on the right shoulder. Once the ritual unction had concluded, the king ascended alone to the altar, took the royal diadem and placed it on his head.[1]

The chronicler's description of these events and of the festivities that followed remind us of similar accounts in other parts of the medieval West. The act of self-coronation and the manner in which Alfonso XI was knighted and anointed might seem a bit peculiar to those acquainted with the rituals of monarchy in other parts of Europe,[2] but the symbols and rites associated with royal authority and sacrality—crown, holy oil, and knighting—were common in other medieval kingdoms. Yet, what makes the anointing and crowning of Alfonso XI so interesting—and a point of departure for a discussion of medieval royal rituals in Castile—was less its familiarity than its peculiar place in Castilian history.[3] For almost two centuries before 1332 no Castilian king had been anointed, and none was anointed afterward. Moreover, the surviving documentary evidence records only one formal crowning of a Castilian king after Alfonso VII's death in 1157, and only another king crowned himself. After Alfonso XI's self-coronation we know of only two more kings who followed his example. In short, from 1135 on, the Castilian and Spanish rulers consciously rejected the traditional emblems of power and authority in use elsewhere in the medieval West and in the early modern period.[4] The Castilian kings did not consider their office sacred, even though they believed that as kings their responsibilities were of the highest order and were entrusted to them by God. Never did the kings of Castile and later of Spain claim seriously to have the power to heal the sick. Nor did their birth, crowning, dying, and burial enjoy any of the elaborate rituals associated with royalty in England and France. The kings of Castile in the late Middle Ages had their rituals and symbols of authority to mark their ascension to the throne and their exercise of political rule, but these differed from those of England, France, and other western medieval kingdoms. The question is why?

In the following pages I would like to describe the symbols of kingship and power that the kings of Castile in fact employed, and to suggest why the evolution of ceremonial in Castile deviated from the experiences of England, France, and, to a lesser extent, the Holy Roman Empire. To do so, we must follow a circuitous road. We begin by examining the Visigothic-Asturian precedents, and then proceed to describe the evolution of rituals after 1135 within the context of Castilian political and institutional history. We should then show how the Castilian kings sought to legitimize their rule, what gave them the right to be kings, and what symbols of authority they chose as representative of their power.[5] The first two tasks are not difficult, inasmuch as it is a story which can be read in the chronicles, and which has already been described, although not in any systematic fashion, by previous historians.[6] Finally, I wish to explain why Castile and thus Spain evolved as it did—and to suggest how events in the medieval period not only explain the peculiarities of Castile, but may help us understand modern Spanish politics.

Visigothic, Asturian, and Navarrese Precedents

By ceasing to be anointed or, in most instances, even crowned, the kings of Castile and León broke with what they believed, and later medieval chronicles maintained, had been a rich and long tradition.[7] For centuries before 1135, most of the Visigothic kings of Spain and, after the mid-eighth century, most of the rulers of Asturias and León were anointed and crowned. Following an ancient Germanic tradition, the Visigothic kings of Toulouse and, later, those of Toledo were also raised upon the shield. They wore no distinctive clothing; nor did they have special emblems of their authority apart from the sword and banner. These early Visigothic kings were elected and acclaimed by the assembly of all free men, although they were generally selected from the members of the ancient family of the Balthi. After Leovigild (568–86) subdued most of the peninsula, he adopted the ceremonial and symbols of the Byzantine court. From his reign on, the Visigothic kings adopted the title Flavius, and the throne, crown, scepter, and purple mantle, the regal symbols of the Late Empire.[8] As the rulers of Visigothic Spain sought to consolidate their rule and turn the realm into their hereditary possession, they were hindered in their efforts by their heretical beliefs and the influence of the Catholic Church. After the conversion of Recared (587), however, the Church was willing to cooperate with the monarchy. The sacral elements of unction, ecclesiastical coronation, and the royal oath to the people and popular oath to the king were added to the imperial symbols introduced by Leovigild half a century before.[9]

Unlike in Frankland, where the hereditary principle became established fairly early and where the monarchs established a theocratic kingship,[10] the sacral elements of Visigothic kingship and the hereditary principle were always tempered by assassination, the survival into post-Visigothic time of the elective principle, and by the law. Dynastic violence and regicide were common among the Visigoths, and the ordinances of the Visigothic church councils, as well as St. Isidore, had stated that any free nobleman of Gothic blood and good character could be king.[11] Theoretically, kingship was the birthright of any Goth and a well-earned reward for deeds of arms. Moreover, a king who acted unjustly and selfishly was considered a tyrant and hence undeserving of royal power.[12] The level of dynastic violence was so high that more than five centuries later the *Primera crónica general* invoked the Visigothic example to explain the fratricidal battles of the Castilian and Leonese kings.[13]

Although the Visigothic church councils, St. Isidore, and other Church fathers supported the theory that all power, including political power, came from God and, although the Visigothic kings attempted to use these sacral trappings to strengthen the hereditary principle, both custom and law restricted the dynastic and theocratic pretensions of the Spanish rulers in the early medieval period. The canons of the Church councils, the *Lex visigothorum*, also stated the duties, conditions, and limitations placed upon the monarch.[14] Thus the idea that kings should be elected survived into the post-Visigothic period always as a dangerous alternative to political stability and dynastic continuity.

When Visigothic Spain fell to the Muslim invaders in 711, the northern mountain region of Asturias and Cantabria remained free from Muslim domination. Slowly, through the eighth, ninth, and tenth centuries, the Christians moved out of these well-protected enclaves into the plain. Most Spanish historians have maintained that the kings of Asturias, León, and Galicia had adopted, as early as the reign of Alfonso II (791–842), the Visigothic rituals of royal anointment and crowning. These sacral ceremonies were accompanied by the acclamation or election of the king by the magnates and the clergy and the elevation or raising of the king if not on a shield, then on a chair. The chronicles and iconography of a later period point to the use of ceremonies and liturgical tokens that emphasized the sacred character of the king and that were similar to the ceremonies of royal ordination prevalent in the kingdoms of northern Europe. Recently, however, Peter A. Linehan has argued for the absence of anointing and sacral ceremonial in the Asturian period. Later chronicles and some present-day historians, above all Don Claudio Sánchez Albornoz, had either fabricated or been misled into believing in the continuity of sacred kingship from Visigothic Spain to the Asturian and Leonese period. I find Linehan's arguments most convincing, although there remain unanswerable questions. What were the aims of late twelfth- and thirteenth-century chroniclers in inventing such ceremonies? Did they believe that they had truly taken place?[15] Whether or not the Asturian kings were ritually anointed, contemporary and later chronicles emphasized the role of the Asturian kings and later the Castilian monarchs as military leaders or, to use a word employed often by the late chroniclers—and put to such forbidding use by Franco—*caudillos.* Indeed, the real test and glory of a king resided in his prowess as a fighter and in his ability to retain and to augment the territory of the kingdom.[16] Within this context one must note that although medieval kings in northern Europe also stressed their roles as military leaders, they often chose to emphasize their sacred functions over the martial aspects of their rule. In the north, unlike Castile or other Iberian kingdoms, there was no sustained struggle (seven centuries) against a well-defined enemy.

In Asturias, León, and later in Castile the position and authority of the king was also qualitatively different from that of rulers north of the Pyrenees. Inasmuch as feudal and vassalic ties may never have developed to the extent that they did in France, England, and Germany, political authority was not as extensively fragmented. Moreover, a combination of factors—the Muslim example, the revival of Visigothic ideology, a reaction to Carolingian influence—led the kings of Asturias and León to lay claim to the imperial dignity and, with the title, exemption from the political relationships that existed in the rest of the western medieval world. The Asturian and Leonese kings and their successors, the kings of Castile, thought themselves exempt from imperial and papal authority in political and sometimes even ecclesiastical issues. The land was theirs because they had conquered it with their swords: not unlike other places in Europe, the kings and their subjects thought of their land as a unique place. Spain, as Isidore of Seville wrote, and as rephrased by the thirteenth-century *Primera crónica general*, was a unique, plentiful land. Nowhere, the *crónica* claimed, had there been as many saints and martyrs: Rome kept the body of St. Paul, but it was Spain, the best place in the whole world, that had kept St. Paul's words.[17]

The Asturian and Leonese kings, it was believed, were solemnly anointed on the head and crowned. The city of León became associated with the imperial claims of the revival of Visigothic rituals and a royal pantheon, blessed with the body of St. Pelayo, served as a reminder of the power and ambitions of the Asturian dynasty.[18] The regal symbols of the Late Empire and the Visigothic period and the title of Flavius were used, although some of the royal tokens—such as the sword and the standard—did not yet play the important role they acquired in the thirteenth and fourteenth centuries. The kings were still acclaimed and elected, even if in a symbolic manner; they were raised upon a shield or chair. After almost three centuries, their rule had become an established tradition by the late tenth and early eleventh centuries, but their time of glory was coming to an end.

Through victories on the battlefield and dynastic marriages, Sancho III of Navarre (1004–1035) became the master of the peninsula by 1030. In 1034 he traveled to the city of León to be crowned and to take for himself the imperial title and the ancient primacy of the Leonese realm. Nevertheless, in spite of the attention Sancho paid to ancient forms, the Navarrese were the vanguard of northern influences and of new ideas. Sancho's children and grandchildren, as rulers of Castile and Aragón, promoted the work of Cluny and the final opening of the road to Compostela to pilgrims from beyond the Pyrenees and, thus, to new social, economic, and political concepts. Moreover, in Navarre the kings were neither anointed nor crowned but raised on a shield at the cry of "Real, real, real." This Navarrese inheritance further reinforced the martial character of Iberian kingship. The *Primera crónica general* traced the origins of the family to an obscure northern knight who wandered into Navarre and "fought so well against the Moors, that the people of the region elected him king because he was a good warrior and defended them well."[19] Clearly, the chronicle once again chose to emphasize military ability over bloodline or saintly origins. In the Iberian kingdom there was not a saintly founder of the dynasty, or a saintly blood connection to sanctify the royal family. There was no Edward the Confessor, Charlemagne, or St. Louis. Ferdinand III, the only royal saint, was not canonized until the early modern period; by then other Spanish saints canonized during those years, St. Ignatius, St. Theresa, and St. John of the Cross, obscured the figure of the medieval king.

The Late Middle Ages: Politics and Rituals

The reigns of Alfonso VI and of his grandson, Alfonso VII (1126–57), are landmarks in the history of Castile. Alfonso VI's conquest of Toledo in 1085, his opening of the realm to the Roman liturgy and the influence of Cluny, his claiming of the imperial title, and his family connections with France and Burgundy, altered the institutional and political development of the realm. Alfonso VII also laid claim to the imperial title, but his pretension of hegemony in the peninsula was tempered by new political realities—a peninsula divided among five kingdoms and the end, at least for that period, of any dream of political unity. In the south, the advances of the reconquest were once again checked, this time, by the invasion of the Almohads. The rule of Alfonso VII's grandson, Alfonso VIII (after the brief reign in Castile of Sancho III), was marked by a long and violent minority. Once the new king reached age, however, he proved to be capable of restoring order and defending the integrity of the realm. Moreover, in 1212 Alfonso VIII won a signal victory at Las Navas de Tolosa, which irrevocably changed the balance of power in the peninsula in favor of the Christians. After one more minority (that of Henry I) and further nobiliary unrest, Ferdinand III, Alfonso VIII's grandson, continued his grandfather's work. The successful campaigns of this king in Andalusia, highlighted by the conquests of Córdoba (1236) and Seville (1248), brought most of this rich and populous region under Castilian rule. Furthermore, under his rule León, which had been an independent kingdom for almost a century, was now united to Castile forever. The mid-thirteenth century, which seemed to promise a golden age, witnessed the point of farthest advance for the Christian armies, but it also marked the beginning of a series of long-lasting economic, social, and institutional crises. These structural dislocations plagued Castile for most of the next hundred years and set new patterns of development for the kingdom.

The reigns of Alfonso X, Sancho IV, Ferdinand IV, and Alfonso XI were often disrupted by civil wars, nobiliary unrest, and turbulent minorities. Only after Alfonso XI came to age in 1325 did Castile return to some semblance of order. In the 1340s Alfonso XI, well in command of the realm, initiated important institutional reforms, aimed at strengthening royal power by taming the nobility and controlling the financial resources of the cities. He also renewed the march of the Reconquest, which for all practical purposes had come to a stop in the 1250s. His untimely demise from the ravages of the Black Death at the siege of Algeciras in 1350, and the subsequent dynastic conflicts that led to the rise of the bastard-royal branch of the Trastámaras, opened a new period in the life of Castile.

From the ascent of Henry II in 1365, after murdering his half-brother and rightful king Peter I, to the beginnings of Isabella's rule in 1474, the rule of the Trastámaras encompassed a period of great political, economic, and social upheaval. Castile became entangled in the Hundred Years War and the power of the high nobility became a threat to the stability of the realm. Frequent minorities, civil wars, economic stagnation, a galloping inflation, and social unrest, manifested in the violent pogroms of 1391, are some of the elements that made this period generally unstable. In short, from the reign of Alfonso VII to that of Isabella I, Castile was seldom stable enough to allow for normal institutional development.

Few of the kings and queens who ruled Castile and León after the death of Alfonso VII, from Sancho III (1157–58) to Isabella the Catholic (1474–1504), enjoyed enough time as rulers to develop coherent policies. Alfonso VIII and Alfonso XI's long reigns included long and troubled minorities. Those kings who did have the time—Alfonso X (1252–1284) and Juan II (1407–59)—were failures.[20] Of these kings, only Alfonso XI was anointed (on the shoulder), as far as we know; Alfonso X crowned himself; Sancho IV (1284–95) was crowned; while Alfonso XI, Henry II (1369–79), and Juan I (1379–90) also crowned themselves. Clearly by the twelfth century the kings of Castile had abandoned a policy of royal theocracy, and the rites and symbols that accompanied such policy had been downgraded or substituted by more secular ceremonies and emblems.

Although solemn coronations did not occur regularly, the kings of Castile in the late Middle Ages had crowns. We know that Sancho IV chose to be buried with the crown of his great-grandfather, but there is no evidence that any other king did so. In the thirteenth and fourteenth centuries two kings bequeathed crowns to their descendants. Moreover, manuscript illuminations, sculptures, and lead seals show the Castilian rulers wearing the royal diadem, though I believe that in most cases it was an artistic device to identify the king.[21]

With the demise of sacred monarchy, new symbols of royal authority emerged. Instead of the rituals found elsewhere or, at times, even together with them, the Castilian monarchy repeatedly used a series of secular ceremonies during the late Middle Ages and into the early modern period. Although most of these formal acts had a distinctive popular character, they were clearly associated with the claims to kingship and political power. Some of these symbols and secular ceremonial dated back to tribal Germanic customs and even earlier precedents, but they remained alive in Castile without too many attempts at disguising them under a Christian veneer. Many of them were unique to Castile or to the Iberian kingdoms and quite different from the royal symbols of England and France. Among them we find the following: (1) the bestowing of regal attributes to those who were not of the blood royal, (2) emphasis on the martial abilities of Castilians as compared to that of foreigners (above all, the French), (3) the role of heredity in the succession to the throne, (4) succession by election, (5) knighting, (6) royal arms, (7) raising of the standards of Castile to a traditional cry, (8) exchange of oaths between people and monarch, (9) a royal horse that could be ridden only by the king, (10) kissing of the king's hand.

One can already identify a few of these practices in the reigns of Alfonso VI and Alfonso VII, and before the Castilian monarchs discarded anointment, coronation, and the ideological trappings of sacral kingship. Before Alfonso VI could claim the kingdom of Castile, he had to swear on the Bible his innocence of his brother's death to the Castilian nobility gathered at the church of Santa Gadea in Burgos. The dramatic ceremony, in which Ruy Díaz de Vivar, the Cid, speaking for the nobility of Castile, pressed the king again and again to swear his innocence, captured the imagination of contemporaries and of later chronicles, and serves as fair evidence of the contractual nature of the Castilian monarchy. Only after he swore his innocence did Alfonso receive the oath of fidelity and homage from the magnates and from the Cid himself. Only then could he be crowned. There is no indication that he was ever anointed. Instead, the

TABLE 4.1

The Kings of Castile in the Late Middle Ages

Name	Year of Birth	Year Became King	Age	Year of Death	Age	Length of Reign	Minority Time	Illegitimate (I) Contested (C)	Relation to Previous King
Sancho III	1134?	1157	23	1158	24	Less than one year	No		son
Alfonso VIII	1156?	1158	2	1214	58?	56 yrs.	Yes	(C)	son
Henry I	1203	1214	11	1217	14	3 yrs.	Yes	(C)	son
Berenguela	1180?	1217	37	1246	66	A few days	No	(C)	eldest sister
Ferdinand III	1200?	1217	17	1252	52	35 yrs.	No	(I) (C) for Leon	son of B nephew of H
Alfonso X	1221	1252	31	1284	63	32 yrs.	No	(C) by his son	son
Sancho IV	1258	1284	26	1295	38	11 yrs.	No	(C) by nephews	second-son
Ferdinand IV	1285?	1295	10	1312	27	17 yrs.	Yes 5 yrs.	(I) uncanonical marriage (C)	son
Alfonso XI	1311	1312	1	1350	38	38 yrs.	Yes 14 yrs.	(C)	son
Peter I	1333/4	1350	16	1369	35	16 yrs.	No	(C)	son
Henry II	1333?	1369	36	1379	46	10 yrs.	No	(I)	half-brother
Juan I	1358	1379	21	1390	32	11 yrs.	No	(C)	son
Henry III	1379	1390	11	1406	27	16 yrs.	Yes 3 yrs.		son
Juan II	1405	1406	1½	1454	49	48 yrs.	Yes 14 yrs.		son
Henry IV	1425	1454	29	1474	49	20 yrs.	No	(C)	son
Isabella I	1451	1474	23	1504	53	30 yrs.	No	(C)	half-sister

ceremonies of investiture with the sword and the exchange of oaths played a more important role. Great attention is paid to the Cid. Inasmuch as Ruy Díaz de Vivar was a thorn in the side of Alfonso VI, it is surprising, regardless of the influence of the *Poem of the Cid* on later writers, to see the regal attributes employed to describe someone who was at best a freelance adventurer. The Cid's heroic deeds of arms are praised to excess by royal chroniclers. After his death in 1099, his body, anointed, embalmed, and dressed in purple, sat uncorrupted in the church of the monastery of San Pedro de Cardeña for ten years. His horse could not be ridden again. Miracles and conversions of Jews took place around his body. These are indeed some of the symbols of royalty: the horse, which would have no other rider; the deeds of arms, which served as means of identifying the rulers of Castile and León rather than unction and crowning. Alfonso VI, the chronicle tells us, marveled at the greatness of the warrior who had increased by his victories over Christians and Moors the size of the kingdom.[22]

Although Alfonso VI sat on the imperial throne in Toledo as emperor of the three religions and heir to Visigothic glory, he chose to be buried at Sahagún. In doing so he broke (as did many Castilian kings) with the practice established by his father and grandfather of burial in the church of St. Isidore in León.[23] Alfonso VI's grandson, Alfonso VII, was raised on the shield as king of Galicia and crowned at Compostela while still a child. In 1135 Alfonso VII traveled to León and, after a solemn meeting of the *curia regis*, he was, according to the *Primera crónica general* (written more than a century later), anointed and crowned, though the contemporary chronicle of Alfonso VII makes no mention of the anointing. The *Primera crónica* describes how his head and body were consecrated with holy oil, and how, after the ceremony had concluded, surrounded by vassal kings from al-Andalús, Aragón, and Navarre, Alfonso was proclaimed "emperor of all the Spains" *(imperator totius Hispaniae)*. One must emphasize the association between León, the imperial title, and the ritual ceremonies of unction and coronation. In coming to the city of León, Alfonso VII was asserting the continuity with three hundred years of Asturian history. In the same fashion he went to Toledo to be crowned once again and finally to be buried there. He thus joined the Visigothic and Asturian heritages under one crown.[24]

Later chronicles compared Alfonso VII, the mighty emperor, to Louis VII, king of France. According to Castilian sources, Louis came across the Pyrenees on the pretense of making a pilgrimage to Compostela, but in reality to learn whether or not his wife, Alfonso VII's daughter, was legitimate. The emperor's court at Toledo, crowded with vassal kings and great lords, where precious metals, jewels, and exotic foreign imports were found in abundance, bedazzled the French king. He returned to Paris assured of his wife's honor and carrying a rare and precious stone, which he donated some time after to the abbey of St. Denis.[25] Here, the chronicles revealed an air of national pride not unlike that found in later royal wills and proclamations. They have, of course, all the medieval trappings of religion and devotion, but there is also a hard, practical outlook, a sense of the uniqueness and superiority of the Castilian-Leonese enterprise, of resolves forged in battle. Furthermore, the chronicles do not limit their unfavorable comparisons of Castilians and Frenchmen to Alfonso VII and Louis VII. The martial superiority of the Castilians and their secular efforts to reconquer their land are themes often found in the writings of the period. Discussing Spanish "nationalism" in general and the works of Vicentius Hispanicus in particular, Gaines Post writes: "His glorification of Spanish virtues appears as early as 1210–15. 'With deeds like a Spaniard,' he says, 'not with words like a Frenchman. . . .' Rejecting Innocent III's praise of the kingdom of the French, Vicentius declares 'that Spain, not France (the French Church), is greater than other ecclesiastical provinces, for when Charles with all the northerners *(Francigenae)* wished to invade Spain, the Spanish blocked their passage, overcame them in battle and killed twelve peers.'"[26] The chronicle of Sancho IV accuses the French of being subtle, deceitful, and always willing to appeal to and bend the law for their own benefit, the implication being that what the French did not have the courage to earn in battle, they sought in litigation. Similar sentiments are found elsewhere in the Castilian chronicles of the late Middle Ages.[27]

In Castile royal succession took place immediately after the reigning monarch's death, but it was closely tied to the acclamation of the new king by the magnates, the prelates, and the people or the acceptance by the Cortes. Here the two claims, consanguinity and primogeniture on the one hand, and the elective principle on the other, met in the single process of making a king. As Schramm has rightly pointed out, the hereditary and elective principles are not exclusive. Such was the case in Castile, whereas in France and England the prestige of specific blood lines had made the election of kings by the magnates and the people a relic of a distant past.[28]

At the death of Alfonso VIII (1158–1214) and after his burial at the monastery of Las Huelgas of Burgos, the archbishop of Toledo, other bishops present at the funeral, and some of the high nobility of Castile took the eleven-year-old Infante Henry, "heir to king Alfonso and to whom was due the kingdom by right and lineage, and with the clergy singing *Te Deum laudamus*, they raised him king."[29] In 1252, according to a later addition to the chronicle of Lucas de Tuy, after the death and burial at Seville of Ferdinand III (1217–52), his son, Alfonso the first-born, told "the prelates and knights present there, 'I am now the king,' and those who were there answered: 'we know certainly that of your father you are the primogenitus and thus it is for you to receive the government of the realm.'" Once the funeral ceremonies had concluded, all came into the church and gave Alfonso the royal horse. In front of the altar of the Blessed Virgin, the magnates raised the king to the horse, calling him with one voice, the Lord King Alfonso. The new monarch changed his mourning clothes into festive royal garments and was led through the streets of Seville at the sound of trumpets and cries of "your king, give him reverence and honor. Obey him for he is our king and prince of all the Spaniards." They sat Alfonso on "his father's chair," and he promised to respect the privileges and charters granted by previous kings and to make no demands that would contravene the customs of the realm. In his biography of Alfonso X, Antonio Ballesteros offers a somewhat different account. "The prince Alfonso," he writes, "was proclaimed king as it has been done during the period of the ancient elective principle; the magnates raised him upon the shield." Citing a charter of 1253, Ballesteros maintains that since no one could crown the king, Alfonso X took the crown from the altar and placed it on his head with both hands. Later in the day a mechanical statue of St. James knighted him.[30]

These two lengthy accounts contain elements of interest. In both cases, Henry I and Alfonxo X undoubtedly had the right to be kings by law and because of primogeniture. The majority of the prelates and great men accepted this without great opposition. In the case of Alfonso X it was not so clear, however, that he could inherit both kingdoms. There was, after all, a long-standing precedent for the separation of Castile and León. Eventually Alfonso X's brother, the Infante Henry, rebeled against his exclusion from the kingdoms, and the king was forced to grant the high nobility large holdings in Andalusia to secure their support.[31] The hereditary principle was also reinforced by the common practice among Castilian kings of demanding recognition of their first-born, male or female, shortly after birth. This was done at two levels, one by the approval of the Cortes, to gain the support of the Castilian cities in case of a minority, the other by an oath taken by the princes of the blood royal and the *ricos hombres*, all of them potential pretenders to the crown.

Unlike England or France, where kingship was vested in one family blessed with thaumaturgical and sacred attributes, the legal and practical requirements to be king in Castile, as set in both the *Fuero juzgo* and the *Siete partidas*, made access to kingship less restrictive than in England or France. The legal codes reveal obvious contradictions. Castilian jurists could not help but be influenced by the theories of royal power, which had been for a long time part of the Christian heritage and which were favored in other medieval kingdoms. Thus, according to the legal codes the king is the head of the realm as God is the head of the Celestial Court. Moreover, kings are vicars of Christ: each is emperor in his realm *(imperator in regno suo)*. As the saints have explained, the king holds the place of God on earth, to enforce justice, to give each person his or her due. The monarch is the heart and soul of the people, put there to protect, guard, and increase the realm.[32]

Yet if we look closer at both the *Fuero juzgo* and the *Partidas*, we find alternative states. Both state that a king is king because he rules. Emperors and kings came into existence because of a social contract. Long ago, differences of opinions and discord had prevailed among the people, a Hobbesian state of nature. The people agreed, therefore, to have a king and later emperors (king preceded emperors) to make things right, to crush the proud and the troublemakers. The old Visigothic law, still in force in most parts of Castile and León until late in the thirteenth century as the *Fuero juzgo*, stated that the king ought to be elected either in Rome or in the place where the last king died, with the advice of the bishops, the great men of the realm, and the people. According to the *Partidas*, the throne could be gained in the following four ways: (1) by inheritance, (2) by agreement (election) of all the people of the realm if there is no heir, (3) by marriage, (4) by grant of the pope or the emperor.[33] The legal codes of medieval Castile also state that the king is king as long as he behaves in a manner befitting his status and the welfare of the realm, as long as he rules according to law and tradition. If the ruler disregards the good customs and abuses his people, he can be challenged and indeed deposed. The codes also state explicitly that the monarch is not above the law but subject to it. These two last points are, of course, commonplace elsewhere in medieval western Europe and found in most medieval legal and political treatises.[34] We must return, however, to the point raised above, that access to the throne in Castile was not as restricted as it was elsewhere.

In Castile royal succession was not always clear; the first-born did not always follow his father to the throne. Unfortunately for Castile there were more troubled than untroubled successions, for many of the kings of Castile had dubious claims to the crown. Their rule was therefore legitimized not only by an appeal to inheritance, even if spurious, but above all by election and acclamation of the nobility and people. When the young king Henry I died in an accident in 1217, the magnates and prelates "gave" the kingdom to his older sister Berenguela, because "she was Alfonso VIII's first-born and all her brothers were dead." The *Primera crónica general* invoked a privilege of Alfonso VIII, kept at the cathedral of Burgos as authority for Berenguela's election as queen. Such care was needed, since it was not clear if her sister Blanca, Louis VIII's wife and mother of St. Louis, had equal rights to the throne. Most probably, the Castilian nobility found the idea of a French prince, the future Louis VIII, ruling Castile unacceptable and the hereditary principle was subverted. Mariana, who believed that to be the case, describes the acclamation of Berenguela under an elm tree in Nájera, accompanied by the cries of "Castilla, Castilla, real for the queen."[35] Days later the citizens of Valladolid, gathered in the public market of the city, acclaimed and recognized Berenguela heir by nature and right to the throne of Castile. Immediately the queen resigned the throne in favor of her son Ferdinand. In a ceremony of distinctly popular flavor, the prince was carried from the open market to the church of Our Lady. There he took the oath as king and received the homage of the magnates (who kissed his hand in obeisance), prelates, and people, as well as their oath of fidelity. Two years later, on 26 November 1219, Ferdinand completed the rituals and ceremonies of becoming king of Castile by keeping vigil through the night over his sword and armor at the main altar of the monastery of Las Huelgas. In the morning, after being knighted by the mechanical arm of St. James, Ferdinand took the sword from the altar and girded it around his waist.[36]

After his father Alfonso IX of León's (1188–1230) death, Ferdinand rushed to León where, through a show of force and the prudent negotiations of his mother and stepmother, he was proclaimed king of León in a ceremony not unlike that of Valladolid. He was neither crowned nor anointed as he joined the two kingdoms, which would never be parted again. This did not imply, however, that heredity and bloodline could be ignored completely. Ferdinand became king because he also had rights to the throne on the basis of heredity. Yet when others appear to contest the throne with better claims, election and military pressure preceded the right of heredity. The chronicle carefully emphasizes, by using the words *lindo* and *lindamente*, the legitimacy of Berenguela and her son and, thus, their right to rule. In fact they had none. Ferdinand was born two years after Pope Innocent III had branded the marriage of Alfonso IX and Berenguela incestuous, and no attempt to legitimize his birth is known to have occurred. Ferdinand was a bastard, and his claims to the thrones of Castile and León were not as valid as those possessed by others. Force of arms and election or acclamation by the magnates and people granted the legitimacy that blood and the right of succession did not.[37] Others could rule in Castile with equally weak or even weaker claims to kingship. Sancho IV, his son Ferdinand IV, the bastard Henry II and, last but certainly not least, Isabella the Catholic, all of them with dubious rights of succession, assumed the throne with ceremonies and rituals that did not differ from those described above.[38]

If bloodline, primogeniture, and election played an important role in the making of the king, what other important rituals and symbols were used in Castile and early modern Spain? The exchange of oaths constituted the binding legal agreement between a king and his people. This ceremony, which remains to this day an important part of the English coronation rites and one of the reasons for the loyalty of the Spanish army to its present king, had specific connotations in medieval Castile. In this context, the king's duties seem far more numerous than his rights.[39] The king, by his oath, entered into a contract with his subjects, and they in turn, bound themselves to him. For the king's part, the agreement involved the exercise of justice, and the protection of the laws and customs of the realm, but, in the thirteenth and fourteenth centuries, it was also a commitment to fight the Moors and recover the lands once held by the Visigoths. Kings who advanced the Reconquest were praised; those who did not were condemned. Unfortunately, we do not have the precise text of the royal oath, but one can gather most of its contents from the chronicles and, above all, from the proceedings of the meetings of the Cortes. When the new monarch came to the Cortes to make his financial requests, he was presented with an elaborate list of demands by the procurators of the Castilian and Leonese cities represented in the Cortes. These petitions, dealing with tax collections, policies toward the religious minorities, municipal rights, monetary policy, control of aristocratic violence, and war, became a contract between the monarch and the urban oligarchy and repeated reign after reign through the next centuries.[40]

Implicit also in the royal oath, in the *cuadernos* of the Cortes, and in the *Partidas* was the duty of the ruler to approach, in the words of Gimeno Casalduero, "the ideal image of the king." The monarch should be a tireless warrior, pious, articulate, a good father, a faithful husband, moderate in his eating and drinking, continent, a good hunter, a scholar. Yet he must also choose his mistresses from good families, be handsome, and dress in silk, gold, and precious jewels and still remain modest. These are the impossible injunctions pressed on the kings of Castile by the law and emphasized in royal writings, as for example, Sancho IV's written admonitions to his son. There is, of course, nothing remarkable in this "mirror of princes" literature. Similar ideals are found in other medieval kingdoms. There are, however, some differences in the emphasis placed in Castile on the Reconquest and the latitude in sexual matters, that is, the choice of concubines from good families, and of having bastards only from noble women.[41] It goes without saying that with the exception of Alfonso VIII and, to a lesser extent, Ferdinand III and Isabella the Catholic, all the Castilian rulers between 1157 and 1504, as their northern counterparts did, fell far short of the ideal. The people, the magnates, the prelates, and municipal councils proved as fickle to their oaths as their kings. Rebellion, conspiracies, wanton nobiliary violence, and frequent urban resistance to royal encroachment were the answers to the errors of the Castilian monarchy.[42]

Another rite associated with kingship was the ceremony of knighting and the self-girding of the sword. On this matter the Castilian kings were insistent. No one could knight them; no one could bear the royal arms except the king. The knighting and the royal arms were, in a sense, magical symbols of their promise as warriors, of their right to be kings. When the time came to be knighted, the Infante Don Sancho, the second-born, refused to be invested by his brother and heir to the throne, Ferdinand de la Cerda, even though his younger brothers had been knighted by him already. Sancho was old enough and ambitious enough to be king, as he did become eventually over the rightful claims of his nephew, Alfonso de la Cerda, and the objections of his father. To receive knighthood from someone implied obligations and service to the person who granted it, which Sancho might not have been willing to accept.[43] The tradition was already so clearly set in the thirteenth century that no exceptions were made for minors. In 1295 Sancho's son, Ferdinand IV (1295–1312), aged nine, was acclaimed king of Castile and León with the traditional cries and elevation. He took the oath to keep the *fueros* (charters), and his hand was kissed by the regents and magnates. With Ferdinand already a king, Don Nuño González de Lara, first among the *ricos hombres* of the realm, put the royal arms around his neck and walked with the young monarch through the streets of Toledo. We should compare this Castilian attitude with Edward's (the future Edward I of England) ready acceptance of knighthood at the hands of Alfonso X at Las Huelgas of Burgos.[44] Edward must not have thought that receiving knighthood from Alfonso X, or having him handle his sword, placed him under any obligation.

Linked to this knightly tradition we find other ceremonies and tokens of royalty, such as the royal horse, the lifting of the *pendones* (standards) of Castile to the cry of "Castilla . . . real for the king" and the *besamanos* or kissing of the king's hand. With the exception of the last ritual, all these ceremonies are linked to the Visigothic tradition. They are martial and secular rites which, while they had diminished in importance elsewhere, still played an important role in medieval Castile and early modern Spain.

On several occasions I have referred above to the royal horse, as for example, those used in the self-coronations of Alfonso X and Alfonso XI. The chronicles do not specify what they mean by the term *cavallo real*, but clearly the king's horse was set apart from other horses. In the seventeenth century if the king of Spain rode a horse, no one else could ride it afterward. The tradition must probably date back to the medieval period and, as with all the others, was associated with the role of the Castilian kings as leaders of the Reconquest.[45]

The raising of the banners of Castile to a traditional acclamation is rooted in Visigothic practice, but it can also be traced back to early medieval Navarre. As the chronicles attest, the raising of the *pendones* of Castile gained in importance through the years. The devotion given to the banner flown at Las Navas de Tolosa and kept at Las Huelgas of Burgos serves as an indication of the importance of these symbols. After Isabella took the oath to the people and kingdom and was acclaimed, she embraced the standard of the realm and offered it to God. The sources of the period stress the fact that the standards were never raised for Juana la Beltraneja, the rightful heir to the throne.[46] In the sixteenth and seventeenth centuries the ceremonial raising of the standards and the ritual cries in the Plaza Mayor of Madrid and elsewhere in the city marked the ascent of the Habsburgs to the throne of Castile and other Iberian kingdoms. The descriptions of these rituals closely parallel the medieval accounts.[47]

If all these rites had a strong martial flavor and were in Castile and later in Spain associated with the glorification of deeds of arms, honor, and courage, the *besamanos* belongs in a somewhat different category. The kiss was a sign of feudal homage and also of the essential equality between two warriors, but the Castilian *besamanos*, while retaining some of its feudal connotations, was far removed from the kiss of peace or the traditional kiss of French feudal custom. As Américo Castro has pointed out, in Castile the kissing of the king's hand and, sometimes, his feet imitated Muslim custom. The ceremonial kissing of the hand, so prominent in the descriptions of enthronement of medieval Castilian kings and early modern Spanish rulers, was an act of submission performed by the great lords of the realm, and even lowly royal officials. Such was the case of the three men commissioned by Sancho IV to undertake an investigation in Ávila, who in their report symbolically stated, "we kiss your hand as natural lord in whose mercy we are." This established a bond of loyalty, which, I should note, was broken again and again.[48]

Unlike Aragon, England, Germany, or France, where quite early a recognizable shrine was associated with the ruling dynasty either as a place of coronation or royal pantheon—Westminster, St. Denis, Reims, Aächen, Zaragoza—Castile never had a specific site around which a tradition crystallized. Lacking a real capital until the sixteenth century, the peripatetic Asturian, Leonese, and Castilian kings were crowned, became kings, and were buried in Oviedo, León, Santiago, Sahagún, Nájera, Burgos, Valladolid, Segovia, Toledo, Seville, and Granada. Their choices of burial places and sites for their enthronement show an obvious association with the Reconquest and the moving frontier. As the Castilians advanced southward, so did the center of power. Most often the kings were buried in the most important city that they had captured. Ferdinand III, for example, was buried in Seville, Alfonso requested to be buried in Murcia, the Catholic kings in Granada. In the late thirteenth and early fourteenth centuries, whenever there were no victories, the kings were laid to rest in Burgos, Toledo, Valladolid, or whatever city was close by. After 1157 only Alfonso VIII and Sancho IV attempted to establish royal pantheons in Las Huelgas of Burgos and Toledo, but their enterprises did not succeed, and no pantheon existed until the building of the Escorial.[49]

Neither did the kings of Castile and León attempt to establish elaborate genealogies by forgery or otherwise. They paid some attention to bloodline and family connections, but in the end such ties had little importance. When the pope asked Sancho IV to reject his wife, María de Molina, and to wed a princess of France, he refused in spite of all the clear political advantages. "Other kings of my house," he said, "had married within similar degree of consanguinity without [ecclesiastical] dispensation, and from the union were born many good kings, adventurous, conquerors against the enemies of the faith who increased [the size] and made their kingdoms better."[50]

There was no tradition of royal names. The kings named their first male child after their fathers or selected other names apparently in arbitrary fashion. Thus Alfonso VIII named his first son Henry, after his father-in-law Henry II of England. Alfonso XI named his first legitimate child Peter, and his first bastard son Henry. Their fathers had been named Sancho and Ferdinand, respectively. Moreover, in their charters and proclamations the Castilian kings seldom referred back beyond their grandfather or at the most great-grandfather. There was no need to appeal to ancient tradition. There was no Charlemagne or Arthur in their past.[51]

Religion, Politics, and Warfare: The Making of Unsacred Monarchy

At first glance it would appear that weak and troubled kings (such as most Castilian rulers were between 1157 and the advent of Isabella I in 1474) would have benefited by adopting an ideology of sacral kingship, by surrounding their rule with all the religious and magical panoply of *rex et sacerdos*, by claiming to belong to a sacred race, to have thaumaturgical powers. This was not difficult to accomplish, and the kings of Castile had what they believed was a rich tradition in the Visigothic past to which they could appeal. If this had been the case, the kings of Castile might have been spared the continuous challenges to constituted authority that so often plagued them and the realm. Convenient as the adoption of sacral kingship would have been, it was, however, unacceptable to the kingdom and to the kings themselves.

The easiest explanation for this rejection or failure to maintain a sacral kingship is one familiar to students of Castilian and Spanish history, the practical character of Castilian religiosity in the Middle Ages. Paradoxically in a reign and a country that have become so identified with exalted religiosity and fanatism, medieval Castile and, later on, Spain have always shown an ambivalent and, at times, quite practical approach to institutionalized religion. Furthermore, the Castilian clergy was certainly notorious for its misbehavior on sexual matters and its lack of regard for Church discipline or obedience to Rome.[52] Castilian kings often accepted the authority of the Church only if it suited their own political ends or did not interfere with their private lives. Spaniards in general and Castilians in particular had, and still have, a rather personal and arbitrary view of religion. Writing about Philip II, John Elliott puts this idea across very well: "He [Philip II] considered religion too serious a matter to be left to the Pope." The tendency toward mysticism, the fierce nationalism and independence of both Church and monarchy, and the well-known arrogance of Castilians toward foreigners were deterrents in the institutionalization of sacred rites that depended to such large extent on the doctrines of a church with its center elsewhere, influenced and dominated by non-Castilians. As the Infante Don Juan Manuel wrote in the early fourteenth century, "he was certain of one thing only: the pope had less power in Castile than anywhere else." That suited the Castilians just fine.[53]

Sánchez Albornoz and others have pointed out the pragmatic nature of the Castilians. One could say that in that respect earlier than in the rest of

Europe, Castilians had a more down-to-earth, practical outlook toward the uses of power and authority. The boundaries between the religious and the secular in the Middle Ages are vague, and one cannot speak of secular attitudes. The Castilians remained religious in spite of their practicality, but perhaps with a different understanding of the ideal relations between the spiritual and the temporal than that of their northern counterparts. When the Cid left Castile for the lands of the Moors, he did so, above all, "to earn his bread." This dichotomy between the spiritual and the practical is a topic in Spanish literature and the other obvious theme of *Don Quixote*. Nevertheless, there are more Sancho Panzas in Spain than Don Quixotes. Nor was there in Castile a mystification of power or history. Castile never had a revival of Celtic lore in the twelfth century nor a Geoffrey of Monmouth to tell the story. There were no fairies, trolls, or witches. If at all, they were imported or confined to remote and backward Galicia or the Basque region. Without myths, the monarchy used and still uses temporal symbols, and they were strengthened through the centuries, while paradoxically in such a Catholic country the royal sacral elements tended to disappear.[54]

In *Cantiga* 321 Alfonso X tells the story of a young girl from Córdoba who was sick for three years with a throat tumor. After the mother tried unsuccessfully to find a doctor to cure her daughter, a man advised her to take the ailing child to the king the next day, "because all Christian kings have the power to heal this sickness by laying of their hands." When the king heard this story, he told them that the advice was "not worth a very bad fig. When you say that I have such power, you are talking nonsense." Instead the king counseled the woman to wash an image of the Virgin Mary with pure water and afterward "drink that water from a chalice . . . for five days, a day for each letter of the name Maria. . . . And so it was that the girl was restored to full health." In the story Alfonso ridiculed the thaumaturgical claims of English and French kings and offered, as an alternative, what Américo Castro has described as Jewish-Muslim magic. The point is, of course, that Alfonso said that kings do not have the power to heal. Someone like Alfonso X, with his well-known interest in science and the occult, would rather trust the magical lore of the East (which for him was rational and scientific) than the hands of a king.[55]

Practicality and the peculiarities of Castilian religiosity, however, do not fully explain the differences that existed between northern medieval kingdoms and Castile. Other explanations can be offered. They are, of course, tentative answers to a question which may not have a single or set of satisfactory answers. Some of them have been implied in previous pages: (a) the institutional example and influence of Islamic political practices, (b) a change in the balance of power between Christians and Moors in favor of the former after 1157, (c) the martial nature, the personal character of kingship and mentality of the Castilian monarchy and people.

The influence of Islam also modified Germanic and Christian concepts of power and authority. For centuries before the Christians gained the upper-hand in the peninsula, Castilian princes and lords had traveled to al-Andalús, had lived in the courts of Muslim rulers as hostages, guests or exiles. After 1085, and above all, 1212, Muslim princes often accompanied the peripatetic Castilian kings, confirmed their charters, were, at times, enemies, often allies. Alfonso X, for example, sought Muslim help against his son Sancho; Alfonso XI often dressed in Muslim garments. In the caliphate of Córdoba and in the kingdoms of *taifas* afterward, religion was subordinated to the ruler. After Almanzor (d. 1002) political power in Muslim Spain was almost always gained because of personal valor, through assassination and intrigue, maintained by personal ability and violence against the continuous conspiracies of the ruler's own family.

Institutional developments in the caliphate of Córdoba and the kingdoms of the *taifas* thus served as models for the kings of Asturias, León, and Castile. There was a cultural, economic, institutional, and scientific interdependence between al-Andalús and the Christian north; and in the schools of the south the kings of Castile, and more importantly their subjects, learned more than astronomy, magic, and chess. Furthermore, Jamous's recent research on aspects of North African society shows that to this day violence is both ritualized and legalized as a means to political power in the Riff. *Baraka* or the charismatic qualities of the leader, is best revealed in his military prowess and in the continuous struggle against internal and external enemies. As Geertz describes aspects of political rule in present Muslim society, "the strong man aspects of his [the Sultan] role inevitably clashed with and usually dominated the holy man aspects." Clearly, there is a strong relationship between the traditional concept of authority and power in medieval and present Islamic societies and those mental attitudes which in Castile led to the development of unsacred monarchy.[56] There is a further point. If the preparations and fighting of a crusade shaped and transformed the reigns of some English and French kings,[57] how would a struggle but also a symbiotic relation of seven hundred years shape a nation and its rulers?

At a more obvious level, one should note the clear connection between a change in the Christian-Muslim balance of power in the peninsula during the reign of Alfonso VII and his successors' apparent failure to use the rites of anointment and coronation. Alfonso VIII's victory at Las Navas de Tolosa (1212) was the final turning point in a five-century conflict. After the early thirteenth century the issue of mastery over al-Andalús was decided once and for all in favor of the Christians. There was no longer any need to invest the figure of the king with sacred trappings, as had been done when the Christian kings were merely puppets of the proud caliphs of Córdoba. Relations with other Christian kingdoms beyond the Pyrenees were never as important as political ties and conflicts in the peninsula, and by 1212 the power of the kings of Castile had been proven and sanctified in the battlefield. Yet the frontier remained open, beckoning the rulers of Castile to one more expedition in the south, one more victory, almost as if those campaigns were the symbolic and necessary equivalent of unction and coronation. It is not a coincidence, after all, that as soon as the last outpost of Muslim power in Spain, Granada, surrendered to the Catholic kings in 1492, other frontiers were opened: one across the Ocean Sea, in the taming, raping, and conversion of new worlds; the other in central Europe in wasteful and ephemeral battles for empire and religion; and finally an inner frontier engaged in battle against crypto-Jews, heretics, purity of blood, and the mystical search for God.

Finally, the law (both Visigothic *Fuero juzgo* and the Roman inspired *Partidas*) opposed the idea of sacral kingship, even if these codes admitted that God chose the king. To a large extent the kings and the kingdom defined their legitimacy in terms of a warrior tradition. There is enough evidence in the previous pages to see that the ruler was, above all, lord of the armies. He was king because he carried on and directed the war against the Moors, because he led the realm in the centuries-old struggle to recover the land from the enemy. This, in spite of the *divinal* or divine aspects emphasized so much by Castro and others, was no racial or religious war. It was not the glorious Reconquest of Spanish historians. Of course, there were strong religious elements, but it was in many respects the response to the dynamics of a frontier society and territorial expansion.[58] When the kings of Spain claimed special rights over the Church in the *Partidas*, they did so because: (1) they conquered the land from the Moors, turned mosques into churches, and drove out the name of Mohammed and brought in the name of Christ; (2) founded churches where there had never been any; (3) gave these churches large gifts.[59] One can read in this a sense of kings and people engaged in the building up of a nation and an ideal, developing over centuries of battle and conflict. In Castile, although kings were to a certain extent special—how could it be otherwise as they held political power and were leaders of the Reconquest?—they made no sacred claims. Castile was a place where a good number of princes of the blood royal, royal bastards, and powerful magnates could and did assert their rights to be king. These princes, bastards, and magnates, as well as most of the Castilian kings in the thirteenth and fourteenth centuries, had a deep belief in their own individual worth. Unlike France or England, the institutional traditions that, through several centuries, had slowly subordinated the king's human personality to the needs of the realm and the strengthening of royal institutions were not as developed in Castile. Those who ruled and those who wanted to rule had, more often than not, one body instead of two. They often placed their own political ambitions, their pursuit of pleasures and revenge, over the welfare of the realm and the survival of royal institutions. We can see that in the wills of Alfonso X, Henry II, Henry III, and Juan I which are, above all, personal statements. In them the kings, as they contemplated their deaths, sought to please their mistresses, concubines, and bastards while they also attempted to placate God. There is little regard for the needs of the kingdom. In one case, Alfonso X's first will, the king sought to punish his undutiful son Sancho by bequeathing the kingdom to his grandsons and in their absence to the king of France. The idea of Philip IV or Edward I willing their kingdoms to the ruler of Castile is absurd. Above all, Alfonso X's poetry, the *Cantigas of Santa Maria*, bespeaks his personal fear of death, his zeal for life, the unbearable pain of his sickness, his passion, his faith. These are not the words of a king in his majesty but the words of a troubled, weak, and interesting human being. There were, of course, other medieval rulers who entertained similar ideas but never with such intensity or through such long periods of time.[60]

Visigothic law opened kingship to anyone of Gothic blood and good character. In thirteenth-, fourteenth-, and fifteenth-century Castile this was almost true. Between the reigns of Alfonso VIII and Henry IV, every ruler had to contend with a rival king or with nobiliary unrest, and in the case of Ferdinand IV and Alfonso XI's minorities, with several kings. Of these pretenders, Sancho IV, Henry II, and Isabella succeeded in becoming rulers, proving that it was not a futile effort after all. In France and England, magnates and princes of the blood rebelled against the king, but they did not claim the crown until the king's death or removal.

This challenge to the authority of kings came about partly owing to the individual sense of self-worth, a social perception in Castile that a nobleman, a warrior, was the equal of a king. In his *King's Touch* Marc Bloch mentions the tradition that lions were afraid of kings. There are three instances in Castilian and Spanish history and literature showing a lion afraid of a man. In all three cases, the characters are rebels or individuals outside the system. They are heroes or fictional characters with the courage and dignity that kings should have: the Cid, the Infante Enrique (Alfonso X's brother), and Don Quixote.[61] Or as Sancho put it in an entirely different context: "I am an Old Christian, and to become an earl that is sufficient." With some poetic license a Castilian noble could have said, Since I am a noble and a warrior, I could be king. In fact, poor *hidalgos* from the ends and dregs of Spain, Extremadura, did conquer worlds and untold wealth by the effort of their swords. Nobility, as Fernando Mexía, a fifteenth-century writer, emphasized, came before kings, and in parts of Old Castile almost everyone was a noble.[62]

Conclusion

Here at the end of the story, we must return to our initial account of Alfonso XI's anointment and self-coronation and, in doing so, complete the circle. The discontinuity of those events between prior and subsequent time is significant and raises questions as to the role of sacral symbols in Castile. Clearly these symbols neither shaped royal policies nor were fundamental in shaping the mentality of Castilians. These symbols of holy oil and coronation, so important elsewhere and so often mentioned in the models of anthropologists and historians of rituals, could be summoned from obscurity, used for one occasion, for a specific purpose and, soon afterward, forgotten, put aside. With far greater consistency, the rulers of Castile, in spite of the law and the tokens of royalty, expressed their power in the crudest and ultimate manifestation of individual power: in personal acts of violence. The chronicler Lucas de Tuy describes these kings as ferocious, taking arms against brothers and fathers. In the thirteenth and fourteenth centuries such was the case of Sancho IV and the fifteen-year-old Alfonso XI, who marked their assumption of power by killing with their own hands rebellious nobles, or Henry II, who killed his own half-brother and king.[63]

Juan de Mariana, a Jesuit and a keen observer of sixteenth-century political life, put it best. After a long discussion on the legal advantages and disadvantages of hereditary or elective kingship, Mariana added that all these legal arguments "were worth little, for it was the custom of men to carry the title of kingship in the point of their lances and in their weapons. The strongest is the one who captures the jewel [the crown]. And he wins it from his opponent without regard for the laws which are silent in the face of the clamor [noise] of arms, of trumpets and drums. And there is no one who, being able to become king by the strength of his hands, will venture his business to the opinion and judgments of jurists."[64]

This exercise of sheer power does not explain all—otherwise the martial rites and ceremonies developed over centuries and identified with the monarchy would not have been necessary. Yet when all the laws were read, and all the banners had been raised, and all the traditional cries given, the Castilian rulers often acted as if power came, as Mariana wrote and Mao rephrased it, from the barrel of a gun. Alas! as we come to the end of this, by far, too long journey, let us remember that Franco's only claim to legitimacy was to be the *caudillo*, the old medieval leader of hosts, by the grace of God, victorious against the Red infidels of the twentieth century, a caretaker, a tenancy held not by law or sacred rites but by the "sanctity" of the force of arms. Unfortunate Castile! Unfortunate Spain!

Notes

This article first appeared in French as "Une royauté sans sacre: La Monarchie castillane du Bas Moyen Age," *Annales E.S.C.*, 3 (May-June 1984); 429–53. The idea for this article came from Professor John H. Elliott's presentation to the Davis Center in 1981. I would like to acknowledge the many suggestions, invaluable ideas and bibliographical leads which I was fortunate to receive from those attending the Davis Center Seminar and, above all, from Professors Elizabeth A. R. Brown, Joseph R. Strayer, John H. Elliott, Charles Radding, and Javier Gil Pujol. A shorter version of this article was presented at the Centre de Recherches Historiques of the Ecole des Hautes Etudes en Sciences Sociales. I would like to thank Professors Jacques Le Goff, Jean-Claude Schmitt, Jacques Revel, and others for their gracious hospitality, valuable comments, and encouragement. Professor Le Goff's seminar on the rites and ceremonies of the French monarchy sharpened for me the distinctions between the French and Castilian models of kingship. Last but certainly not least, I owe an immense debt of gratitude to Peter A. Linehan of Cambridge University for his careful reading of this article and intelligent comments. In truth this has been a collective enterprise, though for the opinions and mistakes, I am solely to blame.

1. There are no suitable monographs on the reign of Alfonso XI. Salvador de Moxó wrote a series of articles on the early fourteenth century in preparation for a book on Alfonso XI and an edition of the royal documents. Moxó's death in 1980 has left the work incomplete. See Salvador de Moxó, "La sociedad política castellana en la época de Alfonso XI," *Cuadernos de historia*, 6 (1975): 187–326 and bibliographical references therein. The best source for the reign of Alfonso XI, besides the thousands of unpublished documents in the Archivo histórico nacional, is the *Crónica de Alfonso XI* in *Crónicas de los reyes de Castilla*, ed. Cayetano Rosell (Biblioteca de autores españoles, 66, Madrid, 1953) where the ceremony is described in detail on pp. 235–37. This volume of the *Crónicas* includes those of Alfonso X, Sancho IV, Ferdinand IV, Alfonso XI, and Peter I (hereafter cited as the chronicle of each individual king). See also *Poema de Alfonso onceno rey de Castilla y de León* in *Poetas castellanos anteriores al siglo XV*, ed. T. A. Sánchez, P. J. Pidal, and F. Janer (Biblioteca de autores españoles, 57, Madrid, 1966), p. 489 (hereafter cited as *Poema de Alfonso XI*). The ceremonial itself, which Claudio Sánchez Albornoz has studied and edited, was composed by a Portuguese bishop. See Claudio Sánchez Albornoz, "Un ceremonial inédito de coronación de los reyes de Castilla," in *Estudios sobre las instituciones medievales españolas* (Mexico, 1965), pp. 739–63 (hereafter cited as *Estudios*). The ceremonial (p. 762) calls for the king to be crowned with a bishop's miter and, above that, the royal diadem. Alfonso XI did not follow this injunction. Included in the text is also an ideal description of the conduct of kings. See below.

   The king is anointed on the shoulder, because as Christ carried the cross and with it the weight of the world, the king carries on his shoulders the burden of his people. See Partida 1, 4.3 in *Los códigos españoles concordados y anotados*, ed. M. Rivadeneyra, 12 vols. (Madrid, 1847–51), 2:39 (hereafter *Códigos*). The *Partidas* make a distinction between the old law (when kings were anointed on the head with holy oil) and the new law (when they are consecrated only on the shoulder). Mariana adds that the queen was not anointed because of her "honesty" and "because she was pregnant." Juan de Mariana, *Historia general de España*, ed. Francisco Oliva, 7 vols. (Barcelona, 1839), 4:7.

   On the king by the "grace of God," Américo Castro points to the widespread use in Spain of formulas taken from the Arabs and employed by the Mozarabs, "que Deus defenda, que Dios mantenga" and their association with the official naming of the king. To this very day in Spain and, above all, in Latin America "con el favor de Dios," by God's favor or grace, is a common epistolary or speech formula, especially among the old. See Américo Castro, *La realidad histórica de España*, 2d. ed. (Mexico, 1962), p. 234.

2. T. F. Ruiz, "The Transformation of the Castilian Municipalities: The Case of Burgos, 1248–1350," *Past & Present*, 77 (1977): 18–20. For the practice of self-coronation Alfonso XI only had to look across the border to Aragón where the practice had been in use since the late thirteenth century, or to the history of Castile itself. There was in addition the example of Frederick II. See Bonifacio Palacios Martín, *La coronación de los reyes de Aragón, 1204–1410: Aportación al estudio*

de las estructuras medievales (Valencia, 1975), pp. 81ff.; Ernst Kantorowicz, *Kaiser Friedrich der Zweite*, 2 vols. (Berlin, 1928–31), 1:183. Note that Jaume I (1213–76) also insisted upon taking the sword himself. For similar emphasis on the taking of the sword see Hartmut Hoffman, "Französische Fürstenweihen des Hochmittelalters," *Deutsches Archiv* (Cologne, 1962), pp. 104–5. Also Percy E. Schramm, *Las insignias de la realeza en la Edad Media española*, trans. L. Vázquez de Parga (Madrid, 1960), pp. 92–93. Ballesteros maintains that Alfonso X crowned himself. Antonio Ballesteros y Beretta, *Alfonso X, el sabio* (Barcelona, 1963), p. 54. There is a notice of an even earlier self-crowning, that of Sancho II (1065–72) in *Primera crónica general: Estoria de España que mando componer Alfonso el sabio y se continuaba bajo Sancho IV en 1289*, ed. Ramón Menéndez Pidal (Nueva biblioteca de autores espanoles, 5, Madrid, 1906), p. 505 (hereafter cited as *Primera crónica general*). See also Carlrichard Brühl, "Fränkischer Krönungsbrauch und das Problem der 'Festkrönungen,'" *Historische Zeitschrift*, 194 (1962): 265–326; "Kronen und Krönungsbrauch im Frühen und Hohen Mittelalter," *Historische Zeitschrift*, 234 (1982): 1–31; also his "Les auto-couronnements d'empereurs et de rois (XIIIe-XIXe S.). Remarques sur la fonction sacramentelle de la royauté au Moyen Age et à l'Epoque Moderne," Académie des Inscriptions & Belles-Lettres. *Comptes rendus des séances de l'année 1984*, January-March (Paris, 1984), pp. 102–18.

3. That Alfonso XI broke with an established tradition of unsacred monarchy is not too difficult to explain. These explanations can be here summarized by pointing to the problems of his minority, prevailing conditions in Castile, and to his personality. The king was deeply influenced by northern examples, and loved chivalrous acts and distinctive ceremonies.
4. For the ordination of Visigothic and Asturian kings see C. Sánchez Albornoz, "La sucesión al trono en los reinos de León y Castilla," in *Estudios*, pp. 639–704; "La '*ordinatio Principis*' en la España goda y postvisigoda," in *Estudios*, pp. 705–37; J. M. Ramos y Loscertales, "La sucesión del rey Alfonso VI," *Anuario de historia del derecho español*, 13 (1941): 36–79. For the tokens of the Asturian, Leonese, and Castilian kingship see Schramm, *Las insignias*, pp. 26–27, 32, 61–63. Schramm limits his discussion to crowns, throne, scepter, etc., a different category from the symbols discussed in this paper.
5. On this point see Clifford Geertz, *The Interpretation of Cultures: Selected Essays* (New York, 1973), pp. 6–7, 29, 362–63: "To commit oneself . . . to an interpretative approach to the study of it [culture] is to commit oneself to a view of ethnographic assertion as, to borrow W. B. Gallie's by now famous phrase, 'essentially contestable.'" See also Edward Evans-Pritchard, *The Divine Kingship of the Shilluk of the Nilotic Sudan* (Cambridge, Eng., 1948); Reinhard Bendix, *Kings or People: Power and the Mandate to Rule* (Berkeley and Los Angeles, 1978). See also the old but still wonderful mine of information in James G. Frazer, *The Golden Bough: A Study in Magic and Religion*, 1-vol. abridged ed. (New York, 1927), pp. 1–10, 83–92, 146–58 et passim. It is not my intention, however, to approach this inquiry with an anthropological or strictly interdisciplinary meth-

odology. Rather, my task here is the modest one of describing the rituals and symbols of Castilian kingship and to advance a tentative explanation for its uniqueness. It might be proper for historians to take to heart Felix Gilbert's review of Richard C. Trexler, *Public Life in Renaissance Florence* in *The New York Review of Books* (21 Jan. 1982), pp. 62–64.

6. A great deal has been done elsewhere. See for example Percy E. Schramm, *A History of the English Coronation*, trans. Leopold C. Wickham (Oxford, Eng., 1937); *Kaiser, Könige und Päpste*, 4 vols. in 5 (Stuttgart, 1970); *Der König von Frankreich*, 2 vols. (Weimar, 1939); Ernst H. Kantorowicz, *The King's Two Bodies: A Study in Mediaeval Political Theology* (Princeton, 1957); *Laudes Regiae: A Study in Liturgical Acclamations and Medieval Ruler Worship* (Berkeley and Los Angeles, 1946); Joseph R. Strayer, "France: The Holy Land, the Chosen People and the Most Christian King," in *Medieval Statecraft and the Perspectives of History: Essays by Joseph R. Strayer*, ed. J. F. Benton and T. N. Bisson (Princeton, 1971), pp. 300–14; also "Defense of the Realm and Royal Power in France," in *Medieval Statecraft*, pp. 291–99; *The Reign of Philip the Fair* (Princeton, 1980), pp. 380–423; Andrew W. Lewis, *Royal Succession in Capetian France: Studies in Familial Order and the State* (Cambridge, Mass., 1981), pp. 118–31. For Castile see nn. 1, 2, 4, and 58. For a good short summary of the rituals and symbols of the medieval Spanish kingdoms see Luis García de Valdeavellano, *Curso de historia de las instituciones españolas* (Madrid, 1968), pp. 186–94, 411–30; Schramm, *Kaiser, Könige*, vol. 4, pt. 1, pp. 316–419, and above all, 319–48. Also Pedro Longás Bartibas, "La coronación litúrgica del rey en la Edad Media," *Anuario de Historia del Derecho Español*, 23 (1953): 371–81 (mostly an edition of a relevant document); Rafael Gibert, *Historia general del derecho español* (Granada, 1968); Manuel Colmeiro, *Reyes cristianos desde Alfonso VI hasta Alfonso XI* (Madrid, 1893).

7. Possibly in imitation of Visigothic rituals, the Frankish kings introduced into Frankland the practice of anointing of the monarch with holy oil, and soon afterward this practice spread to the rest of western Europe. This opinion by Bloch is disputed by others. See n. 2 and Marc Bloch, *The Royal Touch: Sacred Monarchy and Scrofula in England and France*, trans. F. E. Anderson (London, 1973), pp. 37, 262–63.

8. García de Valdeavellano, *Curso de historia*, p. 193; Alfonso García Gallo, *Manual de historia del derecho español*, 3d ed., 2 vols. (Madrid, 1967), 1:532–43. Vol. 2 contains long excerpts of primary sources providing evidence for García Gallo's contentions. Margaret Deanesly, *A History of Early Medieval Europe 476–911*, 2d ed. (London, 1969), p. 99.

9. Deanesly, *History*, p. 102; Bloch, *Royal Touch*, pp. 262–63; García Gallo, *Manual*, 1:544.

10. Kantorowicz, *The King's Two Bodies*, pp. 71, 81 et passim; Walter Ullmann, *A History of Political Thought: The Middle Ages* (Baltimore, 1968), pp. 53–99.

11. *Fuero juzgo*, 1:1.8; "Cuando el rey muere, nadie debe tomar el reino, ni hacerse rey, ni ningun religioso, ni otro hombre extraño, si no hombre del linaje de los

godos, e hijodalgo . . . y noble et digno de costumbre." in *Códigos*, 1:100; García Gallo, *Manual*, 1:540.

12. *Fuero juzgo*, 1. Introducción: "Onde los antigos dicen tal proverbio; Rey seras, si fueres derecho, et si non fecieres derecho, no seras rey." *Códigos*, 1:97; García Gallo, *Manual*, 1:540; Aloysius K. Ziegler, *Church and State in Visigothic Spain* (Washington, D.C., 1930), pp. 55–88.
13. *Primera crónica general*, p. 495: "because the kings of Spain came from the strong blood of the Goths, and many times the Gothic kings killed each other, brother killing brother . . . "
14. *Fuero juzgo*, 1:1; 1:1.2, 3. in *Códigos*, 1:97–98; García Gallo, *Manual*, 1:540. Quoting St. Isidore: "El Poder no existe para provecho de alguno o daño de los demas . . . todo Poder viene de Dios y solo se usa rectamente cuando se ejerce para el bien y la *utilitas populi* 'provecho del pueblo y en defensa de la Iglesia.' " Also García Gallo, *Manual*, 1:627, and 2:F734.12, F811.71.5, F646–49.50.
15. Mariana, *Historia*, 2:148ff.; Sánchez Albornoz, "La '*ordinatio Principis*,' " pp. 720–27 (p. 721): "Como ilustración del '*Officium in ordinatione regis*' del Antifonario de León, se representa al rey postrado ante los obispos y al metropolitano vertiendo sobre su cabeza el óleo santo por la punta de un cuerno litúrgico, que recuerda al que fue empleado segun la Biblia por Samuel para ungir a David." Also Schramm, *Las insignias de la realeza*, pp. 22–27.
16. Castro, *La realidad histórica*, p. 85: quoting the bishop Don Alonso de Cartagena in 1434. "Los reyes de España—entre los quales el principal e primero e mayor, el rey de Castilla e de León—nunca fueron subjectos al Emperador, ca esta singularidad tienen los reyes de España que *nunca fueron subjetos al Imperio Romano* (el Sacro Romano Imperio) *nin a otro alguno mas ganaron et alçaron los regnos de los dientes de los enemigos*" (emphasis mine). The kings of Spain were never subjects of the Holy Roman Empire (or of anyone else), but they gained and raised the kingdom from the teeth of the enemy. The same feelings had been expressed before by Alvarus Pelagius. See Joaquín Gimeno Casalduero, *La imagen del monarca en la Castilla del siglo XIV* (Madrid, n.d.), p. 24; *Primera crónica general*, pp. 356, 382, 475 et passim. See also nn. 26 and 27.
17. On the imperial question see Cayetano J. Socarrás, *Alfonso X of Castile: A Study on Imperialistic Frustration* (Barcelona, 1979), pp. 9–63 (a summary of the bibliography on the subject). Also *Primera crónica general*, pp. 310–12, 356 and below nn. 26 and 27. According to the chronicles and legends, the Spaniards defeated Charlemagne at Roncesvalles (the feat of the legendary Bernardo del Carpio), and by their efforts opened the road to Compostela. Legend and epic poems have given this glory to Charlemagne, but epic and legends, the chronicler maintains, lack the veracity of history.
18. On medieval royal tombs in Castile see Heath Dillard, "Medieval Convent Tombs: Dynastic Burial at Iberian Nunneries," paper given at Kalamazoo, Mich., May 1981. Professor Dillard has kindly given me a copy of her yet unpublished paper.

19. García Gallo, *Manual*, 1:635, 2:F823.1; *Primera crónica general*, pp. 467–68.
20. For the history of Asturias and Castile, which serves as background to the development of rituals of kingship, see Luis García de Valdeavellano, *Historia de España*, vol. 1 (Madrid, 1952); Joseph O'Callaghan, *A History of Medieval Spain* (Ithaca, N.Y., 1975); Angus MacKay, *Spain in the Middle Ages: From Frontier to Empire, 1000–1500* (London, 1977); and the polemical Claudio Sánchez Albornoz, *España: Un enigma histórico*, 2 vols. (Buenos Aires, 1956). Also MacKay, *Spain*, pp. 15–35. How confusing some aspects of Castilian medieval history can be is best expressed in a paragraph from Christopher Brooke, *Europe in the Central Middle Ages, 962–1154* (New York, 1966), p. 380. After attempting to make sense of Iberian affairs in the mid-twelfth century, Brooke writes, "Thus the mid-1150s saw three kingdoms firmly established in Christian Spain, with an Alfonso growing old in Castile, an Alfonso in the prime of life in Portugal, and a small Alfonso growing up to be heir of Aragón, all dedicated to spread moderate confusion among Muslims of their own day, and extreme confusion among historians until the end of the world." On the general crisis of the early fourteenth century Julio Valdeón Baruque, *Los conflictos sociales en el reino de Castilla en los siglos XIV y XV*, 2d ed. (Madrid, 1976), pp. 54–65; "Aspectos de la crisis castellana en la primera mitad del siglo XIV," *Hispania*, 111 (1969): 5–24; Salustiano Moreta Velayos, *Malbechores-feudales: Violencia, antagonismos y alianzas de clases en Castilla, siglos XIII y XIV* (Madrid, 1975), pp. 70ff.; T. F. Ruiz, "Expansion et changement: la conquête de Séville et la société castillane (1248–1350)," *Annales E.S.C.*, vol. 34, no. 3 (1979): 548–65. Also in Ruiz, *Sociedad y poder real en Castilla* (Barcelona, 1981), ch. 1; Antonio Ubieto Arteta, *Ciclos económicos en la Edad Media española* (Valencia, 1969); Ramon Menéndez Pidal, *La España del Cid*, 7th ed., 2 vols. (Madrid, 1969); MacKay, *Spain in the Middle Ages*, pp. 20–29; García de Valdeavellano, *Historia de España*, pp. 768–97, 858. Also Julio Valdeón Baruque, *Enrique II de Castilla; la guerra civil y la consolidación del regimen (1336–1371)* (Valladolid, 1966); Luis Suarez Fernández, *Nobleza y monarquia: Puntos de vista sobre la historia castellana del siglo XV*, 2d ed. (Valladolid, 1959); César Conzález Minguez, *Fernando IV de Castilla (1295–1312). La guerra civil y el predomino de la nobleza* (Vitoria, 1976).
21. Schramm, *Las insignias*, pp. 36–38, 56–57. For sculptures and miniatures see José Guerrero Lovillo, *Las Cantigas, estudio arqueológico de sus miniaturas* (Madrid, 1949); *Miniatura gótica castellana (siglos XIII y XIV)* (Madrid, 1956); Rafael Cómez Ramos, *Las empresas artísticas de Alfonso X, el sabio* (Sevilla, 1979); *Crónica de Enrique III* in *Crónicas de los reyes de Castilla*, ed. C. Rosell (Biblioteca de autores españoles, 68, Madrid, 1877), p. 193. This volume of the *Crónicas* includes those of Henry II, Juan I, Henry III, and Juan II, and will be cited hereafter as the chronicle of each individual king. See also Françoise Dumas, "Le thrône des rois de France et son rayonnement," *La monnaie, miroir des rois* (Paris, 1978), pp. 231–50; R. H. Bautier, "Echanges d'influences dans les chancelleries souveraines du Moyen Age, d'après les types des sceaux de majesté," *Comptes rendús de l'Académie des Inscriptions et Belles-Lettres* (Paris, 1968), fn. 3, pp. 207–8. Bautier notes that al-

though there is a seal from the reign of Alfonso VII, showing the king in his majesty, the seals of the Castilian kings of the thirteenth and fourteenth centuries were equestrian seals.

22. *Primera crónica general*, pp. 560–643. This account is revealing at different levels. The heirs of Navarre and Aragón, by kissing Alfonso VI's hand in the name of the Cid, acknowledge themselves vassals of both the Cid and Alfonso. Miracles are reported, including the conversion of a Jew who comes to Cardeña to mock the body of the Cid. Yet on the same page the miraculous is explained and made rational. Alfonso VI is amazed at seeing the Cid, dead for many days, still uncorrupted and riding his horse, but when the attendants explain to him that the Cid did not eat for the last seven days of life and was embalmed immediately after his death the king was no longer amazed. "He had heard that in the land of Egypt they did that to their *kings*." Ibid., p. 640. See below for the lion's fear of el Cid.
23. *Primera crónica general*, pp. 539, 645; Dillard, "Medieval Convents," p. 10; Mariana, *Historia*, 2:310, 406.
24. For the reign of Alfonso VII see García de Valdeavellano, *Historia de España*, pp. 875–924; Mariana, *Historia*, 2:446–69; *Primera crónica general*, pp. 653–54, 663. Neither Linehan nor Bruhl believe that Alfonso VII was anointed. Again, we are faced with the distortion of the past by later chronicles. Was it a mistake or conscious distortion?
25. *Primera crónica general*, p. 657; Lucas de Tuy, *Crónica de España*, ed. Julio Puyol (Madrid, 1926), p. 339. Lucas de Tuy attributes a quote to Louis VII: "I swear that there is no similar glory [that of Alfonso VII's court] as this in the whole world."
26. See Castro, *La realidad histórica*, pp. 92–96; Gaines Post, *Studies in Medieval Legal Thought: Public Law and the State, 1100–1322* (Princeton, 1964), pp. 482–90; *Primera crónica general*, pp. 310–12, 356. See also Peter Linehan, *The Spanish Church and the Papacy in the Thirteenth Century* (Cambridge, Eng., 1971), pp. 102–6.
27. Lucas de Tuy, *Crónica*, pp. 3–11; José A. Maravall, *El concepto de España en la Edad Media*, 2d ed. (Madrid, 1964), pp. 23, 280 et passim; *Crónica de Sancho IV*, pp. 3, 72. See also Sancho's attitude toward the pope and the papal messengers in *Crónica de Alfonso X*, p. 65. Alfonso X in his first will paid the French a left-handed compliment by commenting on what good businessmen the French were but neither good warriors nor as courageous as the Spaniards. *Memorial histórico español*, 47 vols. (Madrid, 1851–1915), 2:110–22; Schramm, *Kaiser, Könige*, vol. 4, pt. 1, 378–88. See table 4.1. Although there is certainly a religious and mystical aspect to this hard-nosed chauvinism, I find at the heart of it very little of a religious crusade in the sense in which crusades were understood in the north. Anyone who has lived in Spain or dealt with Spaniards for a while will recognize today, even if it is probably a defensive mechanism, that individual and national pride which already existed in the medieval past.
28. Schramm, *A History of the English Coronation*, pp. 1, 141; Lewis, *Royal Succession*, pp. 76–77.

29. *Primera crónica general*, p. 709.
30. Lucas de Tuy, *Crónica*, pp. 449–50. This part of the vernacular chronicle is a later addition. See the introduction by Puyol, pp. xviiff. See also Joseph O'Callaghan, "The *Cantigas de Santa María* as an Historical Source: Two Examples," paper given at a symposium on the *Cantigas* held in New York (November 1981) and forthcoming in the proceedings of the symposium. I would like to thank Professor O'Callaghan for providing me with a copy of his paper. See also Ballesteros, *Alfonso X*, p. 54, who quotes a privilege of Alfonso X of 6 December 1253: "E por mi que fu hy Rey e recebi hy cabelleria." Schramm incorrectly traces self-coronation to Aragón.
31. Ruiz, *Sociedad y poder real*, p. 36; Ballesteros, *Alfonso X*, p. 54; *Crónica de Alfonso X*, p. 7.
32. *Fuero real de Castilla*, 2:2, in *Códigos*, 1:350; *Partida*, 2:1.5, 6 in *Códigos*, 2:317–25.
33. *Fuero juzgo*, 1:1.7, 8, 9 in *Códigos*, 2:319, 326–68. See also Gimeno Casalduero, *La imagen*, pp. 26–37. See also Wilhelm Berges, *Die Fürstenspiegel des hohen und späten Mittelalters* (Leipzig, 1938), pp. 86–88, 93–101.
34. *Fuero juzgo*, 1:1 in *Códigos*, 1:97; 2:1.2, p. 107; "Que el rey e los pueblos deven seer sometidos de las leyes," *Fuero viejo de Castilla*, ley ccxxviii in *Códigos*, 1:337; *Fuero real*, tit 2 in *Códigos* 1:351 instructs how to obtain redress from the evil actions of kings, including "going public." *Partida*, 1:1.16, in *Códigos* 2:16; *Partida*, 2:1.10 in *Códigos*, 2, 329.
35. *Primera crónica general*, p. 713; Mariana, *Historia*, 3:127–28 claims that the succession was not legal and that Doña Blanca was the rightful heir. Commenting on the troubled succession of Henry III, Mariana, *Historia*, 4:350–53, describes how the king's will in favor of his young son, the Infante Don Juan, was challenged. He goes on to show the many instances in thirteenth- and fourteenth-century Castilian history in which the rightful heir did not succeed to the throne. "Seria forzoso confesar," Mariana added, "que los Reyes pasados no tuvieron justo titulo." The throne of Castile was offered to the Infante Fernando (Henry III's brother), who did not accept it. *Crónica de Enrique III*, p. 262. See also, for Isabella I, John H. Elliott, *Imperial Spain 1469–1716* (Harmondsworth, 1975), pp. 22–23.
36. *Primera crónica general*, pp. 713–18; Lucas de Tuy, *Crónica*, p. 417; Rodrigo Ximénez de Rada, *Opera* (reimpression, facsimile of ed. of 1793. Valencia, 1968), pp. 192–96. The Portuguese kings also girded their swords themselves.
37. Ballesteros, *Alfonso X*, pp. 10–50; *Primera crónica general*, pp. 722–23. It is remarkable to see how early the Capetians established dynastic succession and the uniqueness of a bloodline when compared with Castile. See Lewis, *Royal Succession*, pp. 19–20, 35–36, 76, 107–16; Schramm, *A History of the English Coronation*, p. 106.
38. See *Crónica de Sancho IV*, p. 69; *Crónica de Fernando IV*, p. 93; *Crónica de Alfonso XI*, p. 173; *Crónica de Enrique II*, p. 1; *Crónica de Juan* 1, 65; *Crónica de Enrique III*, p. 161; *Crónica de Juan II*, pp. 261–62; Fernando del Pulgar, *Crónica de los Reyes Católicos*, 2 vols. (Madrid, 1943), 1:65–66.

39. García Gallo, *Manual*, 1:628.
40. See Ferdinand III's advice to his son Alfonso: "Sir, I leave you all the lands on this side of the sea which the Moors won from King Roderick of Spain. All this now lies within your power, one part of it conquered and the other laid under tribute. If you should manage to hold it all in the way in which I leave it to you, then you are as good a king as I; and if you should lose any of it, you are not as good as I." Quoted in MacKay, *Spain*, p. 59. According to the *Crónica de Alfonso X*, p. 53, after the death of the Infante de la Cerda, heir to the crown, the magnates requested from Alfonso X that he name Sancho as his successor because "he defended the land and defeated the Moors." See also *Poema de Alfonso XI*, p. 481. For the oath see Mariana, *Historia*, 4:11, describing how Alfonso XI took an oath to the Basques under the famous and ancient tree of Guernica. For the oath of Charles I see Schramm, *Las insignias*, p. 74. For the relations between king and Cortes in the thirteenth and fourteenth centuries see T. F. Ruiz, "Oligarchy and Royal Power: The Castilian Cortes and the Castilian Crisis, 1248–1350," in *Parliaments, Estates & Representation*, vol. 2, no. 2 (1982): 95–101. On contracts in general see H. Hopfl and M. P. Thompson, "The History of Contracts as a Motif in Political Thought," *American Historical Review*, 84 (1979): 929–44; also Ralph E. Giesey, *If Not, Not. The Oath and the Legendary Laws of Sobrarbe* (Princeton, 1968), pp. 158–226. On the emphasis of military symbols and ideal warriors see a different approach in Frances Yates, *Astraea: The Imperial Theme in the Sixteenth Century* (London, 1975), pp. 21–23 and the motif of Hercules in the symbols of the Spanish monarchy of the early modern period in Jonathan Brown and John H. Elliott, *A Palace for a King* (New Haven, 1980), pp. 156ff.
41. *Partida*, 2:4.1–5 in *Códigos*, 2:334–48; *Castigos é documentos del Rey don Sancho*, ed. Pascual de Gayangos (Biblioteca de autores españoles, 51, Madrid, 1952), pp. 79–228; Gimeno Casalduero, *La imagen*, pp. 46–52. On the "mirror of princes" literature in general, see Wilhelm Berges, *Die Fürstenspiegel des hohen und späten Mittelalters*, pp. 86–101. On the sexual mores see Linehan, *The Spanish Church*.
42. See nn. 6 and 36 and Elliott, *Imperial Spain*, pp. 86, 93, 151–56.
43. *Crónica de Alfonso X*, p. 13. This was the same Alfonso de la Cerda who girded Alfonso XI's spurs. See also n. 2.
44. For the knighting of Prince Edward see Ballesteros, *Alfonso X*, p. 101. For Ferdinand IV see *Crónica de Fernando IV*, p. 93.
45. Professor John H. Elliott was kind enough to direct me to this source. "Voyage d'Antoine de Brunel en Espagne," *Revue hispanique*, 30 (1914): 213: "Il est vray que, pour le respect qu'on rend au roy et à ceux qui l'approchent, on a quantité de petites coustumes toutes extraordinaries, et entr'autres on à celle que personne ne monte jamais un cheval quand le roy s'en est servy. L'on raconte qu'après la prise de Barcelonne en la cavalcade que sa Majesté fit à l'Atocha, le duc de Medina de las Torres luy envoya presenter son beau cheval, qui est si fameux à Madrid; mais le roy le renvoya, devant: seria lastima, c'est à dire que seroit dommage qu'il le montast, puisque par là il deviendroit inutile à tout le

monde, et ne seroit monté que de quelques escuyers." See also references to the *cavallo real* in Lucas de Tuy, *Crónica*, p. 450; and Frazer, *Bough*, pp. 174, 459, 639–40 et passim.

46. Schramm, *Las insignias*, p. 67; García de Valdeavellano, *Curso de historia*, p. 193. The proclamation of Isabella as queen of Castile and the description of the ceremonies are found in the minutes of the council of Segovia. The *acta* have been edited and published by M. Grau, *Estudios segovianos*, 1 (1949): 24–36; Luis Suárez Fernández notes that the *pendones* were not raised for the Beltraneja, *Historia de España*, ed. R. Menédez Pidal (Madrid, 1969), vol. 17, pt. 1, pp. 85–87. One should note the similarities with Louis VII of France receiving the standard of St. Denis. See Robert Fawtier, *The Capetian Kings of France: Monarchy and Nation 987–1328*, trans. L. Butler and R. J. Adam (New York, 1965), p. 80. To this very day small towns in Castile and León, such as that of my ancestors in the province of Burgos, keep their banners in the local church, to be paraded in the patron saint's procession. See J. W. and R. L. Fernández, "El escenario de la romería asturiana," *Expresiones actuales de la cultura del pueblo* (Madrid, 1976). Ruth Behar is at work on a study of the *romería* of the Virgin del Camino, forthcoming in *Archivos leoneses*. For the inheritance of the throne by bastards see Charles T. Wood, "Queens, Queans, and Kingship: An Inquiry into Theories of Royal Legitmacy in Late Medieval England and France," in *Order and Innovation in the Middle Ages*, ed. W. C. Jordan, et al. (Princeton, 1976), pp. 387–400.

47. I also owe this note to Professor Elliott. Antonio de León Pinelo, *Anales de Madrid* (Biblioteca de estudios madrileños, 9, Madrid, 1971), pp. 168, 235. The Plaza Mayor also served as a bull ring and as the showcase for great Inquisition trials. It was also one of the scenes of the popular uprising against the Napoleonic armies. It is as if in one place, the Plaza Mayor, the central themes of Castilian and Spanish history—martial monarchy, bullfighting, Inquisition, and popular violence—met within the serene and formal majesty of the square.

48. García de Valdeavellano, *Curso de historia*, p. 384; Marc Bloch, *Feudal Society*, trans. L. A. Manyon, 2 vols. (Chicago, 1966), pp. 162, 180, and for Castile, 182; Schramm, *A History of the English Coronation*, p. 20. Some examples from the chronicles can be seen in *Crónica de Fernando IV*, pp. 96, 117; Castro, *La realidad histórica*, pp. 234–35. For the kissing of feet as a sign of submission see the *Dictatus Papae*, item no. 9, in Brian Tierney, *The Crisis of Church and State 1050–1300* (Englewood Cliffs, N.J., 1964); Linehan, *The Spanish Church*, p. 240; Angel Barrios García, *Documentación medieval de la catedral de Ávila* (Salamanca, 1981), p. 145.

49. Schramm, *A History of the English Coronation*, p. 38; Jofré de Loaysa, *Crónica de los reyes de Castilla: Fernando III, Alfonso X, Sancho IV, Fernando IV (1248–1305)* (Murcia, 1961), p. 141. For the rearranging of tombs as means of advancing dynastic claims and royal funerals see Elizabeth A. R. Brown, "The Ceremony of Royal Succession in Capetian France: The Double Funeral of Louis X," *Traditio*, 34 (1978): 227–71; "Philippe le Bel and the Remains of Saint Louis," *Gazette des Beaux-Arts* (May 1980): 175–82; "The Ceremonial of Royal Succession in

Capetian France: The Funeral of Philip V," *Speculum*, 55 (1980): 266–93; "Death and the Human Body in the Later Middle Ages: The Legislation of Boniface VIII on the Division of the Corpse," *Viator*, 12 (1981): 221–70. Only Alfonso X, a great admirer of Louis IX of France, requested in his will that his body be divided, in imitation, he said, of his German grandfather, but probably because Louis's example was close at hand. All the other Castilian kings avoided the French royal custom of division of the corpse.

50. *Crónica de Sancho IV*, pp. 72–73. See also Gimeno Casalduero, *La imagen*, pp. 93–116, for Henry II's bizarre propaganda against his half-brother, accusing Peter I of being illegitimate, which, of course, made him a bastard as Henry was, and their common father, Alfonso XI, a cuckold.
51. Socarras, *Alfonso X*, p. 79. Nobility in Spain was established when three successive generations were exempted from taxes. See Ruiz, *Sociedad y poder real*, p. 46.
52. Linehan, *The Spanish Church*, pp. 29–30.
53. Ibid., pp. 102–6, 186, 240: "Alvarus Pelagius 'forced to admit that even he was accustomed to kiss the King's hand,—as the vile Spanish prelates' did." For the quote by Don Juan Manuel, p. 224. John H. Elliott, *Imperial Spain, 1469–1716* (London, 1963), p. 230.
54. Claudio Sánchez Albornoz, *España*, 1:316–17. For the attitude toward myths and witches, a thoroughly rational one, see Julio Caro Baroja, *Inquisición, brujeria y criptojudaísmo*, 3d ed. (Barcelona, 1974), pp. 183–282; *The World of the Witches*, trans. O. N. V. Glendinning (Chicago, 1973), pp. 180–89. Think of the attitude toward religion in the Spanish picaresque novels or the debunking of St. James in *Don Quixote*. Also Berges, *Die Fürstenspiegel*, p. 89, and n. 53.
55. *Cantigas de Santa María*, ed. Walter Mettmann, 4 vols. (Coimbra, 1959–72), 3:175–77; O'Callaghan, "The *Cantigas*," p. 2; Evelyn Proctor, *Alfonso X of Castile, Patron of Literature and Learning* (Cambridge, Eng., 1951), pp. 24–45; John Esten Keller, *Alfonso X: El Sabio* (New York, 1967), pp. 64–95; Castro, *La realidad historica*, p. 371; Bloch, *The Royal Touch*, pp. 85–89.
56. García Gallo, *Manual*, 1:561ff.; García de Valdeavellano, *Curso de historia*, pp. 629–76. For the interaction of Islamic and Christian cultures see Thomas F. Glick, *Islamic and Christian Spain in the Early Middle Ages: Comparative Perspective on Social and Cultural Formation* (Princeton, 1979). See also R.P.A. Dozy, *Histoire des musulmans d'Espagne*, ed. E. Leví-Provençal, 3 vols. (Leyde, 1932); E. Leví-Provençal, *L'Espagne musulmane au Xéme siècle: Institutions et vie sociale* (Paris, 1932), pp. 41–114; Raymond Jamous, *Honneur et baraka: Les structures sociales traditionneles dans le Rif* (Cambridge, Eng., 1981), pp. 221–28; Clifford Geertz, *Islam Observed: Religious Development in Morocco and Indonesia* (New Haven, 1969), pp. 44, 53.
57. See William C. Jordan, *Louis XI and the Challenge of the Crusade* (Princeton, 1979); Lewis, *Royal Succession*, p. 125.
58. Quoting Alonso de Cartagena, Castro describes the wars of the *hispano-cristianos* as *divinales*. See Castro, *La realidad histórica*, p. 140. See also p. 246: "El modelo para la estructuración colectiva no fue ni el visigodo, ni el francés, ni el inglés en

los cuales la dimensión política predominaba sobre la religiosa. La base de la nación fue la circumstancia de haber nacido la persona dentro de la casta religiosa a la que pertenecía cada uno de los tres grupos creyentes." Castro contradicts himself on pp. 38–39. He published in parallel columns the epitaph of Ferdinand III, written in Latin, Castilian, Arabic, and Hebrew. Only the Latin version, a clerical production, refers to religious matters: "qui civitatem Hispalensem que capud est et metropolis tocius Hispanie de manibus eripuit paganorum et cultui restituit christiano." The other three versions address Ferdinand's human qualities and his deeds of arms. Sánchez Albornoz, "La *'ordinatio Principis,'* " p. 737, explains the decline in the influence of the Church. To a certain extent he is correct, but it is perhaps more accurate to speak of the peculiar relationship between Church and king in Castile and later in Spain due to the martial tradition, the frontier, and the Muslim influence. On the Castilian church see the excellent work by Peter Linehan, *The Spanish Church and the Papacy in the Thirteenth Century* (Cambridge, Eng., 1971). For the later relations between Church and king see Elliott, *Imperial Spain*, pp. 99–110. Schramm, *A History of the English Coronation*, p. 96, advances a one-line explanation, "the relation of the king to the Estates. . ." for the peculiarities of the Castilian ordination of kings. See also A. Barbero and M. Vigil, *Sobre las orígenes sociales de la Reconquista* (Barcelona, 1974). See also n. 53.

59. *Partida*, 1:5.18 in *Códigos*, p. 82; Castro, *La realidad histórica*, p. 85.

60. See *Memorial histórico español*, 2:110–34. For other wills see *Crónica de Enrique II*, pp. 39–44; *Crónica de Enrique III*, pp. 186–94. Compare with the will of Philip IV of France. See Elizabeth A. R. Brown, "Royal Salvation and Needs of State in Late Capetian France," in *Order and Innovation*, pp. 363–83. For the sense of individuality in Alfonso X's *Cantigas* see Marisel Precillas, "The Image of Death in the *Cantigas* of Santa María," forthcoming, *Proceedings of International Symposium on the Cantigas of Santa María*.

61. Bloch, *The Royal Touch*, p. 142; *Crónica de Alfonso X*, p. 7; *Poema del Cid* (Biblioteca de autores españoles, 57), p. 25; *Don Quixote*, 2: ch. 17. Dumas, "Le throne," p. 247, seal no 41.

62. Fernando Mexía, *Nobiliario perfetamente copulado* (Seville, 1492), f. 164; Mariana, *Historia*, 4:70.

63. Lucas de Tuy, *Crónica*, p. 363: "Ciertamente, los reyes de España se dize aver seydo de tanta ferocidad, que aun en la hedad non cumplida tomaron armas, quier contra hermano, quier contra padre si fuesse bivo, y aparejan contender por sus fuerças que el derecho real solo se lo tenga." Jofré de Loaysa, *Crónica*, p. 121; *Crónica de Sancho IV*, p. 74 (Juan Martínez de Negrita spoke in defense of his lord, and Sancho IV beat him to death with a stick). *Crónica de Fernando IV*, p. 169; *Crónica de Alfonso XI*, p. 202; *Poema de Alfonso XI*, p. 484; *Crónica de Pedro I*, p. 592.

64. Mariana, *Historia*, 4:390.

XIV

IMAGES OF POWER IN THE SEALS OF THE CASTILIAN MONARCHY: 1135-1469

In a long and soon to be published article, "Unsacred Monarchy: The Kings of Castile in the Late Middle Ages", I discuss in detail the peculiar absence of sacral elements and of thaumaturgical claims in the Castilian monarchy after 1157[1]. Unlike France or England which, over a long period of time, developed a sacral and thaumaturgical kingship and, together with these sacral claims, what has been described as "the religion of monarchy", after 1157 the Castilian kings abandoned these exalted claims and formulated consciously or unconsciously an alternative model of kingship[2]. Indeed, after the reign of Alfonso VII, with very few exceptions, the kings of Castile ceased to be anointed or crowned. Instead of these sacral symbols and rites in use elsewhere in medieval Europe, the Castilian kings chose, as they laid their claims to the throne, a series of secular symbols and ceremonies, most of which were of a martial nature.

[1] "Unsacred Monarchy: The Kings of Castile in the Late Middle Ages", paper given to the Davis Center Seminar, Princeton University, Princeton, N.J. 27-III-1982. Forthcoming in a collection of papers given to the Davis Center, 1982-83. Also given in a new version to the Ecole des Hautes Etudes en Sciences Sociales, "Le roi non sacré", 17-I-1983.

[2] On sacred monarchy see MARC BLOCH, *The Royal Touch. Sacred Monarchy and Scrofula in England and France,* trans. F.E. Anderson (London, 1973); PERCY E. SCHRAMM, *Kaiser, Könige und Päpste,* 4 vols. in 5 (Stuttgart, 1970); ERNST H. KANTOROWICZ, *The King's Two Bodies. A Study in Medieval Political Theology* (Princeton, N.J. 1957); also his *Laudes Regiae: A Study in Liturgical Acclamations and Medieval Ruler Worship* (Berkeley and Los Angeles, 1946); JOSEPH R. STRAYER, "France: The Holy Land, the Chosen People and the Most Christian King", in *Medieval Statecraft and the Perspectives of History. Essays by Joseph R. Strayer,* eds. J.F. Benton and T.N. Bisson (Princeton, N.J., 1971), pp.300-14.

These unsacred symbols and ceremonies reflected in part the long struggle for control of the peninsula, the influence of Muslim examples, the Castilian independence from the church, as well as, an ancient military tradition which dated back to the Germanic invaders of Hispania during the last years of the Late Empire[3].

This "rite of passage" from claimant of the crown to king, which as Jacques Le Goff has pointed out, was in France a ceremony filled with religious undertones, was in Castile a secular passage to the assumption of unsacred power[4]. That which made a king in Castile was neither the crowning nor the anointing with holy oil, and even less the royal exercise of thaumaturgical power. Instead, knighting of the king by the mechanical arm of a statue of St. Jacques, the raising of the king on a shield or chair by the magnates, the exchange of oaths between king and people, and the lifting of the standards of Castile at the sound of a traditional cry: Castilla, Castilla por el rey, took the place of sacral ceremonies organized and orchestrated by the church[5].

My interest in these topics began by having one of Don Claudio Sánchez Albornoz's works as a point of departure. In his *Estudios sobre las instituciones medievales españolas* Sánchez Albornoz edited and studied the ceremonial composed by a Portuguese bishop for the coronation and unction of Alfonso XI in 1332[6]. Although Alfonso XI did not follow the above mentioned ceremonial or *ordo* of coronation and anointment, the document serves as an useful beginning for the above mentioned discussion of the symbols and rituals of the Castilian monarchy in the late medieval period, since it sharpened the distinction between the ideal concept of sacred kingship and the real absence in Castile of such rites.

I, would like, however, at this point to move away from a summary of my previous work and to discuss a complementary

[3] "Unsacred Monarchy".

[4] The term rite of passage in this context, as well as, the idea of the Castilian monarchy as a different model of kingship originate with Jacques Le Goff, in his seminary at the Ecole des Hautes Etudes, which I had the honor to attend.

[5] "Unsacred Monarchy", pp.   See also PETER LINEHAN, *The Spanish Church and the Papacy in the Thirteenth Century* (Cambridge, 1971), pp.102-06, 186, 240, 244 for the attitude of the Castilian kings to Church authority.

[6] CLAUDIO SANCHEZ ALBORNOZ, "Un ceremonial inédito de coronación de los reyes de Castilla", in *Estudios sobre las instituciones medievales españolas* (Mexico, 1965), pp.739-63.

aspect of this topic. My aim in the following pages is to show how the kings of Castile in the late middle ages expressed and projected their peculiar concept of kingship and political authority. I refer here to the images and symbols present in the seals of the Castilian monarchy from the reign of Alfonso VII (1126-1157) to that of Isabella I (1474-1504). A study of the seals (wax, plaque but most often made of lead) employed by the kings of Castile and Leon between the mid-twelfth century and the dawn of the modern period confirm some of my conclusions already advanced in "Usacred Monarchy", and raises further questions as to the uses of symbols and images of power in medieval Castile. It also raises question as to the hold of tradition, or better yet the lack of a continuous tradition in the image of kingship. Once again, the Castilian kings chose symbols of political power which differed markedly from those employed elsewhere in the medieval West[7]. Moreover, contrary to England and France where an established tradition set a pattern of seals seldom broken, in Castile the symbols of power and authority were often chosen to serve specific political aims in particular circumstances and were discarded when no longer appropriate or useful. These changes in the ideological and symbolic messages conveyed by the seals did not take place over a long period of time but occurred swiftly from ruler to ruler and in response to immediate needs.

The message of the seals of the Castilian monarchy, in spite of the noted eclecticism in design and imagery, was essentially a martial one between 1157 and 1474. In some specific situations, however, the kings of Castile-Leon resorted to other images of power and authority. In these instances, the selection of lofty symbols of monarchy over the traditional martial motif attempted to legitimize what was otherwise an illegitimate rule. Yet, even when the design of the obverse face of the seals emphasized the majesty of the royal position over its military function, the latter remained a constant theme in the reverse of the seal of the ideal image of the monarch[8].

[7] For seals elsewhere see FRANÇOISE DUMAS, "Le thrône des rois de France et son rayonnement", *La monnaie, miroir des rois* (Paris, 1978), pp.231-50; R.H. BAUTIER, "Echanges d'influence dans les chancelleries souveraines du Moyen Age, d'après les types des sceaux de majesté", *Comptes rendús de l'Académie des Inscriptions et Belles-Lettres* (Paris, 1968), pp.192-220.

[8] On the ideal image of the monarch see JOAQUIN GIMENO CASALDUERO, *La imagen del monarca en la Castilla del siglo XIV* (Madrid, n.d.), p.24. This ideal image was essentially a martial one. *Primera crónica general,* ed.

The royal seals extant at the Archivo historico nacional in Madrid have already been described and catalogued by Araceli Guglieri Navarro[9]. In the cathedral and municipal archives of Castile and Leon, as for example those of Burgos and Segovia, there is also a large collection of royal seals which are still attached to the original charters and privileges. They wait to be catalogued and described by a patient and industrious historian although the task of examining this large collection of royal seals will certainly be long and ardous. In reality, however, the seals kept at the Archivo histórico nacional are more than a representative sample for our purposes, specially since from reign to reign there is little variation in the type of seals used by each individual king.

The chronological series of seals catalogued by Guglieri Navarro begins with a wax seal of Alfonso VII dated from 1152. A majestic seal, it shows on its only face a crowned king seated on a chair or x shaped bench. The king holds in his right hand a sphere or globe and in his left the scepter. The globe, symbolic of the imperial status which Alfonso VII claimed, is reinforced by the legend on the face of the seal: *Adefonsus Imperator Hispaniae*[10]. The majestic design, of course, fits perfectly Alfonso VII's own concept of his regal powers. He had been anointed and crowned with great pomp in the city of Leon and crowned once again in imperial Toledo[11]. The symbolic meaning of the seal was in perfect concordance with the sacral rites of unction with holy oil and ritual coronation which he had received in 1135, and it reveals to us ideological trappings similar to those employed by the kings of England and France.

On the other hand, after Alfonso VII's death in 1157 his grandsons, Alfonso IX of León and Alfonso VIII of Castile, ignored the majestic style of their grandfather. Instead, their seals show on the obverse the equestrian figure of a king, holding in his hand a bare sword. On the reverse there is a lion in the seals of the kingdom of Leon and a castle with three towers in Alfonso VIII's seals. The

R. Menéndez Pidal (Nueva biblioteca de autores españoles, V, Madrid, 1906), pp.356, 382, 475; AMERICO CASTRO, *La realidad histórica de España*, 2nd. ed. (Mexico, 1962), p.85 and my "Unsacred Monarchy", n.40.

[9] ARACELI GUGLIERI NAVARRO, *Catálogo de Sellos de la sección de sigilografía del Archivo Histórico Nacional,* 3 vols. (Valencia, 1974). Royal seals appear in the first volume.

[10] GUGLIERI NAVARRO, I, 1, pp.3-5.

[11] For the reign of Alfonso VII see LUIS GARCIA DE VALDEAVELLANO, *Historia de España,* I, (Madrid, 1952), pp.875-924; *Primera crónica general*, pp.653-54, 663.

most typical among the seals of Alfonso IX is number 7 in Guglieri Navarro's inventory. The king wears a crown or crowned helmet, a broad sword in his hand. The legend: "Adefonsus: Dei Gracia Rex" continues on the reverse of the seal "Legion et Gall." That is Alfonso by the grace of God, king of Leon and Galicia[12]. His cousin, Alfonso VIII, also maintained the same motif with some minor variations. Alfonso VIII's most commonly used seal is number 16 in the catalogue, dating from around 1181. In the obverse it shows an equestrian representation of the king wearing a suit of armor, with a large oval shield hanging from the king's neck and a broad naked sword in his hand. The legend in Latin states: Seal of king Alfonso. The reverse shows a castle with three towers and the continuation of the legend in the obverse: king of Toledo and Castile[13]. It is redundant to go on describing these seals since Guglieri Navarro has done a thorough job of description. The point is, of course, that in both cases the ruler is represented as a warrior, with that image taking exclusive precedence over the majestic one. In fact, in Castile-Leon the symbols of majesty comes to be used after the death of Alfonso VII only in special circumstances and for the purpose of lending to the ruling monarch an image of majesty which he lacks in law.

The seals of Enrique I and Fernando III of Castile preserved the same format: an equestrian figure, crowned and armed with a sword on the face of the seal and the emblems of Castile on the reverse. After 1230, however, when Castile and Leon were joined under Fernando III's rule, a new seal was used concurrently with the equestrian-castle format. This new seal showed a castle on its face and a lion on the reverse. The political message conveyed is simple and direct: the union of Castile and Leon, or to be precise, Leon-Galicia and Castile-Toledo, under one ruler. Furthermore, after 1230 the equestrian seals of Fernando III also showed the crowned rider's shield blazoned with the lions and castles, and on the reverse a similar representation of castles and lions[14]. Fernando's son, Alfonso X, whose rule over the two kingdoms was not secure upon his accession to the throne and who was indeed challenged in the early 1250's by his brother Enrique, revived the format of a castle on

[12] GUGLIERI NAVARRO, I, 7, pp.9-10. There are no descriptions of the seals of Fernando II or Sancho III in the catalogue of Guglieri Navarro.

[13] *Ibíd.*, 16, pp.16-7.

[14] *Ibíd.*, 34, pp.27-8; 35, pp.29-30; 40, pp.33-35, 52, p.42. On Fernando III see JULIO GONZALEZ, *Reinado y diplomas de Fernando III* (Cordoba, 1980), I, pp.528-31.

the obverse and a lion on the reverse for the first three years of his reign. By 1255, when his rule was no longer in dispute, the equestrian seal, with the crowned rider holding in his right hand a naked sword, and castles and lions on the reverse began to alternate with the castle-lions format[15].

In 1284 Alfonso X's son, Sancho IV, came to the throne after a debilitating conflict and waging war on his father. He set aside the legal claims to the throne of his nephew Alfonso de la Cerda and took power by what can only be described as violent means. Sancho was crowned in solemn ceremonies, the only king to be crowned in the entire period since Alfonso VII. The images selected for his seal symbolically asserted his legitimacy. Throughout his reign and without variation his seals showed a king sitting in majesty with the emblems of Castile and Leon on both sides of the throne. An equestrian reverse continued the tradition of the crowned king as a warrior[16]. Nevertheless, at his death in 1295 the regents for his son, Fernando IV, reverted immediately to an equestrian/castle-and-lions seal. All the seals extant in the Seccion de Sigilografia of the Archivo histórico nacional for the reign of Fernando IV belong to this category[17]. The same style was used throughout the minority of Alfonso XI, although it alternated with the type of seal used by Fernando III after 1230 (castle on the obverse, lion on the reverse). Again the choice of seals reveal a political aim. We know that in 1315, when these symbols were reintroduced, there were several claimants to the thrones of Castile and León. In some instances some of the pretenders took the title of king. Most probably the regents, above all Alfonso XI's grandmother, María de Molina, sought to emphasize in the royal seals the indivisibility of the crowns. Once more we see how images of power and authority were drummed out to deal with specific circumstances and discarded when no longer necessary. By 1325, with Alfonso XI in firm control of the realm, the king was again depicted on the face of his seals as a crowned rider with a raised sword in his right hand and castles and lions on the reverse of the seals[18].

[15] GUGLIERI NAVARRO, I, 58, pp.46-7; 63, p.50. On Alfonso X, see ANTONIO BALLESTEROS y BERETTA, *Alfonso X. El sabio* (Barcelona, 1963), p.54.

[16] GUGLIERI NAVARRO, I, 99, pp.76-77; 100, pp.77-9.

[17] *Ibíd.*, I, 125, pp.96-97 *et passim.*

[18] *Ibíd.*, I, 169, pp.126-27; 174, p.130; 196, pp.144-45. For the problems of Alfonso XI's minorities see JULIO VALDEON, "Aspectos de la crisis castellana en la primera mitad del siglo XIV", *Hispania*, 111 (1969), 5-24.

From 1332 on, after Alfonso XI's anointment and selfcoronation at the monastery of Las Huelgas of Burgos, a new seal was introduced. It shows the figure of a crowned king sitting on a throne, holding a scepter with an eagle on his right hand and a globe with a cross on his left. Other regal symbols appeared on the obverse of Alfonso XI's seals, but with equestrian design on the reverse. Throughout the rest of his reign the majestic/equestrian and the standard equestrian/lions-and-castles seals alternated in royal privileges and documents. Clearly, the seals reflected the significance of the events of 1332, Alfonso XI's lofty concept of his own power. As such, these alternating selection of majestic and military symbols reveal the unique character of Alfonso XI's rule and of his use for political ends of the images of power present in the lead seals of his reign[19].

The lead seals of Peter I, Alfonso XI's son, show changes in design, but the themes remained essentially the same. Peter I, who attempted to exercise his rule by direct and violent means, reverted in his seals exclusively to the equestrian/castles-and-lions format, both of them enclosed now within a stylized rose. His half-brother and rival for the crown, Enrique II, adopted as early as 1367, while Peter was still king, the traditional equestrian/castles-and-lions motifs but without the innovations introduced by Peter I.[20]. In 1370, a year after he had murdered his brother at Montiel, Enrique II adopted a lead seal which depicted on its face a crowned king seated on two lions, a naked sword (a sign of judicial authority and the king's power of life and death) in his right hand. On his left hand, the figure holds a globe topped with a large cross. One should notice the introduction of new motifs by the new dynasty and its political pretensions as conveyed by the seals. The globe is a revival of imperial dreams, which were already present in Alfonso XI's seals and ritual unction, even if the imperial claims meant only hegemony in the peninsula. The reverse retained the castles and lions themes, always revived in times of political upheavals, though with the addition of small fleur de lis, probably of French origin. The lead seals of Enrique II's son and heir, Juan I, faithfully followed those of his father[21]. Obviously, the Trastámaras, bastards by birth and kings by murder, wished to

[19] See note 18. The majestic seal coincided with Alfonso XI's renewal in earnest of the Reconquest. To the majestic motif in his seal, he added the real martial behavior.

[20] GUGLIERI NAVARRO, I, 217, pp.160-61; 237, pp.175-76; 239, pp.177-78.

[21] See note 20. Also 254, p.188.

emphasize their role as kings and the majesty of their office while retaining on the reverse the traditional union of the crowns motif. Nevertheless, when Enrique III came to the throne, the dynasty now secured, there was a return to the equestrian/castles-and-lions model. This king and during all of his long reign his son, Juan II, used no other design[22].

The seals of Enrique IV present a radical departure from previous practices, but one which considering Enrique IV's peculiar personality and tastes, seems to me to reflect the person as much as it reflected the new artistic currents entering the peninsula in the mid-fifteenth century. One should note, however, that Enrique IV's seals, a bust of majesty on the face and castles-and-lions on the reverse, is similar to an ancient traditional bust of majesty used by the Ottonians and Carolingian emperors[23].

The variety of motifs employed by the Castilian monarchy in their seals contrasts with the uniformity of the Aragonese seals. The lead seals of Aragon, from the twelfth century on showed a crowned king bearing a naked sword and sitting in majesty in his throne on the obverse and an equestrian figure with a lance on the reverse. In contrast, wax seals and paper plaques are overwhelmingly equestrian until the mid-fourteenth century. Afterwards, they alternate with the majestic/equestrian type. It is not surprising, therefore, that the lead seals of Isabelle the Catholic showed the queen sitting in majesty on her throne on the obverse and an equestrian representation of the king Fernando on the reverse. Since in earlier seals Castilian queens were always depicted standing, the images of the Catholic Kings seals integrated not only the emblems of Aragon and Sicily with those of Castile and Leon, but also the new concepts of power and authority emerging in Castile under Isabella I. One must also add that her rule was not uncontested or fully legitimate and, thus, similar to Sancho IV and Enrique II, the queen chose to emphasize her majesty[24].

[22] *Ibíd.*, 278, pp.206-07; 294, pp.218-19.

[23] *Ibíd.*, 319, p.235. Also BAUTIER, p.196.

[24] *Ibíd.*, 573, pp.425-26. In Guglieri Navarro's description of the seals, one could also find the appropriate and relevant bibliography to individual seals.

This preliminary assessment of the images of power found in the medieval seals of the Castilian monarchy does not do full justice to other types of seals, or indeed, examines in detail other themes and symbols present in these seals. Yet, even a brief examination of the images of the monarch, as these few pages have attempted to present, shows the expedient nature of these rulers, their approach to power, the continuity of martial motifs, and the discontinuity in the use of more sacred or regal themes.

XV

FESTIVITÉS, COULEURS ET SYMBOLES DU POUVOIR EN CASTILLE AU XVe SIÈCLE
LES CÉLÉBRATIONS DE MAI 1428

Vêtus d'écarlate et parés de fourrures précieuses, les fiers magistrats et seigneurs de Burgos conduisirent la procession solennelle par la porte de San Juan vers les faubourgs de la cité. Là, en grande cérémonie et avec force cris d'allégresse, ils accueillirent l'infante doña Blanca, princesse de Navarre, qui venait d'arriver dans le royaume pour épouser l'infant don Enrique, héritier des Couronnes de Castille et de León. Sous un dais écarlate, l'infante fit son entrée dans la cité antique sous les acclamations de la foule en liesse. Pour marquer le passage de l'infante à Burgos, on organisa de somptueux banquets, des lâchers de taureaux dans les rues et l'inévitable joute : ces festivités qui avaient déjà eu pour cadre d'autres cités allaient se répéter tout au long de l'itinéraire qui devait mener l'infante à Valladolid pour ses funestes épousailles [1].

Dans ce court récit, ainsi que dans d'innombrables descriptions d'entrées solennelles et de festivités en Castille à la fin du Moyen Age et au début de l'époque moderne, les chroniqueurs montrent une extrême sensibilité aux couleurs, parures et symboles de la fête. Dans leurs récits, l'art et la réalité se mêlent pour évoquer une tradition de longue date qui identifiait certaines couleurs — le rouge, le blanc et le noir — aux manifestations du pouvoir et au cycle de la vie humaine. On trouve aussi, dans les fêtes et dans la poésie de la fin du Moyen Age et des premiers temps de l'Époque Moderne, des messages tantôt implicites, tantôt fort explicites, concernant la nature de l'autorité. Ils nous renseignent sur les liens unissant ceux qui dirigent et ceux qui obéissent. Quelle était la nature de ce langage symbolique des couleurs et des gestes ? Comment était-il perçu par l'assistance ? Découvrons à présent, dans les cérémonies et les fêtes de la Castille au xve siècle, et dans leur déploiement chatoyant, ces messages du pouvoir à l'aube d'une époque.

I. — La symbolique du pouvoir

Le pouvoir et l'autorité des monarques médiévaux s'accrurent lentement au cours des siècles qui suivent la fin de l'ère wisigothique en Ibérie et de l'Empire carolingien au nord des Pyrénées. L'image idéalisée de la majesté royale — en dépit des sérieux défis que les grands féodaux lancèrent au xve siècle à l'autorité monarchique en Angleterre, en France, dans les royaumes ibériques et ailleurs en Occident — trouvait son origine dans l'entrelacement de motifs religieux, séculiers et populaires complexes et elle servit, avec le temps, de fondement à des modes de gouvernement nouveaux et plus forts. Ce processus s'accompagna souvent de la représentation délibérée de fêtes et de cérémonies ritualisées qui servaient aussi les ambitions politiques des rois et de la grande noblesse.

Nous connaissons les grandes lignes des processus qui permirent aux rois, et parfois aux reines, d'accéder à des positions de majesté et de pouvoir et, plus important encore, de devenir les symboles du royaume et finalement de la nation[2]; il n'est donc pas nécessaire de rappeler ces aspects bien connus de la réalité politique propre à l'époque qui nous intéresse. J'aimerais plutôt mettre en évidence ici la façon dont les dirigeants (rois et grands féodaux) assirent leur pouvoir au moyen de fêtes et de jeux, et grâce à l'utilisation symbolique de costumes et de couleurs[3].

En Castille, comme dans d'autres royaumes, les dirigeants ecclésiastiques et laïques affirmaient leurs prétentions à l'autorité au cours de joutes et d'affrontements, la plupart du temps féroces, mais dans lesquels la violence était soumise aux règles de la chevalerie au moyen de mises en scène dramatiques, de tableaux vivants évocateurs, de montages mécaniques ingénieux et d'entrées solennelles, presque rituelles, dans les villes[4]. C'était là aussi les arènes où les rois — comme ils le firent au sein des parlements, des assemblées représentatives et sur les champs de bataille — établirent les assises de cette « religion de la monarchie », ou religion de l'autorité, qui devint avec le temps la base de l'État-nation naissant[5]. Les significations symboliques des costumes et des couleurs arborés en ces occasions servaient en outre de commentaires sous-jacents aux célébrations elles-mêmes. Il n'est pas toujours aisé de reconnaître ou d'expliquer ces textes que l'on pourrait comparer en quelque sorte à des palimpsestes, mais qui sont aussi importants pour notre compréhension de la nature du pouvoir exercé par la Couronne et par la noblesse que d'autres aspects mieux connus de l'élaboration des images de l'autorité.

Avant d'examiner de façon plus précise ces thèmes en Castille au xve siècle, il convient de replacer ces festivités et cérémonies dans le cadre d'un renouveau somptueux et parfois malsain de la culture courtoise à la fin du Moyen Age. L'accent fut mis de façon exagérée sur les valeurs chevaleresques et les codes de comportement courtois à une époque où l'évolution sociale et politique et la brutalité de la noblesse contredisaient l'hommage de pure forme dont ces valeurs faisaient l'objet[6].

Comme pour certains autres domaines de l'histoire de la Castille à la fin du Moyen Age les recherches les plus importantes restent à faire[7]. Cependant il nous est déjà possible de la replacer dans le cadre plus vaste de ce phénomène européen que Huizinga a magistralement décrit dans *Le déclin du Moyen Age*.

Bien que nous ne disposions pas d'une documentation aussi vaste que pour d'autres régions d'Europe, les chroniques et œuvres littéraires castillanes du xve siècle et les études de Riquer portant sur les chevaliers errants espagnols nous donnent de nombreux exemples de la participation de la Castille aux idéaux chevaleresques de l'Europe à la fin du Moyen Age[8].

J'aimerais faire porter mon analyse sur un cycle particulier de festivités qui eurent lieu à Valladolid en mai 1428. Tout en plaçant ces manifestations dans le cadre plus vaste des rituels ludiques ou des rituels de fête castillans, j'étudierai la signification politique et symbolique de ces célébrations. Quelle était la place de ces festivités dans l'histoire politique du royaume ? Quels étaient les objectifs, autres que politiques, de tels événements ?

Avant de commencer une étude plus détaillée des textes pertinents, il est nécessaire de préciser un point. Même si je considère ici les fêtes comme les instruments de l'affirmation du pouvoir noble et régalien, la vie politique en Castille au xve siècle, et surtout pendant le long règne de Juan II, était trop anarchique pour permettre un exercice efficace de l'autorité[9]. Le roi n'était le plus souvent qu'un simple pion dans les mains de son favori, don Alvaro de Luna, connétable de Castille. Dans les faits Juan II était dominé par ses ennemis jurés, les infants d'Aragon. Fêtes et cérémonies servaient parfois des buts politiques contradictoires ou, peut-être, des buts parfaitement indiscernables. Notre incapacité à définir précisément ce que les fêtes cherchaient à exprimer ou comment ces manifestations étaient comprises et interprétées par les divers groupes sociaux présents dans l'assistance est accentuée par les difficultés qui se présentent lorsqu'on tente de définir les objectifs des festivités royales. Il est nécessaire aussi d'établir une distinction subtile entre la ritualisation ou la représentation du pouvoir et le pouvoir de la ritualisation. Bien qu'un concept soit enchâssé dans l'autre, tous les conflits politiques ne pouvaient être mis en scène au cours de festivités rituelles, et toutes les fêtes ne visaient pas à exprimer un message politique. Néanmoins je pense que les divers témoignages montreront que les fêtes, en particulier celles de mai 1428, entraient souvent dans un programme politique ayant pour objectif de mettre en valeur le pouvoir et l'image des dirigeants[10].

Comme toutes les cérémonies significatives de la fin du Moyen Age et du début de l'époque moderne les fêtes étaient des manifestations publiques[11]. Ainsi la ritualisation du pouvoir en Castille médiévale ou en d'autres lieux (dans ce cas particulier par des festivités, un choix de couleurs et de costumes) était peut-être aussi une tentative pour s'adresser à une audience spécifique et combler le fossé existant entre la culture populaire et celle de l'élite. Les fêtes présentaient souvent une pluralité de voix et de significations qui n'étaient pas toutes intelligibles pour la majorité de l'assistance. Mon propos n'est pas d'entamer ici une analyse des relations entre culture « populaire » et culture « élitaire », une telle approche risquant de nous éloigner des objectifs essentiels de cet essai. De surcroît de telles distinctions sont des constructions intellectuelles modernes qui ont peu de rapports avec la manière dont les hommes et les femmes du xve siècle comprenaient leur univers. Examinons, à présent, les festivités en Castille à la fin du Moyen Age.

II. — Festivités et cérémonies castillanes à la fin du Moyen Age

De nombreuses références à des festivités inscrites ou non dans le calendrier sont éparses dans les innombrables comptes rendus de campagnes contre les Maures, de sièges de villes musulmanes, ainsi que dans les récits des luttes continuelles contre la noblesse et des actes de violence populaire contre juifs et *conversos*, que l'on trouve dans les chroniques privées et royales en Castille à cette époque. Les chroniqueurs interrompent souvent leur narration, non pour signaler simplement l'événement, mais pour décrire avec force détails les costumes, les couleurs et les cérémonies de fêtes particulières. Certains chroniqueurs paraissent avoir été plus sensibles que d'autres aux fêtes et manifestations solennelles, mais ceux du règne de Juan II (1406-1454), et surtout l'auteur des *Hechos del condestable don Miguel Lucas de Iranzo*, prirent un plaisir presque pervers à la description des festivités.

Il est évident que les fêtes étaient à un certain niveau l'expression d'idéaux aristocratiques à une époque où, comme l'écrit Luis Suárez Fernández paraphrasant Riquer, « l'imaginaire et la réalité se rejoignaient, intégrant dans la vie quotidienne les aventures et l'imagerie des chevaliers errants »[12]. Il ne fait pas de doute que les codes de chevalerie et d'hospitalité du XVe siècle définissaient le cadre de la plupart des fêtes castillanes, y compris de celles de 1428. En tant que telles, ces fêtes, et surtout celles que commanditaient le roi et la haute noblesse, créèrent un cérémonial pour la vie de la cour et des courtisans ; les joutes, affrontements et pas d'armes fréquents constituaient pour les jeunes chevaliers un entraînement physique de valeur et un exutoire à leur énergie. Ainsi ces manifestations liaient, encore qu'imparfaitement parfois, des segments des élites dirigeantes au roi ou à de grands seigneurs par le biais des valeurs de la société courtoise. Presque toutes les festivités dans la Castille de la fin du Moyen Age comportaient une gamme variée de célébrations et d'activités en rapport avec les codes d'honneur et les idéaux chevaleresques : entrées solennelles, déploiements de fastes extraordinaires, représentations théâtrales de caractère héroïque ou mythologique, banquets, danses. Par souci de clarté et de commodité, nous tenterons d'esquisser une typologie des célébrations. Les chroniques de l'époque font état de deux types distincts de festivités : les fêtes liturgiques ou inscrites dans le calendrier, et les fêtes non inscrites qui, bien qu'elles aient été souvent programmées pour coïncider avec le calendrier liturgique ou les célébrations établies, visaient à commémorer ou à magnifier un événement particulier.

Les fêtes du calendrier

A cette catégorie appartiennent ces festivités répétées chaque année comme autant d'éléments du cycle liturgique. Certaines d'entre elles, comme la Chandeleur, le Premier Mai et la Saint-Jean (au solstice d'été) bien que correspondant à l'observance chrétienne rappelaient d'anciennes traditions pré-chrétiennes. Il en était de même de la façon dont la cour royale et la haute noblesse célébraient les dates majeures du calendrier chrétien : Noël, l'Épiphanie, Pâques, les fêtes de la Vierge, de saint Michel et de saint Martin. La plupart des chroniqueurs de la fin du XIVe siècle et du XVe siècle ne rapportèrent ces fêtes qu'incidemment. Cependant l'auteur de la chronique privée du connétable Miguel Lucas de Iranzo dresse une liste complète des fêtes du calendrier et décrit de quelle façon elles étaient célébrées [13].

Ces dates importantes rassemblaient des thèmes populaires, sacrés et courtois, selon des modes propres au monde de la fin du Moyen Age. Des manifestations exagérées de piété étaient suivies de repas officiels publics, de tournois, de bals, de combats d'ours et de chiens, et de dépenses ostentatoires. La cour royale s'était engagée depuis longtemps dans la célébration de tels événements inscrits dans le calendrier, mais au cours du xve siècle, période de troubles politiques, les barons, princes de sang et personnages officiels importants imitèrent et souvent surpassèrent les munificences royales [14]. La chronique de Miguel Lucas de Iranzo, qui est pour l'essentiel un panégyrique de celui qui fut connétable de Castille et favori d'Enrique IV (1454-1474), comporte des descriptions détaillées de telles célébrations liturgiques. En fait, les *Hechos del condestable* ne sont guère autre chose qu'un récit interminable de fêtes dont certaines sont si étranges et dispendieuses qu'il est aisé de comprendre pourquoi de tels événements finissaient parfois par remettre en question leurs objectifs premiers, pourquoi la Castille ne connût guère de résultats dans sa guerre contre Grenade au cours de ces années et pourquoi le connétable fut assassiné au cours d'un soulèvement populaire à Jaén — la ville qui avait été le théâtre de presque toutes les manifestations fastueuses qu'il avait organisées et qui avait certainement dû contribuer largement aux dépenses. Il suffira de citer ici un exemple de fête inscrite au calendrier.

La célébration de la Semaine sainte par don Miguel Lucas en 1461 est, dans l'excès de ses manifestations, caractéristique de cette introduction de motifs païens et laïques dans l'observance d'une période sacrée. Ces fêtes donnaient une fois encore au connétable de Castille la possibilité de montrer, à ses amis comme à ses ennemis, qu'ils fussent de la noblesse ou du petit peuple, son pouvoir et sa générosité. Après s'être retiré pour se recueillir dans le sanctuaire de la Vierge à Guadalupe, Miguel Lucas de Iranzo revint à Jaén le Jeudi saint et passa une journée et une nuit entières en prière dans la cathédrale. Le lundi de Pâques le peuple de Jaén, ecclésiastiques et laïcs, pauvres et riches, vint jusqu'au palais du connétable pour recevoir le *fornazo* (ou *hornazo*, pâtisserie typique que l'on confectionne encore pour Pâques en Amérique latine et en Espagne). Comme la foule se rassemblait devant le palais, don Miguel Lucas, entouré de ses hommes et des notables de la ville, contemplait la scène du haut d'une tour. Un grand château de bois monté sur quatre roues de charrette descendit la rue de la Madeleine. A l'intérieur, des hommes armés de boucliers se tenaient prêts au combat. Lorsque la procession et le château artificiel atteignirent la tour, une bataille d'œufs commença au cours de laquelle, dit le chroniqueur, quelque neuf à dix mille œufs servirent de projectiles. Cet exercice ou ce gâchis fut suivi d'un somptueux banquet public. Le festin fut dressé dans un vaste champ à l'extérieur de la ville et l'on servit des montagnes de nourriture sur des tables d'argent. Après le repas, le connétable, son épouse, sa belle-sœur et quelques membres importants de sa suite dansèrent devant les invités. Après cela on fit une sieste réparatrice. A la fin de l'après-midi des tentes furent installées à une demi-lieue de Jaén : là, le connétable organisa un dîner raffiné pour le chapitre de la cathédrale, les notables de la cité, les chevaliers de la *gente menuda* (littéralement le petit peuple, les roturiers) de Jaén. Cela représentait tant de gens, rapporte le chroniqueur, que la ville s'en trouva désertée. Après ce repas un ours de grande taille fut lâché dans les environs et traqué par les chiens. Puis Miguel Lucas reconduisit tous ses hôtes à Jaén au son des trompettes et des tambours et sous les cris de la foule. La soirée s'acheva par un tournoi qui eut lieu sur la place principale de la cité, certainement éclairée de nombreux flambeaux, et par une nouvelle distribution de nourriture avant que chacun ne se retirât pour dormir [15].

Il n'est guère nécessaire d'ajouter quoi que ce soit à cette description détaillée. Le récit traduit l'enthousiasme du chroniqueur devant la magnificence et la générosité de son héros, une largesse financée en majeure partie par des impôts prélevés sur la population de Jaén. Dans ce contexte, de surcroît, la générosité, même lorsqu'elle s'exerçait aux dépens d'une tierce personne, était une forme de pouvoir. Elle impliquait l'obligation pour toute la population de Jaén, pour les puissants comme pour les faibles, d'accepter les dons de nourriture du connétable [16]. La fête de Miguel Lucas de Iranzo associait aussi des motifs de carnaval à des activités sophistiquées propres à la société courtoise telles que danses raffinées, repas rituels, manifestations publiques de piété et tournoi. L'adjonction de la bataille d'œufs, de combat d'ours et de chiens et de la procession populaire pour revenir à Jaén permettait enfin de réunir la population entière dans la glorification du pouvoir et de l'autorité du connétable. Tout cela avait pour arrière-plan les rites du printemps et la résurrection du Christ [17].

Fêtes non inscrites au calendrier

Appartiennent à cette catégorie des festivités célébrant un événement unique et non cyclique. Les fêtes de 1428 à Valladolid, que nous examinerons en détail plus loin, eurent lieu en mai, période de prédilection pour les tournois et les parades courtoises. Elles furent, dit-on, organisées pour honorer l'arrivée dans la ville de l'infante doña Leonor et, comme la plupart des événements ludiques du Moyen Age, elles comportent la gamme habituelle des activités de fête. D'autres célébrations hors calendrier étaient aussi l'occasion d'organiser des déploiements de fastes. Elles servaient à marquer les événements importants de la vie des membres de la famille royale et de la haute noblesse : naissances et baptêmes, mariages ou funérailles. D'autres signalaient divers jalons de la vie politique et sociale du royaume et de ses élites dirigeantes : couronnements ou accessions au trône, entrées solennelles du roi ou de princes. Bien évidemment certaines de ces festivités, en particulier celles qui étaient associées au cycle vital, n'étaient pas le monopole exclusif des puissants. Naissances, mariages et morts transcendaient les limites privées étroites de la famille et étaient l'occasion de manifestations publiques, même si leur portée demeurait modeste. Cependant la différence entre ces affaires privées et les cérémonies ostentatoires du roi et de la noblesse n'était pas simplement une question d'importance ; il s'agissait aussi d'une différence d'objectif. Bien que toutes les formes de festivités remplissent jusqu'à un certain point une fonction sociale, en Castille et en d'autres lieux, les fêtes organisées par les grands correspondaient aussi à un programme politique.

Illustrer chacune de ces catégories par des exemples reviendrait à faire de cet article un simple exercice anecdotique riche en détails curieux mais qui ne permettrait guère de comprendre le monde politique et mental de la Castille du xvᵉ siècle. La plupart des célébrations, que ce soit la fantastique fête de couronnement de Fernando de Antequera ou le célèbre pas d'armes organisé sur la route de Compostelle par Suero de Quiñones, alliaient des éléments martiaux et sacrés, populaires et élitaires, à l'usage symbolique de certaines couleurs (le rouge, le blanc et le noir) et de certaines parures [18]. Au lieu d'examiner brièvement chacune de ces observances hors calendrier, nous nous intéresserons plus particulièrement à un type d'événement qui servira de modèle de célébration dans la Castille de la fin du Moyen Age : les entrées solennelles.

Dans les récits du retour triomphal, en janvier 1428, d'Alvaro de Luna à la cour, après son bref exil, on devine l'intérêt que les chroniqueurs portaient à l'entrée solennelle dans une ville et, plus important encore, à la nature et à la qualité de l'accueil. Dès le xivᵉ siècle les chroniques accordent une attention particulière à ces événements. A la fin du xvᵉ siècle et pendant presque tout le début de l'époque moderne, la première visite d'un roi dans une ville imposait un tel déploiement de fastes que les finances municipales s'en trouvaient grevées. Le développement des liens avec l'Italie par l'intermédiaire de la Couronne d'Aragon et l'adoption de la culture italienne de la Renaissance à la fin du xvᵉ siècle, avec ses exemples de triomphes romains et de pompe impériale, accentuèrent le goût déjà existant pour de telles réceptions publiques de caractère raffiné [19].

Les exemples d'entrées solennelles sont trop nombreux pour être mentionnés ici et je me limiterai à deux récits remarquables [20]. Mais auparavant il peut être utile de signaler quelques traits saillants de ces réceptions publiques, qu'elles fussent royales ou autres. En premier lieu, plutôt qu'une entrée ces cérémonies complexes célébraient soit une rencontre, soit plus précisément une réception. Le caractère de réciprocité des entrées constituait un élément intrinsèque des cérémonies du xvᵉ siècle ; la visite du roi ou d'un grand seigneur imposait une contrepartie, de la part des autorités municipales et des citoyens. Dans leurs récits les chroniqueurs soulignent donc avec soin la distance que parcourait la procession des édiles municipaux, des dignitaires de l'Église et les habitants de la ville pour accueillir et accompagner le visiteur de marque. Plus elle s'éloignait de la cité et plus l'honneur était grand. C'était là, en fait, une caractéristique du comportement castillan, et Huizinga commente, non sans quelque ironie, la courtoisie exagérée des nobles espagnols du xvᵉ siècle qui, contre toute raison, insistaient pour raccompagner leurs invités jusqu'à leur demeure [21]. D'autre part, les symboles, gestes, joutes et couleurs qui servaient de commentaires non écrits à ces entrées véhiculaient des messages suggestifs à l'intention des contemporains sur la nature du pouvoir politique. Enfin, comme pour la plupart des autres cérémonies en Castille au xvᵉ siècle, les entrées solennelles dans les villes réunissaient en un ensemble cohérent images guerrières, religieuses (dans le cas de l'un des exemples décrits ci-dessous des éléments des trois religions ibériques se trouvaient intégrés) et populaires. A la même époque, ces entrées royales et princières, outre leur facette liturgique en tant que reconstitutions laïques de l'entrée de Jésus à Jérusalem, présentaient des aspects magiques et mystérieux qui marquaient le passage de seuils symboliques entre deux mondes distincts [22].

Au xve siècle, parmi les nombreux récits existants, deux descriptions d'entrées solennelles sont fort proches, d'un point de vue thématique et symbolique, des fêtes de 1428 à Valladolid. En 1410, l'infant don Fernando, qui assurait la co-régence pour son neveu le jeune Juan II, s'arrêta à Séville alors qu'il allait assiéger une place forte musulmane sur la frontière. Au cours d'une cérémonie fastueuse et impressionnante dans la cathédrale, il retira de la tombe de Fernando III (1217-1252), son homonyme, l'épée avec laquelle le roi défunt avait conquis la ville en 1248. Après sa remarquable victoire à Antequera, l'infant don Fernando fit une entrée triomphale à Séville. Le 14 octobre 1410, malgré une forte pluie, don Fernando atteignit les abords de la ville en compagnie de nombreux officiers de la Couronne et de grands seigneurs. En procession solennelle, l'archevêque de Séville, tous les notables, nobles et seigneurs sortirent à sa rencontre. Ils accueillirent l'infant à l'extérieur de la ville avec « des jeux, danses et force manifestations de joie de la manière dont on accueille [aussi] les rois ». Les membres de la suite de l'infant et les chevaliers conduisirent le cortège dans la ville ; ils étaient suivis de dix-sept Maures, à pied, portant sur l'épaule les bannières capturées au cours de la bataille. Ainsi qu'il convenait pour des ennemis vaincus, ils laissaient traîner ces bannières dans la boue. Immédiatement derrière venait un des hommes de Fernando avec un grand crucifix, et, derrière lui, deux autres hommes portaient les étendards de la Croisade, l'un rouge et l'autre blanc. Dans la procession, le rang suivant était occupé par l'*adelantado* de la frontière, Per Afán de Ribera, qui tenait à la main, comme une relique, l'épée nue de Fernando III. Seul, au centre du cortège, chevauchait l'infant ; il était suivi par les *ricos hombres* (les grands seigneurs) accompagnés chacun de leurs gens et de leurs bannières. Sur la droite de la procession les chevaliers castillans portaient les bannières de saint Jacques et de saint Isidore de Séville, tandis que sur la gauche d'autres seigneurs arboraient leurs propres étendards. Une fois dans la ville, ils se dirigèrent vers la cathédrale où le chapitre accueillit l'infant sur le parvis en chantant un *Te Deum*. Après avoir adoré la croix, l'infant « avec grande révérence » replaça l'épée entre les mains de marbre de la statue funéraire de Fernando III[23].

La réception de Fernando de Antequera à Séville peut être comparée à celle de l'infante doña Blanca de Navarre lorsqu'elle entra en Castille pour épouser l'infant don Enrique. Le court récit qui ouvre cet article décrit son entrée à Burgos, mais une réception bien plus somptueuse marqua sa première arrivée dans le royaume de Castille. Don Pedro de Velasco, comte de Haro et l'un des plus puissants barons du royaume, fut choisi pour accueillir la princesse et sa mère, la reine de Navarre, à Briviesca, une petite ville sur la route entre les deux royaumes. A deux lieues de Briviesca, lorsque le cortège de doña Blanca fut en vue, cent chevaliers — la moitié d'entre eux en rouge, l'autre en blanc — s'engagèrent dans une mêlée sauvage, brisant des lances et se livrant à de périlleux combats à l'épée, jusqu'au moment où le comte de Haro leur donna l'ordre d'arrêter. La princesse et sa suite se dirigèrent vers la ville, dont tous les habitants sortirent sur le pas de porte pour l'accueillir. Toutes les confréries et corporations de Briviesca allèrent à la rencontre de doña Blanca avec leurs bannières et elles représentèrent des saynètes et des tableaux vivants devant les Navarrais. Les juifs avec la Thora et les musulmans avec le Coran exécutèrent des danses pour doña Blanca « de la manière qu'il sied lorsque des rois viennent pour gouverner le pays ». Au son des trompettes et des tambours, des chants des ménestrels et des cris assourdissants de l'assistance, la princesse entra dans Briviesca pour un somptueux banquet. Les festivités durèrent quatre jours, avec des joutes, des lâchers de taureaux, des pantomimes et des danses, et le tout fut couronné par une fantastique manifestation à l'extérieur de la ville. Le comte de Haro transforma les champs et les bois en une gigantesque salle. Sur une haute estrade recouverte de drap écarlate brodé prirent place la princesse et sa cour pour assister à une chasse, précise le chroniqueur, à l'intérieur même de ses appartements. Enfin de riches présents, des soies et des bijoux, furent offerts à tous les invités [24]. Reprenant leur voyage, l'infante et ses compagnons se virent offrir des réceptions semblables à Burgos et à Valladolid. Bien que nous n'ayons pas de description de ces fêtes, le chroniqueur rapporte qu'elles furent les plus belles jamais données en Espagne. Malheureusement, en dépit de ces prémices extraordinaires, l'infant don Enrique ne put consommer le mariage et quitta son épouse et Valladolid le lendemain des noces [25].

III. — Les festivités de mai 1428

Même si l'on fait la part du penchant quasi obsessionnel des chroniqueurs de Juan II pour la description de telles réjouissances, leurs récits des fêtes de mai 1428 à Valladolid (la plus détaillée de ces descriptions étant l'œuvre d'un témoin visuel qui prit part à ces manifestations) occupent une place particulière dans les narrations du XVe siècle. La fascination que ces festivités exercèrent fut telle que des décennies plus tard leur souvenir résonnait encore dans l'extraordinaire poème de Jorge Manrique (1440-1479), *Coplas por la muerte de su padre* [26].

L'arrière-plan de ces fêtes apparaît clairement dans les chroniques de l'époque ou dans l'ouvrage de Suárez Fernández, *Nobleza y monarquía*; j'en donnerai ici les grandes lignes. Alvaro de Luna, connétable de Castille et favori de Juan II, avait habilement contrecarré les ambitions des infants d'Aragon. En dressant un frère contre l'autre et en faisant appel à l'intérêt personnel des factions nobiliaires, Alvaro de Luna empêcha la branche cadette des Trastámaras de prendre le pas sur le roi et de dominer le royaume. Ce n'était pas là une mince réussite. Les infants d'Aragon, don Juan et don Enrique, avaient le soutien de leur frère Alfonso, roi d'Aragon. Don Juan était lui-même roi de Navarre et, avec son frère, il comptait parmi les grands seigneurs les plus riches de Castille. Au milieu des années 1420 Alvaro de Luna, « le plus grand des hommes non couronnés », devait encore maintenir un savant équilibre entre les diverses forces du royaume. La réconciliation des infants à l'instigation de leur frère Alfonso V, homme ambitieux et de basse extraction, entraînèrent le premier exil du connétable en 1427 [27].

Le bannissement d'Alvaro de Luna loin de la cour ne dura guère. Le roi ne pouvait vivre sans lui et, dès janvier 1428, même ceux qui s'étaient dressés contre lui quelques mois plus tôt imploraient son retour. Après une entrée triomphale don Alvaro réaffirma son autorité sur Juan II, déterminé cette fois à réduire le pouvoir et l'influence des infants d'Aragon [28].

L'arrivée solennelle de l'infante doña Leonor et les fêtes organisées pour sa réception à Valladolid furent suivies d'une joute commanditée par le connétable don Alvaro de Luna, tournoi typique qui opposa cinquante chevaliers vêtus de rouge contre cinquante autres vêtus de blanc [29]. Les festivités organisées par don Alvaro furent les moins importantes du cycle des célébrations. Pour une fois dans sa vie, Juan II occupait le centre de la scène, même si ce n'était que comme simple soutien de son favori, et il répondit aux fastes fantastiques des infants d'Aragon par son propre étalage de symboles et de gestes.

Le véritable point de départ d'une lecture attentive du récit des chroniqueurs est la fête de l'infant don Enrique. Elle entraîna un tel déploiement de fastes et une dépense si excessive qu'Alvar García de Santa María, un des ennemis des infants, dit qu'elle avait coûté entre 12 000 et 15 000 florins d'or, somme extraordinaire, même si l'on prend en considération les critères extravagants de l'époque [30].

La dangereuse passe d'armes, le château artificiel, le bal public, les représentations théâtrales, la roue de la fortune, le griffon, les bannières blanches et rouges véhiculaient des messages hautement symboliques et tendaient probablement à évoquer l'imagerie et les couleurs de la fête mémorable du couronnement de Fernando de Antequera, le père de don Enrique, seize ans auparavant. A Valladolid, Enrique — fils, frère et cousin de monarques, mais qui n'était pas roi lui-même (comme son emblème à la fête le proclamait, *non es*) — affirmait ses prétentions à la royauté et aux honneurs, prétentions qui étaient profondément enracinées dans la croyance des Castillans selon laquelle l'ordre nobiliaire et le courage étaient au-dessus des prérogatives royales [31]. La description que donnent les chroniques du message, fort peu caché, de la mise en scène de don Enrique mériterait une lecture et une analyse attentives que les impératifs de longueur de cet article nous obligent à laisser de côté. J'aimerais donc porter mon attention sur Juan II et examiner les descriptions contemporaines du roi tel qu'il est apparu au cours de ce cycle de festivités.

Le roi de Castille vint au pas d'armes de l'infant don Enrique, revêtu d'habits d'argent (blanc) et d'or, et couvert d'un manteau d'hermine (blanc et noir). Sur la tête il portait un grand panache et un diadème de papillons. Le choix des couleurs de Juan II, le blanc et le noir, ou des nuances de noir, de blanc et d'or, fait partie d'une tradition iconographique bien établie visant à représenter la majesté et la pureté. Il s'agit là aussi des couleurs que l'on associait à la Vierge (blanc, rouge et bleu) et des couleurs portées par Fernando de Antequera avant son couronnement et, par la suite, lors de banquets. L'argent, l'or et surtout l'hermine étaient des matières précieuses qui, à cause de leur valeur monétaire et de leurs couleurs, étaient traditionnellement associées au pouvoir royal et judiciaire. Comme le montrent cependant les chroniques, les infants d'Aragon et le connétable lui-même, n'hésitaient pas à faire leurs ces couleurs et parures jadis réservées en Castille à l'usage exclusif des rois [32].

Les papillons qui ornaient la tête du roi appartenaient à une autre tradition iconographique médiévale. Dans l'art religieux du Moyen Age ils symbolisent la résurrection de l'âme, l'attirance de l'esprit par la lumière divine et la seconde naissance. Connaissant le penchant de la Couronne de Castille pour la sécularisation des images sacrées, ne peut-on suggérer, sans forcer le trait, que les papillons symbolisaient le retour d'exil de don Alvaro de Luna et la renaissance de l'autorité royale ? Après tout, ces représentations théâtrales et symboliques suivaient de près l'exécution sommaire de Juan García de Guadalajara et furent elles-mêmes suivies de l'affranchissement de la Couronne de l'influence néfaste des infants d'Aragon [33].

Cette lecture des symboles et des couleurs arborés par Juan II à la fête de don Enrique illustre bien la séquence complète des apparitions royales au cours du mois de mai 1429, ainsi que les suites politiques de ces célébrations. Les descriptions que les chroniqueurs donnent des vêtements du roi et des mises en scène dramatiques constituent un texte continu et significatif qui doit être lu chronologiquement tout au long du mois de mai.

Aux festivités suivantes, organisées par l'infant don Juan, roi de Navarre, le roi de Castille vint en costume de chasseur, entouré de symboles cynégétiques. Son apparition théâtrale en dieu païen, en roi des bois primitif ou en roi de mai, s'accordait avec les traditions de la saison et avec ces croyances pré-chrétiennes déjà si parfaitement intégrées dans l'apparat de la cour. Les hommes de la suite de Juan II — les chroniqueurs ne parlent pas des couleurs du costume du roi — étaient vêtus de vert foncé (*azeituno pardillo*) et leurs casques étaient ornés de panaches. Le roi portait un javelot et un cor sur le dos ; ses hommes avaient eux aussi des lances et des trompes de chasse. Précédant le roi vers le lieu où devait se dérouler la joute, les chasseurs et leurs chiens poussaient devant eux un lion adulte et un ours enchaînés. Ces deux animaux captifs étaient-ils les symboles des infants d'Aragon ? L'iconographie médiévale voit dans l'ours un homme fruste et cruel et le lion dompté représente la défaite. Des lions et des ours figuraient souvent dans les festivités du XVe siècle en Castille ainsi que dans la littérature et l'art de l'époque. Les combats d'ours et de chiens étaient un passe-temps populaire dans les cours d'Europe ; en Castille ils clôturaient souvent les tournois et les festivités. De plus, le symbolisme politique du lion — souvenons-nous du *Poema de mío Cid*, de la *Primera crónica general* et, plus tard, de l'œuvre de Shakespeare où les lions reconnaissent les rois véritables — était bien connu de la noblesse castillane. En fait, Villasandino, un des poètes et partisans de Juan II, avait représenté le roi en lion libéré lorsqu'il s'était affranchi du pouvoir des infants d'Aragon quelques années plus tôt. Mais le lion et l'ours ont été capturés. Ils sont conduits à la fête enchaînés et domptés, comme soumis à l'autorité du roi. Juan II entre en lice au son des trompettes pour montrer ses prouesses sur le terrain des armes, et le chroniqueur raconte que le roi « brisa une très forte lance » [34].

Nous arrivons enfin aux fêtes et au tournoi offerts par Juan II et qui furent probablement orchestrés par don Alvaro de Luna. Les estrades construites pour cette fête sur la place principale de Valladolid étaient recouvertes de drap d'or ; la lice pour le tournoi était de couleur rouge et probablement couverte de soie. Le roi apparut en Dieu le Père, vêtu de blanc, et ses douze compagnons figuraient des saints. Le groupe montait des chevaux caparaçonnés de drap rouge ; le roi et ses hommes portaient des emblèmes proclamant leur *lardon* (*galardon*), leur droit aux honneurs. Ces étoffes et ces couleurs formaient la toile de fond de la manifestation publique et solennelle de l'autorité royale. C'est là en fait l'apothéose du pouvoir. Au cours du dernier tournoi du cycle de festivités donné en l'honneur de l'infante doña Leonor et qui dura un mois entier, les thèmes courtois, païens et chrétiens des puissants et des érudits retrouvèrent, par le biais des couleurs et du cérémonial, des croyances populaires anciennes. Ce faisant, ils réaffirmaient le pouvoir royal. Juan II apparaît à la fête en Dieu le Père, le tout-puissant dieu d'Israël ; il est accompagné de douze saints, nombre symbolique et magique, comme de nouveaux apôtres ; leurs emblèmes proclament leurs mérites pour leur service et leurs actions chevaleresques. Tous ces symboles et toutes ces attitudes avaient pour toile de fond le rouge, le blanc et, à un moindre degré, le noir. On peut voir les trois fêtes de mai 1428 comme un triptyque avec les entrées solennelles, l'exécution et, en introduction, le tournoi d'Alvaro de Luna. Lorsque l'on passe d'un panneau au suivant, l'histoire se déroule devant nous : le retour du connétable et la renaissance du pouvoir royal, la victoire remportée sur les infants et la soumission de leurs ambitions et, en dernier lieu, la manifestation finale du pouvoir royal avec Juan II en Dieu tout-puissant.

Ces « drames sociaux » sophistiqués n'étaient pas propres à la Castille ; ils n'indiquaient pas davantage une rupture radicale avec la façon dont les rois cherchaient à manifester leur pouvoir. En vérité, depuis longtemps dans l'Occident médiéval les monarques s'efforçaient de donner à leur autorité des attributs sacrés et charismatiques. Même en Castille où les rois montraient quelque réticence à adopter les symboles sacrés de la monarchie — tels que la consécration, le couronnement et l'affirmation de pouvoirs thaumaturgiques — la Couronne ne répugnait pas à assumer des caractères christologiques[35]. Ce qui est inhabituel ici, mais qui concorde cependant tout à fait avec les pratiques castillanes, c'est l'absence complète d'ecclésiastiques — ils ne sont que spectateurs — et de l'Église. Dans les festivités de la monarchie et de la haute noblesse de Castille, ni l'Église ni ses serviteurs n'avaient de rôle officiel ou actif à jouer.

N'allons pas imaginer cependant que Juan II avait soit l'énergie soit la capacité de penser ou d'agir de cette manière. La description lapidaire du roi que nous donne Fernán Pérez de Guzmán dans ses *Generaciones y semblanzas* nous présente un monarque incompétent et peu désireux de régner. Derrière les représentations de mai 1428 nous devinons l'intervention habile et efficace du connétable. Il ne faut pas davantage croire que les fêtes de 1428 n'étaient que des exercices théâtraux vides de sens. C'est le lien direct entre l'imagerie et la réalité qui leur confère une place centrale dans la tradition des cérémonies de la Castille du xve siècle. Deux semaines seulement après le départ de l'infante doña Leonor pour le Portugal, le symbolisme céda la place à une action politique rapide et décisive. L'infant don Enrique dut quitter la cour et fut envoyé sur la frontière faire son devoir contre Grenade. Son frère don Juan, roi de Navarre, selon la paraphrase que Luis Suárez Fernández donne de la chronique, « fut soudain, avec un laconisme proprement insultant, invité à quitter la cour et le royaume, parce que — fut-il simplement dit — il n'y avait pas en Castille de place pour deux rois ». Cette campagne contre les infants d'Aragon fut bientôt suivie du départ du connétable pour la frontière de Grenade et de la reprise de l'offensive contre le dernier poste avancé de l'islam dans la péninsule[36].

Bien qu'il soit possible que les apparitions successives de Juan II aux fêtes de mai ainsi que son choix de symboles, de couleurs et de costumes aient été purement accidentels, le lien étroit entre ces symboles et ces cérémonies et la solution politique apportée à la présence gênante des infants à la cour est trop suggestif pour être passé sous silence. La fin des dissensions civiles, la soumission des barons indisciplinés et le rétablissement de la suprématie du monarque dans le royaume étaient les conditions préalables à l'assaut final contre Grenade. Les contemporains ne cessèrent de souligner ce lien et le *Laberinto de fortuna* de Juan de Mena, l'une des œuvres littéraires les plus admirées à l'époque, développait précisément la même idée [37]. Il ne faut pas davantage, comme nous l'avons dit plus haut, voir dans les fêtes de mai 1428 un événement spécifique et isolé. Chacune des cérémonies ou festivités célébrées à l'aube du xve siècle en Castille tendait à faire passer un message particulier mais important, l'idée que les rois étaient au-dessus de tous les sujets du royaume. La noblesse bien sûr chercha aussi, dans un déploiement de fastes, à exprimer une conception toute différente, celle que certains nobles au moins étaient les égaux des rois, voire, dans le cas des infants d'Aragon, qu'ils leur étaient peut-être même supérieurs. Mais les ressources et le charisme martial de la monarchie castillane devaient se révéler à terme trop puissants pour être combattus avec succès. Un seul exemple suffira à illustrer cela.

En 1425, trois ans avant les festivités légendaires de Valladolid, le roi de Castille, Juan II, réunit les Cortes pour faire reconnaître don Enrique, l'infant nouveau-né, comme héritier du trône. La réunion des grands seigneurs, des représentants des villes et des dignitaires de l'Église avait été reportée de janvier, mois anniversaire de l'infant, au printemps, afin de coïncider avec les grands tournois et les manifestations des fêtes régulières de Pâques et de mai. Une vaste estrade comportant trois gradins fut construite dans le palais où les Cortes devaient se rassembler. En haut de l'estrade on plaça un grand trône de bois et le sol fut recouvert alentour de « riches tapisseries et de tapis royaux rouges ». A droite du trône fut installé un lit « riche » bleu et or, recouvert d'un drap d'or. A gauche, un degré plus bas que le trône, se tenait l'infant don Juan, représentant principal de la branche cadette des Trastámaras et, en tant que seigneur de Lara, représentant et porte-parole traditionnels de la noblesse de Castille. Une marche plus bas encore, assis sur des bancs, se trouvaient les grands seigneurs et, sous eux, au niveau du sol étaient assis les représentants des villes, procureurs aux Cortes. Monté sur une mule, don Alfonso Enríque, amiral de Castille, porta l'infant dans ses bras par les rues de Valladolid, du palais jusqu'au lieu de réunion des Cortes, tandis que les chevaliers et la foule le suivaient à pied en procession solennelle. A son arrivée, l'infant don Enriquez fut placé sur le lit ; des dames de haute naissance et de belles servantes vinrent s'asseoir ou se tinrent debout autour de lui. Le roi plaça un sceptre d'or et une épée dans les mains du jeune infant, puis l'infant don Juan, d'autres grands seigneurs et des prélats présentèrent leur hommage à l'héritier du trône. Cette mise en scène n'a rien d'exceptionnel en Occident au Moyen Age. Nous assistons à la représentation publique d'une initiation rituelle importante. Dans cette cérémonie particulière, les quatre niveaux de la scène rappellent habilement la gradation du pouvoir en Castille au xve siècle et la distance qui séparait le roi de ceux qui étaient placés sous son autorité [38].

IV. — Les usages du pouvoir : fêtes, symboles, couleurs et costumes

Il existe une autre lecture possible des cérémonies décrites plus haut. D'autres textes, sous-jacents aux récits des chroniqueurs, sont peut-être bien plus révélateurs que le symbolisme évident et les actions politiques que nous venons d'étudier. Ces textes doivent également être décodés si nous voulons comprendre les multiples significations véhiculées par les fêtes de 1428. On peut affirmer, en reprenant les thèses de Dilthey et de Victor Turner, que « la représentation culturelle, y compris le rituel, le cérémonial, le carnaval, le théâtre et la poésie, est une explication de la vie »[39]. Les fêtes de 1428 nous permettent de voir comment la lutte terrible pour le pouvoir politique qui opposa la Couronne à diverses factions de la haute noblesse fut mise en scène de manière rituelle et, dans certains cas, remportée grâce à des festivités au cérémonial complexe. En tant qu'espèce de drame social, pour reprendre la formule de Turner, ces fêtes furent aussi, en un certain sens, une représentation ritualisée qui permit au connétable Alvaro de Luna et au monarque qu'il servait, Juan II, de prendre des mesures énergiques pour se libérer et affranchir la Couronne des ambitions néfastes et de la violence des infants d'Aragon.

Bien que mon souci premier dans ces pages ait été de décrypter le symbolisme politique des festivités de mai 1428, d'autres aspects méritent de retenir notre attention. Les célébrations de Valladolid se déroulèrent dans un contexte historique complexe ; il est donc possible de les examiner et de les interpréter à des niveaux divers. J'aborderai sous la forme de remarques rapides, plutôt que sous celle d'une analyse en profondeur, certains de ces aspects.

Topographie, assistance et objet des festivités

Les célébrations en Castille à la fin du Moyen Age furent un élément essentiel de la vie urbaine. La ville était la scène des manifestations royales, aristocratiques et bourgeoises. L'assistance, chaque fois que les chroniques en font état, comprenait l'ensemble de l'ordre social médiéval. Les habitants des villes, les paysans des environs, les visiteurs et les membres de la noblesse envahissaient la place principale ou la grande rue de la cité pour assister à ces spectacles splendides et fantastiques[40]. Le caractère urbain des célébrations castillanes n'était pas remis en question par le choix occasionnel, comme cadre de ces fêtes, des champs environnants. Dans ce cas, les personnes qui organisaient ces événements cherchaient à imposer, à la fois symboliquement et littéralement, un caractère urbain à la campagne. Des chambres imaginaires, des demeures enchantées transformaient la nature en un miroir rationnel de la vie citadine. Dans les premiers exemples nous avons déjà vu comment Miguel Lucas de Iranzo transposa Jaén dans les champs à l'extérieur des murs de la ville. A Briviesca les bois devinrent une salle close où furent organisés une chasse et un combat d'ours et de chiens dans le cadre civilisateur d'une demeure princière. A la même époque cependant, dans des fêtes comme celles du Premier Mai et de la Saint Jean, la verdeur des champs et les symboles de la vie animale et végétale surgissaient et modifiaient le caractère urbain des festivités.

Le caractère public des fêtes, qui rassemblent paysans et étrangers dans l'enceinte de la cité, et le lien entre la ville et la campagne dans ces cérémonies contribuèrent, une fois encore, à faire progresser les politiques des dirigeants. Bien que fêtes royales et princières, entrées solennelles et autres manifestations de même type aient pu peser lourdement sur les finances municipales, les autorités civiles prenaient souvent part de bonne grâce à ces activités. Elles permettaient au pouvoir civil de se manifester et aux hiérarchies sociales de réaffirmer leur existence au sein même de la ville. Non seulement ces fêtes soulignaient les relations de la bourgeoisie avec le peuple, mais elles permettaient aux élites patriciennes de Burgos, Jaén, Valladolid et d'autres villes de Castille de définir leur position vis-à-vis de la Couronne et de la noblesse. Elles regroupaient des participants et des symbolismes divers ; ainsi, personne ne pouvait espérer monopoliser ces fêtes ou les réduire à servir ses seuls intérêts politiques ou sociaux. C'est également vêtues d'écarlate que les autorités municipales de Burgos défilèrent dans la ville et en franchirent la porte pour accueillir l'infante doña Blanca. Vêtues également d'écarlate, les autorités de Valladolid reçurent la visite de Juan II en 1447. Les démonstrations fastueuses du roi et de la noblesse avaient donc leur contrepartie, tantôt complémentaire et tantôt antagoniste, dans le déploiement ostentatoire que la bourgeoisie donnait de sa richesse et de ses prouesses militaires. De surcroît, en Castille où les villes, en particulier à la frontière, étaient des îlots d'activité perdus dans une campagne relativement déserte, les fêtes, qu'elles fussent royales, princières ou bourgeoises, cherchaient à affirmer la suprématie de la cité sur la campagne et elles servaient de scène pour la réunion des différents groupes sociaux.

J'ai déjà parlé du caractère hétérogène de l'assistance ou du « public » présent à ces fêtes. Les chroniques ne sont pas toujours explicites sur le nombre des participants ou sur leur identité. Nous ne disposons de guère plus d'informations sur la réaction des spectateurs ou sur ce qu'ils pouvaient penser des manifestations théâtrales de la fête. Il nous faut assumer que, lors des grandes occasions, presque toute la population de la cité, et la majeure partie des habitants de la campagne environnante, étaient présentes. A Jaén la chronique du connétable, description fidèle dans son exagération, va dans ce sens. Elle décrit l'assistance selon un ordre manifestement descendant : le connétable, sa famille et sa suite, les hauts dignitaires de l'Église, l'élite patricienne et le peuple. Il devait en être de même ailleurs.

L'appropriation de symboles religieux

Les fêtes comme forme de théâtre social urbain servaient aussi d'autres buts. J'ai signalé incidemment plus haut l'absence des autorités ecclésiastiques en tant que participants majeurs à ces festivités. Bien que certaines de ces manifestations aient inclus le *Te Deum* de rigueur et que les dignitaires de l'Église y fussent des hôtes honorés, les ecclésiastiques jouaient un rôle mineur lorsqu'il s'agissait d'organiser ces événements ou de les présider. Il n'y a guère de documents témoignant que l'Église ait tiré quelques bénéfices, financiers ou politiques, de ces fêtes. Cependant il est clair que ces festivités étaient fort soigneusement mises en scène ; elles devaient nécessiter une longue préparation et des dépenses considérables. Nous ne disposons pas de suffisamment d'informations sur l'organisation intérieure des maisons royales ou princières ou sur leurs comptes financiers pour pouvoir indiquer quels étaient les serviteurs royaux ou aristocratiques responsables de la mise en scène. De même, si l'on fait abstraction de quelques remarques au passage, il nous est impossible d'évaluer la part que ces célébrations représentaient dans les budgets de la Couronne et de l'aristocratie. Quels qu'aient été leur coût et leur caractère sophistiqué, ces festivités étaient profondément séculières, complètement ancrées dans la tradition courtoise existante et sans lien important avec la culture religieuse de l'époque. S'il est une chose que montrent les portraits littéraires satiriques d'ecclésiastiques castillans sous le règne de Juan II ce sont les préoccupations mondaines de ces derniers et leur implication dans la politique des factions de l'époque[41]. La Couronne n'hésitait pas, bien sûr, à s'approprier la symbolique religieuse comme autre moyen de consolider sa position politique. On trouvera dans ces pages des références à l'usage de symboles religieux et christologiques, mais il peut être utile de les rappeler brièvement.

Le xve siècle fut une période au cours de laquelle certains chroniqueurs, auteurs littéraires et théologiens cherchèrent à accentuer la nature sacrée de la royauté par opposition au caractère manifestement non sacré de la monarchie castillane. Cela était peut-être dicté par l'agitation politique dominante ; il se peut qu'une royauté de type sacré ait été perçue comme un moyen de contenir les ambitions de la noblesse. Cependant les rois de Castille au xve siècle ne recherchèrent pas la médiation de l'Église, ou n'en eurent pas besoin pour affirmer leurs prétentions au pouvoir ou à l'autorité. Bien que les entrées solennelles et les fêtes liturgiques eussent reproduit des scènes de l'histoire religieuse, ce symbolisme sacré devint finalement un simple ornement pour la ritualisation des valeurs et de la puissance des chevaliers. A la même époque, alors que le xve siècle était témoin de l'ascension triomphale du christianisme, du déclin inexorable de l'islam et de la fin du judaïsme dans la Péninsule, les fêtes réunissaient les trois religions. Cela avait parfois pour but de dévaloriser de manière rituelle une des religions minoritaires, mais, dans d'autres cas, comme à Briviesca, musulmans, juifs et chrétiens participaient ensemble aux célébrations et s'associaient ainsi à la légitimation de ceux qui exerçaient le pouvoir.

Couleurs

Lorsque nous nous penchons sur la question des couleurs et des costumes, tout examen, fût-il superficiel, des chroniques castillanes du xve siècle montre l'intérêt plus que prononcé que les auteurs accordaient aux couleurs et aux motifs décoratifs. Bien que les descriptions détaillées des costumes portés par les grands soient fréquentes, elles ne font pas l'objet du même intérêt que les couleurs. Le choix des couleurs utilisées pour les costumes et les ornements n'était pas le résultat d'une coïncidence ou d'une sélection arbitraire. Les chroniqueurs — pour la plupart des contemporains qui prenaient une part active à la vie politique du royaume — relevaient très fidèlement ces couleurs parce qu'ils en comprenaient l'importance symbolique, en particulier lorsqu'il s'agissait des déploiements massifs de rouge et de blanc. C'était là, et c'est significatif, les couleurs de la Croisade (une bannière rouge et l'autre blanche) qui était depuis longtemps, en 1428, une entreprise martiale et quasi religieuse. La monarchie castillane trouvait sa raison d'être fondamentale et le fondement le plus important de son autorité précisément dans son rôle de chef dans la lutte contre l'islam[42]. Ceux qui cherchaient à défier le pouvoir des rois affirmaient leur droit à agir ainsi précisément pour les mêmes raisons — parce qu'ils pouvaient mener le combat contre Grenade plus efficacement que les gens au pouvoir. Les infants d'Aragon, grâce à la victoire remarquable de leur père à Antequera, qui devint un élément de leurs états de service, arboraient eux aussi fièrement leurs bannières rouges et blanches.

Les couleurs des costumes de fête et leur signification symbolique étaient un trait important de la société à la fin du Moyen Age. La brève analyse que fait Huizinga des couleurs et, chose plus importante, ses nombreux exemples évocateurs de leur utilisation par les puissants mettent en évidence les liens qui existaient entre leur choix et la culture politique et courtoise de l'époque. Michel Pastoureau a lui aussi relevé la place des couleurs, en particulier du rouge, du blanc et du noir, au cœur du Moyen Age, et l'importance grandissante du bleu — ce qu'il décrit comme « la révolution bleue » — en tant que couleur préférée de l'Occident. Bien qu'aujourd'hui le bleu soit la couleur favorite du monde occidental (avec un taux supérieur à 50 % dans les enquêtes), l'Espagne est la seule exception dans cette uniformité plutôt remarquable. La péninsule Ibérique a résisté au penchant d'inspiration française pour le bleu et conserve sa prédilection ancienne pour le rouge et pour les couleurs chaudes [43].

En dépit de l'ascendant du bleu à la fin de l'époque médiévale, le rouge, le blanc et le noir ou des combinaisons de ces couleurs avaient longtemps joué un rôle central dans l'expérience humaine. C'était les couleurs des rites de passage ou d'initiation ; Victor Turner et Mircea Eliade ont montré que les rites de passage importants, quels qu'aient été leurs contextes culturels ou ethnologiques, étaient mis en scène — terme approprié car il s'agissait d'une forme de théâtre social — sur fond rouge, blanc et/ou noir. Le blanc et le rouge symbolisaient aussi les principes mâle et femelle, et l'on peut songer incidemment ici aux aspects libidinaux des tournois et des manifestations courtoises du XVe siècle. En Castille comme ailleurs les tensions opposant les principes mâle et femelle (blanc/rouge) étaient souvent résolues par l'alliance symbolique des couleurs, le travestissement et la littérature. Dans les chroniques du XVe siècle nous trouvons de nombreuses références à des combats simulés entre des chevaliers vêtus de blanc et des chevaliers vêtus de rouge, en nombre égal, le plus souvent cinquante, mais parfois cent. Ces mêlées une fois terminées étaient suivies de banquets auxquels participaient les adversaires en une célébration des idéaux courtois [44].

En plus des déploiements de rouge et de blanc, l'échange des rôles dévolus aux deux sexes et les travestissements jouaient un rôle important dans les cérémonies. Au cours de la réception spectaculaire d'Enrique II à Jaén en 1464, le roi fut accueilli à une demi-lieue de la ville par les dignitaires de la municipalité et de l'Église, cinq cents chevaliers déguisés en Maures avec de fausses barbes, trente autres hommes déguisés en femmes maures jouant du tambourin et agitant des clochettes, quatre mille enfants montés sur des chevaux d'osier et mille autres enfants armés d'arbalètes d'osier et de paille, et un grand nombre d'habitants de Jaén complétaient la réception publique du monarque. Après un repas solennel — le roi fut servi par le connétable et son épouse, et chaque plat fut apporté au son des trompettes — le roi assista à une danse présentée par huit enfants, tous de la même taille et du même maintien, déguisés en flammes [45]. Ces images récurrentes de rouge, de blanc et parfois de noir, ont leurs équivalents dans les nombreuses références à ces couleurs que l'on trouve dans les chroniques contemporaines, la prose et la poésie castillanes, comme dans la littérature de toute l'Europe occidentale [46].

Au Royaume des châteaux et des lions, les lois somptuaires, à partir de la moitié du XIIIe siècle tendirent à réserver certaines étoffes, fourrures et couleurs à la famille royale et, dans quelques cas, à la haute noblesse. La petite noblesse, les officiels de la Couronne, les oligarques des villes et, surtout les Juifs et les Maures ne devaient pas porter de blanc, de bas et de capes écarlates, ni de vêtements de soie, d'hermine, d'or ou d'argent (dans quelques cas l'interdit s'étendait aussi aux étoffes roses, vertes et oranges). Les réglementations somptuaires ne faisaient que refléter l'incapacité de la Couronne à contrôler le port de couleurs, fourrures et vêtements par les personnes de rang inférieur. Ceux qui pouvaient acheter des fourrures et des étoffes de couleur, qu'ils fussent nobles ou pas, chrétiens ou juifs, ignoraient souvent les édits royaux pour suivre les exigences de la mode et du goût [47].

Au XVe siècle le rouge, le blanc et, à un degré moindre, le noir se trouvaient profondément incorporés à la trame des événements ludiques quasi ritualisés, mis en scène par la Couronne et les grands seigneurs. Cela n'apparaît nulle part plus clairement que dans les *Hechos del condestable Don Miguel Lucas de Iranzo*. Cette chronique n'est pas un simple catalogue fastidieux de festivités, c'est aussi en quelque sorte une brochure de mode. En 1461, à l'occasion de l'arrivée d'un nouvel évêque à Jaén, le connétable l'accueillit vêtu de brocard noir orné de parements de zibeline. Quelques semaines plus tard la ville de Jaén assistait au mariage somptueux du connétable (ou, pourrait-on dire, devait supporter ce mariage). Les deux époux portaient des vêtements semblables et de même couleur, pourpoints d'or, atours de couleur rouge pourpre ornés de zibeline, tandis que le connétable était coiffé d'un bonnet noir. Tous deux étaient parés de bijoux précieux et l'épouse montait un petit cheval blanc. Le garçon d'honneur était en noir, la demoiselle d'honneur en vert et noir. Le chroniqueur continue son récit en donnant, avec force détails, la liste des festivités qui suivirent : repas solennels, bal, course de taureaux, représentations musicales, joutes, représentations théâtrales (*entremeses*), et autres réjouissances, et en décrivant les vêtements et couleurs portés par le connétable au cours des jours suivants. Son récit s'achève avec la fête de la Chandeleur pour laquelle don Miguel Lucas de Iranzo s'habilla de blanc comme il le faisait chaque samedi et tous les jours consacrés à la Vierge [48].

A quelque événement que nous nous intéressions en Castille à la fin du Moyen Age — mariages, exécutions, deuils, funérailles, entrées solennelles, combats de chevaliers, tournois, reconnaissance des héritiers par les Cortes — les couleurs dominantes de ces drames sociaux sont le rouge, le blanc et le noir. L'Ordre de la *Banda,* la distinction honorifique la plus importante à la cour de Castille, était noir et blanc. La rançon d'un captif était payée au sultan du Levant en étoffe écarlate. Le pape exigea d'Enrique II qu'il portât ses couleurs et il lui envoya pour cela trois pièces d'étoffe pourpre. Les chevaliers de l'Ordre de Saint Jacques portaient des tuniques blanches ornées de croix rouges lors de leur initiation, et nous avons vu que le rouge et le blanc étaient les couleurs dominantes des fêtes de mai 1428, des entrées solennelles de Fernando de Antequera à Séville et de doña Blanca en Castille [49].

La signification symbolique du rouge et du blanc intéressait également les personnes de rang inférieur. Comme l'affirme Linda Woodbridge, l'usage du rouge et du blanc « fait partie d'un code sémiotique visible dans toute l'histoire humaine ». Elle fait remonter les origines des images construites sur le rouge et le blanc dans la poésie de la Renaissance à des sources littéraires classiques et aux Pères de l'Église, mais elle rattache aussi ces images à certains aspects de la culture populaire : danses (*morris dances*, ou danses maures), pantomimes et fêtes du Premier Mai. Bien que le petit peuple portât des vêtements simples et sans couleur (toile grossière, toile à sac, laines naturelles non teintées), les couleurs de leurs festivités et de leurs vêtements de fête étaient le rouge et le blanc. Ce sont les couleurs des mimes et des danses populaires en Castille et ailleurs ; ce sont aussi les couleurs des vêtements du peuple en Navarre, au Pays basque, en Galice et dans certaines régions de Castille encore de nos jours [50]. D'une part entrées solennelles, tournois, pas d'armes biens réglés et autres représentations courtoises réaffirmaient aux yeux des spectateurs et des participants la hiérarchie existante du pouvoir, des idéaux chevaleresques et des valeurs de la culture élevée, ce que James Scott a pu décrire comme la transcription publique, pour poser le problème en termes bakhtiniens, de la « culture officielle ». D'autre part ces mêmes manifestations de la culture et du pouvoir étaient mises en scène sur un fond rouge et blanc auquel les dirigeants comme ceux qui leur devaient obéissance étaient sensibles.

★

Le symbolisme des couleurs et des vêtements ainsi que les buts des festivités rituelles ne sont pas demeurés immuables. Au début de l'époque moderne la signification de bon nombre de ces représentations et des couleurs portées par les puissants avait changé à cause de facteurs économiques et culturels. La manière dont le pouvoir était mis en scène par les dirigeants dans des spectacles ludiques et la façon dont ces fêtes étaient perçues par les personnes de rang inférieur changeaient aussi selon le contexte politique. Vers la moitié du XVIe siècle, les enfants des grands seigneurs rebelles et querelleurs du XVe siècle étaient devenus les serviteurs obéissants de la monarchie des Habsbourg. Dans la longue durée j'ai cherché à saisir un moment éphémère, mais la description de ce tableau vivant nous renseigne sur la nature de la société castillane, sur ses valeurs au XVe siècle, ainsi que sur son bon ou son mauvais usage du pouvoir. Dans les fêtes du XVe siècle et du début du XVIe siècle en Castille, les thèmes courtois et populaires sont souvent mêlés. Les symboles du pouvoir, religieux et séculier, étaient associés à des manifestations de la culture populaire. La transcription publique et privée, la culture officielle et la paillardise carnavalesque, la glorification et la dégradation des symboles de l'autorité ne faisaient parfois qu'un. Il suffit de se rappeler la farce d'Avila remarquablement étudiée par Angus MacKay pour comprendre comment ces mélanges du « haut » et du « bas », du théâtre et de la politique, étaient utilisés dans ce cas par une fraction de la haute noblesse pour ses propres fins hégémoniques. Mais dans l'ensemble, et en particulier au cours des fêtes de 1428, Juan II nous apparaît (ou est présenté par don Alvaro de Luna, son favori) comme un roi et un homme de même valeur et de même importance que Fernando de Antequera, l'idole adorée des chroniqueurs du début du XVe siècle et le fondateur d'une dynastie rivale. Au cours de ces festivités le roi de Castille faisait sienne l'essence même de la Castille, sa mission religieuse, guerrière et séculière. Chevalier errant par excellence, roi de Mai, représentant de Dieu, le roi conjugait la mentalité du royaume avec des couleurs et les symboles populaires et courtois facilement compréhensibles par tous au niveau le plus fondamental. Là, au point où les cultures et les mentalités des puissants et des faibles se recoupaient, les rois posaient les fondements du pouvoir absolu.

Il est difficile de ne pas s'intéresser, fût-ce brièvement, au début de l'Époque moderne pour mettre en évidence la continuité de la signification des costumes, couleurs et symboles du pouvoir — alors renforcés par l'héritage bourguignon — dans l'Espagne des Habsbourg, même lorsque le sens et le cadre eurent changé. Les exemples sont certes nombreux pour le XVIe et le XVIIe siècle mais, souhaitant terminer cet essai comme je l'ai commencé, j'aimerais évoquer les portraits austères des membres de l'élite patricienne de Tolède, tous de blanc et de noir vêtus, peints par Le Greco, qui bien que d'origine étrangère fut le plus espagnol des peintres d'Espagne[51]. Rappelons-nous surtout la magistrale galerie de portraits de « L'Enterrement du Comte d'Orgaz ». Le tableau est une scène où les puissants sont rassemblés pour recommander le corps du comte à Dieu. Le ciel et la terre sont réunis en un instant précis, celui d'un enterrement, d'une célébration. Et là, en suspens entre les espaces sacré et séculier, les fiers chevaliers de Saint Jacques lèvent les yeux vers le ciel, baissent leurs regards vers la dépouille mortelle du comte ou fixent le spectateur. Leurs costumes sont noirs et blancs et la croix de leur ordre, symbole de leur état et de leur pouvoir, est écarlate.

NOTES

* Cet essai a été présenté sous une forme abrégée à la troisième réunion annuelle d'un groupe de recherches du CNRS-ATP à Madrid en novembre 1987, publiée ensuite dans les Actes de ce colloque sous le titre « Fiestas, torneos y simbolos de realeza en la Castilla del siglo XV. Las fiestas de Valladolid de 1428 », dans A. RUCQUOI éd., *Realidad e imágines del poder. España a fines de la Edad Media,* Valladolid, 1988, pp. 249-265, et présenté enfin sous une forme développée au Shelby Cullom Davis Center for Historical Studies, à Princeton University, le 3 mars 1989. L'idée de ce travail m'a été fort généreusement suggérée par Angus MacKay. Je tiens à remercier Scarlett Berkowitz, Ruth Behar, Elizabeth A. R. Brown, Peter Brown, Hilario Casado, Remie Constable, Natalie Davis, John H. Elliott, David Frye, Xavier Gil Pujol, William Jordan, Denis Menjot, Charles Radding, Adeline Rucquoi et Lawrence Stone.

1. « Crónica del rey don Juan II », dans *Crónica de los reyes de Castilla*, vol. II, C. ROSSELL éd., Biblioteca de autores españoles, vol. LXVIII, Madrid, 1953, p. 566, ci-dessous repris sous le titre « Crónica del rey don Juan II ». Le terme souvent utilisé dans les chroniques en Castille au XVe siècle est *carmesí* (kermes) que l'on peut traduire par cramoisi ou écarlate.

2. Cf. Marc BLOCH, *Les rois thaumaturges*, Strasbourg, 1924, pp. 185-260 ; Ernst KANTOROWICZ, *The King's Two Bodies. A Study in Medieval Political Theology,* Princeton, 1957, pp. 42-227 (éd. frse, *Les deux corps du roi*, Paris, 1989) ; Joseph R. STRAYER, « France : the Holy Land, the Chosen People and the Most Christian King », dans *Medieval Statecraft and the Perspectives*

of History, Princeton, 1971, pp. 300-314 ; Teofilo F. Ruiz, « Une royauté sans sacre : la monarchie castillane du Bas Moyen Age », *Annales ESC*, n° 3, 1984, pp. 429-453. Il en existe une version révisée dans Sean Wilentz éd., *Rites of Power. Symbolism, Ritual and Politics since the Middle Ages*, Philadelphie, 1985, pp. 109-144. Voir aussi dans *Rites of Power* les articles de Clifford Geertz, pp. 13-38 ; Ralph E. Giesey, pp. 41-64, et surtout les pp. 51-53 sur les entrées royales. Cf. aussi John H. Elliott, « Power and Propaganda in the Spain of Philip IV », dans *Rites of Power*, pp. 145-173.

3. Voir Johan Huizinga, *Homo Ludens. Essai sur la fonction sociale du jeu*, Paris, 1951, pp. 150-157, et aussi son *The Waning of the Middle Ages*, New York, 1954, pp. 67-106 (éd. frse, *L'automne du Moyen Age*, Paris, 1975) et *passim* ; Harvey Cox, *The Feast of Fools. A Theological Essay on Festivity and Fantasy*, New York, 1969, pp. 3-35, ainsi que Mikhaïl Bakhtin, *Rabelais and his World*, Bloomington, 1984, pp. 219-231 (éd. frse : M. Bakhtine, *L'œuvre de François Rabelais et la culture populaire au Moyen Age et sous la Renaissance*, Paris, 1970).

4. Sur les fêtes princières en Castille voir les exemples cités ci-dessous. Pour les fêtes organisées en d'autres lieux en Europe à la fin de l'époque médiévale et au début de l'époque moderne, voir Huizinga, *The Waning of the Middle Ages*, pp. 51, 135 ss, 250 ss, et *passim* ; Maurice Keen, *Chivalry*, Londres, Yale Univ. Press, 1984, pp. 200-212.

5. Sur la religion de la monarchie, voir Strayer, *op. cit.*, pp. 302-312 et note 4 ; Adeline Rucquoi éd., *Genèse médiévale de l'État moderne : la Castille et la Navarre, 1250-1370*, Valladolid, 1987, et *Realidad e imágenes del poder, op. cit.*

6. Cf. Huizinga, *The Waning of the Middle Ages*, Chap. I, pp. 127 ss, et *passim*. Thomas Malory, l'auteur de la glorieuse *Morte d'Arthur*, fut emprisonné deux fois pour viol. Voir Lacey B. Smith, *This Realm of England, 1399-1688*, Lexington, 1983, p. 26. Norbert Elias, *The Civilizing Process*, 2 vols, New York, 1982, I, pp. 190-205 (éd. frse, *La civilisation des mœurs*, Paris, 1973 ; et *La dynamique de l'Occident*, Paris, 1975) .

7. Voir note 8 *infra*. On trouvera des études portant sur les festivités et la chevalerie dans Rosana de Andrés Díaz, « Las fiestas de caballería en la Castilla de los Trastámaras », *En la España medieval. V. Estudios en memoria del profesor D. Claudio Sánchez Albornoz*, 2 vols, Madrid, 1986, I, pp. 81-108 ; Luis Suárez Fernández, *Nobleza y monarquía. Puntos de vista sobre la historia castellana del siglo XV*, Valladolid, 1975, pp. 101-179 ; Francisco Rico, « Unas coplas de Jorge Manrique y las fiestas de Valladolid en 1428 », *Anuario de estudios medievales*, 2, 1965, pp. 515-524 ; l'article inédit en anglais d'Angus MacKay, « The Coronation Banquet of Ferdinand of Antequera », a été publié en espagnol sous le titre « Don Fernando de Antequera y la Virgen Santa María », dans *Homenaje al profesor Juan Torres Fontes*, Murcie, 1987, pp. 949-957. J'aimerais remercier le professeur MacKay qui m'a aimablement autorisé à lire une première version en anglais de cet article.

8. Huizinga, dans *The Waning of the Middle Ages*, ne consacre que quelques observations à la Castille. Keen adopte une approche semblable dans *Chivalry*. Voir Martín de Riquer, *Caballeros andantes españoles*, Madrid, 1967, pp. 10-15, et *passim*. Voir aussi ses *Lletres de batalla. Cartells de deseiximents i capitols de passos d'armes*, 3 vols, Barcelone, 1963-1968. Voir introduction à Pero Rodríguez de Lena, *El passo honroso de Suero de Quiñones*, introduction et édité par A. Labandeira Fernández, Madrid, 1977. Voir aussi T. F. Ruiz, « The Transformation of the Castilian Municipalities. The Case of Burgos (1248-1350) », *Past and Present*, 77, 1977, pp. 3-33.

9. Voir Angus MacKay, *Spain in the Middle Ages. From Frontier to Empire, 1000-1500*, Londres, 1977, pp. 121-212 ; Suárez Fernández, pp. 71-222 ; Joseph O'Callaghan, *A History of Medieval Spain*, Ithaca, 1975, pp. 549-624.

10. Lawrence Stone, dans sa réponse à ma conférence au Davis Center, a défendu la thèse selon laquelle certaines fêtes pourraient n'avoir eu aucun but précis, ou l'idée que peut-être, par leur répétition, elles en étaient venues à perdre leur signification et leur symbolisme politiques. Il est clair que dans cet article je m'efforce de montrer que certaines fêtes au moins avaient un symbolisme politique.

11. Huizinga, *The Waning of the Middle Ages*, pp. 50-51, 250-253 et *passim* ; Ruiz, « Une royauté sans sacre », pp. 439-440. Voir plus bas pour d'autres exemples.

12. SUÁREZ FERNÁNDEZ, p. 105. Il s'agit là, bien sûr, de la formulation de Huizinga, c'est-à-dire : « La conception de la chevalerie comme forme sublime de la vie séculière pourrait se définir comme un idéal esthétique qui assumerait l'apparence d'une idée éthique. » HUIZINGA, *The Waning of the Middle Ages,* p. 69. Keen rejette ce « modèle littéraire » de la chevalerie. KEEN, p. 3 et *passim.*

13. *Hechos del condestable Don Miguel Lucas de Iranzo,* Juan DE MATA CARRIAZO éd., Madrid, 1940, pp. 152-183. Ci-dessous *Hechos del condestable.* Dans ces pages le chroniqueur dresse la liste de toutes les fêtes du calendrier et décrit leur célébration. Sur le cycle des fêtes dans l'Espagne moderne, voir Nina EPTON, *Spanish Fiestas,* Londres, 1968, et pp. 1-41 et 227-240. Pour les fêtes de mai et de la Saint Jean, voir Julio CARO BAROJA, *La estación de amor. Fiestas populares de mayo a San Juan,* Madrid, 1979, pp. 18-28, 119-122 et *passim.*

14. Voir exemples ci-dessous, en particulier ceux impliquant le connétable don Miguel Lucas de Iranzo, ainsi que les fêtes des infants d'Aragon de 1428. Voir *supra*, note 4, et pour d'autres exemples, Jacob BURCKHARDT, *The Civilization of the Renaissance in Italy,* 2 vols, New York, 1975, II, pp. 401-425 ; Jean JACQUOT éd., *Les fêtes de la Renaissance,* 3 vols, Paris, 1956, en particulier le vol. II qui décrit les fêtes et les entrées solennelles de l'empereur Charles Quint (Charles I et Castille et la Couronne d'Aragon).

15. *Hechos del condestable,* pp. 63-65 et pp. 32-41.

16. Voir Marcel MAUSS, *The Gift. Forms and Functions of Exchange in Archaic Societies,* Glencoe, 1954, pp. 35-39 (éd. frse : « Essai sur le don. Formes et raison de l'échange dans les sociétés archaïques », dans *Sociologie et anthropologie*, Paris, PUF, 1980) et *passim.*

17. BAKHTINE, pp. 78-81 ; Caro BAROJA, pp. 112-116, 289-302 ; James G. FRAZER, *The Golden Bough. A Study in Magic and Religion,* New York, 1957, pp. 119-135 et *passim.* Voir aussi Francis X. WEISER, *Handbook of Christian Feasts and Customs. The Year of the Lord in Liturgy and Folklore,* New York, 1958, p. 253 ; en Angleterre, rapporte l'auteur, le dimanche de la Pentecôte était un jour de courses de chevaux, de pièces de théâtre et d'agapes.

18. Pour le couronnement de Fernando de Antequera et la fête organisée à cette occasion, cf. Angus MACKAY, « Don Fernando de Antequera y la Virgen Santa Maria ». Pour le célèbre *paso* de Suero de Quiñones, voir Pero RODRÍGUEZ DE LENA, *El passo honroso de Suero de Quiñones.*

19. Peter RUSSELL, « Arms Versus Letters : Towards a Definition of Spanish Fifteenth Century Humanism », dans *Aspects of the Renaissance. A Symposium,* Archibald R. LEWIS éd., Austin, 1967, pp. 51-57. Voir aussi Ottavio DI CAMILLO, *El humanismo castellano del siglo XV*, Valence, 1976, pp. 111-133, 229-265 ; Helen NADER, *The Mendoza Family in the Spanish Renaissance, 1350-1550,* New Brunswick, 1979, pp. 77-100 ; Alonso DE PALENCIA, « Tratado de la perfección del triunfo militar », dans *Dos tratados de Alfonso de Palencia,* Madrid, 1876, pp. 105-163 : l'ouvrage s'achève par un chapitre sur les pompes triomphales et les *juegos* (jeux et festivités).

20. On trouvera des exemples d'entrées solennelles dans « Crónica del rey don Alfonso el Onceno », dans *Crónica de los reyes de Castilla, op. cit.*, I, LXVI, 1953, pp. 204, 289, 329, 390-392 ; « Crónica del rey don Pedro I », dans *idem*, I, pp. 540-541 ; et dans les diverses chroniques des règnes d'Enrique IV et des monarques catholiques, Ferdinand et Isabelle, réunies dans *idem*, III, 7, pp. 108, 323, 424, 441, 622-623 et 735. Voir aussi, pour les entrées royales en Castille, Rosana DE ANDRÉS DÍAZ, « Las entradas reales castellanas en los siglos XIV y XV, segun las crónicas de la época », dans *En la España medieval,* IV, Madrid, 1984, pp. 47-62.

21. Cf. Bernard GUENÉE et Françoise LEHOUX, *Les entrées royales françaises de 1328 à 1515,* Paris, 1968 ; Victor E. GRAHAM et W. MCALLISTER JOHNSON, *The Royal Tour of France by Charles IX and Catherine of Medici : Festivals and Entries, 1564-1566,* Toronto, 1979. Voir l'entrée solennelle de Louis XI, de pourpre, d'or et de blanc, à Paris, dans Paul MURRAY KENDALL, *Louis XI. The Universal Spider,* New York, 1971, pp. 111-113. Voir aussi Lawrence M. BRYANT, *The King and the City in the Parisian Royal Entry Ceremony : Politics, Ritual, and Art in the Renaissance,* Genève, 1986. Comme Bryant le met en évidence (p. 15), à partir du XIVe siècle, « l'*entrée royale* française fut l'une des cérémonies principales employées pour dramatiser les concepts politiques ». Les couleurs pour l'entrée de Henry II à Paris sont le noir et l'argent, et le connétable porte une épée nue (p. 57). Pour les rencontres hors des murs de la cité, habituellement à une demi-lieue, une lieue ou deux au plus, voir tous les exemples cités.

22. Sur l'importance magique du passage des seuils, c'est-à-dire ici des portes de la cité, voir Arnold VAN GENNEP, *The Rites of Passage,* Chicago, 1960, pp. 15-25 (éd. frse : *Les rites de passage,* Paris, 1969). A ma connaissance il n'existe pas de preuve que dans le cas des entrées royales en Castille au xve siècle la première visite du roi dans une ville immédiatement après son accession au trône avait déjà la signification politique que l'on trouve dans les entrées royales françaises. Les deux exemples que j'étudie dans mon article ne sont pas des entrées royales mais les cérémonies qui marquaient l'arrivée d'une princesse royale venue pour se marier, ou une importante victoire militaire remportée sur l'Islam.

23. *Crónica de Juan II de Castilla,* Juan DE MATA CARRIAZO éd., Madrid, 1982, pp. 398-400 ; « Crónica del rey don Juan II », pp. 332-333.

24. « Crónica del rey don Juan II », pp. 566-566.

25. *Idem,* p. 567 : « ... quedando la Princesa tal qual nascio,... ». Si l'on me permet de jouer sur les mots je dirai que Blanca (Blanche) demeura telle, sans être tachée de rouge. En bref, le prince, à cause de son homosexualité ou pour toute autre raison, fut incapable de consommer le mariage.

26. Francisco RICO, « Unas coplas de Jorge Manrique y las fiestas de Valladolid en 1428 », p. 517 :

« Qué se fizo el rey don Juan ?
Los infantes de Aragón,
qué se fizieron ?
Qué fué de tanto galán ?
Qué fué de tanta invención
como truxieron ?
Las justas y los torneos,
paramentos, bordaduras,
y cimeras,
fueron sino devaneos ?
qué fueron sino verduras
de las eras ? »

27. SUÁREZ FERNÁNDEZ, pp. 119-167 ; Nicholas ROUND, *The Greatest Man Uncrowned. A Study of the Fall of Don Alvaro de Luna,* Londres, 1987, pp. 1-31. Les chroniques du règne de Juan II s'intéressent essentiellement au combat entre le connétable et les factions nobiliaires en conflit. Pour un récit du soulèvement civil des années 1420, voir Alvar GARCÍA DE SANTA MARÍA, *Crónica de Juan II de Castilla*, 2 vols (ci-dessous Alvar GARCÍA DE SANTA MARÍA), dans *Colección de documentos inéditos para la historia de España,* vol. I C et C, Madrid, 1891, I C, pp. 447-461 ; Pero CARRILLO DE HUETE, *Crónica del halconero de Juan II*, J. DE MATA CARRIAZO éd., Madrid, 1946, pp. 1-18 ; *Refundición de la crónica del halconero*, J. DE MATA CARRIAZO éd., Madrid, 1946, pp. 48-58 ; « Crónica del rey don Juan II », pp. 430-446.

28. Voir ROUND, pp. 1-31.

29. La « Crónica del rey don Juan II » place la fête du connétable après celle du roi. Il y aurait eu à l'occasion un affrontement entre cinquante chevaliers en blanc et cinquante en rouge (p. 447). La *Crónica del halconero de Juan II,* le récit le plus fiable d'un témoin visuel, précise que la fête eut lieu au début, le 2 mai, avec une joute au cours de laquelle le connétable et sept de ses chevaliers affrontèrent en lice les infants d'Aragon et le roi de Castille (pp. 18-19). Alvar García de Santa María place aussi ces festivités au début. Elles concernèrent Alvaro de Luna et « quarante ou cinquante chevaliers » vêtus d'or, de soie et d'hermine » (vol. C, p. 15).

30. Alvar GARCÍA DE SANTA MARÍA, *op. cit.,* p. 16.

31. Cf. RUIZ, « Une royauté sans sacre », p. 447.

32. Pero CARRILLO DE HUETE, *Crónica del halconero de Juan II*, pp. 19-27 ; Alvar GARCÍA DE SANTA MARÍA, *op. cit.*, pp. 14-20 ; « Crónica del rey don Juan II », pp. 446-447. Sur les lois somptuaires des Cortes, voir les archives municipales de Burgos (AMB), classif. 1391 (12-X-1252), publiées dans Ismael GARCÍA RÁMILA, « Ordenamiento de posturas y otros capítulos generales otorgados a la ciudad de Burgos por el rey Alfonso X », *Hispania,* XIX (1945), pp. 179-235 ; XX (1945), pp. 385-439 ; XXI (1945), pp. 605-650 ; *Cortes de los antiguos reinos de León y Castilla,* 5 vols, Madrid, 1861-1903 (ci-dessous *Cortes*), I, 1338, p. 451. Voir ci-dessous. Pour les couleurs utilisées pour représenter la royauté et la Vierge dans la tradition iconographique primitive, voir les enluminures qui accompagnent les *Cantigas de Santa María,* parag. XV, XVII, XVIII et *passim.* Les atours d'or et d'argent dans la société médiévale sont analysés dans Françoise PIPONNIER, *Costume et vie sociale. La cour d'Anjou, XIVe-XVe siècle*, Paris, 1970, en particulier pp. 195-260.

33. Sur l'exécution de Juan García, voir note 32. Cf. Gertrude G. SILL, *A Handbook of Symbols in Christian Art,* New York, 1975, pp. 18 pour les papillons, pp. 29-30 pour les couleurs; Juan E. CIRLOT, *A Dictionary of Symbols,* 2e éd., New York, 1971, p. 35 pour les papillons, pp. 52-60 pour les couleurs ; George FERGUSON, *Signs and Symbols in Christian Art*, New York, 1954, p. 7 (papillons), pp. 271-275 (couleurs). Des papillons figurent aussi dans un tableau de Velázquez représentant une infante d'Espagne. Ils sont cousus sur sa coiffure. Voir aussi le symbolisme des papillons dans *Les Versets sataniques* de Salman RUSHDIE, Paris, 1989.

34. SILL, p. 23; CIRLOT, pp. 23, 189; FERGUSON, pp. 5, 20-21. Voir l'usage symbolique des lions dans le *Poema de mío Cid* (cantar tercero), vers 2280-2299. Le récit est repris presque littéralement dans la *Primera crónica general,* œuvre rédigée au milieu du XIIIe siècle. Dans le *Henry IV* de SHAKESPEARE, Première partie, Acte II, scène 4, 1. pp. 271 ss: « Jamais le lion ne touche à un vrai prince ». Pour l'image du lion libéré chez Villasandino (mort en 1425), voir Angel VALBUENA PRAT, *Historia de la literatura española*, 2e éd., Barcelone, 1946, pp. 213-214; « ... dans un de ses poèmes, Villasandino fait référence à des prophéties de Merlin. Le lion sortant de la caverne est Juan II échappant au pouvoir de l'infant Don Enrique ». Le poème date de 1421. Voir aussi Juan DE MENA, *Laberinto de fortuna,* John G. CUMMINS éd., Madrid, 1984, p. 157. Dans une note l'auteur raconte que Juan II avait presque toujours à ses côtés un lion apprivoisé. Quand il trônait sur la *silla real,* il posait ses mains sur le lion. *Hechos del condestable,* pp. 35, 169 et *passim*. Sur l'utilisation iconographique de lions et d'ours, cf. Cesare RIPA, *Iconologia*, Padoue, 1611, éd. en fac-similé, New York, 1976. Pour les lions, cf. pp. 9, 13, 66, 78, 84-85, 111, 126, 132, 145, 170, 175, 179, 321, 453, etc. Pour les ours, pp. 264, 407, 473. Olivier DE LA MARCHE dans ses *Mémoires...*, livre I, chap. 29, décrivant les tableaux vivants présentés lors du banquet donné par Philippe le Bon de Bourgogne, montre l'utilisation de lions à des fins symboliques dans deux des tableaux présentés.

35. Huizinga montre que Molinet compare Maximilien (le fils de l'empereur Frédéric III) à Dieu le Père lors de son arrivée aux Pays-Bas pour épouser Marie de Bourgogne. Maximilien, Frédéric III et Philippe le Beau sont aussi comparés à la Trinité. HUIZINGA, *The Waning of the Middle Ages,* pp. 157-158. Sur le thème christologique, lorsque l'infant don Enrique (le fils de Juan II) fut reconnu par les Cortes, l'évêque don Alvaro de Osorno prononça la bénédiction ou le discours de salutation sur le thème: *Puer natus est nobis* (un enfant nous est né). Voir aussi Françoise AUTRAND, *Charles VI,* Paris, 1986, et son analyse de la signification politique des fêtes organisées en mai 1389 à Saint Denis, pp. 214-240.

36. SUÁREZ FERNÁNDEZ, p. 135; « Crónica del rey don Juan II », p. 448.

37. Juan DE MENA, *Laberinto de fortuna,* pp. 16, 126-127. Voir également Alan DEYERMOND, « La ideología del estado moderno en la literatura española del siglo XV », *Realidad e imágenes del poder*, pp. 178-179.

38. Les tapis étaient presque toujours rouges. Il existe de nombreuses références dans les chroniques à des tapis qui auraient été ajoutés pour renforcer la dominante rouge dans les cérémonies et les lieux publics. Sur les tapis en Espagne et sur leurs couleurs, voir Ernst KUHNEL, *Catalogue of Spanish Rugs: Twelfth Century to the Nineteenth Century*, Washington, D.C., 1953. Sur la reconnaissance par les Cortes de l'infant don Enrique comme héritier, cf. « Crónica del rey don Juan II », p. 429. Pour une cérémonie semblable, le serment prêté à l'infante Catalina quelques années plus tard, voir pp. 422-423. Cf. aussi ci-dessous, pour d'autres exemples. Voir également Joseph O'CALLAGHAN, *The Cortes of Castile-León, 1188-1350,* Philadelphie, 1989, pp. 82-89.

39. Victor TURNER, *From Ritual to Theatre. The Human Seriousness of Play,* New York, 1982, pp. 13-14.

40. Il existe de nombreux exemples de cela dans le texte mais, même dans les récits plus anciens, nous percevons l'hétérogénéité de l'assistance rassemblée dans un cadre urbain. Voir « Crónica de Alfonso XI », dans *Crónica de los reyes de Castilla*, I, 235-237.

41. Voir, par exemple, « Coplas de la Panadera », dans *Poesía crítica y satírica del siglo XV*, Julio RODRÍGUEZ PUÉRTOLAS, Madrid, 1981, pp. 131-147.

42. RUIZ, « Une royauté sans sacre », pp. 440, 443-447. Voir aussi MACKAY, *Spain in the Middle Ages,* p. 59.

43. *The Waning of the Middle Ages* de Huizinga comporte, pp. 270-273, une excellente analyse de l'utilisation des couleurs dans la société médiévale. On retrouve dans cet ouvrage des références aux couleurs des vêtements portés à l'occasion des fêtes, funérailles, entrées solennelles, etc. Michel Pastoureau, « Les couleurs ont aussi une histoire », *L'Histoire*, 29, sept. 1986, pp. 46-52, ainsi que son « Et puis vint le bleu », dans *Figures et couleurs. Étude sur la symbolique et la sensibilité médiévales,* Paris, 1986, pp. 15-22 ; également dans le même ouvrage, « Les couleurs médiévales : systèmes de valeurs et modes de sensibilités », pp. 35-49 (cf. p. 40 un tableau sur le symbolisme des couleurs). Voir également « L'État et son image emblématique », pp. 61-69. Également J. Le Goff, « Codes vestimentaire et alimentaire dans *Erec et Enide* », dans *L'imaginaire médiéval. Essais,* Paris, 1985, pp. 188-201. Faber Birren, *Selling Colors to People,* New York, 1956, pp. 149-155. Nous apprenons ainsi que les femmes brunes et les Latins préfèrent le rouge. Voir aussi pp. 173-174. Birren, *The Story of Color. From Ancient Mysticism to Modern Science,* Westport, 1941, pp. 90, 323-326 : la couleur héraldique mythique d'Adam est le rouge, celle d'Eve le blanc. Voir aussi Jacques Heers, « La mode et les marchés des draps de laine : Gênes et la montagne à la fin du Moyen Age », *Annales ESC*, 26, n° 5, 1971, pp. 1093-1117 : à la fin du XVe siècle et au début du XVIe les testaments montrent que les marchands gênois avaient une préférence pour les teintes rouges.

44. Victor W. Turner, « Color Classification in Ndembu Ritual. A Problem in Primitive Classification », dans *The Forest of Symbols,* Ithaca, 1967, pp. 59-90 ; Mircea Eliade, *Rites and Symbols of Initiation. The Mysteries of Birth and Rebirth,* New York, 1958, pp. 26, 105, 122, 125. Pour une lecture critique de Turner et pour une discussion fort instructive de la dynamique de l'usage des couleurs, voir Jane Schneider, « Peacocks and Penguins. The Political Economy of European Cloth and Colors », *American Ethnologist,* V, 3, 1978, pp. 413-447. Sur les aspects libidinaux du tournoi et de la culture courtoise, voir Huizinga, *The Waning of the Middle Ages,* pp. 79-89 et *passim* ; F. Heer, *The Medieval World. Europe, 1100-1350,* Cleveland, 1962, pp. 143-147. Sur les affrontements entre chevaliers en blanc et chevaliers en rouge, voir plus bas.

45. *Hechos del condestable,* pp. 195-196.

46. Voir Linda Woodbridge, « Black and White and Red All Over : The Sonnet Mistress Amongst the Ndembu », *Renaissancce Quaterly,* XL, 2, 1987, pp. 247-297. Dans le *Libro de buen amor* (années 1330) de Juan Ruiz il est dit que la femme idéale a un visage fort blanc et une bouche rouge (pp. 431-434). Dans Fernán Pérez de Guzmán, *Generaciones y semblanzas*, Biblioteca de autores españoles, LXVIII, Madrid, 1953, pp. 697-719, les rois de Castille sont toujours décrits comme étant blonds, avec un visage d'un blanc pur et des joues rouges.

47. Voir plus haut. Cf. également *Cortes,* I, Burgos, 1338, p. 451 ; *Cortes,* II, Valladolid, 1351, pp. 14-15, 19 ; *Cortes,* III, Palenzuela, 1425, p. 70 et *passim.* Voir l'édition récente établie par Francisco Hernández d'un *Cuaderno de Cortes* jusqu'alors inconnu, dans son « Las cortes de Toledo de 1207 », dans *Las cortes de Castilla y León en la edad media,* 2 vols, Valladolid, 1988, I, pp. 221-263 : Hernández montre l'intérêt déjà accordé à l'époque aux étoffes importées de grand prix, et surtout à l'*escarlata*. Sur les restrictions imposées uniquement aux Juifs et aux Maures, voir S. Berkowitz et T. F. Ruiz, « Jewish and Christian Relations in Urban Northern Castile, 1200-1350 », à paraître dans les Actes d'un colloque sur les relations entre juifs et chrétiens au Moyen Age qui s'est tenu à Seton Hall University en mai 1988. Un inventaire inédit datant du 22 juin 1442, aimablement communiqué par Adeline Rucquoi, montre que les étoffes étaient de couleurs variées, sans préférence marqué pour la combinaison blanc/rouge. Cela renforce la signification de l'accent mis sur ces deux couleurs dans les fêtes. F. Autrand montre, dans *Charles VI*, pp. 217-219, que les couleurs utilisées de manière exclusive pour la fête royale de mai 1389 étaient celles du roi, « vert-blanc-vermeil ». Tout le monde portait les mêmes couleurs et les distinctions de rang social se manifestaient seulement dans la qualité de l'étoffe : « Les robes du roi, de la reine, des princes, sont de satin doublé de taffetas, celles de chevaliers sont de velours ou de fine écarlate, celles des écuyers sont de simple drap ou de brunette. »

48. *Hechos del condestable,* pp. 41-57.

49. Voir *Crónica de Alfonso XI,* pp. 231, 329 ; *Crónica de Pedro I,* p. 431 : un chevalier de l'Ordre de la Banda (blanc et noir) porte aussi un emblème rouge ; également p. 432 mariage du roi (en argent, or et hermine), p. 472 affrontement de cinquante chevaliers contre cinquante autres (rouge et blanc). *Crónica de Enrique II,* pp. 33-34 ; « Crónica del rey don Juan II », pp. 332-333, 359-361, 365, 422-424, 428-430, 514, 516, 524, 526-527, 655-656, 683 : la dernière référence

comporte une description de l'exécution théâtrale de don Alvaro de Luna. Mosén Diego de Valera, « Memorial de diversas hazañas » dans *Crónicas de los reyes de Castilla, op. cit.*, Biblioteca de autores españoles, LXX, vol. III, p. 33 ; Diego Enríquez del Castillo, p. 108 ; dans la deuxième *Partida,* tit. xix, ley 18, Alfonso X recommande que les jeunes chevaliers soient vêtus de rouge et de vert pour qu'ils soient heureux. Voir les utilisations iconographiques du rouge, du blanc et du noir dans Ripa, *Iconologia,* blanc : pp. 16-17, 74, 124, 162, 203, 250, 273, 318, 418, 478, 483 et *passim* ; noir : pp. 25, 54, 126, 255, 265, 335, 418, 420, 450, 500 ; rouge : pp. 37, 72, 86, 102, 135, 139, 170, 256, 264, 351, 426 et *passim*.

50. Woodbridge, pp. 268-272.

51. Voir Schneider, pp. 430-431.

XVI

The Holy Office in Medieval France and in Late Medieval Castile: Origins and Contrasts

For most people the mention of the Spanish Inquisition calls up the image of a sinister and peculiar institution. Whether that response is fairly correct or incorrect, partly the result of long-standing prejudices with regard to early modern Spanish history or a remnant of the Black Legend, does not matter. In spite of the revisionist work which has been done for the last few decades on the histories of Castile, Spain, and the Inquisition itself (mostly by English historians), the reputation of the Holy Office has remained one of cruelty and excessive violence. Moreover, in spite of evidence to the contrary, the Inquisition has been seen as a fatal flaw in the social, intellectual, and institutional development of Spain and, thus, in its present claim to modernity and democracy.

Just before his return to Spain, where he died a few weeks later, Vicente Llorens, by both scholarly research and inclination an exponent of romantic liberalism, gave a farewell lecture at Princeton University on the tragic impact of the Inquisition on Spanish life. His vehement and heartfelt presentation condensed in a magisterial manner the arguments of Enlightenment thinkers and Spanish nineteenth-century liberals (for there were liberals in Spain in spite of the Inquisition) agreeing with the view of the Holy Office long held by non-Spaniards and best exemplified by the work of Henry C. Lea.

I do not disagree with Llorens's and others' condemnation of the Spanish Inquisition. Certainly its evils far outweigh any imaginable benefit. Nevertheless, it may prove worthwhile to compare the origins and work of the Holy Office in Castile and, later on, in Spain with those of its medieval counterpart and to examine to what extent the Inquisition in Spain followed rather than dictated institutional and cultural patterns. In short, I would like to compare briefly the medieval and Spanish Inquisitions and to offer a few preliminary comments on the historical origins of the Holy Office in Castile. Whereas most historians distinguish between the Spanish and the Papal Inquisitions (the great Lea, of course, by treating them as separate subjects), it is important to keep in mind their intrinsic similarity. We know that the Inquisition was at work in other parts of Western Europe in the early modern period and that its methods and far-reaching influence in Italy or France were not too different from those of the Holy Office in Spain. Carlo Ginzburg's excellent recent book, *Il formaggio e i vermi,* though a study of the cosmology of a sixteenth-century miller, shows this quite conclusively. If they were similar in organization and methods, what, then, gave the Spanish Inquisition its peculiar character?

The rise and growth of the medieval Inquisition are topics which have been already well studied and with which most historians of medieval and early modern Europe are acquainted.[1] The Papal Inquisition was born out of the struggle against heretics, Waldenses and Cathars, in Occitania and was the last resort in that conflict after everything else had failed.[2] From the mid-twelfth century on, the dualist heresy known as Catharism found a home in southern France and unexpectedly prospered. The corruption and laxity of the southern clergy, the cosmopolitan culture of Languedoc, and the still anarchic and feudal nature of Occitanian politics made the area a haven for new and peculiar beliefs. Whether Catharism (as opposed to Waldensian beliefs) was a heretical doctrine or in reality a different religion dating back to ancient Manichaean practices is not a question which ought to be examined here.[3] What is important, however, is that the leaders of the Cathar church found ample support in the region among the bourgeoisie and at least benign neglect and even support from the ruling feudal class.

The medieval church, then at its zenith, had no mechanism for dealing with such threats; its ancient means of dealing with heretics, the episcopal inquisition, had proved inadequate. Furthermore, the humanistic currents of the late eleventh and twelfth centuries made for toleration.[4] The first attempt at quelling widespread heresy was through preaching and conversion of heretics—a preaching by example carried on in 1206 by the

Castilian bishop of Osma and his more celebrated companion, St. Dominic, and later on by the latter's new order, the Dominicans. Though later Dominican sources claimed success, their preaching did not seem to have turned the tide in favor of orthodoxy. Moreover, when Peter of Castelnau, the papal legate in Languedoc, was assassinated in 1208, this opened a new and more violent phase in the conflict between church and heresy.[5]

The slow progress of the preaching mission and the murder of his legate prompted Innocent III to call for a crusade in 1208. The political and religious aspects of the Albigensian Crusade, as the enterprise is now known, have been examined elsewhere. In short, the crusade was a foreign invasion of the South, and a large number of Occitanians, both Catholics and Cathars, fought side by side against the French and northern crusaders. The violence of the war, highlighted by the massacres at Beziers and Marmande, and the death of Peter the Catholic, king of Aragon, fighting on the side of the Cathars, are reminders of the political overtones of this conflict. Not surprisingly, therefore, victory on the battlefield and the eventual extinction of Occitanian independence did not bring an end to heresy.[6] Further measures were necessary, specifically, an agency capable of identifying and dealing with heretics throughout the region. Thus, the Papal Inquisition was born.

Well grounded in medieval legal practices, the Inquisition "was a method of inquiry to ascertain facts in all kinds of affairs. It also designated one of several procedures in civil and canon law for detecting and punishing violation."[7] The new Inquisition was manned by the Dominicans and, to a lesser extent, the Franciscans and responsible to the pope. Although the Mendicant orders were in the thirteenth century, as they were also in the fifteenth and sixteenth, the tribunes of popular pressures and fears, the Inquisition in Occitania did not meet with popular support as it did in Spain. On the contrary, the amount of resistance and popular hostility which the inquisitors found throughout the region was remarkable and a clear sign of the identification of inquisitor with foreign occupation—this despite the fact that, notwithstanding Lea's long list of inquisitorial inequities, Dossat's recent research shows the moderation of the penalties imposed by the Holy Office and the fact that almost one out of every four persons indicted by the Inquisition was able to escape its wrath.[8] Regardless of its harshness or lack of it, the Inquisition was able to control heresy in southern France and elsewhere. It succeeded because after the defeat and submission of the Occitanian lords, the secular authorities were either willing or compelled to do the Inquisition's bidding. Furthermore, the Inquisition's methods of inquiry allowed its agents to gather an ever-wider list of suspects. Since ready confession and implication of others was a way of lessening one's own sentence, the identification of heretics, sympathizers, or indifferent Catholics progressed at a fast pace. This, as we know, also worked well in Spain.[9]

A further point should be made in this brief summary of the birth of the medieval Inquisition. Its beginning in southern France and elsewhere in Western Europe coincided with drastic changes in medieval mentalities and institutions. The closing of the "open" twelfth century, the final condemnation of the ideals of courtly love in 1277, the changes in the liturgy of the Mass, the bureaucratization of the church, and the beginnings of the nation-state in England and France brought a climate of uncertainty and fear to what had been a vigorous, vital culture. The twelfth century was remarkably exempt from excesses and fear. The optimism of the age was, however, waning, and the new feelings of despair brought with them a revival of millennial expectations, evident in the flagellant movement of 1260, growing misogyny, anti-Semitism, and popular and secular demands for execution by fire of these scapegoats. Jean Delumeau's assessment of these new ways of combatting popular fear fits well here. In many respects, the medieval Papal Inquisition was a dike against the onslaught of new modes of behavior–against the first symptoms of the breaking up of feudal society and of social and cultural change.[10]

Certain generalizations can be advanced. The medieval Inquisition was born only after other measures had failed to contain the very real threat of heresy. Its inception did not break with established medieval legal tradition. Moreover, in Occitania the Inquisition served a political purpose and thus often received the cooperation and support of those in power, above all the newcomers from the North and the southern allies. Popular and nobiliary opposition to the Inquisition was the result partly of its heavy-handed methods but more than anything else of its identification with foreign occupation. Most important, the first Papal Inquisition operated in a society which was culturally and ethnically homogeneous. Thus, once Catharism was subdued or driven underground, inquisitorial activities and their role in society diminished.

When we turn to Spain, conditions and circumstances were sometimes similar but more often than not quite different. In twelfth- and thirteenth-century Iberia we find a heterogeneous society unlike that of northern Europe. Although there was an active Papal Inquisition in Aragon, paralleling that of Languedoc, there was no Inquisition in Castile. Our parallels and contrasts must, then, be drawn between Castile and the North. After all, the creation of the Inquisition under Castilian control and its extension to Aragon in 1483 marked the beginning of the Holy Office in Spain.

Although recent research has called attention to inquisitorial activities in Castile before the 1470s, the Inquisition was never formally constituted in the kingdom. Lea attempts a few explanations for this absence, but although he is essentially correct in his assessment, a great deal more is needed. If heresy was not as widespread in Castile as it had been in Occitania, there were, nevertheless, heretics and Judaizers in late medieval Castile. We find references to them in the legal codes, in literary works, and in the chronicles and documents of the period. Moreover, the road to Compostela opened Castile to all influences, orthodox and heterodox. Yet, Castilians on the whole, both secular and ecclesiastic, were not overly concerned with the purity of religion. The Castilian church in the thirteenth century and afterward was less inclined to follow papal direction than any other church in the West. Its behavior in sexual matters and ecclesiastical discipline, above all, in obedience to Rome was, as Peter Linehan has shown, nothing short of contumacious. The church hierarchy already had enough problems fending off the financial extortions of the Castilian kings in the late Middle Ages, protecting their domains and privileges from rapacious nobles and royal officials, and simply surviving in the midst of the social, economic, and political upheavals which plagued Castile after 1250 to worry also about the purity of the faith. In the mid-thirteenth century, when the example of inquisitorial success in Languedoc, Aragon, and other kingdoms was fresh and could have been adopted in Castile, the realm turned inward to deal with a series of protracted crises which transformed and shaped Castile for centuries to come.[11]

Unlike the rulers of France, England, and almost all the other countries of the West, the kings of Castile after 1157 had consciously or unconsciously rejected the sacralization and ritualization of power associated with medieval kingship. The kings of Castile in the Middle Ages and those of Spain in the early modern period and until today, with very few and notable exceptions, were not crowned or, if at all, crowned themselves and were not anointed with holy oil. The rituals of kingship were secular and martial ones: knighting by the mechanical arm of Saint James, acclamation and rasing on the shield or chair by the *ricos hombres*, prelates, and people, exchange of oaths, lifting of the *pendones* (standards) of Castile to a traditional cry, and kissing of the king's hand in obeisance. The medieval Castilian monarchy, neither sacral nor thaumaturgical, did not need the sanction of the church to claim its power. Its authority came from the sword, harking back to a pre-Christian, Germanic military tradition. This is not to say that the Castilian kings and people were not religious. Of course they were, but in a manner which differed from the religiosity of northern realms. Both law and tradition had long subordinated the church and obedience to Rome to the political necessity of the kingdom. Alvarus Pelagius, a noted theologian and papal apologist of the early fourteenth century, was "forced to admit that even he was accustomed to kiss the king's hand–as the vile Spanish prelates did." As the Infante Don Juan Manuel wrote a few years later, "he was certain of one thing only: the pope had less power in Castile than anywhere else."[12]

It is not difficult to understand, then, why there was no Inquisition in medieval Castile and why, when it came time to be organized, it was under the authority of the monarchs. The first distinction, therefore, is between the relationship of unsacred monarchy and church in Castile and sacral kingship and religion elsewhere.[13] The question, however, remains, why the Inquisition in 1478-83? The stock answer has been to point to the Judaizing problem, specifically the activities of New Christians or conversos who practiced their old religion in secret. Yet, the problem was not new. Why not the Inquisition in the 1390s or early 1400s, when the secret practice of Judaism was probably more common than a century later? Here Benzion Netanyahu's arguments (in this volume) seem most convincing. Although the 1391 pogroms led to a large number of forced conversions, some of the most notable ones, for example, that of Rabbi Selemoh Ha-Levi (better known to us as Pablo de Santa María), took place before the violence began. The Jewish community in Castile had long been in turmoil. The secularism of some, the failed messianic expectations of others, the virulent anti-Judaism of some conversos (Abner of

Burgos, Pablo de Santa María, Gerónimo de Santafé, and Pedro de la Caballería among them), and increased social pressure left the Castilian Jews vulnerable to conversion and intimidation. There were, of course, New Christians who still practiced Judaism in secret, but I do not think their number was large enough to justify the claims of the supporters of the Holy Office. If we add all those who were handed over to the secular authorities or punished by the Inquisition in its first ten years, as many as they were, they only represent a small percentage of all conversos. After the Edict of Expulsion of 1492, when many more converted, conditions of course worsened.[14]

We see, therefore, that in contrast to the situation in Occitania, where Catharism was a fomidable rival of the church, Judaizing was not such a threat in Spain, though it may have been perceived as such. The question remains, nevertheless, why the Inquisition then?

As John H. Elliott has pointed out, the Inquisition "gave official sanction to already existing attitudes and practices. Suspicion of those who deviated from the common norm was deeply rooted in a country where deviation was itself more normal than elsewhere."[15] The Holy Office in Castile and Spain in the early modern period followed and expressed deeply rooted popular sentiments; it did not create or formulate them. Many of these popular attitudes had been present in Castile for centuries, coming to their fullness in the late fifteenth century. If the Inquisition found widespread support, as it did especially in Castile, it was essentially because its aims were well grounded in popular culture.

One must emphasize anew that, unlike Occitania, Castile, Spain as a whole, was a racially and religiously heterogeneous society. Harmonious relations between races, if they ever existed, were often confined to the level of the court or among intellectuals. Certainly, after the Battle of Las Navas de Tolosa (1212) the treatment of the Muslims had deteriorated. Their massive expulsions from conquered cities showed clearly how Christians were going to behave now that they had the upper hand. In Andalusia after 1248, for example, the conquerors left no doubt as to the nature of the relations between Christians and Moors, that of master and servant.[16] In northern Castile, specifically the area of Burgos which I have long studied, there is no evidence of conviviality between Jews and Christians. Jews rendered services to the Christian population, lent money, farmed and collected taxes, and engaged in many other economic activities, but they did so amidst growing racial and social hatred. What were the roots of this antagonism?

Besides the well-known causes of anti-Semitism, there were other explanations for this sentiment in Castile. The writings of Saint Isidore, the *Fuero juzgo*, the Partidas, and other medieval legal codes emphasized the superiority and importance of Gothic blood, good behavior, and military prowess. Here the legal codes were in line with a societal sense of self-worth, with noble and martial traditions associated not with religion but with race. Of course, we know how Cervantes ridiculed this racial prejudice through Sancho's well-known utterances: "I am an Old Christian and to become an earl that is sufficient." Yet, his choice of words only shows how widespread was the belief in the connection between blood, martial spirit, and innate nobility. This idea, which, I should add, ran counter to Christian doctrine, has remained one of the motifs of Spanish history down to the present. We are left, then, in the late Middle Ages with a racial and social perception of the superiority of one group over another because of blood and martial tradition. When Maravall describes the humanism of arms in *Don Quixote* as superior to, albeit not as profitable as, the humanism of letters, we come closer to that feeling of racial superiority to which the martial enterprises of Castilians, first in the peninsula, then in Central Europe and America, were vivid testimonies.[17] We ought to contrast the exemplary knightly code of Don Quixote, the ideal nobility of his heart, with the military inadequacies of the New Christians. Whereas the urban elites of late medieval Castile had fulfilled a military role and maintained their skills as warriors, the bourgeoisie of the late fifteenth century, with its large converso component, had ceased to do so. In the pages of *La Celestina* we see the pathos of an urban aristocracy in the pursuit of pleasure. Its reward in *La Celestina* and in real life was doom.[18] In thirteenth- and early fourteenth-century Castile, Jews, Moors, and Christians interacted only in the peculiar setting of Alfonso X's court and *scriptoria* or in the narrow circles of other Castilian kings. In the street, where it counted, we find suspicion, segregation, and growing hatred. The upheavals of the late fourteenth century and, above all, the fifteenth only augmented the underlying animosity and violence.[19]

Alas, prejudice and violence were not the monopoly of Castilians or of Christians. Wherever we look in the fifteenth century, wherever we look in the sixteenth century, wherever we look today, peaceful coexistence of diverse racial and religious groups is seldom a reality. We should not, then, expect to find it in medieval Castile, and to do so is only the delusion of romantic historians. Moreover, in Castile racial prejudices were compounded by the unavoidable realization of how unreal racial exclusivity truly was.

Racial and social animosity found a vocal expression in the ordinances of the Cortes. From the mid-thirteenth century on, a large portion of the petitions presented to the king at the meetings of the Cortes can only be described as anti-Semitic. The urban oligarchs who controlled the Castilian cities and served as procurators to the Cortes sought to segregate Jews and Moors from the rest of the population. Moors had to wear their hair short and their beards long. Jews and Moors were forbidden to wear certain types of cloth and colors, and Jews had to wear a yellow circle on their garments as a sign of their religion. They could not marry Christians, bear Christian names, or be hired as nannies for Christian babies.[20] Furthermore, the urban procurators repeatedly petitioned for economic sanctions, requesting reduction of interest rates and partial or total cancellation of debts to Jewish moneylenders. Politically, the city councils of Castile pressed to end the influence of Jews at the court and their role as tax collectors and royal administrators. Within the cities the local liogarchies had long been engaged in jurisdictional conflicts with Jews and Moors, seeking to end their exemption from municipal authority.[21]

The urban oligarchies were not always successful in their petitions. The kings of Castile had good reasons, both financial and administrative, to protect Jews from the animosity of other groups. One should emphasize that this active antagonism toward the Jews was not limited to the lower classes. While we have evidence of popular anti-Semitism only when expressed on pogroms or violent actions, the evidence for the anti-Jewish sentiments of the medieval urban elites–long in competition with the Jews in financial affairs and for administrative posts–is overwhelming. Moneylending, for example, was partially in Christian hands in late thirteenth-century Burgos and in those of foreign Christian merchants in Seville. The Jews were clearly under attack on all fronts.[22]

I have noticed elsewhere that Castile did have, at least in some northern cities, a dynamic bourgeoisie in the Middle Ages. Unlike other parts of Western Europe, however, when the Castilian bourgeoisie moved into the ranks of the lower nobility in the late fourteenth century, the void was filled not by the "new men" whom we see coming to the fore in other European cities, such as Salvestro de Medici in Florence, but by conversos. The traditional alliance between the lower nobility and oligarchic urban groups was imperiled by these developments.[23] The conversos came to fulfill their new role in the midst of serious economic and political upheaval and with a tradition of racial and social hatred already well established. That they prospered in spite of this did not help their cause.

I have argued in the past, in connection with Stephen Haliczer's excellent article, "The Castilian Urban Patriciate and the Jewish Expulsions of 1480-92," that the conversos supported the Edict of Expulsion partly because they had inherited the anti-Jewish program of the late medieval urban elites rather than exclusively as a reaction to the presence of Jewish communities in their midst. If conversos were active in inquisitorial affairs, and they were in the early years, this also followed from their new roles. Moreover, as members of the bourgeoisie they also continued their age-old struggle against the high aristocracy, but now no longer assured of the support of the lower nobility or the church. In this connection even their political role changed. The success of the Catholic Kings in putting an end to the political ambitions of the high nobility in Castile eliminated one of the political advantages of the bourgeoisie in its relations with the crown. They were no longer as needed for the well-being of the monarchy as they had been before. If one looks at the chronology of Ferdinand and Isabella's reforms, the establishment of the Holy Office in Castile in 1478 followed the taming of the nobility and almost coincides with the final extension of royal authority over the cities which resulted from the Cortes of Toledo in 1480.[24] The Inquisition was, to a certain degree, another instrument in weakening the political and economic role of some segments of the bourgeoisie and keeping under a tight rein the disfranchised lower bourgeoisie.

We should look at the early victims of the Inquisition in terms of social class rather than racial background. In this connection, a superficial examination of the *Catálogo de las Causas contra la fe seguidas ante el Tribunal del Santo Oficio de la Inquisición de Toledo* raises a series of questions which deserve a more thorough investigation. I should begin by confessing that I do not know how accurate this catalog is or to what extent it reflects the reality of the Toledan Holy Office. The catalog lists the names of those charged by the Inquisition, the date and nature of the charges, the final disposition of the case, the town of residence, and the marital status of the accused. In addition, the occupation of the accused or of his or her parents or spouse is sometimes included. In a few cases the catalog indicates whether torture was administered and the type of torture.[25]

Since my concern here is the origins of the Inquisition in Castile, I have examined the evidence of the catalog only up to 1530, after which, theoretically, the persecution of Judaizers would have slackened, not to be renewed in earnest until the influx of Portuguese conversos into Spain in the seventeenth century. Between the beginnings of the Inquisition in Toledo and 1530, there are twenty-one different charges, ranging from bigamy and blasphemy to sacrilege and including, of course, Judaizing. During this period, 137 persons were charged of crimes or improper behavior other than Judaizing. Of those only 4 were tried before 1499, 24 between 1500 and 1515, and 109 between 1516 and 1530. The breakdown of these cases by sex and disposition is shown in table 1. Clearly, the proportion of males to females is considerable. Further, while the number tried for reasons other than Judaizing increased after 1515, the number tried for Judaizing decreased (table 2). The bulk of the persecution on charges of Judaizing came before 1500 (320 cases), decreasing to just 49 cases between 1516 and 1530. The number of women charged, 223, or 45.88 percent of the total, is remarkable. This may be the result of the greater spirituality and concern of medieval women for public demonstration of their religious beliefs; perhaps the wives of conversos maintained the Judaic traditions more faithfully than their husbands.[26] This explanation, however, presupposes that there was widespread practice of Judaism in secret, and I am not entirely convinced by it. The larger percentage of females absolved also points to some extent to the weakness of this argument. Again, looking at the accused from the perspective of their social class suggests a different explanation. Of the 195 persons identified either by their professions or by those of their husbands or fathers, only 16 can be recognized as belonging to the urban ruling elites or to the clergy: 8 clergymen, 5 regidors, 1 "comendador de Santiago," 1 corregidor. The rest belong to what may be described as the petty bourgeoisie, ranging from weavers and hat makers

TABLE 1

Persons Charged with Crimes Other than Judaizing by the Inquisition in Toledo to 1530, by Sex and Disposition of Case

	Absolved	Condemned	Penanced	Incomplete	Suspended	Reprimanded	Total
Males	3	76	20	15	6	1	121
Females	0	13	3	0	0	0	16

TABLE 2

Number and Percent of Persons Charged with Judaizing by the Inquisition in Toledo to 1530, by Sex, Time Period, and Disposition of Case

Sex and Disposition	Time Period				Total
	Up to 1494	1495-1500	1501-15	1516-30	
Females					
Absolved	15 (5.5)	4 (7.84)	15 (12.82)	6 (12.24)	40 (8.31)
Condemned	96 (35.69)	18 (35.29)	36 (30.77)	17 (34.69)	167 (34.36)
Sentence Incomplete	7 (2.60)	5 (9.80)	3 (2.56)	0	15 (3.08)
Sentence Suspended	0	0	1 (0.85)	0	1 (0.20)
Total	118 (43.86)	27 (52.94)	55 (47.01)	23 (46.94)	223 (45.88)
Males					
Absolved	10 (3.71)	1 (1.96)	16 (13.67)	5 (10.20)	32 (6.58)
Condemned	131 (48.69)	21 (41.17)	44 (37.60)	19 (38.77)	215 (44.24)
Sentence Incomplete	8 (2.97)	1 (1.96)	2 (1.71)	2 (4.08)	13 (2.67)
Sentence Suspended	2 (0.7)	0	0	0	2 (0.41)
Reprimanded	0	1 (1.96)	0	0	1 (0.20)
Total	151 (56.14)	24 (47.06)	62 (52.99)	26 (53.06)	263 (54.10)
Grand Total	269	51	117	49	486

Note: The chronological division here is designed to emphasize the distinction between those accused before the expulsions of 1492-94, who in theory had been Christians for almost a century, and those who converted in 1492-94 as a way of avoiding expulsion. The percentages condemned or absolved in relation to the totals by sex are as follows: 85.55 percent of all males condemned, 12.17 percent absolved; 74.89 percent of all females condemned, 17.93 percent absolved.

to a seller of spices; there are 26 shoemakers or their relatives, 13 tailors, and 14 merchants. The implications are clear. The victims of the Inquisition in the early years were overwhelmingly from a particular social group. Were they persecuted because of their social identity or because, being less well-to-do than the conversos in positions of power in the royal and municipal administration and the church, they retained some of the practices of their former faith? Without a more careful examination of the evidence it is difficult to offer a conclusive assessment, but my own inclination is to describe the early work of the Inquisition in Toledo as resulting from social antagonism aggravated by racial hatred.

A few more observations are in order. A very large number of those condemned, 114, were already dead or had escaped. Moreover, according to the catalog, of those accused of Judaizing, 26 persons were tortured before 1530. The figure seems minimal and runs counter to the widespread belief in the excesses of the Holy Office. Again, only a thorough examination of the documentation can provide a true answer. Of these 26 individuals, 16 were female (7 found guilty and condemned, 7 innocent and released, 1 sentence suspended, 1 sentence incomplete) and 10 male (7 condemned, 3 released).

If these figures are correct, and if the Inquisition of Toledo was representative of the Inquisition in the rest of Castile, then in the light of the numbers condemned postmortem or in absentia, the numbers absolved, and the small percentages of those tortured, our long-standing views of the work of the Holy Office in Spain require a radical reinterpretation.

I know too little about this period or the Inquisition to venture into far-reaching theories. Yet, if the Inquisition reflected latent antagonism against certain social and racial groups and against women, why these new methods of persecution in the late fifteenth century? Judaizing practices can only have been a pretext. We must look elsewhere, to the changing political, social, and intellectual conditions of late-fifteenth-century Castile, Aragon, and Western Europe. Political centralization in Castile coincided with the naming of an inquisitor general for the realm, a position unheard of in the medieval Inquisition. Isabella's rough reform of the Castilian church paralleled royal control of the Inquisition, again, unprecedented in terms of the medieval Inquisition but in line with the traditional control of the church by the kings of Castile.

The waning of the medieval order, to paraphrase Huizinga, in Castile and elsewhere in Europe brought with it peculiar beliefs, extreme forms of popular piety and religion, wanton violence, and a sense of doom and despair. In Castile we find examples of this mood in some of its most remarkable literary monuments: Jorge Manrique's *Coplas por la muerte de su padre* and *Coplas contra el mundo* and Fernando de Rojas's *Celestina*. Manrique's pessimistic outlook, his rejection of the vanity and mundane concerns of his society, reveals the anguish of the man and his times. Américo Castro writes of *Celestina* as emerging "de un sentimiento trágico de la vida." There is no need here to go into details as to the social aspects of *La Celestina*; Maravall's book is an excellent treatment of the subject. Correctly, he sees *La Celestina* as a moral work, a clear example of the Gospel's admonition that the wages of sin is death everlasting. In Fernando de Rojas's novel we contemplate the birth of the modern world, attuned no longer to the natural order but to the mechanical movement of clocks, a world in which relations between master and servant are based on money rather than loyalty. We find echoes of these sentiments in *Don Quixote*: What despicable age is this that uses firearms? What despicable age is this in which a knight errant needs money to wander through the roads of La Mancha?[27]

The idealized perception of the Middle Ages had been on the wane for more than two centuries, but in the late fifteenth and early sixteenth century it gave way to new economic concepts and a new social order. Celestin does not think of her squalor as the gift of God; the medieval idea of the blessings of poverty be damned. Among the charges listed against Alabert de Almazán, condemned by the Inquisition in 1486, was that he had stated that "el Parayso era tener dinero," and one could add, then and now, that to have none is Hell.[28]

One should not be surprised either at the zealous preaching of the mendicants against Judaizing practices or the virulent anti-Jewish writings submitted to the monarchs of Castile in the last quarter of the fifteenth century. The tone, the vehemence is present elsewhere in Western Europe. The establishment of the Holy Office in Spain in 1483 preceded by barely a year Innocent VIII's bull, *Summis desiderantes affectibus* (December 9, 1484) in which the pope lamented the spread of witchcraft and commissioned two Dominican inquisitors, Heinrich Kramer and James Sprenger, to investigate and deal with that threat. In 1486 they wrote and published the *Malleus Maleficarum*, the most influential book in the development of the European witch craze. In the *Malleus* and throughout

Europe we see the final identification of the Jew with Satan and the extreme misogyny of the age. Castile was not exempted from the pattern. Although most of those condemned by the Inquisition in the early years were charged with Judaizing, we find from time to time charges of sexual misconduct and references to succubus and to the adoration and ritual kissing of the anus of Satan's agents.[29] Here, as in other parts of Europe, Judaizing, fornication, and necromancy were seen as one.

We must turn again to Delumeau's perceptive analysis of the way in which the established institutions of Europe abetted popular fears. The new monarchies in England and France dealt as harshly with witches and dissenters as the Inquisition did in Spain. In contrast to the situation in the northern countries, however, where royal rule, though often contested by the nobility, lay uniformly over the land, in Spain political centralization in Castile was not paralleled by similar developments in Aragon. The Inquisition was the only true national institution and the only one capable of dealing with what was perceived as a serious threat to the realm.

While the medieval Inquisition was born to meet a specific challenge, Catharism, and was the extension of existing institutions, the Spanish Inquisition came about from societal forces long in the making rather than as a result of an immediate and justifiable threat. Both inquisitions came to the fore in times of change and upheaval. However, while the thirteenth century was still grounded in the optimistic expansion of the twelfth, in the late fifteenth century one could only look back to more than two hundred years of hard times. The methods, the tone of the Spanish Inquisition could not but reflect the tenor of the times and be shaped by the historical development of Castilian institutions. Yet, the inquisitorial mind was not exclusive to the agents and familiars of the Holy Office but sprang from popular culture, nor were its choices of victims and scapegoats in Castile very different from those being made in other parts of early modern Europe.

Notes

1. For the medieval Inquisition, see the old but still formidable Henry C. Lea, *A History of the Inquisition in the Middle Ages,* 3 vols.

(New York, 1880); Yves Dossat, *Les crises de l'Inquisition toulousaine au XIIIéme siècle (1233-1273)* (Bordeaux, 1959); Jean Guiraud, *Histoire de l'Inquisition au moyen-âge*, 2 vols. (Paris, 1935-38); Joseph R. Strayer, *The Albigensian Crusades* (New York, 1971); Walter L. Wakefield, *Heresy, Crusade, and Inquisition in Southern France 1100-1250* (London, 1974).

2. On the use of the term "Occitania" and social and economic conditions there, see Strayer, *Albigensian Crusades*, chap. 1.

3. Wakefield, *Heresy, Crusade, and Inquisition*, pp. 77-81; Strayer, *Albigensian Crusades*, pp. 15-39; Lea, *Inquisition in the Middle Ages*, 1: 136-38.

4. Lea, *Inquisition in the Middle Ages*, 1:219-31; Colin Morris, *The Discovery of the Individual 1050-1200* (New York, 1973), pp. 139-44; Wakefield, *Heresy, Crusade, and Inquisition*, pp. 82-83.

5. Wakefield, *Heresy, Crusade, and Inquisition*, pp. 84-91; Lea, *Inquisition in the Middle Ages*, 1:141-45.

6. On the political aspects of the Albigensian Crusades, see Strayer, *Albigensian Crusades*, pp. 55-142.

7. Wakefield, *Heresy, Crusade, and Inquisition*, p. 133.

8. Lea, *Inquisition in the Middle Ages*, 2:12-28, 35, 82 et passim; Dossat, *L'Inquisition toulousaine*, pp. 297-320, quoted in Wakefield, *Heresy, Crusade, and Inquisition*, pp. 183-85. See also Friedrich Heer, *The Medieval World* (New York, 1962), p. 139. For the role of the mendicants in the early modern period, see H. R. Trevor-Roper, *The European Witch-Craze of the Sixteenth and Seventeenth Centuries and Other Essays* (New York, 1967), pp. 90-192.

9. Lea, *Inquisition in the Middle Ages*, 1:369-405; Wakefield, *Heresy, Crusade, and Inquisition*, p. 135.

10. See Charles N. Radding, *A World Made of Men* (Chapel Hill, N.C., 1985); Heer, *Medieval World*, pp. 147-56, 249-51, 321-23 et passim; Lea, *History of the Inquisition*, 1:222; Joseph R. Strayer, *On the Medieval Origins of the Modern State* (Princeton, 1973), pp. 27-56; Norman Cohn, *The Pursuit of the Millennium* (New York, 1970), pp. 127-30; Jean Delumeau, *La peur en Occident, XIVe-XVIIIe siècles* (Paris, 1978), pp. 49-50.

11. Lea, *Inquisition in the Middle Ages*, 2:180-85. On the Spanish church in the thirteenth century, see Peter Linehan, *The Spanish Church and the Papacy in the Thirteenth Century* (Cambridge, 1971). On the

crisis of late medieval Castile, see Teófilo F. Ruiz, "Expansion et changement: La conquêt de Seville et la société castillane (1248-1350)," *Annales: Economies, Sociétés, Civilisations.* 34, no. 3 (1979):548-65.

12. See my "Une royauté sans sacre: La monarchie castillane du bas Moyen-Age," *Annales: Economies, Sociétés, Civilisations,* 39, no. 3 (1984): 429-53; Linehan, *Spanish Church,* pp. 102-6, 186, 240, and, for the quote from Don Juan Manuel, 244.

1970), p. 107. For sacral kingship elsewhere in Europe, see Ernst H. Kantorowicz, *The King's Two Bodies: A Study in Medieval Political Theology* (Princeton, 1957).

14. Yitzhak Fritz Baer, *The History of the Jews in Christian Spain,* 2 vols. (Philadelphia, 1961), 1:327-29; Henry C. Lea, *A History of the Inquisition of Spain,* 4 vols. (New York, 1906-7), 1:114-19; 3:551-54, 561-63. See also B. Netanyahu, *The Marranos of Spain: From the Late Fourteenth to the Early Sixteenth Century* (New York, 1966).

15. Elliott, *Imperial Spain,* p. 220.

16. See Ruiz, "Expansion et changement," pp. 550-51.

17. See Ruiz, "Une royauté sans sacre"; see also José Antonio Maravall, *El humanismo de las armas en Don Quijote* (Madrid, 1948), pp. 109-64.

18. On this topic see José Antonio Maravall, *El mundo social de "La Celestina,"* 2d ed. (Madrid, 1968); on the military tradition of medieval urban oligarchies, see Teófilo F. Ruiz, "The Transformation of the Castilian Municipalities: The Case of Burgos 1248-1350," *Past and Present,* no. 77 (1977), pp. 3-33 and bibliographic references therein.

19. Ruiz, "Expansion et changement,"; see also Angus MacKay, "Popular Movements and Pogroms in Fifteenth-Century Castile," *Past and Present,* no. 55 (1972), pp. 36-37; Philippe Wolff, "The 1391 Pogrom in Spain: Social Crisis or Not?" *Past and Present,* no. 50 (1971), pp. 4-18.

20. *Cortes de los antiguos reinos de León y Castilla,* 5 vols. (Madrid, 1861-), 1:59, 68-69, 227, 231, 244, 280 et passim.

21. *Cortes,* 1:60, 80-84, 114, 127, 195, 227, 230, 280-82, 285, 352-56, 414, 421-22, 464-65, 486, 598-99 et passim. See also Teófilo F. Ruiz, *Sociedad y poder real en Castilla* (Barcelona, 1981), pp. 116-19; also appropriate chapters of my *Historia de Burgos en la Edad Media,* ed. Julio Valdeón (Valladolid, 1984)

22. Teófilo F. Ruiz, "Una nota sobre la estructura y relaciones fiscales del Burgos bajomedieval," in *La España medieval,* vol. 3 (Madrid, 1982), pp. 387-98; see also Antonio Ballesteros, *Sevilla en el siglo XIII* (Madrid, 1913).

23. Teófilo F. Ruiz, "Oligarchy and Royal Power: The Castilian Cortes and the Castilian Crisis 1248-1350," *Parliaments, Estates and Representation* 2, no. 2 (1982):95-101.

24. Elliott, *Imperial Spain,* pp. 86-94. On royal control of Castilian cities, see Ruiz, "The Transformation."

25. *Catálogo de las causas contra la fe seguidas ante el Tribunal del Santo Oficio de la Inquisición de Toledo* (Madrid, 1903). Similar evidence is found in the records of the autos de fe held in Zaragoza from 1482 to 1492 published in Lea, *Inquisition of Spain,* 1:592-611.

26. I would like to thank David Berger for this reference, as well as for his enlightened discussion of some of these issues. Baer (*Jews in Christian Spain,* 2:442-43) quotes R. Joseph Ya'abetz's *Or ha-Hayyim* to the effect that those with knowledge did not keep their faith but women and the common people were willing to be martyrs to their beliefs.

27. Maravall, *El mundo social* and *El humanismo de las armas.*

28. Lea, *Inquisition of Spain,* 1:601.

29. Ibid., 1:592, 597. My argument here is not original; Trevor-Roper has said as much in the article on the witch craze cited above (see n. 8).

INDEX

The names of individuals who lived before 1500 are indexed by first name. Royal and municipal officials listed in the appendix to chapter VI are not included here.